The
Unpredictable Past

The Unpredictable Past

EXPLORATIONS IN AMERICAN CULTURAL HISTORY

Lawrence W. Levine

New York   Oxford
OXFORD UNIVERSITY PRESS
1993

Oxford University Press

Oxford   New York   Toronto
Delhi   Bombay   Calcutta   Madras   Karachi
Kuala Lumpur   Singapore   Hong Kong   Tokyo
Nairobi   Dar es Salaam   Cape Town
Melbourne   Auckland   Madrid

and associated companies in
Berlin   Ibadan

Copyright © 1993 by Lawrence W. Levine

Published by Oxford University Press, Inc.,
200 Madison Avenue, New York, New York 10016

Oxford is a registered trademark of Oxford University Press

Library of Congress Cataloging-in-Publication Data
Levine, Lawrence W.
The unpredictable past : explorations in American cultural history/
Lawrence W. Levine.
p. cm.   Includes bibliographical references and index.
ISBN 0-19-508296-6.—ISBN 0-19-508297-4 (pbk.)
1. United States—Popular culture—History.   2. Afro-Americans—
History.   3. United States—Historiography.   I. Title.
E169.1.L5374   1993
973'.0496073—dc20   92-32258

4 6 8 9 7 5 3

Printed in the United States of America
on acid-free paper

For all my children

   Alex, Joshua, Isaac, Jennie, and Stephanie

      with love

The future is certain, it is only the past that is unpredictable.

Soviet joke

Preface

The amusing epigraph that opens this volume should not lead us to conclude that it is only in totalitarian societies that the past is contested terrain. Disagreements—that not infrequently expand into protracted disputes—about the meaning and significance of past events and people have been part of the landscape in our own society from its inception and continue to be. Thus I have chosen as the title for this collection of essays the title of my contribution to a debate at the American Historical Association meetings in 1988 which signified the ongoing struggle over the shape and meaning of the past. Though this particular essay appears as only one of fourteen, its title, I believe, characterizes the entire volume.

These essays, written over the past twenty-four years, were part of the dialogue that has helped to fashion a number of the approaches and perceptions that guide us to a sense of our history quite unpredictably divergent in important ways from the one I grew up with. During the years I was in high school, college, and graduate school, it would not have been possible to predict that the past, as it was then understood, would change in the future in the many ways and directions it has. Our notion of the groups and events worthy of serious exploration and the role they played in shaping American culture and society has expanded considerably, and these essays are a testament to some of the directions that expansion has taken. That there is at present severe opposition to many of these changes makes it all the more important to understand their nature and meaning; a task to which I trust these essays will contribute.

All of the essays in this volume have been published before in collections and journals. Several of them were later expanded and incorporated into two of my books. Nonetheless, I have reprinted them here both because of my conviction that they are substantially different and retain certain virtues in their essay form and because—alas—everyone cannot be counted on to have read my books. With some exceptions, which have been noted and explained, these essays are presented as they originally appeared. I have added introductions that identify the date, place, and occasion of their original publication, and in some instances the state of mind of their author.

My friend Elliott Gorn, after reading an early draft of this manuscript, urged me to be more reflective. "I really think we need a more introspective introduction here," he admonished me. I trust that in the introductions to the individual essays (which he did not see) as well as in essays 1, 2, and 14, in which I think more openly and directly about the writing of history, I achieve some of the reflection he urged upon me. Nevertheless, I do want to add here one introspective note concerning a familiar subject: the putative conflict between teaching and research. As I look back upon this work of almost a quarter of a century, I realize how indebted to my teaching so much of it is. It was in the classroom that I was first able to explore and test approaches to folk and popular culture. It was in the classroom that I received my first critical responses to those approaches. The challenges of interesting and absorbing my students in the past, of teaching them to locate, hear, and understand the voices of the past wherever we can find them, of guiding them to the realization that no cultural artifact of a people and a society is unworthy of serious study, of helping them comprehend how much we have to learn from people we have hitherto ignored, of struggling along with them to the conclusion that the historian has to become a participant in the past whose primary purpose is not judgment but understanding, have honed and developed my own historical skills far beyond what they would be had I never entered a classroom. Certainly, there are tensions between the demands of teaching and those of research and writing, which are best resolved by research leaves and sabbaticals. Without frequent time off from teaching, I undoubtedly would have written significantly less. But without my teaching, significantly less of what I have written would be worth as much.

Berkeley, California   L.W.L.
July 4, 1992

Acknowledgments

Many scholars with a healthy sense of their work are led ultimately to feel that their poor scattered articles and essays ought to be gathered up and made available to a potentially eager public. Occasionally, publishers agree, and I am grateful to Sheldon Meyer—who has been my editor and my friend since the beginning of my career—and Oxford University Press for doing so in this instance.

Were I to attempt to adequately recognize all of the people who contributed to this work of more than two decades, the Acknowledgments might well become the longest piece in the collection. Let me simply say that I could not have researched or written these essays without the friends, colleagues, students, and family who have nurtured, taught, advised, and helped me over the years. I have been especially fortunate in the many invitations I've had to contribute papers to universities, museums, and scholarly meetings and to publish my essays in journals and books. I have never learned to take any of this for granted, and I feel deep gratitude to the many colleagues involved in according me these opportunities and privileges.

The idea for this collection was conceived and the most recent essay—"The Folklore of Industrial Society"—was written amidst the incomparable scholarly environment that prevails at the Center for Advanced Study in the Behavioral Sciences where I was fortunate enough to spend the academic year, 1990–1991. Peter Agree and Elliott Gorn read the manuscript in its entirety, and the final organization of this volume was strongly influenced by their suggestions. Madelon Powers and Lauren Smith helped me turn these essays into a book. Their assistance, their friendship, and their unfailingly candid counsel were indispensable. In the final stages, Jay Cook and Brigitte Koenig provided generous advice and assistance and Leona Capeless of Oxford University Press made valuable editorial suggestions.

"Once more again," as one of our children used to say, my wife Cornelia was there when I needed her, which was often.

L.W.L.

Contents

I

THINKING ABOUT HISTORY

I

1

The Unpredictable Past: Reflections on Recent American Historiography

On the evening of December 27, 1988, at the opening session of the annual meeting of the American Historical Society in Cincinnati, Ohio, I participated, along with Theodore S. Hamerow, Gertrude Himmelfarb, Joan Wallach Scott, and John E. Towes, in a vigorous debate concerning the state of history and the historical profession in the contemporary United States. I had for some time been upset at what I considered attacks on the "new" historiography which had blossomed forth in the 1970s and 1980s. I was troubled not by the fact of the opposition—ferment is a healthy state for historians and their work—but by its nature. Instead of attempting to refute the findings of the new cultural and social historians, who were doing so much to illuminate peoples and subjects hitherto neglected or ignored, the critics were simply dismissing their work as irrelevant, or trivial, or fragmentary. Suddenly we were suffused with cries for "synthesis," for an end to "specialization," for greater communication with the intelligent layman, for greater relevance or "significance," for a more "holistic" approach and an end to "Balkanization."

My own feeling—then and now—is that those who don't appreciate the current historiography are free to show the way by creating a better one. I felt this way in the 1960s and 1970s when some of my colleagues were almost making a profession of calling for what they termed "history from the bottom up." I agreed with what they wanted to see more of; indeed, that was precisely the kind of history I myself was trying to write. I simply had limited patience with people who spent so much of their time professing something they were not themselves practicing. If history from the bottom up was so important, why in the world didn't they *write* some? I feel precisely this way today about those who spend much of their time calling for

"synthesis." If historical synthesis is so crucial, why don't they stop calling
for it and put their energy into *doing* it? I confess that I worried—and still
worry—about what the issues really were. Thus I welcomed the invitation
to join in the AHA debate—which was held before a very large and responsive audience—in order to express some of my own views and misgivings
about what was transpiring. My paper, together with the others, was subsequently published in a forum entitled "The Old History and the New," in
The American Historical Review, 94 (June 1989). It appears here with a few
minor alterations.

"The future is certain," a Soviet joke assures us, "it is only the past that
is unpredictable."[1] For historians, alas, the future is hardly certain, and the
fact that the past is unpredictable has become no laughing matter. Indeed, it
has caused a good deal of concern in recent years and the growing conviction among many that the venerable craft of the historian is in a state of
crisis.

This was not always so. The unpredictability of the past was an accepted fact to those who thought seriously about history. The dialectic between the past and the present was seen not only as inescapable but as
salutary. History, Henry James observed, "is never, in any rich sense, the
immediate crudity of what 'happens,' but the finer complexity of what we
read into it and think of in connection with it."[2] This truth was built into
the graduate program at Columbia University when I was a student there
thirty years ago. On our comprehensive written examinations, there was one
question that was repeated year after year: "Discuss the changing interpretations of: . . ." which was followed by a varying list of the basic events:
the American Revolution, the creation of the Constitution, Jeffersonian Democracy, the causes of the Civil War, the nature of the Populist revolt, and
on and on.

Historians were, and I think still are, comfortable with the fact that our
understanding of these standard historical occurrences inevitably varies from
generation to generation because they perceive that, of necessity, we view
them through the prism of a changing present. Nor have historians conceived of this prism as a prison that condemned them to a flawed vision.
There was confidence that, although we might operate in cycles of historical
interpretations, the general movement was upward toward an increasingly
sophisticated understanding of the past. The present was not merely a hin-
drance; it could provide new ways of seeing things, new tools, new perceptions of human motivation or economic forces that helped us to gain a surer

sense of past generations. When the French historian Marc Bloch made the familiar observation, "Misunderstanding of the present is the inevitable consequence of ignorance of the past," he quickly added, "But a man may wear himself out just as fruitlessly in seeking to understand the past, if he is totally ignorant of the present."[3]

There is one area of historiographical unpredictability, however, with which many historians have not learned to make their peace. This involves not changing interpretations of well-agreed-upon standard events but changing notions of which events—and which people—should constitute the focus of the historian's study.

The direction in which American historiography has moved during the past several decades becomes clear by discussing the ideas of a prominent and influential American historian, John Higham of Johns Hopkins University. In two articles, "The Cult of the 'American Consensus' " and "Beyond Consensus," that he published in 1959 and 1962 respectively, Higham took his colleagues to task for treating our history much the way dairy companies treated our milk: homogenizing it so that all the separate particles were blended together in one indistinguishable mass. Earlier historians, Higham insisted, "had painted America in the bold hues of conflict": class against class, section against section, ideology against ideology, and had viewed the American past as jagged and discontinuous, filled with cataclysms and sudden change. For historians in the conservative years after World War II, on the other hand, American history looked more like one long, happy voyage with few fundamental differences and with an enduring consensus. "The phrase '*the* American experience' has become an incantation," Higham charged, as he pointed to his colleagues' emphasis on uniformity, stability, "the persistence of a national character, the triumph of a single homogeneous culture."[4]

More than twenty years later, at the 1983 annual meeting of the Organization of American Historians, Higham issued another critique of the direction in which his colleagues were moving. In a paper titled "Beyond Pluralism: the Historian as American Prophet," Higham argued that somewhere in the late 1960s the ruling paradigms of homogeneity and consensus were replaced by the paradigms of fragmentation and heterogeneity. The ideal of the national community was replaced by the ideal of the local community: the town, the parish, the family, the ethnic group. Thus the very things Higham had been decrying in the late 1950s and early 1960s—the exaggerated belief in consensus and homogeneity—had been vanquished. But Higham was far from pleased. The more we learned about the specific, he complained, the less we understood about the larger scheme of things. Historians had lost their sense of coherence and direction. Higham described his colleagues by using the metaphor of a field of solitary gophers, each digging its own hole. Our task now, Higham concluded, was to rediscover our national unity and our national identity.[5]

What had happened between the early 1960s and the early 1980s to lead Higham to change the title of his critique from "Beyond Consensus" to "Beyond Pluralism," and to lament at the end of this period the demise of the very thing he seemed to be inveighing against at its beginning? For our purposes, the most decisive factor was the advent of a stream of modern American historiography beginning in the late 1960s and blossoming in the mid-1970s that was—and is—convinced that there can be no real sense of the whole without exploring the parts, without understanding—often for the first time—the consciousness and actions of workers, women, ethnic, religious, racial, and national minorities, immigrants and their progeny, who participated in a myriad of separate geographical, occupational, fraternal, and religious communities that together constituted the larger society.

This shift was never total or inclusive. Throughout the years since the mid-1970s, historians continued to explore all the standard phenomena that have traditionally concerned them. Revisionism characteristically and perhaps inevitably tends to overstate. But these overstatements—especially the occasionally stupid ones—should not be elevated into an expression of what the new approaches are all about. The great majority of those who have sought to expand our historical vision to new groups of people and new areas of expressive culture mean to do just that: to *expand* our knowledge, to *supplement* our approaches, not to erect new fences and shut still more doors.

In 1965, I published a study of the politician William Jennings Bryan that tried to use him to understand his small-town and agrarian midwestern and southern constituencies. In the years following the publication of my Bryan study, I turned to a history of black protest thought in America and attempted to utilize the same approach: that is, I began by focusing on the thought of the black leadership. Increasingly, I was troubled by my assumption that one necessarily can derive the consciousness of people from the goals and aspirations of their leaders, and I turned gradually and then decisively to folk materials to enable me to hear more directly the voices of people who had not left traditional historical sources behind them. Although I felt quite lonely and vulnerable as I was writing this work, this, as it turned out, was precisely the direction in which many historians, especially younger ones, were moving.[6]

The new historiography was fashioned by what has been perhaps the most important intellectual breakthrough by historians in the past two decades: their changed attitude toward the folk whom they now began to see not as inarticulate, impotent, irrelevant historical ciphers continually processed by forces over which they had no control but rather as actors in their own right who, to a larger extent than we previously imagined, were able to build a culture, create alternatives, affect the situation they found themselves in, and influence the people they found themselves among.

This historiographical trend has brought forth a series of laments from both within and without the profession. Once, we have been told, American history was written by those who had a sense of the entire tradition, who wrote of a nation, not of its bits and pieces, whose writings did not divide the American people into their constituent elements but helped unite them by giving them a sense of a common tradition and a shared past. In 1982, C. Vann Woodward deplored the "fragmentation of the profession into highly specialized fields." "People of a democratic tradition," he insisted, "can surely be interested in the historic plight of the powerless, but they have a natural and abiding concern for power and those who have wielded i. and to what effect—a concern that historians should never have neglected anyway. If they can now revive the art of the craft, historians can also reclaim a general public."[7]

This tendency to decry the historiographical present and look with nostalgia upon the historians of the nineteenth and early twentieth centuries, whose sweeping, politically focused narratives supposedly encompassed the whole tradition and communicated with a wide audience, smacks of what Eric Hobsbawm has called "invented tradition."[8] In reality, for the most part, these earlier historians were concerned overwhelmingly with a decided minority of the population in terms of class, ethnicity, region, and gender, and tended to confuse the history of one group with the history of the nation. Moreover, historians today probably communicate with a much broader public than their predecessors ever did, both through the secondary schools and colleges, which contain a far larger portion of the population than at any other time, and through such institutions as the National Museum of American History, whose recent popular exhibits on the black migration and the internment of Japanese-Americans after Pearl Harbor could not have taken place without the new scholarship, whose ultimate influence cannot be measured by the direct sales of books, which is never the way to gauge the influence of scholarship either in the sciences or the humanities.

But, if the practice of creating a Golden Age of Historiography, in comparison with which current historians pale, cannot be taken literally, it helps us to understand the nature of the debate we are engaged in. This practice was manifest at least as early as 1962, when the current historiographical stream was still a trickle. In his presidential address to the American Historical Association that year, Carl Bridenbaugh of Brown University painted a bleak picture of the future of the historical profession in the United States. In former days, Bridenbaugh maintained, the ablest historians were amateur scholars, men who had known life at first hand, and shared a common culture. This was no longer the case; now many younger historians and apprentices "are products of lower middle-class or foreign origins, and their emotions not infrequently get in the way of historical reconstructions. They find themselves in a very real sense outsiders on our past . . . and the chasm between them and the Remote Past widens every hour." The result, he feared, "will make it impossible for them to communicate and to reconstruct the past for future generations."[9]

Bridenbaugh's jeremiad was met with embarrassed silence and treated, when it was treated at all, as some sort of idiosyncratic aberration. While it is true that no other scholars have picked up his unfortunate tendency to read an entire group of young historians out of the profession by asserting that the culture they were raised in forever barred them from comprehending the American past, it is also true that Bridenbaugh was quite prescient in one important respect: the young historians then preparing to take their place in the profession *were* different from the generations before them in their greater degree of heterogeneity and marginality and these differences *did* leave their mark on the generation's historical work.

Where he went wrong was in his prediction that that mark would have primarily negative results. In fact, it is no accident that the heterogeneous historical generation Bridenbaugh so feared turned out to understand one fundamental aspect of the American past—its heterogeneity—infinitely better than its predecessors had. The decades following Bridenbaugh's presidential address were characterized historiographically by an exciting and pioneering dynamic in which historians explored unchartered groups and institutions; made the expressive culture of the folk and of popular entertainment part of American culture; wondered openly about the direction of cultural diffusion and hypothesized that cultural influence could proceed from the socioeconomic bottom to the top as well as vice-versa. The generation that Bridenbaugh predicted would not and could not understand the American past has done more to enable us to understand it in its full complexity and diversity than any preceding generation of historians.

It is this very accomplishment that has proven to be most troubling to so many. Although the current debate is usually billed as political versus social and cultural history, or narrative history versus analytic history, or fragmentary history versus synthetic history, it makes complete sense only when it is seen as what, at its root, it really is: a debate about the extent to which we should widen our historical net to include the powerless as well as the powerful, the followers as well as the leaders, the margins as well as the center, popular and folk culture as well as high culture. The primary criticism of contemporary historiography has little to do with what kind of history we practice and almost everything to do with the subjects of that history. This is really what is objected to by those who so fear the directions in which many contemporary historians are moving. When Gertrude Himmelfarb, who has written of what she terms "the current prejudice against greatness," charges, on page 17 of her book, *The New History and the Old,* that for the social historian "the infrastructure is what the historian thinks it is, not what contemporaries may have judged to be the most significant aspects of their lives and times," we arrive at the nub of the problem: how broad, how comprehensive must our history be to know what "contemporaries" thought was significant? How far must we go beyond the political, economic, and military leaders even to begin our understanding of political, economic, and military history? Himmelfarb tells us on the very next page by the insertion of two revealing adjectives before the word "contemporaries." Social history, she writes, by devaluing the political realm "makes meaningless those aspects of the past which *serious* and *influential* contemporaries thought most meaningful" (italics added). The point is made even more clearly eight pages later when Himmelfarb complains that "the social historian, rejecting any such 'elitist' idea as the good life, seeking only to understand *any* life, indeed regarding it as a triumph of the historical imagination to explore the lowest depths of life, to probe the unconscious, unreflective, irrational aspects of life, denies that man is the distinctive, indeed unique animal Aristotle thought him to be—a rational animal, which is to say, a political animal." Indeed, Himmelfarb goes so far as to assert that the new history "involves a radical redefinition of human nature.[10]

To comprehend why such apocalyptic language is used—and it is used often, as witness Theodore Hamerow's charge that many of the new historians feel "they must be ruthless in destroying conventional methodology"— it is necessary to locate the historiographical debate within the larger debate concerning the current directions of American culture itself; a debate in which William Bennett, while he was still Secretary of Education, accused those faculty desiring to expand the cultural canon of "trashing" Plato and Shakespeare.[11] The larger contemporary debate between those like Allan Bloom on the one side who "know" what culture is and what it is not, who have a map of its fixed perimeters and a profile of the identity of its creators and its followers, who perceive culture to be something finite and fragile, which needs to be conserved and protected from the incessant Philistinism that threatens it; and those on the other side who believe that worthy, enduring culture is not the possession of any single group or genre or period, who conceive of culture as neither finite nor fixed but dynamic and expansive, helps to frame our own specific historical debate and makes it clear that our discussions are not taking place in some academic vacuum apart from the outside world.[12]

But there is still another context that helps to elucidate the full meaning of our debate. The complaints against the current historiography center not just on its subject matter but on its degree of complexity and relative inaccessibility to a larger public. We first heard charges like these not in the discipline of history but in that of physics and the sciences in general. During the 1920s, the New York *Times* published a series of editorials bitterly lamenting the fact that educated people could no longer grasp those theories on the cutting edge of science. "What common folk must be content to do in regard to Dr. Einstein," the *Times* concluded reluctantly in 1921, "is to accept the judgment of experts on his work, just as they do in many other domains of specialized knowledge." The *Times* seemed loath to accept its own advice, however, and continued to return to the problem throughout the decade, always with the same negative results. In a 1923 editorial titled "IT SIMPLY CAN'T BE DONE" the *Times* asserted, "The attempt to explain his theory to people who know only the elements of arithmetic, algebra and geometry is quite hopeless. The thing cannot be done, and, however humiliating the confession may be, most of us will be obliged either to take our Einsteinism on trust or just ignore it." Five years later, the paper used an editorial titled "A MYSTIC UNIVERSE" to proclaim, "Countless textbooks on Relativity have made a brave try at explaining and have succeeded at most in conveying a vague sense of analogy or metaphor . . . Understanding the new physics is like the new physical universe itself . . . We can only hope for dim enlightenment. The situation is all the harder on the public because physics has become unintelligible precisely in an age when the citizen is supposed to be under the moral obligation to try to understand everything. Nor are things made easier for the common man . . . when theory changes from year to year." [13]

In a recent survey of modern physics, Nick Herbert wrote of "the reality crisis in physics." Quantum theory, he observed, "irreparably smashed Newton's clockwork" and taught us that the world is *not* a deterministic mechanism, but did not teach us what the world *is*. [14] The late Nobel Laureate Richard Feynman had this advice for those interested in quantum mechanics: "Do not keep saying to yourself, if you can possibly avoid it, 'But how can it be like that?' because you will go 'down the drain' into a blind alley from which nobody has yet escaped. Nobody knows how it can be like that." [15]

History, of course, is not physics, and historians neither can nor want to claim the level of complexity and abstraction attained by Albert Einstein and his colleagues. Nonetheless, historians today are engaged in a similar debate centering on matters of synthesis, complexity, and accessibility because their own discipline and related humanistic disciplines do not inhabit a planet apart from the sciences; they are part of the same cultural matrix out of which the new scientific attitudes and approaches have sprung.

In 1928, the New York *Times* observed that, while Alfred Tennyson defined faith as believing what we cannot prove, "The new physics comes perilously close to proving what most of us cannot believe; at least until we have rid ourselves completely of established notions and forms of thought . . . The Quantum invites us to think of something which can be in two places at the same time." [16] Much of contemporary historiography invites us to rid ourselves of established notions and to stretch our imaginations in similar ways.

If the *Times* had trouble with the concept that something can be in two places at the same time, what are we to say when we learn, for instance, that a culture can move in two directions at the same time? In my own work on Afro-American folk thought, I was searching for that moment in post-Civil War history when American blacks, whose culture during slavery had remained so very African in so many ways and so autonomous in so many respects from the white culture that surrounded it, crossed over into the process of unmistakable cultural amalgamation. But I found that, every time I focused on a new form of cultural expression that seemed to function as a mechanism for deep acculturation to the larger society, I discovered important degrees of cultural revitalization as well. In so many modern forms of their expressive culture, Afro-Americans exhibited the tendency to surge outward into the larger society even as they nurtured a strong centripetal urge that continually drew them back to central aspects of their traditions. My own findings were duplicated by the sociologist Mark Slobin in his study of Jewish music in America. We each independently found that such recent developments as the modern recording industry acted not only as a force for cultural amalgamation but also served to preserve important elements of group tradition. That is, developments that common sense and logic tell us *must* have reduced a group's cultural autonomy turn out on closer inspection to have been more complex and to have enabled people to move simultaneously outward and inward. Thus it is difficult to disagree with Slobin's rejection of the older progressive models of cultural change and accommodation in favor of the recognition that what we are faced with is "a dynamic state of flux." [17]

Contemporary scholars have demonstrated again and again that, in penetrating the culture of a neglected group, historians often find more than they bargained for. What looked like a group becomes an amalgam of groups; what looked like a culture becomes a series of cultures. Americans on the eve of World War II might have seen only a monolith when they looked at Japanese-Americans, but historians must see something vastly more complicated: the *Issei* born in Japan and legally barred from becoming U.S. citizens, the *Nisei,* born and raised here and thus citizens by birth, the *Kibei,* born here but raised in Japan and thus legally Americans and culturally

Japanese, as well as those who lived in cities and those who lived on farms, those who struggled to maintain the old ways and those who hungered for acculturation. The complexity I speak of is not the complexity of specialized languages or esoteric methodologies but the complexity of people and the cultures they create.

This is not to say that we must fragment every group we study to the point where generalizations become impossible, but if we generalize the things we study right out of their complexity, we are doomed to futility. There can be no meaningful political history of labor or industry in the United States without understanding the cultures and social structures of the urban-industrial working class—the bulk of them immigrant and black—at the turn of the century. There can be no complete political history of women's rights in the United States without an understanding of the impact of the new immigrants, so many of whom came from Southern and Eastern European cultures in which women occupied a decidedly subordinate place. We have not begun to understand our political history sufficiently because we have too frequently artificially separated it from the larger cultural context of which it was a part.

Just as scientists have traveled light years from Copernicus's conviction that the Ptolemaic universe must be a misconception because God would not have expressed Himself in such complicated terms, and have spent much of their time attempting to articulate the complexities of the universe we do inhabit, so, too, historians find themselves again and again complicating simple pictures, finding intricacies where before we had certainties, turning unity into multiplicity, clarity into ambiguity. It is possible to see this development, as a number of critics have, as an act of perversity and failure. It is also possible to view it, as I do, as a sign of the maturation and seriousness of our profession. In any case, it is in the midst of this fluid state that we are hearing increasingly insistent demands that we get our act together, carry the enterprise forward, formulate syntheses that allow us to make our current findings immediately intelligible to a broad public, and incorporate larger doses of narrative style in our work, as our illustrious scholarly ancestors did.

We have to comprehend, finally, that we ourselves have a good deal to do with the reception of the history we write and teach. If we tell people continually that history is invariably narrative storytelling about those whose power, position, and influence are palpable, then that is precisely what they will expect from us. But this is only one form of history, and it is incumbent upon us to inform the public, by deed and word, that there is no exclusive preferred form for the writing of history and that no single group in history and no one aspect of the past—the social, the political, the cultural, the economic—is inherently more important, or more essential, or more relevant than the others. If we have respect for our audience, then we must realize that ambiguity and paradox and uncertainty are not strangers to them. They know these things are part of life, and they certainly can be taught to see them as part of history.

But historians will be in no position to teach these lessons if we ourselves do not strive to increase not only our tolerance for and acceptance of the complexities of the past but our tolerance for and acceptance of the complexities and ambiguities of our own profession.

2

The Historian and
the Culture Gap

In the late 1960s my Berkeley colleague Perry Curtis frequently spoke with me about a book he hoped to edit in which historians would write about their craft in a personal and introspective way in order to convey to their colleagues and readers the *human* dimensions of what they did. It was his original intention to invite only the leaders of the profession, with a great deal of experience and substantial accomplishments. While he certainly did attract a number of senior historians, he was turned down sufficiently to appreciate more fully the French historian Marc Bloch's lament about the "curious modesty which, as soon as we are outside the study, seems to forbid us to expose the honest groping of our methods before a profane public." Ultimately, he was forced to widen his net, and I was one of the younger historians he caught. His invitation came at a time when several developments were compelling me to think more concertedly and more personally than I yet had about the *act* of historical writing and creativity and I was delighted to become one of the contributors to L. P. Curtis, Jr., ed., *The Historian's Workshop: Original Essays by Sixteen Historians* (New York: Alfred A. Knopf, 1970).

At some point in his studies (for many historians at *all* points), the historian is faced with a situation where there is little continuity or connection between his own cultural conditioning and expectations and that of his subjects. He is faced with a culture gap that must be bridged both by painstaking historical reconstruction and by a series of imaginative leaps that allow him to perform the central act of empathy—figuratively, to crawl into the skins of his subjects. This situation is a familiar one, which any good historian has had to face and overcome. It is, in fact, the primary function of the historian and gives the study of history much of its excitement and importance.

Less familiar is the assertion, made increasingly of late, that some historians, regardless of their talents or determination, cannot bridge the culture gap. I first heard this charge in 1962, six months after my dissertation on William Jennings Bryan had been completed and accepted by Columbia University and while I was revising it—stylistically more than substantively—into a book.[1] In December of that year, Professor Carl Bridenbaugh of Brown University, in his presidential address to the American Historical Association, delivered a long lament on the future of the historical profession in the United States. Professor Bridenbaugh's main point is worth quoting at some length:

> In former days, the ablest historians were educated amateurs, or perhaps a better term would be amateur scholars. They were men who had previously been men of action: Herodotus, Thucydides, Caesar, Comines, Macaulay, the Americans Bancroft and Adams, and today, Churchill. These great writers knew life at first hand, life which they described critically and interpreted reflectively for their readers. Historians of our Recent Past shared a common culture, a body of literary knowledge to which allusion could be usefully made. . . .
>
> Today we must face the discouraging prospect that we all, teachers and pupils alike, have lost much of what this earlier generation possessed, the priceless asset of a shared culture. Today imaginations have become starved or stunted. . . . Furthermore, many of the younger practitioners of our craft, and those who are still apprentices, are products of lower middle-class or foreign origins, and their emotions not infrequently get in the way of historical reconstructions. They find themselves in a very real sense outsiders on our past and feel themselves shut out. This is certainly not their fault, but it is true. They have no experience to assist them, and the chasm between them and the Remote Past widens every hour. . . . What I fear is that the changes observant in the background and training of the present generation will make it impossible for them to communicate to and reconstruct the past for future generations.[2]

In part, Bridenbaugh was indulging in historical mythology. As if such historians as Herodotus, Macaulay, Bancroft, and Adams were a golden race of men whose emotions never got in *their* way. Insofar as they were important historians, they recognized their emotions and either overcame them or channeled them constructively. Not infrequently, they failed to do either.

In part, Bridenbaugh was repeating a warning which historians have long recognized. As E. H. Carr put it in his George Macaulay Trevelyan Lectures in 1961: "Before you study the history, study the historian. . . .

Before you study the historian, study his historical and social environment.''
This was necessary because, as Carr also noted, ''The historian, being an
individual, is also a product of history and of society; and it is in this twofold
light that the student of history must learn to regard him.''[3] This is a fair
enough warning, the validity of which most historians would admit. But
Ernest Nagel has indicated some of the dangers of taking it too literally. To
do so would mean that before one could study a work of history, it would
be necessary to re-create the environment in which the historian lived, which
would mean going to the work of other historians whose own histories could
not be relied upon until one had in turn studied their environments, which
would entail going to the work of still other historians whose work again
could not be trusted until their backgrounds were researched, which would
mean going to the work of other historians and so on and on until one was
mired in the quicksands of infinite regression.[4]

Professor Bridenbaugh, of course, went beyond Carr's caveat. It was
not merely that all historical creations were affected by the environment in
which the historian lived and matured, but also that certain environments
literally made it impossible for historians to understand and re-create the
American past. I found it difficult to take Bridenbaugh's lament imperson-
ally since it would have been hard to find a better example of the incongruity
he seemed to be warning against than the spectacle of the historian Lawrence Levine and the historical figure William Jennings Bryan enlisted in a
joint endeavor to throw new light on the American past. Indeed, what
connections had I with that America for which Bryan was such a crucial and
central figure? My paternal grandfather was a butcher in a Jewish *shtetl* in
Lithuania buying cattle from neighboring farmers, slaughtering them according to Jewish ritual, selling the rear half to the town's Gentiles and the rest
to his own people. He died in 1904 leaving his wife with eight young children, all of whom gradually wandered from their birthplace and came even-
tually to America. My own father followed his older brothers and sisters
here just a year before World War I engulfed Europe. My maternal grandfather deserted from the Russian army during the Russo-Japanese War of
1904–1905, wandered across a vast expanse of Russia to tell his teen-age
future wife he would send for her, and then made his way over the border
and ultimately to America where he both sustained himself and saved enough
to send for my grandmother by working as a house painter in the halls and
classrooms of the College of the City of New York. My mother was born
in 1907 and spent her youth in the Jewish and Italian immigrant neighborhood
of East Harlem, living with her parents and her siblings in a small apartment
behind the hand laundry my grandfather maintained until he was in his sev-
enties. I was born and raised in a lower-middle-class area of Manhattan in
which my father kept a tiny fruit and vegetable store and where almost

everyone I knew was either an immigrant or the child of immigrants—mostly Jews, but with a strong sprinkling of Greeks. For me "Americans" meant the Irish Catholic kids who lived on the other side of the trolley tracks, crossing them occasionally to engage us in battle.

My upbringing was filled with the cultural confusion so common to the lives of second-generation Americans. Among my oldest childhood memories of my father are those of him wearing a stained white apron, lugging heavy crates of fruits and vegetables, rushing to wait on customers, skillfully stacking high rows of fruit which would need to be repacked almost as soon as he had finished. The amazing amount of labor and attention demanded by that small, dark store where one froze in the winter and sweated in the summer and where my father worked fourteen hours a day, six and one-half days a week, drove both my parents to want their children to "succeed," which in their terms meant simply to be able to live an easier life with more material rewards than they had known—especially if this could be done as a "professional" of one sort or another who relied upon his mind rather than his hands. Since the route to this "better" life lay in that semimysterious world outside the confines of the subculture in which I was raised, I was encouraged to venture forth away from the familiar world of my childhood. At the same time, I was expected to remain at home spiritually, to retain the values so carefully inculcated in me for so long. The result of this dual mandate was a cultural ambivalence which I retain to this day.

My schooling, right through the City College of New York, whose walls my grandfather had once painted, may have introduced me to strange worlds and new concepts, but my teachers and classmates were more often than not people very much like myself whose roots in America were just as tenuous, whose ambivalence was as profound, and whose English would have sounded equally alien to a William Jennings Bryan. Even in my graduate school days at Columbia University, half my fellow students of history came from backgrounds almost identical to my own. It was in this environment that I first began to come to grips with Bryan. More than two years after I had begun work on Bryan, I finally crossed the Alleghenies and the Mississippi and saw the America in which he grew to maturity and for which he spoke for so long and with such fervor. What I saw, of course, was primarily the geographical reality of Bryan's America. Culturally, the America that had nurtured and formed Bryan had begun to fade at the turn of the century. His people were the farmers and townsfolk, his politics the agrarian democracy, his religion the Presbyterian fundamentalism, his speech the full-blown rhetoric, his moral universe the simple world in which one took it for granted that good was rewarded, evil punished, and progress assured, which had flourished during the nineteenth century.

Here then was I—the epitome of Bridenbaugh's lower-middle-class "outsider" of foreign origins, and Bryan—the personification of that America from which I was supposed to feel myself shut out. It was little wonder that I took Professor Bridenbaugh's address very seriously indeed. But no matter how closely I pondered it, I simply could not see its relationship to my own experience in studying Bryan's final years. I was willing to admit that unconsciously I might well have been led to study Bryan originally in order to catch up with a past that had become my own through adoption rather than experience or direct heritage, though even here I remain unconvinced. (It might be much truer to say that this was why I gravitated into the study of *American* history in the first place.)

Settling upon this topic seemed more accident than design. As a first-year student in Richard Hofstadter's graduate seminar, I knew too little American history to devise with any confidence the master's thesis topic that would occupy me for the next year or so. After several timorous attempts to come up with a subject (each one of which was rejected by Hofstadter and my fellow students as either unimportant or not feasible), I vaguely suggested the possibility of studying the social and political philosophy of William Jennings Bryan. I knew little enough about Bryan at the time, except that he was an important figure whom I tended to admire because he had been a force for reform. At this point Hofstadter, who had just finished his *Age of Reform* (in which Bryan and his world played an important role), suggested that if I were really interested in Bryan, I might look at his final years, during which he went through a metamorphosis from reform to reaction. At Hofstadter's suggestion, I read C. Vann Woodward's *Tom Watson,* the latter part of which examined a similar transformation. Before finishing Woodward, I knew I had a topic that thoroughly engaged me—a condition Hofstadter insisted upon before he encouraged his students to begin their theses. Without a day's research, I even had a title: "The Decline of William Jennings Bryan as a Progressive." Years of research may have made my premature title inappropriate, but only deepened my sense of engagement. When my master's thesis did not begin to exhaust the potentialities of the problem, I continued to explore it in my doctoral dissertation and book.

In retrospect, then, my subject seems to have been born out of a combination of my own inexperience and timidity and my professor's interests. Even if my ethnicity had a relationship to my choice of a subject, that connection ended once my research began. The forces that threatened from the very beginning to cut me off from Bryan and his universe had less to do with my ethnic and environmental background than with my choice of a profession. In deciding to spend my life as a historian and teacher, I had taken my place in a milieu in which, ideally, the life of the mind was paramount, in which there was a commitment to thought in general rather than to any one set of ideas, in which there was a dedication to the dissection and understanding of institutions rather than to their perpetuation or alteration, in which comprehension of the past took precedence over the task of keeping its values alive. These goals in themselves, of course, constituted a set of ideals that potentially weakened the ability of the historian to understand a populist figure like Bryan. Even at the height of his reformist glory, Bryan's militant egalitarianism, his tendency to *use* ideas rather than to value them, the simplistic lines of his moral and spiritual universe, were enough to make even the most sympathetic historian shudder. When, during his last years, these qualities no longer seemed tied to a dedication to social, political, and economic reform, the scholar's inward misgivings were transformed into overt anger and ridicule. Bryan became more a target than a subject.

I still remember vividly the anger and incredulity with which I read of Bryan's failure to oppose the activities of the Ku Klux Klan in the 1920s, his anti-urban proclivities, his defense of the Southern attitude toward Negroes, his "fanatical" campaign for prohibition, and, above all, his crusade to drive the teaching of evolution out of the public schools. Ironically, my Eastern European, Jewish family would have understood Bryan instinctively far better than I at first could. If they had been more politically conscious in the 1920s, they undoubtedly would have opposed many of his activities, especially those aimed at rendering the new urban, immigrant wing of the Democratic party impotent and thwarting the rising power of the new polyglot cities. Nevertheless, they would have *understood* the Bryan who insisted that "it is better to trust in the Rock of Ages than to know the ages of rocks," who urged his audiences to remember that "man is infinitely more than science; science, as well as the Sabbath, was made for man," who admitted that "the objection to evolution, however . . . is not, primarily, that it is not true. . . . The principal objection to evolution is that it is highly harmful to those who accept it," who put faith above reason, who spent his final days on this earth protecting a culture and a way of life from the erosions of the outside world. If I had trouble understanding the meaning of these things initially, it was not because I had come from a particular cultural and ethnic milieu, but to a certain extent because I had strayed—had been encouraged to stray—from it.

Professor Bridenbaugh was correct in maintaining that there is a culture gap separating the mid-twentieth-century historian from the American past. His error was in identifying the nature of that gap. The problem the historian faces in confronting Bryan and those he represented is not primarily whether the historian is urban or rural, immigrant or native-born, Jewish or Protestant, white or black; the problem often is his intellectuality and the complex of values attached to it. For all the differences in the cultural background of Bridenbaugh and myself, as professional historians we share values that transcend our upbringing. I doubt that he would have found the Tennessee anti-evolution law of 1925 and the resultant Scopes trial any less repugnant than I, or have been any more detached from the issues involved in these events than I was. Nor should either of us necessarily have been detached. Objectivity does not necessitate detachment; it does not entail the abandonment of passion or the emasculation of ideals. It means simply and profoundly the ability to keep one's mind open and to allow one's powers of empathy to range widely. It means, above all, the desire to understand. It means perceiving the truth of John Higham's observation, "The serious historian may not wrap himself in judicial robes and pass judgment from on high; he is too much involved in both the prosecution and the defense. He is not a judge of the dead, but rather a participant in their affairs, and their only trustworthy intermediary." [5]

These qualities of mind may come instinctively, but more often than not I suspect they have to be sought after and learned. What enables one individual to assimilate these lessons and approach these goals more successfully than another is, for me, still wrapped in mystery. It is at this precise point that my own teaching often breaks down. I can tell my students what it is they have to strive for, but I have yet to learn to show them concretely how to accomplish what they must accomplish if they are to be good at what they want to do. All I can say with any certainty is that in studying the careers of my predecessors, my peers, and my students, I have not discovered any cultural preconditions that allow some of us to be more successful than others. Certainly by now we have sufficient evidence that a sense of social and cultural marginality can be as conducive to the development of historical skills and insights as the feeling of a shared culture—that "priceless asset" which Professor Bridenbaugh argues contemporary historians are the worse off for having lost. Both, of course, can also constitute impediments to historical understanding. It is not the mere existence of marginality or cultural sameness, but the way they act upon the historian, and the manner in which he reacts to them that is crucial. Becoming a sensitive and perceptive historian still remains an individual process, the meaning of which demands more study and thought than we have devoted to it.

All these lessons still lay before me when I began my research into Bryan's final years. At that point, I had no reason to challenge the prevalent image of Bryan drawn so indelibly by H. L. Mencken in his famous eulogy: "He came into life a hero, a Galahad, in bright and shining armor. He was passing out a poor mountebank." The assumption that Bryan had passed through the relatively familiar evolutionary pattern from angry idealism to angry conservatism was useful in the initial stages, since it provided a focus for my research and thought. It enabled me to concentrate on that phase of Bryan's long career in which the change I set out to understand appeared to have taken place. And it allowed me to winnow from his prolific writings those materials that seemed relevant to the problem with which I was concerned. As I worked my way carefully through Bryan's invaluable periodical *The Commoner,* however, I began to discover evidence that simply did not fit the traditional image. Even as Bryan was stumping the country on behalf of prohibition and fundamentalism, even as he became increasingly interested in the moral and religious purity of his countrymen, even as his ideological constituency became narrower and narrower, his efforts to secure political, economic, and social reform not only continued but broadened, and his interest in wielding political power within the Democratic party remained as great as ever.

At first this evidence was only mildly troubling. Not even neophyte historians should expect too much in the way of perfect symmetry. I had little hope of finding a clear point at which Bryan dropped his reform proclivities and became an intractable anachronism. Even then I realized that no man was ever totally one thing or another, and I fully anticipated discovering ambivalence and contradiction. But as I continued working through Bryan's speeches, his personal correspondence, the press of the period, the private papers of his contemporaries, the evidence mounted well beyond these contingencies. My research was making clear what no other historian, a number of whom had been through the identical materials, had so much as indicated: that in the decade between his resignation from Woodrow Wilson's Cabinet in 1915 and his death at the close of the Scopes trial in 1925, Bryan had moved to the Left on political and economic questions. He now advocated more government ownership, development, and regulation than at any previous point in his career; his relatively narrow reform program of 1896 was by 1925 far more comprehensive and bold.

It was becoming clear, even to so reluctant a revisionist as I was at that stage of my career, that I had been asking the wrong questions. The problem was not why Bryan had abandoned reform, for clearly he had not, nor why he had deserted the area of political activity for the hazier regions of religious and moralistic panaceas, for again he had not, but rather why he supplemented his traditional reform endeavors with new activities in the 1920s. How could he continue to espouse political and economic innovations while at the same time forging alliances with the antiurban, xenophobic, backward-looking Ku Klux Klan, and participating actively in the militant fundamentalist and antievolution movements? And what implications did all this have for our understanding of the decline of progressivism in America after World War I? Merely by posing these and similar questions, I was forced to rethink and challenge the accepted picture of Bryan in his later years and perhaps that of his followers as well. This was not in itself an easy task, for, my evidence aside, the traditional interpretation seemed so firmly based.

First of all, Bryan had reasons for abandoning reform and becoming "the bitter and malignant old man of the Scopes trial" whom Richard Hofstadter had portrayed in his influential essay on Bryan.[6] His tenure as Secretary of State from 1913 to 1915 saw the frustration of his efforts to bring about world peace, and his failure to convince Wilson and his fellow cabinet officers of the correctness of his course forced him to resign the only important official position he ever held (with the exception of his four years as a Congressman from Nebraska in the 1890s). His resignation during a time of heightened international tension brought him more criticism and ridicule than he had known at any time during his career. His efforts to secure prohibition further divided his old followers and clouded his reputation. His attempts to hold on to his power within the Democratic party and continue his crusade for reform were constantly thwarted. Although he was treated with respect and even affection during the Democratic National Convention of 1920, every one of his reform proposals was voted down, and a man he considered reactionary was nominated for the Presidency. Four years later, even the respect and affection were gone, and he could scarcely get his fellow Democrats gathered at the New York convention to listen to him. Postwar America was in general a strange and difficult place for Bryan.

The reasons for Bryan's apostasy were certainly present, and there even appeared to be a confession of that apostasy in a widely quoted letter Bryan wrote in 1923:

> . . . my power in politics is not what it used to be and, therefore, my responsibility is not so great. While my power in politics has waned, I think it has increased in religious matters and I have invitations from preachers in all the churches. An evidence of the change is found in the fact that my correspondence in religious subjects is much larger than my correspondence in political subjects. My interest is deeper in religious subjects. . . .

Yet in spite of all the alleged reasons for his transformation, and in spite of what Bryan himself seemed to be saying, I had uncovered massive evidence to show that during these very years Bryan was spending much of his time and energy going before political rallies to plead for progressive labor legislation, liberal tax laws, government aid to farmers, public ownership of railroads, telegraph, and telephone, federal development of water resources, minimum wages for labor, minimum prices for agriculture, maximum profits for middlemen, and government guarantee of bank deposits, while maneuvering endlessly and always optimistically to regain power within his party.

At this point I reached an impasse in my work. I spent day after day rereading my notes, reshuffling my cards, rethinking my evidence. The conundrum posed by the letter was easy enough to resolve: Although historians had quoted it widely, none of them had discussed the context in which it was written. In 1923, in an effort to strengthen his antievolution crusade within the churches, Bryan decided to run for the position of Moderator of the Presbyterian Church. Accordingly, he wrote a series of letters to prominent Presbyterian ministers asking their support. One of them, the Reverend John A. Marquis of New York, responded by warning Bryan that should he be elected to the position, his chances of attaining high political office would be ruined. Bryan's answer was the letter quoted above, and it clearly was intended as an argument in favor of his increased activity in the religious sphere rather than as a serious admission of a diminished interest in politics. In 1922 Bryan had been far more accurate when he told a New York political rally, ''I am not yet out of politics,'' and he meant just that, as his numerous political activities throughout the 1920s showed. (Significantly, statements such as this—and there were many of them—were never quoted by his biographers and historians.)

As satisfying as this explanation may have been, the fact remained that Bryan, after all, *had* attempted to be elected to his church's highest position, *had* enlisted in the crusade against evolution in the schools and modernism in the pulpit, and *had* placed himself in opposition to such newly emerging urban reformers as Al Smith and Fiorello LaGuardia. I had by now convinced myself that these activities supplemented rather than replaced his traditional reformist efforts, but I still had the obligation of explaining them, of understanding why he had chosen to engage himself in these new areas in his final years. The explanation lay in those copious notes I continued to ponder, although I could not see it at first. My dilemma remained until I began to reconceive the entire nature of my work.

Since Bryan was a political figure, I thought of my study as the reconstruction of the activities of a politician. That is, I saw it as primarily political history. My late colleague Joseph Levenson defined intellectual history as the history not of thought, but of men thinking. Sitting there before my notes, I reached a similar conclusion. I came to the realization that I was engaged fundamentally in the study of Bryan's mind, of his world view. Bryan, after all, was a prolific writer. In his last ten years alone he had written five books, dozens of pamphlets, hundreds of editorials, and uncounted speeches. The problem was that most historians had merely used this large body of work to document Bryan's essential ''vulgarity'' and show the ludicrous nature of his mind. They had quoted ad nauseam Bryan's indictment of Darwin for having men descend ''not even from American monkeys but from Old World monkeys,'' and his own version of the evolution of the leg:

> The leg, according to evolutionists, developed also by chance. One guess
> is that a little animal without legs one day discovered a wart on the belly,

it had come without notice or premonitory symptoms; if it had come on the back instead of the belly the whole history of the world might have been different. But fortunately this wart came on the belly, and the little animal finding that it could use the wart to work itself along, used it until it developed into a leg. And then another wart and another leg. Why did man stop at two legs while the centipede kept on until it got a hundred?

But aside from having great fun with selected quotations from Bryan's writings, they really had not studied or come to terms with the thought of his later years. It was only when I realized that if Bryan was not an intellectual, he was nevertheless a "man thinking," and that as such, his thought, *as thought,* was worthy of study, that I was able to become, in John Higham's phrase, a "participant" in his affairs. It was then that the pieces in my puzzle began to fall into place, and I was able to understand the meaning of his last years. In short, only when I was willing to take Bryan seriously as a man and a mind, as well as a political force, was he willing to reveal himself to me.

Bryan had been a fundamentalist all his life and had objected to the religious and social implications of Darwin's work as early as 1904 in his popular speech, "The Prince of Peace." Why was it not until the 1920s that he became a *militant* fundamentalist and an *active* opponent of the promulgation of Darwinian thinking? The answers were all embodied in Bryan's writings. World War I came as a profound shock to him. At no point could he allow the spectacle of Christians slaughtering rather than loving their neighbors to stand as proof of the bankruptcy of the very Christian ideals that had always provided the basis of his reformist endeavors. Rather, he was led to search for those forces that had driven men away from the teachings of Christ. In 1916 he began to tie Nietzsche's philosophy (which he saw as the philosophical underpinning of German militarism) to Darwin's theory of the survival of the fittest. By 1920 he had become certain that Nietzsche in propounding a philosophy "that condemned democracy . . . denounced Christianity . . . denied the existence of God, over-turned all standards of morality, eulogized war . . . praised hatred . . . and endeavored to substitute the worship of the superman for the worship of Jehovah," had merely carried Darwin's teachings to their logical conclusions.

The shock of the war was intensified for Bryan in the postwar era. The significant accomplishments of the progressive years seemed threatened by what appeared to be one of the most extensive displays of political apathy and indifference in American history. No matter how hard Bryan tried, all his efforts to continue the reform spirit of the past were rebuffed. Nor was Bryan's trauma exclusively political. If the economic primacy of agrarian America had been overturned at the beginning of Bryan's long career, his writings make clear that at the end of that career he saw its cultural primacy being eroded by what Walter Lippmann called the "acids of modernity." No institution seemed safe from assault. Not the churches, not the schools, not even the reliable Democratic party. Again Bryan frantically sought to convince himself and his followers that the fault lay not in the inefficacy of his ideals but in some new force that was paralyzing the will of the people and undermining the religious, cultural, and political certainties of his past. And again the finger pointed to the new science and the new theology that were so closely tied to it.

Bryan's letters, speeches, and books make it possible to travel with him as he made his way through the country on his endless lecture tours and help us relive his experiences as he encountered, or heard of, a professor of geology at Columbia University who told his students to throw away all they had learned in Sunday school, a professor at the University of Wisconsin who taught his students that the Bible was a collection of myths, a congress-man's daughter at Wellesley who glibly remarked, "Nobody believes in Bible stories now," and a teacher in a Methodist college in Ohio who taught his classes that Christ was a bastard. All of this—and there was a great deal of it—presented Bryan with an explanation of the postwar decline in prog-ressivism. Bryan had fought plutocracy and imperialism, war and liquor, in part because he felt they dehumanized man. Now he found abroad in the land an intellectual force that he was convinced also tended to dehumanize man by supplying him with a brute heritage. The younger generation was indifferent and apathetic not because they did not care, but because the doctrines taught them in their schools caused them to lose faith in man's ability to become anything other than what he was. No longer could they believe in the ultimate triumph of righteousness or in a life after death where their virtue and patience would be rewarded.

For Bryan, morality and reform had always been inextricably bound together. At the height of his political power he had argued: "If one actually thinks that man dies as the brute dies, he will yield more easily to the temptation to do injustice to his neighbour when the circumstances are such as to promise security from detection." In his last years he repeated this message endlessly: "How can one fight for a principle unless he believes in the triumph of right? How can he believe in the triumph of right if he does not believe that God stands back of the truth and that God is able to bring victory to His side?" Science and rationality were not enough. The science that was demanding absolute freedom in the classroom was "the same sci-ence that manufactured poisonous gases to suffocate soldiers. . . . Science has no morality. Science gives us weapons and means for escape but not the means for control." Bryan presented the graphic picture of a child reared in a pious home going to college and learning that man descended from the

beasts below, that his development was not part of God's plan, and that
even his morality was man-made:

> And the child goes out with its faith in God shaken, and its faith in the
> Bible shaken, and its faith in immortality shaken, and its faith in prayer
> shaken.

> Oh, are you surprised that men become brutish as they deal with each
> other?

> That is the sentiment today. "There is no God; there is no future; we will
> do as we please." And doing as we please is bringing the world into
> dangerous ground.

If many of his former followers saw tensions between his religious and
political crusades, Bryan did not: "People often ask me why I can be a
progressive in politics and a fundamentalist in religion. The answer is easy.
Government is man-made and therefore imperfect. It can always be improved.
But religion is not a man-made affair. If Christ is the word, how can anyone
be a progressive in religion? I am satisfied with the God we have, with the
Bible and with Christ." He was more than satisfied; he was convinced that
without them there could be no reform. Bryan saw himself wielding "a
double-barreled shotgun, firing one barrel at the [Republican] elephant as he
tries to enter the treasury and another at Darwinism—the monkey—as he
tries to enter the school room." At the heart of all Bryan's writings and
polemics one message became increasingly evident: that Bryan joined the
fundamentalist and anti-evolution crusades not in order to retreat from politics, but in order to combat a force he held responsible for sapping American
politics of its idealism and progressive spirit. He remained a progressive in
the only way he knew how: by attempting to preserve and strengthen the
values and faith of that part of America—the rural West and South—with
which he had always been most closely identified.

The argument and evidence I presented in my book are, of course, more
detailed and complex than I can indicate here. I want only to illustrate how
taking Bryan's words seriously—entering into them rather than merely using
them—allowed me a number of insights not only into Bryan, but also into
the movements he was engaged in. The fundamentalist movement of the
1920s, for instance, has too easily been seen as a politically conservative
force. This was certainly true of many of its leaders, who were convinced
that the function of religion was to save individual souls and not society at
large and who reacted against liberalism wherever they found it, in politics
as well as in theology. This was never true of Bryan, who continued to
espouse the social gospel and to see in Christianity a set of infallible beliefs
leading to eternal salvation *and* a social movement leading to the reforma-

tion of society. Bryan's ability to combine these two aspects of Christian belief and his great influence as one of the nation's leading fundamentalist proponents in his last years force one to wonder whether he may not have been more characteristic of the mass of fundamentalist followers than his more conservative colleagues.

Bryan's last years not only reopen this question, but lead one to think again about the entire fate of progressivism in postwar America. Bryan's career in the 1920s gives evidence for supposing that the decline of progressivism as a movement was due less to economic and political factors than to the growing cultural schism that engulfed America in that decade. There were no yawning political or economic gaps that prevented Al Smith and Bryan from combining their programs and their followers into a new progressive movement. But there were cultural reasons: the Americas for which these two leaders spoke were increasingly different and threatening to each other. The progressive urge in the 1920s, then, did not disappear; it fractionalized and was rechanneled into the struggles waged over prohibition, religion, immigration restriction, evolution, the rights of Catholics and Jews. The primary issues of the twenties were not political or economic, but cultural, and over these issues the old progressive coalition disintegrated.

If I have one great regret about the book I published, it is that it does not go into these matters more fully. At the time, I thought of doing enough research to test, in some areas at least, my supposition that Bryan's urges, motives, and actions in the 1920s were representative of those of large segments of rural America, but I feared this would involve me in writing another book and would structurally and esthetically interfere with the book I had written. I may well have been right, but I allow myself the luxury of some regrets anyway.

I am sorry, too, that I did not have either the materials or the knowledge to do more with Bryan's personality structure. Bryan lacked all introspection; he left behind no truly personal revelations for any part of his life; he appeared almost incapable of having a private life. He seemed to me a particularly inappropriate subject for psychic analysis. One better versed in psychoanalytic theory than I might well have been able to make something of these very qualities, as well as such salient personality characteristics as his compulsive optimism, his inability to question any of his own actions, his propensity to see himself as a vessel carrying out God's ends, his devotion to men in the mass rather than men as individuals, his unfailing ability to rationalize all events so that they confirmed his expectations and the fundamentals of his faith. Traits such as these struck me as more indicative of a cultural than a personal syndrome and more suitable, therefore, for societal rather than individual psychoanalysis. For me, the real question was, and is, not how Bryan got this way, but why the United States produced so many leaders like him at the turn of the century and why the American people were so willing to follow them; it was a question that I was in no way qualified to answer, though I do wish I had raised it more explicitly. Nevertheless, the mere recognition and identification of Bryan's personal qualities tended to confirm my historical thesis, for this kind of personality simply did not lend itself to the traditional image of a man who became so frustrated and disillusioned that he could throw aside the work of a lifetime and end his career leading a cranky religious crusade.

At the time I published my book, I had other misgivings as well. I worried about writing what amounted to a sympathetic study of a man whose actions in the twenties I would have opposed vehemently had I been alive then. One or two friends who read my manuscript were similarly troubled by my failure to inject a sense of moral outrage into my account of many of Bryan's activities. I thought seriously of doing so and rejected the urge largely because so many previous studies of Bryan had been written in just such a manner—as dialogues between Bryan and his contemporary critics, with Bryan invariably coming out second best. I had no illusions that I could keep moral judgment out of my work; I felt only that this should not be my primary object. Bryan had been too often judged and too little understood, and I decided that comprehension, not judgment, should be my basic purpose. I decided also to get off my back, once and for all, the old dictum that to understand is to forgive. For the historian, understanding can be an end in itself with no moral goals attached. About this decision I have no regrets at all, as the earlier parts of this essay undoubtedly make clear. It was this determination that allowed me to bridge the gulf that had for so long separated Bryan from his historical interpreters.

I have written thus far as if my work on Bryan was composed in splendid isolation with no outside influences. No one who has attempted a work of history will believe this, of course. Ultimately, I had to make my own decisions and come to my own conclusions, and this *is* a lonely process. But along the way the influences upon me of other historians, of colleagues, and of friends were crucial and probably more numerous and decisive than I am aware of even now. Two men will serve to illustrate the nature of this debt. John William Ward's study of the ideology of Jacksonian America and his article on Charles Lindbergh[7] taught me both the possibilities for and the necessity of taking *all* thought seriously and provided a methodology for discovering the tensions, ambivalences, and symbolic meanings embodied in thinking. My personal friendship with him, which began while I was finishing my dissertation, has driven these lessons home and opened new vistas that have largely altered the way I look at the past. Richard Hofstadter, who first suggested my study and supervised it at every stage, played a central role. His own work on the reform ethos in America[8] taught me much about its subtleties and tensions and allowed me to understand that the past must not be viewed in absolute terms—that although we may prefer our reformers and conservatives pure, men may harbor reactionary and progressive impulses not only at the same time, but also for the same reasons. Although my study of Bryan contradicted his own essay on Bryan at several points, and although I am sure that to this day he has important reservations about my interpretations, it was he who urged me to expand my master's thesis into a doctoral dissertation and then helped me to publish it. In this respect he was instrumental in teaching me that it is possible to transcend the very human tendency to defend our own specific conclusions and engage in a truly scholarly dialogue. I have tried to incorporate this example into all my own work—especially my teaching.

Unfortunately, it is not an easy lesson to get across in today's political and social atmosphere. Professor Bridenbaugh's insistence that the products of certain cultural environments have little hope of understanding the historical products of others has won a host of new allies. I have learned this unmistakably in the past few years. Shortly after completing the Bryan book, I became engaged in a new study of Negro protest movements in twentieth-century America. I soon found that I was less interested in the organizational aspects of black protest and more concerned with the problem of to what extent the leaders of these movements were reflecting the attitudes and desires of the larger mass of Negroes in America. If my study of Bryan was a tentative attempt to understand the ethos of rural America by examining the attitudes of one of its leaders, I now wanted to reverse the process. I wanted to study the feelings and thought of a group of historically inarticulate people not by looking at their spokesmen, but by examining the cultural records they left behind. Thus, for the past few years I have been attempting to learn how to work with materials hitherto unfamiliar to me: folk music, folk tales, humor, popular culture, as well as with more traditional sources. I have found this work difficult, but illuminating and exciting. I have found it also a bit depressing, for once again I was destined to discover that I am the wrong man working in the wrong field.

Just as six years ago I was told that as the child of lower-middle-class, urban-immigrant parents, the door to the American past in all likelihood would remain closed to me, so today I am told that as the child of white parents, I have little chance of understanding the black past. This message is repeated endlessly. Negro students tend to stay away from classes in black history taught by white men. Negro intellectuals proclaim stridently that they alone are qualified to study and interpret Negro history. In the recently published critique by ten black writers of William Styron's novel, *The Confessions of Nat Turner,* a number of contributors argue not only that Styron failed to transcend his own culture to penetrate that of Nat Turner (a

criticism worth making and exploring), but that no white man could be expected to do so. A few illustrations will make the point:

> . . . it is likely too much to expect a white, twentieth-century American
> novelist to be able to conceive of the world of a black, Old Testament-type
> Messiah.

> There can be no common history until we have first fleshed out the linea-
> ments of our own, for no one else can speak out of the bittersweet bowels
> of our blackness.

> Just as it was impossible for the slave master to look at slavery from the
> point of view of the slave, it has proven impossible for the slave master's
> grandson to look at slavery or at the contemporary black-and-white con-
> frontation from the perspective of Rap Brown and Stokely Carmichael or
> Floyd McKissick or any other black revolutionary, or black non-
> revolutionary, for that matter. The first mistake was for Styron to attempt
> the novel.

> . . . it is impossible for the slavemaster's grandson to see the revolution-
> ary black man in the sense that Gabriel saw himself, as the "George Wash-
> ington" of his people, ready to lay down his life for their liberation.

> Historical fiction about Negroes that has real characters and is true to his-
> tory is almost impossible even for the most understanding white writers in
> the racist, separatist United States.[9]

Nor is this attitude confined to Negroes. White graduate students studying black history are too frequently sheepish not only about their ability, but
about their very right to do so. A number of white scholars in one way or
another have publicly or privately apologized for their own work or the work
of their white colleagues on the grounds that the black man is eminently
more fit to penetrate his own past than the white man. Although some of
these white scholars and students are themselves doing important work in
the area of Negro history, they somehow feel it necessary to put their *mea
culpa* on record. More tragic is the number of young scholars capable of
writing important studies who may be frightened away from this much-
neglected field by the irrelevancies stressed by this rigid cultural and pig-
mental determinism.

The emotional and psychic content of this new argument is so strong it
almost seems futile to point out that such white scholars as Roger Abrahams, Charles Keil, and Elliot Leibow have recently made important strides
toward a greater understanding of Negro culture and society in the United
States.[10] Yet it is necessary to do so, just as it is necessary to assert continually the truth that there are no impassable culture gaps in the realm of

historical scholarship. If too many previous historians have tripped over their own cultural umbilical cords, it is because they were poor historians and not because they were tragic prisoners of an inevitable cultural myopia. The historian who cannot significantly transcend the culture of his youth, the needs of his present, and the hopes of his future in order to come to terms with the past deserves repudiation, but we must take care not to transform his failures into unbending laws governing all historians.

Historians have always had to combat what Marc Bloch called "the virus of the present" and what I would call the virus of culture-boundness. Many historians today are overcoming these handicaps. They are beginning to cast their nets wider to take in not only the articulate leadership classes, but the historically inarticulate lower and lower-middle classes. They are paying attention to the materials of folk and popular culture as well as to those of élite culture. They are finally taking seriously the lessons that cultural anthropologists, psychoanalysts, sociologists, and other social scientists have to offer them. It is ironic that at this very important and pivotal stage in the development of their discipline, historians are being asked to pay obeisance to rigid judgments which seek to tell them who is most fit to study what. I can only hope that when my own study of Negro culture in twentieth-century America is completed, it will be but one of an increasing number of serious studies of black history by scholars from every conceivable cultural background that will help to discredit this new historical obscurantism, just as I like to think that my study of Bryan helps to point out the central fallacy of Professor Bridenbaugh's lament.

II

PATTERNS OF AFRICAN-AMERICAN CULTURE

3

Slave Songs and Slave Consciousness: Explorations in Neglected Sources

In early 1969, John William Ward, whose colleague I had been at Princeton University, phoned in his capacity as Chair of the Program Committee for the American Historical Association's annual meeting in December of that year and invited me to deliver a paper based on the materials I was examining for my book on African-American folk culture. "You're doing interesting work," Ward was kind enough to say, "why not share some of it with us?" I needed little urging to accept his generous offer of a session featuring my paper and the comments of several scholars. The book I was "writing" was still on innumerable bits and pieces of paper in the form of notes and fragments. Here was the opportunity not only to get both exposure and feedback but, most importantly, to be obliged finally to articulate some of my ideas in an organized, intelligible way. I immediately began work on the paper I told Ward I would give on twentieth-century African-American music. It was in trying to come to terms with and comprehend those materials that I found myself being pushed back into the antebellum period to a consideration of both slavery and the African cultural background. It was in the process of writing this paper that the nature of the book I was working on became much clearer to me: before I could write on modern Black culture, I needed to understand its roots in slavery and beyond—a subject then still largely neglected. The resulting paper on slave songs, which surprised me as much as it surprised Bill Ward, became the heart of the opening chapter of my book *Black Culture and Black Consciousness* which was published in 1977. Shortly after the 1969 AHA meetings, I was invited to include an expanded version of the paper in the collection edited by Tamara Hareven, *Anonymous Americans: Explorations in*

Nineteenth-Century Social History (Englewood Cliffs, N.J.: Prentice-Hall, 1971).

Negroes in the United States, both during and after slavery, were anything but inarticulate. They sang songs, told stories, played verbal games, listened and responded to sermons, and expressed their aspirations, fears, and values through the medium of an oral tradition that had characterized the West African cultures from which their ancestors had come. By largely ignoring this tradition, much of which has been preserved, historians have rendered an articulate people historically inarticulate, and have allowed the record of their consciousness to go unexplored.

Having worked my way carefully through thousands of Negro songs, folktales, jokes, and games, I am painfully aware of the problems inherent in the use of such materials. They are difficult, often impossible, to date with any precision. Their geographical distribution is usually unclear. They were collected belatedly, most frequently by men and women who had little understanding of the culture from which they sprang, and little scruple about altering or suppressing them. Such major collectors as John Lomax, Howard Odum, and Newman White all admitted openly that many of the songs they collected were "unprintable" by the moral standards which guided them and presumably their readers. But historians have overcome imperfect records before. They have learned how to deal with altered documents, with consciously or unconsciously biased firsthand accounts, with manuscript collections that were deposited in archives only after being filtered through the overprotective hands of fearful relatives, and with the comparative lack of contemporary sources and the need to use their materials retrospectively. The challenge presented by the materials of folk and popular culture is neither totally unique nor insurmountable.

In this essay I want to illustrate the possible use of materials of this kind by discussing the contribution that an understanding of Negro songs can make to the recent debate over slave personality. In the process I will discuss several aspects of the literature and problems related to the use of slave songs.

The subject of Negro music in slavery has produced a large and varied literature, little of which has been devoted to questions of meaning and function. The one major exception is Miles Mark Fisher's 1953 study, *Negro Slave Songs in the United States,* which attempts to get at the essence of slave life through an analysis of slave songs. Unfortunately, Fisher's rich insights are too often marred by his rather loose scholarly standards, and despite its continuing value his study is in many respects an example of how *not* to use Negro songs. Asserting, correctly, that the words of slave songs "show both accidental and intentional errors of transmission," Fisher changes the words almost at will to fit his own image of their pristine form. Arguing persuasively that "transplanted Negroes continued to promote their own culture by music," Fisher makes their songs part of an "African cult" which he simply wills into existence. Maintaining (again, I think, correctly), that "slave songs preserved in joyful strains the adjustment which Negroes made to their living conditions within the United States," Fisher traces the major patterns of that adjustment by arbitrarily dating these songs, apparently unperturbed by the almost total lack of evidence pertaining to the origin and introduction of individual slave songs.[1]

Fisher aside, most other major studies of slave music have focused almost entirely upon musical structure and origin. This latter question especially has given rise to a long and heated debate.[2] The earliest collectors and students of slave music were impressed by how different that music was from anything familiar to them. Following a visit to the Sea Islands in 1862, Lucy McKim despaired of being able "to express the entire character of these negro ballads by mere musical notes and signs. The odd turns made in the throat; and that curious rhythmic effect produced by single voices chiming in at different irregular intervals, seem almost as impossible to place on score, as the singing of birds, or the tones of an Aeolian Harp."[3] Although some of these early collectors maintained, as did W. F. Allen in 1865, that much of the slave's music "might no doubt be traced to tunes which they have heard from the whites, and transformed to their own use, . . . their music . . . is rather European than African in its character,"[4] they more often stressed the distinctiveness of the Negro's music and attributed it to racial characteristics, African origins, and indigenous developments resulting from the slave's unique experience in the New World.

This tradition, which has had many influential twentieth-century adherents,[5] was increasingly challenged in the early decades of this century. Such scholars as Newman White, Guy Johnson, and George Pullen Jackson argued that the earlier school lacked a comparative grounding in Anglo-American folk song. Comparing Negro spirituals with Methodist and Baptist evangelical religious music of the late eighteenth and early nineteenth centuries, White, Johnson, and Jackson found similarities in words, subject matter, tunes, and musical structure.[6] Although they tended to exaggerate both qualitatively and quantitatively the degrees of similarity, their comparisons were often a persuasive and important corrective to the work of their predecessors. But their studies were inevitably weakened by their ethnocentric assumption that similarities alone settled the argument over origins. Never could they contemplate the possibility that the direction of cultural diffusion might have been from black to white as well as the other way. In fact, insofar as white evangelical music departed from traditional Protestant hymnology and embodied or approached the complex rhythmic structure, the percussive qualities, the polymeter, the syncopation, the emphasis on overlapping call and response patterns that characterized Negro music both in West Africa and the New World, the possibility that it was influenced by slaves who attended and joined in the singing at religious meetings is quite high.

These scholars tended to use the similarities between black and white religious music to deny the significance of slave songs in still another way. Newman White, for example, argued that since white evangelical hymns also used such expressions as "freedom," the "Promised Land," and the "Egyptian Bondage," "without thought of other than spiritual meaning," these images when they occurred in Negro spirituals could not have been symbolic "of the Negro's longing for physical freedom."[7] The familiar process by which different cultural groups can derive varied meanings from identical images is enough to cast doubt on the logic of White's argument.[8] In the case of white and black religious music, however, the problem may be much less complex, since it is quite possible that the similar images in the songs of both groups in fact served similar purposes. Many of those whites who flocked to the camp meetings of the Methodists and Baptists were themselves on the social and economic margins of their society, and had psychic and emotional needs which, qualitatively, may not have been vastly different from those of black slaves. Interestingly, George Pullen Jackson, in his attempt to prove the white origin of Negro spirituals, makes exactly this point: "I may mention in closing the chief remaining argument of the die-hards for the Negro source of the Negro spirituals. . . . How could any, the argument runs, but a natively musical and sorely oppressed race create such beautiful things as 'Swing Low,' 'Steal Away,' and 'Deep River'? . . . But were not the whites of the mountains and the hard-scrabble hill country also 'musical and oppressed'? . . . Yes, these whites were musical, and oppressed too. If their condition was any more tolerable than that of the Negroes, one certainly does not get that impression from any of their songs of release and escape."[9] If this is true, the presence of similar images in white music would merely heighten rather than detract from the significance of these images in Negro songs. Clearly, the function and meaning of white religious music during the late eighteenth and early nineteenth centuries demands far more attention than it has received. In the interim, we must be wary of allowing the mere fact of similarities to deter us from attempting to comprehend the cultural dynamics of slave music.

Contemporary scholars, tending to transcend the more simplistic lines of the old debate, have focused upon the process of syncretism to explain the development of Negro music in the United States. The rich West African

musical tradition common to almost all of the specific cultures from which
Negro slaves came, the comparative cultural isolation in which large numbers of slaves lived, the tolerance and even encouragement which their white
masters accorded to their musical activities, and the fact that, for all its
differences, nothing in the European musical tradition with which they came
into contact in America was totally alien to their own traditions—all these
were conducive to a situation which allowed the slaves to retain a good deal
of the integrity of their own musical heritage while fusing to it compatible
elements of Anglo-American music. Slaves often took over entire white hymns
and folk songs, as White and Jackson maintained, but altered them significantly in terms of words, musical structure, and especially performance before making them their own. The result was a hybrid with a strong African
base.[10]

One of the more interesting aspects of this debate over origins is that
no one engaged in it, not even advocates of the white derivation theory,
denied that the slaves possessed their own distinctive music. Newman White
took particular pains to point out again and again that the notion that Negro
song is purely an imitation of the white man's music "is fully as unjust and
inaccurate, in the final analysis, as the Negro's assumption that his folksong is entirely original." He observed that in the slaves' separate religious
meetings they were free to do as they would with the music they first learned
from the whites, with the result that their spirituals became "the greatest
single outlet for the expression of the Negro folk-mind."[11] Similarly, George
Pullen Jackson, after admitting that he could find no white parallels for over
two-thirds of the existing Negro spirituals, reasoned that these were produced by Negro singers in true folk fashion "by endless singing of heard
tunes and by endless, inevitable and concomitant singing differentiation."
Going even further, Jackson asserted that the lack of deep roots in Anglo-
American culture left the black man "even freer than the white man to make
songs over unconsciously as he sang . . . the free play has resulted in the
very large number of songs which, though formed primarily in the white
man's moulds, have lost all recognizable relationship to known individual
white-sung melodic entities."[12] This debate over origins indicates clearly
that a belief in the direct continuity of African musical traditions or in the
process of syncretism is not a necessary prerequisite to the conclusion that
the Negro slaves' music was their own, regardless of where they received
the components out of which it was fashioned; a conclusion which is crucial
to any attempt to utilize these songs as an aid in reconstructing the slaves'
consciousness.

Equally important is the process by which slave songs were created and
transmitted. When James McKim asked a freedman on the Sea Islands during the Civil War where the slaves got their songs, the answer was elo-

quently simple: "Dey make em, sah." [13] Precisely *how* they made them
worried and fascinated Thomas Wentworth Higginson, who became familiar
with slave music through the singing of the black Union soldiers in his Civil
War regiment. Were their songs, he wondered, a "conscious and definite"
product of "some leading mind," or did they grow "by gradual accretion,
in an almost unconscious way"? A freedman rowing Higginson and some
of his troops between the Sea Islands helped to resolve the problem when
he described a spiritual which he had a hand in creating:

> Once we boys went for some rice and de nigger-driver he keep a-callin'
> on us; and I say, "O de ole nigger-driver!" Den anudder said, "Fust ting
> my mammy tole me was, notin' so bad as nigger-driver." Den I made a
> sing, just puttin' a word, and den anudder word.

He then began to sing his song:

> O, de ole nigger-driver!
>   O, gwine away!
> Fust ting my mammy tell me,
>   O, gwine away!
>
> Tell me 'bout de nigger-driver,
>   O, gwine away!
> Nigger-driver second devil,
>   O, gwine away!

Higginson's black soldiers, after a moment's hesitation, joined in the singing of a song they had never heard before as if they had long been familiar
with it. "I saw," Higginson concluded, "how easily a new 'sing' took root
among them." [14]

This spontaneity, this sense of almost instantaneous community which
so impressed Higginson, constitutes a central element in every account of
slave singing. The English musician Henry Russell, who lived in the United
States in the 1830's, was forcibly struck by the ease with which a slave
congregation in Vicksburg, Mississippi, took a "fine old psalm tune" and,
by suddenly and spontaneously accelerating the tempo, transformed it "into
a kind of negro melody." [15] "Us old heads," an ex-slave told Jeanette Robinson Murphy, "use ter make 'em up on de spurn of de moment. Notes is
good enough for you people, but us likes a mixtery." Her account of the
creation of a spiritual is typical and important:

> We'd all be at the "prayer house" de Lord's day, and de white preacher
> he'd splain de word and read whar Esekial done say—
>
> *Dry bones gwine ter lib ergin.*

And, honey, de Lord would come a-shinin' thoo dem pages and revive dis ole nigger's heart, and I'd jump up dar and den and holler and shout and sing and pat, and dey would all cotch de words and I'd sing it to some ole shout song I'd heard 'em sing from Africa, and dey'd all take it up and keep at it, and keep a-addin' to it, and den it would be a spiritual.[16]

This "internal" account has been verified again and again by the descriptions of observers, many of whom were witnessing not slave services but religious meetings of rural southern Negroes long after emancipation. The essential continuity of the Negro folk process in the more isolated sections of the rural South through the early decades of the twentieth century makes these accounts relevant for the slave period as well. Natalie Curtis Burlin, whose collection of spirituals is musically the most accurate one we have, and who had a long and close acquaintance with Negro music, never lost her sense of awe at the process by which these songs were molded. On a hot July Sunday in rural Virginia, she sat in a Negro meeting house listening to the preacher deliver his prayer, interrupted now and then by an "O Lord!" or "Amen, Amen" from the congregation.

Minutes passed, long minutes of strange intensity. The mutterings, the ejaculations, grew louder, more dramatic, till suddenly I felt the creative thrill dart through the people like an electric vibration, that same half-audible hum arose,—emotion was gathering atmospherically as clouds gather—and then, up from the depths of some "sinner's" remorse and imploring came a pitiful little plea, a real "moan," sobbed in musical cadence. From somewhere in that bowed gathering another voice improvised a response: the plea sounded again, louder this time and more impassioned; then other voices joined in the answer, shaping it into a musical phrase; and so, before our ears, as one might say, from this molten metal of music a new song was smithied out, composed then and there by no one in particular and by everyone in general.[17]

Clifton Furness has given us an even more graphic description. During a visit to an isolated South Carolina plantation in 1926, he attended a prayer meeting held in the old slave cabins. The preacher began his reading of the Scriptures slowly, then increased his tempo and emotional fervor, assuring his flock that "Gawd's lightnin' gwine strike! Gawd's thunder swaller de ert!"

Gradually moaning became audible in the shadowy corners where the women sat. Some patted their bundled babies in time to the flow of the words, and began swaying backward and forward. Several men moved their feet alternately, in strange syncopation. A rhythm was born, almost without reference to the words that were being spoken by the preacher. It seemed to take shape almost visibly, and grow. I was gripped with the feeling of a mass-intelligence, a self-conscious entity, gradually informing the crowd and taking possession of every mind there, including my own.

In the midst of this increasing intensity, a black man sitting directly in front of Furness, his head bowed, his body swaying, his feet patting up and down, suddenly cried out: "Git right—sodger! Git right—sodger! Git right—wit Gawd!"

> Instantly the crowd took it up, moulding a melody out of half-formed familiar phrases based upon a spiritual tune, hummed here and there among the crowd. A distinct melodic outline became more and more prominent, shaping itself around the central theme of the words, "Git right, sodger!"
>
> Scraps of other words and tunes were flung into the medley of sound by individual singers from time to time, but the general trend was carried on by a deep undercurrent, which appeared to be stronger than the mind of any individual present, for it bore the mass of improvised harmony and rhythms into the most effective climax of incremental repetition that I have ever heard. I felt as if some conscious plan or purpose were carrying us along, call it mob-mind, communal composition, or what you will.[18]

Shortly after the Civil War, Elizabeth Kilham witnessed a similar scene among the freedmen, and described it in terms almost identical to those used by observers many years later. "A fog seemed to fill the church," she wrote, ". . . an invisible power seemed to hold us in its iron grasp; . . . A few moments more, and I think we should have shrieked in unison with the crowd."[19]

These accounts and others like them make it clear that spirituals both during and after slavery were the product of an improvisational communal consciousness. They were not, as some observers thought, totally new creations, but were forged out of many preexisting bits of old songs mixed together with snatches of new tunes and lyrics and fit into a fairly traditional but never wholly static metrical pattern. They were, to answer Higginson's question, *simultaneously* the result of individual and mass creativity. They were products of that folk process which has been called "communal recreation," through which older songs are constantly recreated into essentially new entities.[20] Anyone who has read through large numbers of Negro songs is familiar with this process. Identical or slightly varied stanzas appear in song after song; identical tunes are made to accommodate completely different sets of lyrics; the same song appears in different collections in widely varied forms. In 1845 a traveler observed that the only permanent elements in Negro song were the music and the chorus. "The blacks themselves leave out old stanzas, and introduce new ones at pleasure. Travelling through the South, you may, in passing from Virginia to Louisiana, hear the same tune a hundred times, but seldom the same words accompanying it.''[21] Another observer noted in 1870 that during a single religious meeting the freedmen would often sing the words of one spiritual to several different tunes, and then take a tune that particularly pleased them and fit the words of several different songs to it.[22] Slave songs, then, were never static; at no time did Negroes create a "final" version of any spiritual. Always the community felt free to alter and recreate them.

The two facts that I have attempted to establish thus far—that slave music, regardless of its origins, was a distinctive cultural form, and that it was created or constantly recreated through a communal process—are essential if one is to justify the use of these songs as keys to slave consciousness. But these facts in themselves say a good deal about the nature and quality of slave life and personality. That black slaves could create and continually recreate songs marked by the poetic beauty, the emotional intensity, the rich imagery which characterized the spirituals—songs which even one of the most devout proponents of the white man's origins school admits are "the most impressive religious folk songs in our language"[23]—should be enough to make us seriously question recent theories which conceive of slavery as a closed system which destroyed the vitality of the Negro and left him a dependent child. For all of its horrors, slavery was never so complete a system of psychic assault that it prevented the slaves from carving out independent cultural forms. It never pervaded all of the interstices of their minds and their culture, and in those gaps they were able to create an independent art form and a distinctive voice. If North American slavery eroded the African's linguistic and institutional life, if it prevented him from preserving and developing his rich heritage of graphic and plastic art, it nevertheless allowed him to continue and to develop the patterns of verbal art which were so central to his past culture. Historians have not yet come to terms with what the continuance of the oral tradition meant to blacks in slavery.

In Africa, songs, tales, proverbs, and verbal games served the dual function of not only preserving communal values and solidarity, but also of providing occasions for the individual to transcend, at least symbolically, the inevitable restrictions of his environment and his society by permitting him to express deeply held feelings which he ordinarily was not allowed to verbalize. Among the Ashanti and the Dahomeans, for example, periods were set aside when the inhabitants were encouraged to gather together and, through the medium of song, dance, and tales, to openly express their feelings about each other. The psychological release this afforded seems to have been well understood. "You know that everyone has a *sunsum* (soul) that may get hurt or knocked about or become sick, and so make the body ill," an Ashanti high priest explained to the English anthropologist R. S. Rattray:

> Very often . . . ill health is caused by the evil and the hate that another has in his head against you. Again, you too may have hatred in your head against another, because of something that person has done to you, and that, too, causes your *sunsum* to fret and become sick. Our forbears knew this to be the case, and so they ordained a time, once every year, when every man and woman, free man and slave, should have freedom to speak out just what was in their head, to tell their neighbours just what they thought of them, and of their actions, and not only their neighbours, but also the king or chief. When a man has spoken freely thus, he will feel his *sunsum* cool and quieted, and the *sunsum* of the other person against whom he has now openly spoken will be quieted also.

Utilization of verbal art for this purpose was widespread throughout Africa, and was not confined to those ceremonial occasions when one could directly state one's feelings. Through innuendo, metaphor, and circumlocution, Africans could utilize their songs as outlets for individual release without disturbing communal solidarity.[24]

There is abundant internal evidence that the verbal art of the slaves in the United States served many of these traditional functions. Just as the process by which the spirituals were created allowed for simultaneous individual and communal creativity, so their very structure provided simultaneous outlets for individual and communal expression. The overriding antiphonal structure of the spirituals—the call and response pattern which Negroes brought with them from Africa and which was reinforced by the relatively similar white practice of "lining out" hymns—placed the individual in continual dialogue with his community, allowing him at one and the same time to preserve his voice as a distinct entity and to blend it with those of his fellows. Here again slave music confronts us with evidence which indicates that however seriously the slave system may have diminished the strong sense of community that had bound Africans together, it never totally destroyed it or left the individual atomized and emotionally and psychically defenseless before his white masters. In fact, the form and structure of slave music presented the slave with a potential outlet for his individual feelings even while it continually drew him back into the communal presence and permitted him the comfort of basking in the warmth of the shared assumptions of those around him.

Those "shared assumptions" can be further examined by an analysis of the content of slave songs. Our preoccupation in recent years with the degree to which the slaves actually resembled the "Sambo" image held by their white masters has obscured the fact that the slaves developed images of their own which must be consulted and studied before any discussion of slave personality can be meaningful. The image of the trickster, who through cunning and unscrupulousness prevails over his more powerful antagonists, pervades slave tales. The trickster figure is rarely encountered in the slave's religious songs, though its presence is sometimes felt in the slave's many allusions to his narrow escapes from the devil.

> The Devil's mad and I'm glad,
> He lost the soul he thought he had.[25]

> Ole Satan toss a ball at me.
> O me no weary yet . . .

> Him tink de ball would hit my soul.
> O me no weary yet . . .

> De ball for hell and I for heaven.
> O me no weary yet . . .[26]

> Ole Satan thought he had a mighty aim;
> He missed my soul and caught my sins.
> Cry Amen, cry Amen, cry Amen to God!

> He took my sins upon his back;
> Went muttering and grumbling down to hell.
> Cry Amen, cry Amen, cry Amen to God![27]

The single most persistent image the slave songs contain, however, is that of the chosen people. The vast majority of the spirituals identify the singers as "de people dat is born of God," "We are the people of God," "we are de people of de Lord," "I really do believe I'm a child of God," "I'm a child ob God, wid my soul sot free," "I'm born of God, I know I am." Nor is there ever any doubt that "To the promised land I'm bound to go," "I walk de heavenly road," "Heav'n shall-a be my home," "I gwine to meet my Saviour," "I seek my Lord and I find Him," "I'll hear the trumpet sound/In that morning."[28]

The force of this image cannot be diminished by the observation that similar images were present in the religious singing of white evangelical churches during the first half of the nineteenth century. White Americans could be expected to sing of triumph and salvation, given their long-standing heritage of the idea of a chosen people which was reinforced in this era by the belief in inevitable progress and manifest destiny, the spread-eagle oratory, the bombastic folklore, and, paradoxically, the deep insecurities concomitant with the tasks of taming a continent and developing an identity.

But for this same message to be expressed by Negro slaves who were told endlessly that they were members of the lowliest of races *is* significant. It offers an insight into the kinds of barriers the slaves had available to them against the internalization of the stereotyped images their masters held and attempted consciously and unconsciously to foist upon them.

The question of the chosen people image leads directly into the larger problem of what role religion played in the songs of the slave. Writing in 1862, James McKim noted that the songs of the Sea Island freedmen "are all religious, barcaroles and all. I speak without exception. So far as I heard or was told of their singing, it was all religious." Others who worked with recently emancipated slaves recorded the same experience, and Colonel Higginson reported that he rarely heard his troops sing a profane or vulgar song. With a few exceptions, "all had a religious motive."[29] In spite of this testimony, there can be little doubt that the slaves sang nonreligious songs. In 1774, an English visitor to the United States, after his first encounter with slave music, wrote in his journal: "In their songs they generally relate the usage they have received from their Masters or Mistresses in a very satirical stile and manner."[30] Songs fitting this description can be found in the nineteenth-century narratives of fugitive slaves. Harriet Jacobs recorded that during the Christmas season the slaves would ridicule stingy whites by singing:

> Poor Massa, so dey say;
> Down in de heel, so dey say;
> Got no money, so dey say;
> God A'mighty bress you, so dey say.[31]

"Once in a while among a mass of nonsense and wild frolic," Frederick Douglass noted, "a sharp hit was given to the meanness of slaveholders."

> We raise de wheat,
> Dey gib us de corn;
> We bake de bread,
> Dey gib us de crust;
> We sif de meal,
> Dey gib us de huss;
> We peal de meat,
> Dey gib us de skin;
> And dat's de way
> Dey take us in;
> We skim de pot,
> Dey gib us de liquor,
> And say dat's good enough for nigger.[32]

Both of these songs are in the African tradition of utilizing song to bypass both internal and external censors and give vent to feelings which could be expressed in no other form. Nonreligious songs were not limited to the slave's relations with his masters, however, as these rowing songs, collected by contemporary white observers, indicate:

> We are going down to Georgia, boys,
> Aye, aye.
> To see the pretty girls, boys,
> Yoe, yoe.
> We'll give 'em a pint of brandy, boys,
> Aye, aye.
> And a hearty kiss, besides, boys,
> Yoe, yoe.[33]

> Jenny shake her toe at me,
> Jenny gone away;
> Jenny shake her toe at me,
> Jenny gone away.
> Hurrah! Miss Susy, oh!
> Jenny gone away;
> Hurrah! Miss Susy, oh!
> Jenny gone away.[34]

The variety of nonreligious songs in the slave's repertory was wide. There were songs of in-group and out-group satire, songs of nostalgia, nonsense songs, songs of play and work and love. Nevertheless, our total stock of these songs is very small. It is possible to add to these by incorporating such post-bellum secular songs which have an authentic slavery ring to them as "De Blue-Tail Fly," with its ill-concealed satisfaction at the death of a master, or the ubiquitous

> My ole Mistiss promise me,
> W'en she died, she'd set me free,
> She lived so long dat 'er head got bal',
> An' she give out'n de notion a dyin' at all.[35]

The number can be further expanded by following Constance Rourke's suggestion that we attempt to disentangle elements of Negro origin from those of white creation in the "Ethiopian melodies" of the white minstrel shows, many of which were similar to the songs I have just quoted.[36] Either of these possibilities, however, forces the historian to work with sources far more potentially spurious than those with which he normally is comfortable.

Spirituals, on the other hand, for all the problems associated with their being filtered through white hands before they were published, and despite the many errors in transcription that inevitably occurred, constitute a much more satisfactory source. They were collected by the hundreds directly from slaves and freedmen during the Civil War and the decades immediately following, and although they came from widely different geographical areas they share a common structure and content, which seems to have been characteristic of Negro music wherever slavery existed in the United States. It is possible that we have a greater number of religious than nonreligious songs because slaves were more willing to sing these ostensibly innocent songs to white collectors who in turn were more anxious to record them, since they fit easily with their positive and negative images of the Negro. But I would argue that the vast preponderance of spirituals over any other sort of slave music, rather than being merely the result of accident or error, is instead an accurate reflection of slave culture during the ante-bellum period. Whatever songs the slaves may have sung before their wholesale conversion to Christianity in the late eighteenth and early nineteenth centuries, by the latter century spirituals were quantitatively and qualitatively their most significant musical creation. In this form of expression slaves found a medium which resembled in many important ways the world view they had brought with them from Africa, and afforded them the possibility of both adapting to and transcending their situation.

It is significant that the most common form of slave music we know of is sacred song. I use the term "sacred" not in its present usage as something antithetical to the secular world; neither the slaves nor their African forebears ever drew modernity's clear line between the sacred and the secular. The uses to which spirituals were put are an unmistakable indication of this. They were not sung solely or even primarily in churches or praise houses, but were used as rowing songs, field songs, work songs, and social songs. On the Sea Islands during the Civil War, Lucy McKim heard the spiritual "Poor Rosy" sung in a wide variety of contexts and tempos.

> On the water, the oars dip "Poor Rosy" to an even andante; a stout boy and girl at the hominy-mill will make the same "Poor Rosy" fly, to keep up with the whirling stone; and in the evening, after the day's work is done, "Heab'n shall-a be my home" [the final line of each stanza] peals up slowly and mournfully from the distant quarters.[37]

For the slaves, then, songs of God and the mythic heroes of their religion were not confined to any specific time or place, but were appropriate to almost every situation. It is in this sense that I use the concept sacred—

not to signify a rejection of the present world but to describe the process of incorporating within this world all the elements of the divine. The religious historian Mircea Eliade, whose definition of sacred has shaped my own, has maintained that for men in traditional societies religion is a means of extending the world spatially upward so that communication with the other world becomes ritually possible, and extending it temporally backward so that the paradigmatic acts of the gods and mythical ancestors can be continually reenacted and indefinitely recoverable. By creating sacred time and space, man can perpetually live in the presence of his gods, can hold on to the certainty that within one's own lifetime "rebirth" is continually possible, and can impose order on the chaos of the universe. "Life," as Eliade puts it, "is lived on a twofold plane; it takes its course as human existence and, at the same time, shares in a transhuman life, that of the cosmos or the gods." [38]

This notion of sacredness gets at the essence of the spirituals, and through them at the essence of the slave's world view. Denied the possibility of achieving an adjustment to the external world of the antebellum South which involved meaningful forms of personal integration, attainment of status, and feelings of individual worth that all human beings crave and need, the slaves created a new world by transcending the narrow confines of the one in which they were forced to live. They extended the boundaries of their restrictive universe backward until it fused with the world of the Old Testament, and upward until it became one with the world beyond. The spirituals are the record of a people who found the status, the harmony, the values, the order they needed to survive by internally creating an expanded universe, by literally willing themselves reborn. In this respect I agree with the anthropologist Paul Radin that

> The ante-bellum Negro was not converted to God. He converted God to himself. In the Christian God he found a fixed point and he needed a fixed point, for both within and outside of himself, he could see only vacillation and endless shifting. . . . There was no other safety for people faced on all sides by doubt and the threat of personal disintegration, by the thwarting of instincts and the annihilation of values.[39]

The confinement of much of the slave's new world to dreams and fantasies does not free us from the historical obligation of examining its contours, weighing its implications for the development of the slave's psychic and emotional structure, and eschewing the kind of facile reasoning that leads Professor Elkins to imply that, since the slaves had no alternatives open to them, their fantasy life was "limited to catfish and watermelons." [40] Their spirituals indicate clearly that there *were* alternatives open to them—alternatives which they themselves fashioned out of the fusion of their African

heritage and their new religion—and that their fantasy life was so rich and
so important to them that it demands understanding if we are even to begin
to comprehend their inner world.

The God the slaves sang of was neither remote nor abstract, but as
intimate, personal, and immediate as the gods of Africa had been. "O when
I talk I talk wid God," "Mass Jesus is my bosom friend," "I'm goin' to
walk with [talk with, live with, see] King Jesus by myself, by myself,"
were refrains that echoed through the spirituals.[41]

> In de mornin' when I rise,
> Tell my Jesus huddy [howdy] oh,
> I wash my hands in de mornin' glory,
> Tell my Jesus huddy oh.[42]

> Gwine to argue wid de Father and chatter wid de son,
> The last trumpet shall sound, I'll be there.
> Gwine talk 'bout de bright world dey des' come from.
> The last trumpet shall sound, I'll be there.[43]

> Gwine to write to Massa Jesus,
> To send some Valiant soldier
> To turn back Pharaoh's army, Hallelu![44]

The heroes of the Scriptures—"Sister Mary," "Brudder Jonah,"
"Brudder Moses," "Brudder Daniel"—were greeted with similar intimacy
and immediacy. In the world of the spirituals, it was not the masters and
mistresses but God and Jesus and the entire pantheon of Old Testament
figures who set the standards, established the precedents, and defined the
values; who, in short, constituted the "significant others." The world described by the slave songs was a black world in which no reference was
ever made to any white contemporaries. The slave's positive reference group
was composed entirely of his own peers: his mother, father, sister, brother,
uncles, aunts, preacher, fellow "sinners" and "mourners" of whom he sang
endlessly, to whom he sent messages via the dying, and with whom he was
reunited joyfully in the next world.

The same sense of sacred time and space which shaped the slave's portraits of his gods and heroes also made his visions of the past and future
immediate and compelling. Descriptions of the Crucifixion communicate a
sense of the actual presence of the singers: "Dey pierced Him in the side
. . . Dey nail Him to de cross . . . Dey rivet His feet . . . Dey hanged
him high . . . Dey stretch Him wide. . . ."

> Oh sometimes it causes me to tremble,-tremble,-tremble,
> Were you there when they crucified my Lord?[45]

The Slave's "shout"—that counterclockwise, shuffling dance which frequently occurred after the religious service and lasted long into the night—often became a medium through which the ecstatic dancers were transformed into actual participants in historic actions: Joshua's army marching around the walls of Jericho, the children of Israel following Moses out of Egypt.[46]

The thin line between time dimensions is nowhere better illustrated than in the slave's visions of the future, which were, of course, a direct negation of his present. Among the most striking spirituals are those which pile detail upon detail in describing the Day of Judgment: "You'll see de world on fire . . . see de element a meltin', . . . see the stars a fallin' . . . see the moon a bleedin' . . . see the forked lightning, . . . Hear the rumblin' thunder . . . see the righteous marching, . . . see my Jesus coming . . . ," and the world to come where "Dere's no sun to burn you . . . no hard trials . . . no whips a crackin' . . . no stormy weather . . . no tribulation . . . no evil-doers . . . All is gladness in de Kingdom."[47] This vividness was matched by the slave's certainty that he would partake of the triumph of judgment and the joys of the new world:

> Dere's room enough, room enough, room enough in de heaven, my Lord
> Room enough, room enough, I can't stay behind.[48]

Continually, the slaves sang of reaching out beyond the world that confined them, of seeing Jesus "in de wilderness," of praying "in de lonesome valley," of breathing in the freedom of the mountain peaks:

> Did yo' ever
> Stan' on mountun,
> Wash yo' han's
> In a cloud?[49]

Continually, they held out the possibility of imminent rebirth; "I look at de worl' an' de worl' look new, . . . I look at my hands an' they look so too . . . I looked at my feet, my feet was too."[50]

These possibilities, these certainties were not surprising. The religious revivals which swept large numbers of slaves into the Christian fold in the late eighteenth and early nineteenth centuries were based upon a *practical* (not necessarily theological) Armianism: God would save all who believed in Him; Salvation was there for all to take hold of if they would. The effects of this message upon the slaves who were exposed to and converted by it have been passed over too easily by historians. Those effects are illustrated graphically in the spirituals which were the products of these revivals and which continued to spread the evangelical word long after the revivals had passed into history.

The religious music of the slaves is almost devoid of feelings of depravity or unworthiness, but is rather, as I have tried to show, pervaded by a sense of change, transcendence, ultimate justice, and personal worth. The spirituals have been referred to as "sorrow songs," and in some respects they were. The slaves sang of "rollin' thro' an unfriendly world," of being "a-trouble in de mind," of living in a world which was a "howling wilderness," "a hell to me," of feeling like a "motherless child," "a po' little orphan chile in de worl'," a "home-e-less child," of fearing that "Trouble will bury me down.' "[51]

But these feelings were rarely pervasive or permanent; almost always they were overshadowed by a triumphant note of affirmation. Even so despairing a wail as "Nobody Knows the Trouble I've Had" could suddenly have its mood transformed by lines like: "One morning I was a-walking down, . . . Saw some berries a-hanging down, . . . I pick de berry and I suck de juice, . . . Just as sweet as de honey in de comb."[52] Similarly, amid the deep sorrow of "Sometimes I feel like a Motherless chile," sudden release could come with the lines: "Sometimes I feel like/A eagle in de air. . . . Spread my wings an'/Fly, fly, fly."[53] Slaves spent little time singing of the horrors of hell or damnation. Their songs of the Devil, quoted earlier, pictured a harsh but almost semicomic figure (often, one suspects, a surrogate for the white man), over whom they triumphed with reassuring regularity. For all their inevitable sadness, slave songs were characterized more by a feeling of confidence than of despair. There was confidence that contemporary power relationships were not immutable: "Did not old Pharaoh get lost, get lost, get lost, . . . get lost in the Red Sea?"; confidence in the possibilities of instantaneous change: "Jesus make de dumb to speak. . . . Jesus make de cripple walk. . . . Jesus give de blind his sight. . . . Jesus do most anything"; confidence in the rewards of persistence: "Keep a' inching along like a poor inch-worm,/ Jesus will come by'nd bye"; confidence that nothing could stand in the way of the justice they would receive: "You kin hender me here, but you can't do it dah," "O no man, no man, no man can hinder me"; confidence in the prospects of the future: "We'll walk de golden streets/Of de New Jerusalem." Religion, the slaves sang, "is good for anything, . . . Religion make you happy, . . . Religion gib me patience . . . O member, get Religion . . . Religion is so sweet."[54]

The slaves often pursued the "sweetness" of their religion in the face of many obstacles. Becky Ilsey, who was 16 when she was emancipated, recalled many years later:

'Fo' de war when we'd have a meetin' at night, wuz mos' always 'way in
de woods or de bushes some whar so de white folks couldn't hear, an'
when dey'd sing a spiritual an' de spirit 'gin to shout some de elders would

go 'mongst de folks an' put dey han' over dey mouf an' some times put a clof in dey mouf an' say: "Spirit don talk so loud or de patterol break us up." You know dey had white patterols what went 'roun' at night to see de niggers didn't cut up no devilment, an' den de meetin' would break up an' some would go to one house an' some to er nudder an' dey would groan er w'ile, den go home.[55]

Elizabeth Ross Hite testified that although she and her fellow slaves on a Louisiana plantation were Catholics, "lots didn't like that 'ligion."

We used to hide behind some bricks and hold church ourselves. You see, the Catholic preachers from France wouldn't let us shout, and the Lawd done said you gotta shout if you want to be saved. That's in the Bible.

Sometimes we held church all night long, 'til way in the mornin'. We burned some grease in a can for the preacher to see the Bible by. . . .

See, our master didn't like us to have much 'ligion, said it made us lag in our work. He jest wanted us to be Catholicses on Sundays and go to mass and not study 'bout nothin' like that on week days. He didn't want us shoutin' and moanin' all day'-long, but you gotta shout and you gotta moan if you wants to be saved.[56]

The slaves clearly craved the affirmation and promise of their religion. It would be a mistake, however, to see this urge as exclusively other-worldly. When Thomas Wentworth Higginson observed that the spirituals exhibited "nothing but patience for this life,—nothing but triumph in the next," he, and later observers who elaborated upon this judgment, were indulging in hyperbole. Although Jesus was ubiquitous in the spirituals, it was not invariably the Jesus of the New Testament of whom the slaves sang, but frequently a Jesus transformed into an Old Testament warrior: "Mass' Jesus" who engaged in personal combat with the Devil; "King Jesus" seated on a milk-white horse with sword and shield in hand. "Ride on, King Jesus," "Ride on, conquering King," "The God I serve is a man of war," the slaves sang.[57] This transformation of Jesus is symptomatic of the slaves' selectivity in choosing those parts of the Bible which were to serve as the basis of their religious consciousness. Howard Thurman, a Negro minister who as a boy had the duty of reading the Bible to his grandmother, was perplexed by her refusal to allow him to read from the Epistles of Paul.

When at length I asked the reason, she told me that during the days of slavery, the minister (white) on the plantation was always preaching from the Pauline letters—"Slaves, be obedient to your masters," etc. "I vowed to myself," she said, "that if freedom ever came and I learned to read, I would never read that part of the Bible!"[58]

Nor, apparently, did this part of the Scriptures ever constitute a vital element in slave songs or sermons. The emphasis of the spirituals, as Higginson himself noted, was upon the Old Testament and the exploits of the Hebrew children.[59] It is important that Daniel and David and Joshua and Jonah and Moses and Noah, all of whom fill the lines of the spirituals, were delivered in *this* world and delivered in ways which struck the imagination of the slaves. Over and over their songs dwelt upon the spectacle of the Red Sea opening to allow the Hebrew slaves past before inundating the mighty armies of the Pharaoh. They lingered delightedly upon the image of little David humbling the great Goliath with a stone—a pretechnological victory which post-bellum Negroes were to expand upon in their songs of John Henry. They retold in endless variation the stories of the blind and humbled Samson bringing down the mansions of his conquerors; of the ridiculed Noah patiently building the ark which would deliver him from the doom of a mocking world; of the timid Jonah attaining freedom from his confinement through faith. The similarity of these tales to the situation of the slave was too clear for him not to see it; too clear for us to believe that the songs had no worldly content for the black man in bondage. "O my Lord delivered Daniel," the slaves observed, and responded logically: "O why not deliver me, too?"

> He delivered Daniel from de lion's den,
>   Jonah from de belly ob de whale,
> And de Hebrew children from de fiery furnace,
>   And why not every man?[60]

These lines state as clearly as anything can the manner in which the sacred world of the slaves was able to fuse the precedents of the past, the conditions of the present, and the promise of the future into one connected reality. In this respect there was always a latent and symbolic element of protest in the slave's religious songs which frequently became overt and explicit. Frederick Douglass asserted that for him and many of his fellow slaves the song, "O Canaan, sweet Canaan,/I am bound for the land of Canaan," symbolized "something more than a hope of reaching heaven. We meant to reach the *North,* and the North was our Canaan," and he wrote that the lines of another spiritual, "Run to Jesus, shun the danger,/I don't expect to stay much longer here," had a double meaning which first suggested to him the thought of escaping from slavery.[61] Similarly, when the black troops in Higginson's regiment sang:

> We'll soon be free, [three times]
> When de Lord will call us home.

a young drummer boy explained to him, "Dey think *de Lord* mean for say *de Yankees.*" [62] Nor is there any reason to doubt that slaves could have used their songs as a means of secret communication. An ex-slave told Lydia Parrish that when he and his fellow slaves "suspicioned" that one of their number was telling tales to the driver, they would sing lines like the following while working in the field:

> O Judyas he wuz a 'ceitful man
> He went an' betray a mos' innocen' man.
> Fo' thirty pieces a silver dat it wuz done
> He went in de woods an' e' self he hung. [63]

And it is possible, as many writers have argued, that such spirituals as the commonly heard "Steal away, steal away, steal away to Jesus!" were used as explicit calls to secret meetings.

But it is not necessary to invest the spirituals with a secular function only at the price of divesting them of their religious content, as Miles Mark Fisher has done. [64] While we may make such clear-cut distinctions, I have tried to show that the slaves did not. For them religion never constituted a simple escape from this world, because their conception of the world was more expansive than modern man's. Nowhere is this better illustrated than during the Civil War itself. While the war gave rise to such new spirituals as "Before I'd be a slave/I'd be buried in my grave./And go home to my Lord and be saved!" or the popular "Many thousand Go," with its jubilant rejection of all the facets of slave life—"No more peck o' corn for me, . . . No more driver's lash for me, . . . No more pint o' salt for me, . . . No more hundred lash for me, . . . No more mistress' call for me" [65]—the important thing was not that large numbers of slaves now could create new songs which openly expressed their views of slavery; that was to be expected. More significant was the ease with which their old songs fit their new situation. With so much of their inspiration drawn from the events of the Old Testament and the Book of Revelation, the slaves had long sung of wars, of battles, of the Army of the Lord, of Soldiers of the Cross, of trumpets summoning the faithful, of vanquishing the hosts of evil. These songs especially were, as Higginson put it, "available for camp purposes with very little strain upon their symbolism." "We'll cross de mighty river," his troops sang while marching or rowing,

> We'll cross de danger water, . . .
> O Pharaoh's army drownded!
> My army cross over.

"O blow your trumpet, Gabriel," they sang,

> Blow your trumpet louder;
> And I want dat trumpet to blow me home
> To my new Jerusalem.

But they also found their less overtly militant songs quite as appropriate to warfare. Their most popular and effective marching song was:

> Jesus call you, Go in de wilderness,
>   Go in de wilderness, go in de wilderness,
> Jesus call you. Go in de wilderness
>   To wait upon de Lord.[66]

Black Union soldiers found it no more incongruous to accompany their fight for freedom with the sacred songs of their bondage than they had found it inappropriate as slaves to sing their spirituals while picking cotton or shucking corn. Their religious songs, like their religion itself, was of this world as well as the next.

Slave songs by themselves, of course, do not present us with a definitive key to the life and mind of the slave. They have to be seen within the context of the slave's situation and examined alongside such other cultural materials as folk tales. But slave songs do indicate the need to rethink a number of assumptions that have shaped recent interpretations of slavery, such as the assumption that because slavery eroded the linguistic and institutional side of African life it wiped out almost all the more fundamental aspects of African culture. Culture, certainly, is more than merely the sum total of institutions and language. It is also expressed by something less tangible, which the anthropologist Robert Redfield has called "style of life." Peoples as different as the Lapp and the Bedouin, Redfield has argued, with diverse languages, religions, customs, and institutions, may still share an emphasis on certain virtues and ideals, certain manners of independence and hospitality, general ways of looking upon the world, which give them a similar life style.[67] This argument applies to the West African cultures from which the slaves came. Though they varied widely in language, institutions, gods, and familial patterns, they shared a fundamental outlook toward the past, present, and future and common means of cultural expression which could well have constituted the basis of a sense of community and identity capable of surviving the impact of slavery.

Slave songs present us with abundant evidence that in the structure of their music and dance, in the uses to which music was put, in the survival of the oral tradition, in the retention of such practices as spirit possession which often accompanied the creation of spirituals, and in the ways in which the slaves expressed their new religion, important elements of their shared African heritage remained alive not just as quaint cultural vestiges but as vitally creative elements of slave culture. This could never have happened if slavery was, as Professor Elkins maintains, a system which so completely closed in around the slave, so totally penetrated his personality structure as to infantalize him and reduce him to a kind of *tabula rasa* upon which the white man could write what he chose.[68]

Slave songs provide us with the beginnings of a very different kind of hypothesis: that the preliterate, premodern Africans, with their sacred world view, were so imperfectly acculturated into the secular American society into which they were thrust, were so completely denied access to the ideology and dreams which formed the core of the consciousness of other Americans, that they were forced to fall back upon the only cultural frames of reference that made any sense to them and gave them any feeling of security. I use the word "forced" advisedly. Even if the slaves had had the opportunity to enter fully into the life of the larger society, they might still have chosen to retain and perpetuate certain elements of their African heritage. But the point is that they really had no choice. True acculturation was denied to most slaves. The alternatives were either to remain in a state of cultural limbo, divested of the old cultural patterns but not allowed to adopt those of their new homeland—which in the long run is no alternative at all—or to cling to as many as possible of the old ways of thinking and acting. The slaves' oral tradition, their music, and their religious outlook served this latter function and constituted a cultural refuge at least potentially capable of protecting their personalities from some of the worst ravages of the slave system.

The argument of Professors Tannenbaum and Elkins that the Protestant churches in the United States did not act as a buffer between the slave and his master is persuasive enough, but it betrays a modern preoccupation with purely institutional arrangements.[69] Religion is more than an institution, and because Protestant churches failed to protect the slave's inner being from the incursions of the slave system, it does not follow that the spiritual message of Protestantism failed as well. Slave songs are a testament to the ways in which Christianity provided slaves with the precedents, heroes, and future promise that allowed them to transcend the purely temporal bonds of the Peculiar Institution.

Historians have frequently failed to perceive the full importance of this because they have not taken the slave's religiosity seriously enough. A people cannot create a music as forceful and striking as slave music out of a mere uninternalized anodyne. Those who have argued that Negroes did not oppose slavery in any meaningful way are writing from a modern, political context. What they really mean is that the slaves found no *political* means to oppose slavery. But slaves, to borrow Professor Hobsbawm's term, were prepolitical beings in a prepolitical situation.[70] Within their frame of reference there were other—and from the point of view of personality development, not necessarily less effective—means of escape and opposition. If mid-twentieth-century historians have difficulty perceiving the sacred universe created by slaves as a serious alternative to the societal system created by southern slaveholders, the problem may be the historians' and not the slaves'.

Above all, the study of slave songs forces the historian to move out of his own culture, in which music plays a peripheral role, and offers him the opportunity to understand the ways in which black slaves were able to perpetuate much of the centrality and functional importance that music had for their African ancestors. In the concluding lines of his perceptive study of primitive song, C. M. Bowra has written:

> Primitive song is indispensable to those who practice it. . . . they cannot
> do without song, which both formulates and answers their nagging ques-
> tions, enables them to pursue action with zest and confidence, brings them
> into touch with gods and spirits, and makes them feel less strange in the
> natural world. . . . it gives to them a solid centre in what otherwise would
> be almost chaos, and a continuity in their being, which would too easily
> dissolve before the calls of the implacable present . . . through its words
> men, who might otherwise give in to the malice of circumstances, find
> their old powers revived or new powers stirring in them, and through these
> life itself is sustained and renewed and fulfilled.[71]

This, I think, sums up concisely the function of song for the slave. Without a general understanding of that function, without a specific understanding of the content and meaning of slave song, there can be no full comprehension of the effects of slavery upon the slave or the meaning of the society from which slaves emerged at emancipation.

4

"Some Go Up and Some Go Down": The Meaning of the Slave Trickster

Not long after Richard Hofstadter's death at the tragically early age of fifty-four in 1970, Eric McKitrick and Stanley Elkins, who, like myself, had been students of Hofstadter at Columbia University, asked me to contribute an essay to a memorial volume which they were editing. At the time I was writing a chapter on African-American slave folk tales, and I decided to focus my contribution on the meaning of animal trickster tales, probably the best known genre of Black folk tales. It was not a random choice. The last time Dick Hofstadter visited my wife and me in Berkeley, probably some time in late 1968 or early 1969, he spoke about his projected three-volume study of American political culture. He was then working on the colonial period and, as he was sometimes wont to do, he made a comment in the form of a question: ''Melville Herskovits was wrong about American slaves and Africa, wasn't he?'' My research, in fact, had been leading me to exactly the opposite conclusion; the arguments put forward by the anthropologist Melville Herskovits in *The Myth of the Negro Past* concerning the continuities of African culture in the United States, while sometimes weak in detail, on the whole seemed increasingly persuasive to me, but I could not yet articulate a solid case. Although, alas, Hofstadter was no longer there to convince, I began to answer his question in a more cohesive and, I hope, more convincing manner in the preceding essay on slave songs and this one on slave tales, which was published in Eric McKitrick and Stanley Elkins, eds., *The Hofstadter Aegis: A Memorial* (New York: Alfred A. Knopf, 1974).

For the historian interested in slave culture, folk tales constitute a crucial source. Although few black tales were collected until the decades following the Civil War, their distribution was so widespread throughout the South, their content so similar, and their style and function so uniform that it is evident they were not a sudden post-emancipation creation. "All over the South the stories of Br'er Rabbit are told," Octave Thanet reported in 1892. "Everywhere not only ideas and plots are repeated, but the very words often are the same; one gets a new vision of the power of oral tradition."[1] The variations in patterns of mobility, educational and vocational opportunities, cultural expression, and life styles brought about by emancipation produced inevitable changes in black folklore. Still, throughout the remainder of the nineteenth century—and well into the twentieth in many parts of the South— the large body of slave tales remained a vital and central core of Afro-American expression.

As with other aspects of their verbal art, slaves established in their tales important points of continuity with their African past. This is not to say that slave tales in the United States were necessarily African. Scholars will need more complete indices of African tale types and motifs than now exist before they can determine the origin of slave tales with any definitiveness. Comparison of slave tales with those guides to African tales that do exist reveals that a significant number were brought directly from Africa; a roughly similar percentage were tales common in both Africa and Europe, so that while slaves may have brought the tale type with them, its place in their lore could well have been reinforced by their contact with whites; and, finally, a third group of tales were learned in the New World both through Euro-American influence and through independent creation.[2]

Unfortunately, extended debate concerning the exact point of origin of these tales has taken precedence over analysis of their meaning and function. Cultural continuities with Africa were not dependent upon importation and perpetuation of specific folk tales in their pristine form. It was in the place that tales occupied in the lives of the slaves, the meaning slaves derived from them, and the ways in which slaves used them culturally and psychically that the clearest resemblances with their African past could be found. Thus, although Africans brought to the New World were inevitably influenced by the tales they found there and frequently adopted white tale plots, motifs, and characters, what is most important is not the mere fact of these borrowings but their nature. Afro-American slaves did not borrow indiscriminately from the whites among whom they lived. A careful study of their folklore reveals that they tended to be most influenced by those patterns of

Euro-American tales which in terms of functional meaning and aesthetic appeal had the greatest similarity to the tales with deep roots in their ancestral homeland. Regardless of where slave tales came from, the essential point is that with respect to language, delivery, details of characterization, and plot, slaves quickly made them their own and through them revealed much about themselves and their world. These processes can be illustrated through an examination of the slaves' animal trickster tales.

I

Contrary to the stereotype established by such early collectors and popularizers of slave tales as Joel Chandler Harris, slave lore was not monopolized by the adventures of Brer Rabbit and his fellow creatures. Afro-American slaves, like their African progenitors, told a wide variety of tales covering many aspects of life and experience and fulfilling a myriad of needs. Slaves related human as well as animal trickster tales; they told Bible stories, explanatory tales, moralistic and didactic tales, supernatural tales and legends, humorous anecdotes, and stories featuring local traditions and personal experiences. The range of slave tales was narrow in neither content nor focus. In spite of this, it is not surprising or accidental that the tales most easily and abundantly collected in Africa and among Afro-Americans in the New World were animal trickster tales. Because of their overwhelmingly paradigmatic character, animal tales were, of all the narratives of social protest or psychological release, among the easiest to relate both within and especially outside the group.

The propensity of Africans to utilize their folklore quite consciously to gain psychological release from the inhibitions of their society and their situation is by now well known, but it needs to be reiterated here if the popularity and function of animal trickster tales is to be understood. After listening to a series of Ashanti stories that included rather elaborate imitations of afflicted people—an old woman dressed in rags and covered with sores, a leper, an old man suffering from the skin disease yaws—which called forth roars of laughter from the audience, the English anthropologist R. S. Rattray suggested that it was unkind to ridicule such subjects. "The person addressed replied that in everyday life no one might do so, however great the inclination to laugh might be. He went on to explain that it was so with many other things: the cheating and tricks of priests, the rascality of a chief—things about which every one knew, but concerning which one might not ordinarily speak in public. These occasions gave every one an opportunity of talking about and laughing at such things; it was 'good' for every one concerned," he said. Customs such as these led Rattray to conclude "beyond a doubt, that West Africans had discovered for themselves the truth of the psychoanalysts' theory of 'repressions', and that in these ways they sought an outlet for what might otherwise become a dangerous complex."[3]

Certainly this was at the heart of the popularity of animal trickster tales. Whether it is accurate to assert, as Rattray has done, that the majority of "beast fables" were derived from the practice of substituting the names of animals for the names of real individuals whom it would have been impolitic or dangerous to mention, there can be no question that the animals in these tales were easily recognizable representations of both specific actions and generalized patterns of human behavior. "In the fable," Léopold Senghor has written, "the animal is seldom a totem; it is this or that one whom every one in the village knows well: the stupid or tyrannical or wise and good chief, the young man who makes reparation for injustice. Tales and fables are woven out of everyday occurrences. Yet it is not a question of anecdotes or of 'material from life'. The facts are images and have paradigmatic value."[4] The popularity of these tales in Africa is attested to by the fact that the Akan-speaking peoples of the West Coast gave their folk tales the generic title *Anansesem* (spider stories), after the spider trickster Anansi, whether he appeared in the story or not, and this practice was perpetuated by such New World Afro-American groups as the South American Negroes of Surinam who referred to all their stories, whatever their nature, as *Anansitori,* or the West Indian blacks of Curaçao who called theirs *Cuenta de Nansi.*[5]

For all their importance, animals did not monopolize the trickster role in African tales; tricksters could, and did, assume divine and human form as well. Such divine tricksters as the Dahomean Legba or the Yoruban Eshu and Orunmila did not survive the transplantation of Africans to the United States and the slaves' adaptation to Christian religious forms. Human tricksters, on the other hand, played an important role in the tales of American slaves. By the nineteenth century, however, these human tricksters were so rooted in and reflective of their new cultural and social setting that outside of function they bore increasingly little resemblance to their African counterparts. It was in the animal trickster that the most easily perceivable correspondence in form and usage between African and Afro-American tales can be found. In both cases the primary trickster figures of animal tales were weak, relatively powerless creatures who attain their ends through the application of native wit and guile rather than power or authority: the Hare or Rabbit in East Africa, Angola, and parts of Nigeria; the Tortoise among the Yoruba, Ibo, and Edo peoples of Nigeria; the Spider throughout much of West Africa including Ghana, Liberia, and Sierra Leone; Brer Rabbit in the United States.[6]

In their transmutation from their natural state to the world of African and Afro-American tales, the animals inhabiting these tales, though retaining enough of their natural characteristics to be recognizable, were almost thoroughly humanized. The world they lived in, the rules they lived by, the emotions that governed them, the status they craved, the taboos they feared, the prizes they struggled to attain, were those of the men and women who lived in this world. The beings that came to life in these stories were so created as to be human enough to be identified with but at the same time exotic enough to allow both storytellers and listeners a latitude and freedom that came only with much more difficulty and daring in tales explicitly concerning human beings.

This latitude was crucial, for the one central feature of almost all trickster tales is their assault upon deeply ingrained and culturally sanctioned values. This of course accounts for the almost universal occurrence of trickster tales, but it has not rendered them universally identical. The values people find constraining and the mechanisms they choose to utilize in their attempts at transcending or negating them are determined by their culture and their situation. "It is very well to speak of 'the trickster,' " Melville and Frances Herskovits have noted, "yet one need but compare the Winnebago trickster [of the North American Indians] . . . with Legba and Yo in Dahomey to find that the specifications for the first by no means fit the second." [7] The same may be said of the slave trickster in relation to the trickster figures of the whites around them. Although animal trickster tales do not seem to have caught strong hold among American whites during the eighteenth and the first half of the nineteenth centuries, there were indigenous American tricksters from the tall, spare New Englander Jonathan, whose desire for pecuniary gain knew few moral boundaries, to the rough roguish confidence men of southwestern tales. But the American process that seems to have been most analogous in function to the African trickster tale was not these stories so much as the omnipresent tales of exaggeration. In these tall tales Americans were able to deal with the insecurities produced by forces greater than themselves not by manipulating them, as Africans tended to do, but by overwhelming them through the magnification of the self epitomized in the unrestrained exploits of a Mike Fink or Davy Crockett. "I'm . . . half-horse, half-alligator, a little touched with the snapping turtle; can wade the Mississippi, leap the Ohio, ride upon a streak of lightning, and slip without a scratch down a honey locust; can whip my weight in wildcats, . . . hug a bear too close for comfort, and eat any man opposed to Jackson," the latter would boast. [8]

It is significant that mythic strategies such as these played almost no role in the lore of nineteenth-century slaves; not until well after emancipation do tales of exaggeration, with their magnification of the individual, begin to assume importance in the folklore of Afro-Americans. Nor did the model of white trickster figures seem to have seriously affected the slave whose own tricksters remained in a quite different mold—one much closer to the cultures from which they had come. In large part African trickster tales revolved around the strong patterns of authority so central to African cultures. As interested as they might be in material gains, African trickster figures were more obsessed with manipulating the strong and reversing the normal structure of power and prestige. Afro-American slaves, cast into a far more rigidly fixed and certainly a more alien authority system, could hardly have been expected to neglect a cycle of tales so ideally suited to their needs. This is not to argue that slaves in the United States continued with little or no alteration the trickster lore of their ancestral home. The divergences were numerous: divine trickster figures disappeared; such important figures as Anansi the spider were at best relegated to the dim background; sizable numbers of European tales and themes found their way into the slave repertory. But we must take care not to make too much of these differences. For instance, the fact that the spider trickster retained its importance and its Twi name, Anansi, among the Afro-Americans of Jamaica, Surinam, and Curaçao, while in the United States Anansi lived only a peripheral existence in such tales as the Aunt Nancy stories of South Carolina and Georgia, has been magnified out of proportion by some students. "The sharp break between African and American tradition," Richard Dorson has written, "occurs at the West Indies, where Anansi the spider dominates hundreds of cantefables, the tales that inclose songs. But no Anansi stories are found in the United States."[9] The decline of the spider trickster in the United States can be explained by many factors from the ecology of the United States in which spiders are less ubiquitous and important than in either Africa or those parts of the New World in which the spider remained a central figure, to the particular admixture of African peoples in the various parts of the Western Hemisphere. Anansi, after all, was but one of many African tricksters and in Africa itself had a limited influence. Indeed, in many parts of South America where aspects of African culture endured overtly with much less alteration than occurred in the United States, Anansi was either nonexistent or marginal.[10]

What is more revealing than the life or death of any given trickster figure is the retention of the trickster tale itself. Despite all of the changes that took place, there persisted the mechanism, so well developed throughout most of Africa, by means of which psychic relief from arbitrary authority could be secured, symbolic assaults upon the powerful could be waged, and important lessons about authority relationships could be imparted. Afro-Americans in the United States were to make extended use of this mechanism throughout their years of servitude.

II

In its simplest form the slaves' animal trickster tale was a cleanly delineated story free of ambiguity. The strong assault the weak, who fight back with any weapons they have. The animals in these tales have an almost instinctive understanding of each other's habits and foibles. Knowing Rabbit's curiosity and vanity, Wolf constructs a tar-baby and leaves it by the side of the road. At first fascinated by this stranger and then progressively infuriated at its refusal to respond to his friendly salutations, Rabbit strikes at it with his hands. kicks it with his feet, butts it with his head, and becomes thoroughly enmeshed. In the end, however, it is Rabbit whose understanding of his adversary proves to be more profound. Realizing that Wolf will do exactly what he thinks his victim least desires, Rabbit convinces him that of all the ways to die the one he is most afraid of is being thrown into the briar patch, which of course is exactly what Wolf promptly does, allowing Rabbit to escape.[11]

This situation is repeated in tale after tale: the strong attempt to trap the weak but are tricked by them instead. Fox entreats Rooster to come down from his perch, since all the animals have signed a peace treaty and there is no longer any danger: "I don' eat you, you don' boder wid me. Come down! Le's make peace!" Almost convinced by this good news, Rooster is about to descend when he thinks better of it and tests Fox by pretending to see a man and a dog coming down the road. "Don' min' fo' comin' down den," Fox calls out as he runs away. "Dawg ain't got no sense, yer know, an' de man got er gun."[12] Spotting a goat lying on a rock, Lion is about to surprise and kill him when he notices that Goat keeps chewing and chewing although there is nothing there but bare stone. Lion reveals himself and asks what he is eating. Overcoming the momentary paralysis which afflicts most of the weak animals in these tales when they realize they are trapped, Goat saves himself by saying in his most terrifying voice: "Me duh chaw dis rock, an ef you dont leff, wen me done . . . me guine eat you."[13]

At its most elemental, then, the trickster tale consists of a confrontation in which the weak use their wits to evade the strong. Mere escape, however, does not prove to be victory enough, and in a significant number of these tales the weak learn the brutal ways of the more powerful. Fox, taking advantage of Pig's sympathetic nature, gains entrance to his house during a storm by pleading that he is freezing to death. After warming himself by the fire, he acts exactly as Pig's instincts warned him he would. Spotting a pot of peas cooking on the stove, he begins to sing:

> Fox and peas are very good,
> But Pig and peas are better.

Recovering from his initial terror, Pig pretends to hear a pack of hounds, helps Fox hide in a meal barrel, and pours the peas in, scalding Fox to death.[14] In one tale after another the trickster proves to be as merciless as his stronger opponent. Wolf traps Rabbit in a hollow tree and sets it on fire, but Rabbit escapes through a hole in the back and reappears, thanking Wolf for an excellent meal, explaining that the tree was filled with honey which melted from the heat. Wolf, in his eagerness to enjoy a similar feast, allows himself to be sealed into a tree which has no other opening, and is burned to death. ''While eh duh bun, Buh Wolf bague an pray Buh Rabbit fuh leh um come out, but Buh Rabbit wouldnt yeddy [hear] um.'' [15] The brutality of the trickster in these tales was sometimes troubling (''Buh Rabbit . . . hab er bad heart,'' the narrator of the last story concluded), but more often it was mitigated by the fact that the strong were the initial aggressors and the weak really had no choice. The characteristic spirit of these tales was one not of moral judgment but of vicarious triumph. Storytellers allowed their audience to share the heartening spectacle of a lion running in terror from a goat or a fox fleeing a rooster; to experience the mocking joy of Brer Rabbit as he scampers away through the briar patch calling back to Wolf, ''Dis de place me mammy fotch me up,—dis de place me mammy fotch me up''; to feel the joyful relief of Pig as he turns Fox's song upside down and chants:

> Pigs and peas are very good,
> But Fox and peas are better.

Had self-preservation been the only motive driving the animals in these stories, the trickster tale need never have varied from the forms just considered. But Brer Rabbit and his fellow creatures were too humanized to be content with mere survival. Their needs included all the prizes human beings crave and strive for: wealth, success, prestige, honor, sexual prowess. Brer Rabbit himself summed it up best in the tale for which this essay is named:

> De rabbit is de slickest o' all de animals de Lawd ever made. He ain't de biggest, an' he ain't de loudest but he sho' am de slickest. If he gits in trouble he gits out by gittin' somebody else in. Once he fell down a deep well an' did he holler and cry? No siree. He set up a mighty mighty whistling and a singin', an' when de wolf passes by he heard him an' he stuck his head over an' de rabbit say, ''Git 'long 'way f'om here. Dere ain't room fur two. Hit's mighty hot up dere and nice an' cool down here. Don' you git in dat bucket an' come down here.'' Dat made de wolf all de mo' onrestless and he jumped into the bucket an' as he went down de rabbit come up, an' as dey passed de rabbit he laughed an' he say, ''Dis am life; some go up and some go down.'' [16]

There could be no mistaking the direction in which Rabbit was determined to head. It was in his inexorable drive upward that Rabbit emerged not only as an incomparable defender but also as a supreme manipulator, a role that complicated the simple contours of the tales already referred to.

In the ubiquitous tales of amoral manipulation, the trickster could still be pictured as much on the defensive as he was in the stories which had him battling for his very life against stronger creatures. The significant difference is that now the panoply of his victims included the weak as well as the powerful. Trapped by Mr. Man and hung from a sweet gum tree until he can be cooked, Rabbit is buffeted to and fro by the wind and left to contemplate his bleak future until Brer Squirrel happens along. "This yer my cool air swing," Rabbit informs him. "I taking a fine swing this morning." Squirrel begs a turn and finds his friend surprisingly gracious: "Certainly, Brer Squirrel, you do me proud. Come up here, Brer Squirrel, and give me a hand with this knot." Tying the grateful squirrel securely in the tree, Rabbit leaves him to his pleasure—and his fate. When Mr. Man returns, "he take Brer Squirrel home and cook him for dinner."[17]

However, it was primarily advancement not preservation that led to the trickster's manipulations. Among a slave population whose daily rations were at best rather stark fare and quite often a barely minimal diet, it is not surprising that food proved to be the most common symbol of enhanced status and power. In his never ending quest for food the trickster was not content with mere acquisition which he was perfectly capable of on his own; he needed to procure the food through guile from some stronger animal. Easily the most popular tale of this type pictures Rabbit and Wolf as partners in farming a field. They have laid aside a tub of butter for winter provisions, but Rabbit proves unable to wait or to share. Pretending to hear a voice calling him, he leaves his chores and begins to eat the butter. When he returns to the field he informs his partner that his sister has just had a baby and wanted him to name it. "Well, w'at you name um?" Wolf asks innocently. "Oh, I name um Buh Start-um," Rabbit replies. Subsequent calls provide the chance for additional assaults on the butter and additional names for the nonexistent babies: "Buh Half-um," "Buh Done-um." After work, Wolf discovers the empty tub and accuses Rabbit, who indignantly denies the theft. Wolf proposes that they both lie in the sun, which will cause the butter to run out of the guilty party. Rabbit agrees readily, and when grease begins to appear on his own face he rubs it onto that of the sleeping Wolf. "Look, Buh Wolf," he cries, waking his partner, "de buttah melt out on you. Dat prove you eat um." "I guess you been right," Wolf agrees docilely, "I eat um fo' trute."[18] In some versions the animals propose a more hazardous ordeal by fire to discover the guilty party. Rabbit successfully jumps over the flames but some innocent animal—Possum, Terrapin, Bear— falls in and perishes for Rabbit's crime.[19]

In most of these tales the aggrieved animal, realizing he has been tricked, desperately tries to avenge himself by setting careful plans to trap Rabbit, but to no avail. Unable to outwit Rabbit, his adversaries attempt to learn from him, but here too they fail. Seeing Rabbit carrying a string of fish

Fox asks him where they came from. Rabbit confesses that he stole them
from Man by pretending to be ill and begging Man to take him home in his
cart which was filled with fish. While riding along, Rabbit explains, he
threw the load of fish into the woods and then jumped off to retrieve them.
He encourages Fox to try the same tactic and Fox is beaten to death, as
Rabbit knew he would be, since Man is too shrewd to be taken in the same
way twice.[20]

And so it goes in story after story. Rabbit cheats Brer Wolf out of his
rightful portion of a cow and a hog they kill together.[21] He tricks Brer Fox
out of his part of their joint crop year after year "until he starved the fox to
death. Then he had all the crop, and all the land too."[22] He leisurely watches
all the other animals build a house in which they store their winter provisions and then sneaks in, eats the food, and scares the others, including
Lion, away by pretending to be a spirit and calling through a horn in a
ghostly voice that he is a "better man den ebber bin yuh befo."[23] He convinces Wolf that they ought to sell their own grandparents for a tub of
butter, arranges for his grandparents to escape so that only Wolf's remain
to be sold, and once they are bartered for the butter he steals that as well.[24]

The many tales of which these are typical make it clear that what Rabbit
craves is not possession but power and this he acquires not simply by obtaining food but by obtaining it through the manipulation and deprivation of
others. It is not often that he meets his match, and then generally at the
hands of an animal as weak as himself. Refusing to allow Rabbit to cheat
him out of his share of the meat they have just purchased, Partridge samples
a small piece of liver and cries out, "Br'er Rabbit, de meat bitter! Oh, 'e
bitter, bitter! bitter, bitter! You better not eat de meat," and tricks Rabbit
into revealing where he had hidden the rest of the meat. "You is a damn
sha'p feller," Partridge tells him. "But I get even wid you."[25] Angry at
Frog for inviting all the animals in the forest but him to a fish dinner, Rabbit
frightens the guests away and eats all the fish himself. Frog gives another
dinner, but this time he is prepared and tricks Rabbit into the water. "You
is my master many a day on land, Brer Rabbit," Frog tells him just before
killing and eating him, "but I is you master in the water."[26]

It is significant that when these defeats do come, most often it is not
brute force but even greater trickery that triumphs. Normally, however, the
trickster has more than his share of the food. And of the women as well,
for sexual prowess is the other basic sign of prestige in the slaves' tales.
Although the primary trickster was occasionally depicted as a female—Ol'
Molly Hare in Virginia, Aunt Nancy or Ann Nancy in the few surviving
spider stories[27]—in general women played a small role in slave tales. They
were not actors in their own right so much as attractive possessions to be
fought over. That the women for whom the animals compete are frequently

the daughters of the most powerful creatures in the forest makes it evident that the contests are for potency as well as pleasure. When Brer Bear promises his daughter to the best whistler in the forest, Rabbit offers to help his only serious competitor, Brer Dog, whistle more sweetly by slitting the corners of his mouth, which in reality makes him incapable of whistling at all. If Rabbit renders his adversaries figuratively impotent in their quest for women, they often retaliate in kind. In the story just related, Dog chases Rabbit, bites off his tail, and nothing more is said about who wins the woman.[28] More often, though, Rabbit is successful. In the most well known and symbolically interesting courting tale, Rabbit and Wolf vie for the favors of a woman who is pictured as either equally torn between her two suitors or leaning toward Wolf. Rabbit alters the contest by professing surprise that she could be interested in Wolf, since he is merely Rabbit's riding horse. Hearing of this, Wolf confronts Rabbit, who denies ever saying it and promises to go to the woman and personally refute the libel as soon as he is well enough. Wolf insists he go at once, and the characteristic combination of Rabbit's deceit and Wolf's seemingly endless trust and gullibility allows Rabbit to convince his adversary that he is too sick to go with him unless he can ride on Wolf's back with a saddle and bridle for support. The rest of the story is inevitable. Approaching the woman's house Rabbit tightens the reins, digs a pair of spurs into Wolf, and trots him around crying, "Look here, girl! what I told you? Didn't I say I had Brother Wolf for my riding-horse?"[29] It was in many ways the ultimate secular triumph in slave tales. The weak doesn't merely kill his enemy: he mounts him, humiliates him, reduces him to servility, steals his woman, and, in effect, takes his place.

Mastery through possessing the two paramount symbols of power—food and women—did not prove to be sufficient for Rabbit. He craved something more. Going to God himself, Rabbit begs for enhanced potency in the form of a larger tail, greater wisdom, bigger eyes. In each case God imposes a number of tasks upon Rabbit before his wishes will be fulfilled. He must bring God a bag full of blackbirds, the teeth of a rattlesnake or alligator, a swarm of yellowjackets, the "eyewater" (tears) of a deer. Rabbit accomplishes each task by exploiting the animals' vanity. He tells the blackbirds that they cannot fill the bag and when they immediately prove they can, he traps them. He taunts the snake, "dis pole *swear* say you aint long as him." When Rattlesnake insists he is, Rabbit ties him to the stick, ostensibly to measure him, kills him, and takes his teeth. Invariably Rabbit does what is asked of him but finds God less than pleased. In some tales he is chased out of Heaven. In others God counsels him, "Why Rabbit, ef I was to gi' you long tail aint you see you'd 'stroyed up de whol worl'? Nobawdy couldn' do nuttin wid you!" Most commonly God seemingly complies with Rabbit's request and gives him a bag which he is to open when he returns home. But

Rabbit cannot wait, and when he opens the bag prematurely "thirty bull-dawg run out de box, an' bit off Ber Rabbit tail again. An' dis give him a short tail again." [30]

 The rabbit, like the slaves who wove tales about him, was forced to make do with what he had. His small tail, his natural portion of intellect— these would have to suffice, and to make them do he resorted to any means at his disposal: means which may have made him morally tainted but which allowed him to survive and even to conquer. In this respect there was a direct relationship between Rabbit and the slaves, a relationship which the earliest collectors and interpreters of these stories understood well. Joel Chandler Harris, as blind as he could be to some of the deeper implications of the tales he heard and retold, was always aware of their utter seriousness. "Well, I tell you dis," Harris had Uncle Remus say, "ef deze yer tales wuz des fun, fun, fun, en giggle, giggle, giggle, I let you know I'd a-done drapt um long ago." From the beginning Harris insisted that the animal fables he was collecting were "thoroughly characteristic of the negro," and commented that "it needs no scientific investigation to show why he selects as his hero the weakest and most harmless of all animals, and brings him out victorious in contests with the bear, the wolf, and the fox." [31] Harris's interpretations were typical. In the preface to her important 1892 collection of black tales, Abigail Christensen noted, "It must be remembered that the Rabbit represents the colored man. He is not as large nor as strong, as swift, as wise, nor as handsome as the elephant, the alligator, the bear, the deer, the serpent, the fox, but he is 'de mos' cunnin' man dat go on fo' leg' and by this cunning he gains success. So the negro, without education or wealth, could only hope to succeed by stratagem." [32] In that same year Octave Thanet, in an article on Arkansas folklore, concluded, "Br'er Rabbit, indeed, personifies the obscure ideals of the negro race. . . . Ever since the world began, the weak have been trying to outwit the strong; Br'er Rabbit typifies the revolt of his race. His successes are just the kind of successes that his race have craved." [33]

These analyses of the animal trickster tales have remained standard down to our own day. [34] They have been advanced not merely by interpreters of the tales but by their narrators as well. Prince Baskin, one of Mrs. Christensen's informants, was quite explicit in describing the model for many of his actions:

You see, Missus, I is small man myself; but I aint nebber 'low no one for to git head o' me. I allers use my sense for help me 'long jes' like Brer Rabbit. 'Fo de wah ol' Marse Heywood mek me he driber on he place, an' so I aint hab for work so hard as de res'; same time I git mo' ration ebery mont' an' mo' shoe when dey share out de cloes at Chris'mus time. Well,

dat come from usin' my sense. An' den, when I ben a-courtin' I nebber
'lowed no man to git de benefit ob me in dat. I allers carry off de purties'
gal, 'cause, you see, Missus, I know how to play de fiddle an' allers had
to go to ebery dance to play de fiddle for dem.[35]

More than half a century later, William Willis Greenleaf of Texas echoed
Baskin's admiration: "De kinda tales dat allus suits mah fancy de mo'es'
am de tales de ole folks used to tell 'bout de ca'iens on of Brothuh Rabbit.
In de early days Ah heerd many an' many a tale 'bout ole Brothuh Rabbit
what woke me to de fac' dat hit tecks dis, dat an' t'othuh to figguh life
out—dat you hafto use yo' haid fo mo'n a hat rack lack ole Brothuh Rabbit
do. Ole Brothuh Rabbit de smaa'tes' thing Ah done evuh run 'crost in mah
whole bawn life."[36]

This testimony—and there is a great deal of it—documents the enduring
identification between black storytellers and the central trickster figure of
their tales. Brer Rabbit's victories became the victories of the slave. This
symbolism in slave tales allowed them to long outlive slavery itself. So long
as the perilous situation and psychic needs of the slave continued to characterize large numbers of freedmen as well, the imagery of the old slave
tales remained both aesthetically and functionally satisfying. By ascribing
actions to semi-mythical actors, Negroes were able to overcome the external
and internal censorship that their hostile surroundings imposed upon them.
The white master could believe that the rabbit stories his slaves told were
mere figments of a childish imagination, that they were primarily humorous
anecdotes depicting the "roaring comedy of animal life." Blacks knew better. The trickster's exploits, which overturned the neat hierarchy of the world
in which he was forced to live, became their exploits; the justice he achieved,
their justice; the strategies he employed, their strategies. From his adventures they obtained relief; from his triumphs they learned hope.

To deny this interpretation of slave tales would be to ignore much of
their central essence. The problem with the notion that slaves completely
identified with their animal trickster hero whose exploits were really protest
tales in disguise is that it ignores much of the complexity and ambiguity
inherent in these tales. This in turn flows from the propensity of scholars to
view slavery as basically a relatively simple phenomenon which produced
human products conforming to some unitary behavioral pattern. Too frequently slaves emerge from the pages of historians' studies either as docile,
accepting beings or as alienated prisoners on the edge of rebellion. But if
historians have managed to escape much of the anarchic confusion so endemic in the "peculiar institution," slaves did not. Slaveholders who considered Afro-Americans to be little more than subhuman chattels converted
them to a religion which stressed their humanity and even their divinity.

Masters who desired and expected their slaves to act like dependent children also enjoined them to behave like mature, responsible adults, since a work force consisting only of servile infantiles who can make no decisions on their own and can produce only under the impetus of some significant other is a dubious economic resource, and on one level or another both masters and slaves understood this. Whites who considered their black servants to be little more than barbarians, bereft of any culture worth the name, paid a fascinated and flattering attention to their song, their dance, their tales, and their forms of religious exercise. The life of every slave could be altered by the most arbitrary and amoral acts. They could be whipped, sexually assaulted, ripped out of societies in which they had deep roots, and bartered away for pecuniary profit by men and women who were also capable of treating them with kindness and consideration and who professed belief in a moral code which they held up for emulation not only by their children but often by their slaves as well. It would be surprising if these dualities which marked the slaves' world were not reflected in both the forms and the content of their folk culture. In their religious songs and sermons slaves sought certainty in a world filled with confusion and anarchy;[37] in their supernatural folk beliefs they sought power and control in a world filled with arbitrary forces greater than themselves; and in their tales they sought understanding of a world in which, for better or worse, they were forced to live. All the forms of slave folk culture afforded their creators psychic relief and a sense of mastery. Tales differed from the other forms in that they were more directly didactic in intent and therefore more compellingly and realistically reflective of the irrational and amoral side of the slaves' universe. It is precisely this aspect of the animal trickster tales that has been most grossly neglected.

III

Although the vicarious nature of slave tales was undeniably one of their salient features, too much stress has been laid on it. These were not merely clever tales of wish-fulfillment through which slaves could escape from the imperatives of their world. They could also be painfully realistic stories which taught the art of surviving and even triumphing in the face of a hostile environment. They underlined the dangers of acting rashly and striking out blindly, as Brer Rabbit did when he assaulted the tar-baby. They pointed out the futility of believing in the sincerity of the strong, as Brer Pig did when he allowed Fox to enter his house. They emphasized the necessity of comprehending the ways of the powerful, for only through such understanding could the weak endure. This lesson especially was repeated endlessly. In the popular tales featuring a race between a slow animal and a swifter opponent, the former triumphs not through persistence, as does his counterpart in the Aesopian fable of the Tortoise and the Hare—which always remained more popular among whites than blacks—but by outwitting his opponent and capitalizing on his weaknesses and short-sightedness. Terrapin defeats Deer by placing relatives along the route with Terrapin himself stationed by the finish line. The deception is never discovered, since to the arrogant Deer all terrapins ''am so much like one anurrer you cant tell one from turrer.'' ''I still t'ink Ise de fas'est runner in de worl','' the bewildered Deer complains after the race. ''Maybe you air,'' Terrapin responds, ''but I kin head you off wid sense.''[38] Rabbit too understands the myopia of the powerful and benefits from Mr. Man's inability to distinguish between the animals by manipulating Fox into taking the punishment for a crime that Rabbit himself commits. ''De Ole Man yent bin know de diffunce tween Buh Rabbit an Buh Fox,'' the storyteller pointed out. ''Eh tink all two bin de same animal.''[39] For black slaves whose individuality was so frequently denied by the whites above them, this was a particularly appropriate and valuable message.

In many respects the lessons embodied in the animal trickster tales ran directly counter to those of the moralistic tales so popular among ante-bellum slaves. Friendship, held up as a positive model in the moralistic tales, was pictured as a fragile reed in the trickster tales. In the ubiquitous stories in which a trapped Rabbit tricks another animal into taking his place, it never occurs to him simply to ask for help. Nor when he is being pursued by Wolf does Hog even dream of asking Lion for aid. Rather he tricks Lion into killing Wolf by convincing him that the only way to cure his ailing son is to feed him a piece of half-roasted wolf liver.[40] The animals in these stories seldom ask each other for disinterested help. Even more rarely are they caught performing acts of altruism—and with good reason. Carrying a string of fish he has just caught, Fox comes upon the prostrate form of Rabbit lying in the middle of the road moaning and asking for a doctor. Fox lays down his fish and hurries off to get help—with predictable results; ''Ber Fox los' de fish. An' Ber Rabbit got de fish an' got better. Dat's da las' of it.''[41] Brer Rooster learns the same lesson when he unselfishly tries to help a starving Hawk and is rewarded by having Hawk devour all of his children.[42]

Throughout these tales the emphasis on the state of perpetual war between the world's creatures revealed the hypocrisy and meaninglessness of their manners and rules. Animals who called each other brother and sister one moment were at each other's throats the next. On his way to church one Sunday morning, Rabbit meets Fox and the usual unctuous dialogue begins. ''Good-mornin', Ber Rabbit!'' Fox sings out. ''Good-morning', Ber Fox!'' Rabbit sings back. After a few more pleasantries, the brotherliness ends as quickly as it had begun and Fox threatens, ''Dis is my time, I'm hungry dis morning'. I'm goin' to ketch you.'' Assuming the tone of the weak suppli-

cant, Rabbit pleads, "O Ber Fox! leave me off dis mornin'. I will sen' you
to a man house where he got a penful of pretty little pig, an' you will get
yer brakefus' fill.'' Fox agrees and is sent to a pen filled not with pigs but
hound dogs who pursue and kill him. Reverting to his former Sabbath piety,
Rabbit calls after the dogs, "Gawd bless yer soul! dat what enemy get for
meddlin' Gawd's people when dey goin' to church.'' "I was goin' to school
all my life,'' Rabbit mutters to himself as he walks away from the carnage,
"an' learn every letter in de book but *d,* an' D was death an' death was de
en' of Ber Fox.''[43]

Such stories leave no doubt that slaves were aware of the need for role
playing. But animal tales reveal more than this; they emphasize in brutal
detail the irrationality and anarchy that rules man's universe. In tale after
tale violence and duplicity are pictured as existing for their own sake. Rabbit
is capable of acts of senseless cruelty performed for no discernible motive.
Whenever he comes across an alligator's nest "didn' he jes scratch the aigs
out fur pure meanness, an' leave 'em laying' around to spile.''[44] In an
extremely popular tale Alligator confesses to Rabbit that he doesn't know
what trouble is. Rabbit offers to teach him and instructs him to lie down in
the broom grass. While Alligator is sleeping in the dry grass, Rabbit sets it
on fire all around him and calls out, "Dat's trouble, Brer 'Gator, dat's
trouble youse in.''[45] Acts like this are an everyday occurrence for Rabbit.
He sets Tiger, Elephant, and Panther on fire, provokes Man into burning
Wolf to death, participates in the decapitation of Raccoon, causes Fox to
chop off his own finger, drowns Wolf and leaves his body for Shark and
Alligator to eat, boils Wolf's grandmother to death and tricks Wolf into
eating her.[46] These actions often occur for no apparent reason. When a motive is present there is no limit to Rabbit's malice. Nagged by his wife to
build a spring house, Rabbit tricks the other animals into digging it by telling them that if they make a dam to hold the water back they will surely
find buried gold under the springbed. They dig eagerly and to Rabbit's surprise actually do find gold. "But Ole Brer Rabbit never lose he head, that
he don't, and he just push the rocks out the dam, and let the water on and
drown the lastest one of them critters, and then he picks up the gold, and of
course Ole Miss Rabbit done get her spring house.''[47] It is doubtful, though,
that she was able to enjoy it for very long, since in another tale Rabbit
coolly sacrifices his wife and little children in order to save himself from
Wolf's vengeance.[48]

Other trickster figures manifest the identical amorality. Rabbit himself
is taken in by one of them in the popular tale of the Rooster who tucked his
head under his wing and explained that he had his wife cut his head off so
he could sun it. "An' de rabbit he thought he could play de same trick, so
he went home an' tol' his ol' lady to chop his head off. So dat was de las'

of his head."[49] All tricksters share an incapacity for forgetting or forgiving. In a North Carolina spider tale, Ann Nancy is caught stealing Buzzard's food and saves herself only by obsequiously comparing her humble lot to Buzzard's magnificence, stressing "how he sail in the clouds while she 'bliged to crawl in the dirt," until he takes pity and sets her free. "But Ann Nancy ain't got no gratitude in her mind; she feel she looked down on by all the creeters, and it sour her mind and temper. She ain't gwine forget anybody what cross her path, no, that she don't, and while she spin her house she just study constant how she gwine get the best of every creeter." In the end she invites Buzzard to dinner and pours a pot of boiling water over his head, "and the poor old man go baldheaded from that day."[50] At that he was lucky. When Rabbit's friend Elephant accidentally steps on Rabbit's nest, killing his children, Rabbit bides his time until he catches Elephant sleeping, stuffs leaves and grass in his eyes, and sets them on fire.[51] Hare, unable to forgive Miss Fox for marrying Terrapin instead of himself, sneaks into her house, kills her, skins her, hangs her body to the ceiling, and smokes her over hickory chips.[52]

The unrelieved violence and brutality of these tales can be accounted for easily enough within the slave-as-trickster, trickster-as-slave thesis. D. H. Lawrence's insight that "one sheds one's sickness in books" is particularly applicable here. Slave tales which functioned as the bondsmen's books were a perfect vehicle for the channelization of the slaves' "sicknesses": their otherwise inexpressible angers, their gnawing hatreds, their pent-up frustrations. On one level, then, the animal trickster tales were expressions of the slaves' unrestrained fantasies: the impotent become potent, the brutalized are transformed into brutalizers, the undermen inherit the earth. But so many of these tales picture the trickster in such profoundly ambivalent or negative terms, so many of them are cast in the African mold of not depicting phenomena in hard-and-fast, either-or, good-evil categories, that it is difficult to fully accept Bernard Wolfe's argument that it is invariably "the venomous American slave crouching behind the Rabbit."[53] Once we relax the orthodoxy that the trickster and the slave are necessarily one, other crucial levels of meaning and understanding are revealed.

"You nebber kin trus Buh Rabbit," a black storyteller concluded after explaining how Rabbit cheated Partridge. "Eh all fuh ehself; an ef you listne ter him tale, eh gwine cheat you ebry time, an tell de bigges lie dout wink eh yeye."[54] Precisely what many slaves might have said of their white masters. Viewed in this light, trickster tales were a prolonged and telling parody of white society. The animals were frequently almost perfect replicas of whites as slaves saw them. They occasionally worked but more often lived a life filled with leisure-time activities: they fished, hunted, had numerous parties and balls, courted demure women who sat on verandas dressed in white. They mouthed lofty platitudes and professed belief in noble ideals but spent much of their time manipulating, oppressing, enslaving one another. They surrounded themselves with meaningless etiquette, encased themselves in rigid hierarchies, dispensed rewards not to the most deserving but to the most crafty and least scrupulous. Their world was filled with violence, injustice, cruelty. Though they might possess great power, they did not always wield it openly and directly but often with guile and indirection. This last point especially has been neglected; the strong and not merely the weak could function as trickster. Jenny Proctor remembered her Alabama master who was exceedingly stingy and fed his slaves badly: "When he go to sell a slave, he feed that one good for a few days, then when he goes to put 'em on up the auction block he takes a meat skin and greases all round that nigger's mouth and makes 'em look like they been eating plenty meat and such like and was good and strong and able to work."[55]

Slave tales are filled with instances of the strong acting as tricksters: Fox asks Jaybird to pick a bone out of his teeth, and once he is in his mouth, Fox devours him; Buzzard invites eager animals to go for a ride on his back, then drops them to their deaths and eats them; Wolf constructs a tar-baby in which Rabbit almost comes to his end; Elephant, Fox, and Wolf all pretend to be dead in order to throw Rabbit off guard and catch him at their "funerals"; Fox tells Squirrel that he had a brother who could jump from the top of a tall tree right into his arms, and when Squirrel proves he can do the same, Fox eats him.[56] Tales like these, which formed an important part of the slaves' repertory, indicate that the slave could empathize with the tricked as well as the trickster. Again the didactic function of these stories becomes apparent. The slaves' interest was not always in being like the trickster but often in avoiding being like his victims from whose fate they could learn valuable lessons. Although the trickster tales could make a mockery of the values preached by the moralistic tales—friendship, hard work, sincerity— there were also important lines of continuity between the moralistic tales and the trickster stories. Animals were taken in by the trickster most easily when they violated many of the lessons of the moralistic tales: when they were too curious, as Alligator was concerning trouble; too malicious, as Wolf was when he tried to kill Rabbit by the most horrible means possible; too greedy, as Fox and Buzzard were when their hunger for honey led to their deaths; overly proud and arrogant, as Deer was in his race with Terrapin; unable to keep their own counsel, as Fox was when he prematurely blurted out his plans to catch Rabbit; obsessed with a desire to be something other than what they are, as the Buzzard's victims were when they allowed their desire to soar in the air to overcome their caution.

The didacticism of the trickster tales was not confined to tactics and personal attributes. They also had important lessons to teach concerning the nature of the world and of the beings who inhabited it. For Afro-American slaves, as for their African ancestors, the world and those who lived in it were pictured in naturalistic and unsentimental terms. The vanity of human beings, their selfishness, their propensity to do anything and betray anyone for self-preservation, their drive for status and power, their basic insecurity, were all pictured in grim detail. The world was not a rational place in which order and justice prevailed and good was dispensed. The trickster, as Louise Dauner has perceived, often functioned as the eternal "thwarter," the symbol of "the irrational twists of circumstance." His remarkably gullible dupes seldom learned from their experience at his hands any more than human beings learn from experience. There was no more escape from him than there is escape from the irrational in human life.[57] The trickster served as agent of the world's irrationality and as reminder of man's fundamental helplessness. Whenever animals became too bloated with their power or importance or sense of control, the trickster was on hand to remind them of how things really were. No animal escaped these lessons; not Wolf, not Lion, not Elephant, indeed, not the trickster himself. Throughout there is a latent yearning for structure, for justice, for reason, but they are not to be had, in this world at least. If the strong are not to prevail over the weak, neither shall the weak dominate the strong. Their eternal and inconclusive battle served as proof that man is part of a larger order which he scarcely understands and certainly does not control.

If the animal trickster functioned on several different symbolic levels—as black slave, as white master, as irrational force—his adventures were given coherence and continuity by the crucial release they provided and the indispensable lessons they taught. In the exploits of the animal trickster, slaves mirrored in exaggerated terms the experiences of their own lives. It can be argued, of course, that slave tales, by channelizing the bondsmen's discontent, reducing their anxieties, and siphoning off their anger, served the master as well as the slave. In a sense they did, and the fact that tales and songs were often encouraged by the masters may indicate a gleaning of this fact on their part as well. But in terms of the values they inculcated, the models of action they held up for emulation, the disrespect and even contempt they taught concerning the strong, the psychic barriers they created against the inculcation of the white world's values, it would be difficult to maintain that they should be viewed largely as a means of control. What the tales gave to the masters with one hand they more than took back with the other. They encouraged trickery and guile, they stimulated the search for ways out of the system, they inbred a contempt for the powerful and an admiration for the perseverance and even the wisdom of the undermen. In short, they constituted an intragroup lore which must have intensified feelings of distance from the world of the slaveholder.

5

African Culture
and U.S. Slavery

This essay is the result of an invitation I received from Professor Joseph Harris of Howard University to participate in the First African Diaspora Studies Institute, to be held on his campus in the Summer of 1979, where more than 130 scholars from Africa, the Caribbean, Europe, and the United States would gather. The very idea that there had been a diaspora from Africa, not only of peoples but of cultures, which had to be studied and understood before we could comprehend the modern world, helped me to place my own work in a larger and more meaningful perspective. I accepted the invitation gratefully both because I was eager to meet and exchange ideas with those from around the world, and especially from Africa, who had been grappling with issues that had occupied me for so many years and because it gave me the opportunity to restate in brief compass, and to add some points to, one of the fundamental themes of my study, *Black Culture and Black Consciousness*. Twenty-three of the conference papers, including my own, were subsequently published in Joseph E. Harris, ed., *Global Dimensions of the African Diaspora* (Washington, D.C.: Howard University Press, 1982).

A number of assumptions have rendered it difficult, until very recently, to seriously pursue and understand the role that African culture has played in the development of thought and society in the United States.

The first of these assumptions is that political and economic subordination leads inevitably to cultural emasculation. The subordinate groups, according to this dictum, become a tabula rasa on which their political and economic superiors can engrave what they will.[1] This tendency to equate political and economic subordination with rapid deculturation has structured scholars' treatments of other groups in America as well, especially the new immigrant groups from eastern and southern Europe and from Asia. But in no instance was their cultural erosion seen to be as thorough as that of the Africans. "Other peoples," the sociologist Robert Park wrote, "have lost . . . much of their cultural heritage. None has been so utterly cut off and estranged from their ancestral land, traditions and people."[2]

At the heart of the belief that the Africans thoroughly lost their culture was the assumption that one could arrange cultures in a neat hierarchy with Western Europe at the top and Africa at the bottom. The history of music, Frederick Root told the 1893 International Folk-Lore Congress, was a development "from the formless and untutored sounds of savage people to the refined utterances of our highest civilization." Cultural diffusion, therefore, could proceed in only one irreversible direction: from the top to the bottom, from white to black. Guided by these comfortable evolutionary predispositions, scholars attributed almost every aspect of Afro-American culture to the influence of Euro-Americans. Distinctive patterns of black speech, for example, even the Gullah and Geechee dialects of the South Carolina and Georgia coasts, were devoid of African linguistic influences. Rather, black speech was "frozen Elizabethan English," the product of the "slovenly and careless" speech that was "the natural result of a savage and primitive people's endeavor to acquire for themselves the highly organized language of a very highly civilized race."[3]

Africa could be so readily excluded from any cultural influence because of still another pervasive assumption. It was believed that the peoples of Africa came from societies marked by a wide variety of languages, religions, customs and institutions, making it impossible for them to maintain their traditional cultures when they were mixed together indiscriminately in the United States.[4]

These views, in various combinations, affected American scholarship from Emancipation until the mid-twentieth century. They were by no means monolithic and there were important dissenting voices, especially those of W. E. B. DuBois and Melville Herskovits. But it has not been until the last decade that important breakthroughs have been made on a wide front. Scholars have come to understand that for all the culturally disintegrating forces present in the United States, there were also factors conducive to the perpetuation of aspects of African culture.

The same environmental conditions that helped to maintain African cultural patterns in the Caribbean and South America were at work in parts of the United States as well. Africans brought with them highly developed agricultural technologies which were far more relevant to the ecology of the Southern colonies than were those of the Europeans. Thus, in South Carolina the stereotype of black dependency on whites was reversed. It was to the Africans that the Europeans looked for advice on the cultivation of rice, indigo and cotton; the use of such indigenous plants as gourds and the palmetto; knowledge of the medicinal properties of wild plants, herbs and roots which either duplicated or resembled those that slaves had been familiar with in Africa. It was the Africans, not the Europeans, who knew how to deal with such native wildlife as the alligator, and who had the experience necessary to develop the dugout canoe as the prime means of fishing and transportation.[5]

In addition to economic and environmental factors, there were attitudinal forces working for the continuation of African culture. Whites had an unconscious vested interest in seeing their slaves maintain much of their cultural distinctiveness since it was far more difficult to justify the enslavement of a kindred folk than of a people whose behavior patterns were sufficiently different to allow one to apply such commonly used epithets as "primitive," "barbaric," "childlike." This was at the root of the protracted controversy over whether the slaves should be converted to Christianity. And long after a substantial percentage of slaves were converted, the whites were often content to see them develop and continue their own forms of religious worship. Charles C. Jones, who devoted much of his life to the conversion of the slaves, admitted in 1842 that those among whom he was spreading the Gospel still "believe in second-sight, in apparitions, charms, witchcraft. . . . The superstitions brought from Africa have not been wholly laid aside."[6]

This situation, which so pained Jones and his fellow ministers, was far less troubling to many masters who used it to justify their stereotype of uncivilized Africans. "We don't care what they do when their tasks are over," a rice planter asserted in 1828, "we lose sight of them till next day. Their morals and manners are in their own keeping."[7] Thus, slave dancing, with its openly African style of gliding, dragging steps, flexed, fluid bodily position, propulsive rhythm and concentration upon movement outward from the pelvic region, which whites found lewd, was decried by ministers but tolerated and even encouraged by a substantial number of masters.[8]

The reluctance of whites to fully acculturate their slaves was, of course, communicated to the slaves in myriad ways. "I was once whipped," a freedman testified shortly after the Civil War, "because I said to missis, 'My mother sent me.' We were not allowed to call our mammies 'mother.' It made it come too near the way of the white folks."[9] Such attitudes not only allowed slaves to develop their own culture but often enhanced that development. While slave culture was in continual interaction with the white cultures surrounding it, slaves understood that the world of the whites, attractive as it might appear at times, offered little but the certainty of arbitrary and perpetual bondage. This understanding threw slaves back upon their own cultural world in which the peer group and role models—the significant others—remained black. In slavery, the surest way of attaining those things that would alter life positively, short of escape or rebellion, was not through mindless acculturation to the ways of the whites but through Afro-American culture with its comforting precedents and promises, its strategies and alternative sources of power. It was not until Emancipation and the invasion of the South by 5000 Northern school teachers anxious to prove their longstanding belief that blacks were as inherently capable of freedom as whites, that slaves were exhorted in a massive way to turn their backs on the past and their traditional ways of thought and action. "Our work," one of these teachers wrote, "is just as much a missionary work as if we were in India or China." [10] That this messianic impulse to totally change the traditional ways of blacks had been largely absent in the slave South helps to explain the distinctiveness and continuity that marked slave culture.

Finally, and perhaps most importantly, in this catalog of factors conducive to cultural continuity among Africans and their descendants, was the perpetuation of oral culture in slavery. Historians still have not fully understood the structural relationship between the slaves' preliterate world and the culture they created. The Africans from whom the slaves had descended lived in a world of sound; a world in which the spoken, chanted, sung, or shouted word was the primary form of communication. This world of sound contrasts dramatically with the world of vision characteristic of literate Western European cultures in which ideas are held to be distinct from behavior and verbal thought is separable from action. In nonliterate societies such distinctions are not made. Ideas and words are seen as part of the same reality as the events to which they refer; words are powerful parts of the real world in their own right.

It is because they came from such societies, and were not inducted into the literate world of their white masters, that slaves invested their songs, tales and the spoken word in general with the same central importance they enjoyed in Africa. Their world remained a world of sound in which words were actions. To speak or sing of the heroes and exploits of the Old Testament, to relate orally the events that occurred in dreams or visions, was to give them a substance, a reality, to make them literally come alive. To learn of the past through the personally related spoken word was to give the past a contemporary, personal significance missing from the more compartmentalized sense of time characteristic of literate societies in which knowledge of the past is derived largely from the more abstract and detached printed page. [11]

If one is to understand the distinctiveness of slave religion, it is crucial to understand the intimate relationship between the world of sound and the world of sacred time and space in which there were no clear lines between the past and the present, between the sacred and the secular.[12] This was a world common to the traditional societies of Africa and it remained common to the societies created by slaves in the United States. If the slaves had lost many of the specific religious ceremonies and almost all of the gods they had known in Africa, they retained an African world view which became embedded in their form of Christianity. The God the slaves sang of was neither remote nor abstract, but as intimate, personal and immediate as the gods of Africa had been: "O when I talk I talk wid God," "Mass Jesus is my bosom friend," "I'm goin' to walk with [talk with, live with, see] King Jesus by myself, by myself." The heroes of the Scriptures—"Sister Mary," "Brudder Jonah," "Brudder Moses," "Brudder Daniel"—were greeted with similar intimacy and immediacy. In their conversions and ceremonies, slaves often actually saw and conversed with their God. In their counterclockwise religious dance, known as the "ring shout," ecstatic dancers were often transformed into actual participants in historic actions: Joshua's army marching around the walls of Jericho, the children of Israel following Moses out of Egypt. In their songs such events as the Crucifixion and the Day of Judgment were described with a poetic intensity that transformed singers and listeners into participants: "You'll see de world on fire . . . see de element a meltin', . . see the stars a fallin' . . . see the moon a bleedin' . . . see the forked lightning. . . . Hear the rumblin' thunder . . . see the righteous marching . . . see my Jesus coming. . . ."

In their varied network of religious folk beliefs, too, slaves perpetuated much of the cosmology that had characterized the African cultures from which they had come. Man was conceived as part of, not alien to, the Natural Order, attached to the Oneness that bound together all matter, animate and inanimate, all spirits, visible or not. It was necessary to understand the world because one was inexorably linked to it. Thus, survival, happiness and health depended upon being able to read the signs that existed everywhere in the natural world, to understand the visions that recurrently visited one, to commune with the spirits that filled the world.[13]

This discussion of world view helps us to identify a methodological fallacy which has for too long bedeviled scholarship: the preoccupation with the problem of origins. A great deal of energy has been invested in the question of whether a specific song, tale, folk belief or behavioral practice can be traced directly back to Africa. This question, while interesting and often relevant, has also been misleading and has tended to mask the extent to which African cultural patterns continued to influence and shape the culture of the slaves. Cultural continuities with Africa were not dependent upon the importation and perpetuation of specific tales, songs or folk beliefs in their pure form. In the place that tales, songs and folk beliefs occupied in the lives of slaves and in the meaning slaves derived from them, they had the clearest resemblances with their African past.

Thus, the fact that few slave songs of satire and derision could be traced back to Africa is not important. Most of these songs, of course, were on-the-spot improvisations using the local and immediate context and characters. What is important is that the ubiquitous African practice of utilizing songs of satirical derision as a central mode of expression and a crucial safety valve continued to live on in slavery and continued to afford slaves the same avenues of cultural self-assertion and psychological release it had provided their African ancestors. Similarly, the fact that in slave tales all of the divine and many of the animal tricksters of Africa were lost is far less important than the retention of the trickster tale itself. Despite all of the changes that took place, slaves managed to keep alive the mechanism, so well developed throughout most of Africa, by means of which psychic relief from arbitrary authority could be secured, symbolic assaults upon the powerful could be waged and important lessons about authority relationships could be imparted.[14]

Precisely the same argument can be advanced with regard to expressive style. Despite the fact that many—perhaps most—slave songs were the product of black interaction with whites, the nature of their song style with its overriding antiphony, its group performance, its pervasive functionality, its improvisational character, its strong relationship to dance and bodily movement, remained closer to the musical styles of Africa than to those of Western Europe. Similarly, in their tales, aphorisms, proverbs, anecdotes and jokes, slaves, following the practices of their African past, encouraged and rewarded verbal improvisation, emphasized group participation and utilized the spoken arts functionally to voice criticism as well as to uphold traditional values and group cohesion.[15]

An emphasis upon cultural style helps to undercut still another of the assumptions mentioned at the beginning: that the wide variety of languages, religions and institutions differentiating African societies made it impossible for their peoples to reconstitute a significant semblance of African culture on American soil. Historians are finally learning that culture is more than the sum total of institutions and language. It is also expressed by an emphasis upon certain virtues, ideals, manners, modes of hospitality, outlooks toward the past, present and future—in short, by a common style of life.[16] One has only to picture the ways in which Western Europeans, with their diversity of languages, religions and customs, could have reconstituted a common European culture had they been subjected to the same process of enslavement and forced resettlement to understand what in fact the African peoples were able to achieve in the New World.

We have been misled by the scholarly search for "survivals" which embodies the mistaken belief that only those elements of slave culture were African which remained largely unchanged from the African past. Culture is not a fixed, static condition but a process; a product of interaction between the past and the present. The question, as VèVè Clark has put it so well, is not one of survivals but of transformations.[17] The creation of Afro-American culture was not a simple process of radical deculturation followed by forced acculturation. It was, rather, the product of a complex process of syncretism, the nature of which we are only beginning to appreciate. Our understanding of this process has been retarded by the longstanding assumption that the gulf between African and European culture was impossibly wide and virtually unbridgeable. While African slaves were transported to an environment that was unquestionably alien, it was not as invariably alien as we have supposed. For example, nothing in the European musical tradition with which slaves came into contact in America was totally foreign to their own traditions, while a number of important features such as the diatonic scale were held in common and a number of practices such as the lining-out of hymns in Protestant churches and the African practice of antiphonal call-and-response were analogous. Thus, slaves were able to maintain the integrity of their own musical heritage while fusing to it compatible elements of Euro-American music. The same situation held true in the area of folk beliefs. From the seventeenth to the nineteenth century, African slaves met large numbers of Euro-American people who believed the universe was populated by spirits and witches, by supernatural omens and signs, by charms and magic, by conjuring and healing; who held beliefs, in short, that the slaves could adopt or adapt without doing essential violence to their own world view. It is within this context that we must understand the point made by a number of folklorists that Afro-American folk beliefs often were more specifically European in form than African. Slaves could absorb so many Euro-American beliefs not because their own African culture had been reduced to a negligible force but because these beliefs fit so easily beside and often in place of their traditional outlooks and convictions and constituted a source of comfort, familiarity and cultural reinforcement.[18]

Obviously, we have just begun to scratch the surface of this question. We need many studies of such areas as language, material culture and ethical values. These studies will be aided immensely by what has been perhaps the most important breakthrough by historians: their changed attitude toward the slave folk. Recent books on slavery by such historians as John Blassingame, Eugene Genovese, Herbert Gutman, Nathan Huggins, Leon Litwack, Leslie Howard Owens, Albert Raboteau, George Rawick and Peter Wood have pictured the slave folk not as inarticulate, impotent historical ciphers who were continually being acted upon by forces over which they had no control but, rather, as actors in their own right who, to a larger extent than we previously imagined, were able to build a culture, create alternatives and affect the situation they found themselves in.

To further pursue this crucially important subject we need to encourage more active interaction and cooperation between African and American scholars who have much to teach one another. That, hopefully, will be one of the results of this conference.

6

The Concept of the New Negro
and the Realities of Black Culture

The catalyst for this essay was a misunderstanding. My good friend Nathan Huggins, who had chaired my session on slave songs at the American Historical Association meetings in 1969, had assumed I would publish that paper in the collection of essays on African-American history he was co-editing. I honestly can't recall that he ever articulated that assumption to me, but I do recall that he was less than enthusiastic when he heard that I had agreed to publish the paper in Tamara Hareven's collection. I tried to assuage his upset and my sense of guilt at having let a friend down by promising to write an essay for his collection. The subject was not difficult to find. In my teaching, I had for some time worried about the meaning and accuracy of the ubiquitous notion of a "New Negro" appearing periodically in postbellum American society. I also had all that material on twentieth-century Black music which I had been sifting through for my AHA paper before I changed my focus to slave songs. Since the entire notion of the New Negro rested almost exclusively on evidence emanating from a restricted portion of the population—primarily the upper middle and professional classes—I decided to test the notion by examining black folk song. Nat Huggins gracefully accepted both my apology and my paper which was published in Nathan I. Huggins, Martin Kilson, and Daniel M. Fox, eds., *Key Issues in the Afro-American Experience* (New York: Harcourt Brace Jovanovich, 1971).

The Ubiquitous New Negro

Americans in general and American scholars in particular have not yet really come to terms with a challenge posed by Ralph Ellison a number of years ago: "Everybody wants to tell us what a Negro is. . . . But if you would

tell me who I am, at least take the trouble to discover what I have been."[1]
Most scholars have failed to penetrate with sufficient energy and imagination
the rich and varied cultural sources of the black masses. I want to consider
not the reasons for but the effects of this failure. It has left scholars as
vulnerable as other Americans to the mood that prevailed in the decades
following World War II, which, in terms of race relations, might well be
called the period of the rediscovery of the Negro in American life.

White Americans, to be sure, have always been preoccupied with Negroes, but rarely since the years immediately preceding and following the
Civil War have black people occupied so important a place in the national
consciousness as they have in the past several decades. The standard mechanisms by which whites were able to repress their recognition of the Negro's
plight were rendered increasingly ineffective by the middle of the twentieth
century. The belief that Negroes, being inferior, could not really object to
an inferior status, that they were in fact quite content with the caste-ridden
life they were thrust into after the Civil War, and that if there was any
problem, it centered on a handful of white and black radicals, agitators, and
neurotic malcontents was undermined as black Americans became more and
more able to articulate and act upon their dissatisfactions and their aspirations. The fantasy, indulged in by so many whites at the turn of the century,
that what they liked to call the "Negro problem" was at best temporary,
since Negroes, unable to stand the rigors of either the Northern climate or
of free competition, were in the process of extinction as a people, was belied
by the increasing presence of blacks in all parts of the country. Not even
the comfortable conviction that, since the United States was an open society,
those Negroes on the bottom of the socioeconomic ladder had no one to
blame but themselves (though it is a conviction that retains potency to this
day) could be totally persuasive to a people who had just experienced the
irrationality and injustice of the Great Depression.

That Negroes came to occupy an increasingly prominent place in the
national consciousness has been one of the healthier aspects of the postwar
era. Nevertheless, it is important to recognize that this rediscovery has taken
place in a historical vacuum. Knowledge of the historical Negro is still obscured by the myths and stereotypes of the past. Whites have construed their
dawning awareness of the feelings of blacks as a change in Negroes rather
than as a change in themselves. This has given rise to the tendency to think
in cataclysmic terms such as the "New Negro" when characterizing black
people in contemporary America.

In one sense the concept of the New Negro is undeniably valid. The
twentieth century has witnessed striking changes in the status and situation
of black Americans. While at the beginning of the century 90 percent of the
Negroes in the United States lived in the South and 75 percent were rural,

by the middle of the century more than 50 percent lived in the North and 73 percent were urban. These demographic changes have had important social, economic, and political implications. As Negroes moved from rural to urban areas their economic position and occupational opportunities increased markedly. As they moved from the South to the North their political position improved greatly. And both shifts enhanced their opportunities for an improved education. Thus by mid-century Negroes were in a better position to make their demands felt than ever before in American history. But this has been a gradual and cumulative change; it has not been cataclysmic and its effects have been manifest throughout the twentieth century. If black people were more and more able to confront the white man directly and to articulate their feelings, this was not necessarily an indication that the feelings were new.

The problem with the concept of the New Negro is that it has not centered upon these crucial external developments but has taken more important internal changes for granted. It is predicated on the assumption that Negroes before World War II had internalized the white man's image of themselves so that they believed they were somehow inferior and deserving of their fate and consequently did not protest in any effective way. Blacks, to borrow Norbert Wiener's telling phrase, have been seen as reaching up to kiss the whip that lashed them. This image has been enhanced by much of the scholarship of the past few decades. One study, which has had enormous influence in spite of the fact that it totally ignored almost every aspect of slave culture from religion to music to folklore, concluded that Negroes were infantilized by the system of slavery, that they were virtually reduced to a state of perpetual childhood in which their sense of self was derived from the master class upon whom they depended and who constituted their only "significant others."[2] Other studies, paying equally little attention to black culture, have projected this picture into the era of freedom. Confusing group consciousness and a firm sense of self with political consciousness and organization, manhood with armed rebellion, and resistance with the building of a revolutionary tradition, these scholars have been able to find little more than dependence, servility, and apathy in the black masses until relatively recently.[3]

The tendency to see Negroes primarily as reactors to white society rather than as actors in their own right has been intensified by contemporary social scientists who have been unable to perceive a distinctive set of black folkways or institutions at least potentially capable of sustaining Negroes against the worst ravages of the system they live in. "The key to much in the Negro world," two sociologists maintained in their study of ethnic groups in New York City, is that "the Negro is only an American, and nothing else. He has no values and culture to guard and protect."[4] A 1965 government report on the Negro family found that "it was by destroying the Negro family under slavery that white America broke the will of the Negro people. *Al-though that will has reasserted itself in our time,* it is a resurgence doomed to frustration unless the viability of the Negro family is restored."[5] "Being a Negro in America," a psychologist asserted in 1964, "is less of a racial identity than a necessity to adopt a subordinate social role."[6] Nor has this line of argument been confined to white scholars. The sociologist E. Franklin Frazier summed up much of his research by concluding in 1957 that "unlike any other racial or cultural minority, the Negro is not distinguished by culture from the dominant group. Having completely lost his ancestral culture, he speaks the same language, practices the same religion, and accepts the same values and political ideals as the dominant group."[7]

The thrust of these studies has been to see black history in the United States as an almost straight line from slavery to the recent past and to envision the distinctive features of that history not as cultural forms but as disorganization or pathology. Thus a scholarly foundation for the concept of the New Negro has been constructed. That it is a foundation without much substance is due not to the necessary invalidity of its central arguments but to the narrow and culture-bound research that has gone into the construction of these arguments. The easy assumption that black history has merely been a pathological version of white history and that the Negro has been little more than "an exaggerated American," as Gunnar Myrdal put it, has worked to inhibit the open and painstaking study of all areas of Negro life and history, without which a complete understanding of the validity of the concept of the New Negro is impossible.

In fact, of course, Negro protest is not new. Indeed, as August Meier has shown, the term "New Negro" itself has been a ubiquitous one. It was used at least as early as 1895 by the *Cleveland Gazette* to describe a group of Negroes who had just secured a New York civil rights law. Booker T. Washington spoke of a New Negro who was emerging as a result of his policies of self-help and economic betterment. The journalist Ray Stannard Baker wrote in 1908 that while "the old-fashioned Negro preferred to go to the white man for everything . . . the New Negro . . . urges his friends to patronize Negro doctors and dentists, and to trade with Negro storekeepers." In 1916 Dean William Pickens of Morgan College wrote a series of essays entitled *The New Negro,* in which he saw the Negro on the threshold of a renaissance of civilization and culture. For W. E. B. Du Bois, the New Negro was embodied in the group of businessmen who were developing a group economy.[8] The term was used most frequently in the decade after World War I to describe the young artists and poets who were engaged in what was hopefully called a Negro Renaissance. Alain Locke, in his 1925 anthology of Negro writing, *The New Negro,* was virtually alive with the possibilities of the golden day that was dawning:

> There is ample evidence of a New Negro in the latest phases of social change and progress, but still more in the internal world of the Negro mind and spirit. . . . We are witnessing the resurgence of a people. . . . Negro life is not only establishing new contacts and founding new centers, it is finding a new soul. . . . There is a renewed race-spirit that consciously and proudly sets itself apart. . . . The day of "aunties," "uncles" and "mammies" is equally gone. Uncle Tom and Sambo have passed on, . . . the Negro is becoming transformed. . . . The American mind must reckon with a fundamentally changed Negro.[9]

Statements like these stemmed not only from the demographic changes already referred to but also from the ferment that was taking place among Negroes throughout the nation. Although this ferment was not often marked by direct mass action, there was nonetheless more action than has been recognized. August Meier and Elliott Rudwick have demonstrated that the bus boycotts in Montgomery, Alabama, and other Southern cities during the mid-1950's were by no means a radical break with the past. Negroes had adopted similar tactics in the late nineteenth and early twentieth century to oppose segregation in Southern transportation and Northern education. As early as Reconstruction, Negroes in Richmond, New Orleans, Charleston, and Louisville conducted successful boycotts against the introduction of segregated horsecars. During the 1890's, Negroes in Atlanta, Augusta, and Savannah successfully boycotted attempts to segregate local transportation facilities. Between 1900 and 1906, similar protest movements occurred in more than twenty-five cities in every state of the former Confederacy. For periods ranging from several weeks to several years, Negroes in these cities refused to ride on newly segregated streetcars. Negro hackmen and draymen developed informal transit systems to accommodate the protesters, and in Portsmouth, Norfolk, Chattanooga, and Nashville all-black transportation lines were created. Similarly, in Alton, Illinois, in 1897 and in East Orange, New Jersey, in 1899, Negro residents refused to send their children to schools in which they were being segregated. Identical movements took place in Springfield and Dayton, Ohio, in the 1920's. All these movements were ultimately suppressed, as they had to be, with no aid or encouragement from the courts or the government. But, considering the power relationships existing at the time, the important thing about them, as Meier and Rudwick have concluded, is not that they failed "but that they happened in so many places and lasted as long as they often did."[10]

In all this protest there was so great a diversity of means and ends, so frequent a blurring of tactical differences, that it is hard to categorize it without oversimplifying. Bearing this in mind and recalling also that throughout the twentieth century there has always been an important strain of militant action—from the boycotts at the turn of the century, to the campaigns during the Depression to force stores in black neighborhoods to employ Negroes, to the 1941 march on Washington movement to bring about the hiring of Negroes in defense industries, to the accelerating activities of the postwar years—it is possible to isolate several major streams of action that predominated at different times. The political abandonment of the freedmen by the Republican party in the 1870's and 1880's abruptly ended the dream that Negro rights could be secured through conventional political behavior and gave rise to the line of thought epitomized by Booker T. Washington's emphasis upon self-help and economic activity. Operating in an age imbued with the belief that man could progress according to the Horatio Alger model and confronted with the blocking of political channels by federal indifference and Southern disfranchisement, Negro leadership preached the possibilities of advancement through moral and economic development: Negroes must band together and further their own cause through mutual aid and self-help; Negroes must show themselves the equal of white men by developing their own capabilities. Although this philosophy of Negro progress persists with some interesting variations on the theme, World War I dealt it a blow from which it never fully recovered.

With few exceptions, Negroes flocked into the American army during the war and served with enthusiasm and hope. When 200 Negro college graduates were asked to volunteer for officer training, 1,500 responded almost immediately. Here was a situation made to order for the Alger philosophy, whose heroes had always proved their worth through inspired acts of heroism and devotion. "We believe that our second emancipation will be the outcome of this war," the Texas Grand Master of the Negro Masons announced in 1918.[11] This loyalty and hope was rewarded by a hardening of the lines of discrimination, by increased humiliation, and by the bloody Red Summer of 1919, which saw major race riots in city after city. Blacks had played the game by the rules and had discovered definitively that the rules simply did not apply to them. The anxiety that accompanied this discovery was marked by the dramatic rise of Marcus Garvey and his Back to Africa movement and by the Negro Renaissance, whose poets and writers flirted with the dream of Africa and a separate Negro people. In organizational terms it was marked by the emergence of the NAACP, with its emphasis upon legalism as the dominant form of protest. If black leaders in the Reconstruction era put their faith in the political process, and those of Booker T. Washington's time stressed the American dream of self-help and success, the new postwar spokesmen turned to the American system of justice. There were endless appeals to the courts to force the application of the rules of the game to Negroes as well as everyone else.

Ironically, it was the very success of this movement that brought about its demise. In the wake of its greatest legal victory, the *Brown v. Board of Education of Topeka* school desegregation decision of 1954, the NAACP found itself beleaguered by the challenges of new organizations and new tactics. It was not long before it began to appear as though the school victory had only symbolic importance. More than ten years after the court spoke, only 8 percent of the Negro youths in the South attended integrated schools. New organizations—CORE, SNCC, SCLC—abandoned legalism for direct action, the courts for the streets. Their appeal was directly to the American conscience; their tactic was the graphic demonstration of the injustices and brutalities of the system, along with added economic pressure from boycotts and picket lines. Their results were in many ways impressive, and yet in the more than ten years in which they dominated the Civil Rights movement the relative economic position of the Negro masses declined and the stubborn problems of the urban ghettos became even more intense. As a result of these developments there is the crisis of our own day, in which we are witnessing the rise of new leadership and the use of new methods lumped under the rubric "Black Power."

The variegated and shifting spectrum of Negro protest thought and action has provided still another fertile seedbed for the concept of the New Negro. It has been in periods of transition from the dominance of one set of leaders and tactics to that of another that we have most frequently heard the assertion that a New Negro was arising in the land. The failure to see the Negro rights movements as a totality has made it easy to confuse the rise of new organizations and the adoption of new methods with the birth of a New Negro. But there has been an even greater error. In attempting to understand the reaction of Negroes to the society in which they lived, there has been far too great a concentration on organized movements and on the articulate middle-class and upper-class Negroes upon whom the title of "Negro leaders" has been bestowed. The larger masses of lower-class and lower-middle-class Negroes, who are anything but inarticulate in their own lives, have thus been rendered silent, and this silence in turn has been interpreted as acquiescence or apathy. Failure to understand the reaction of the Negro masses has stemmed directly from failure to look seriously at their lives and their culture. It is precisely at this point that the concept of the New Negro is weakest.

The long-standing notion that blacks have understood whites far better than whites have understood blacks can be overdone, but there is much to substantiate its essential validity. It has been true not simply because of white indifference to Negro feelings but because Negroes have taken pains— have had to take pains—not to let whites understand them too well. W. E. B. Du Bois spoke of a "veil" that prevented whites from seeing the inner world of blacks.[12] Paul Laurence Dunbar spoke of a mask:

> Why should the world be overwise,
> In counting all our tears and sighs?
> Nay, let them only see us, while
> We wear the mask.[13]

This has been a constant message in Negro letters from the late nineteenth century to the present. Ralph Ellison wrote in 1964:

> I found the greatest difficulty for a Negro writer was the problem of re-
> vealing what he truly felt, rather than serving up what Negroes were sup-
> posed to feel, and were encouraged to feel. And linked to this was the
> difficulty, based upon our long habit of deception and evasion, of depicting
> what really happened within our areas of American life, and putting down
> with honesty and without bowing to ideological expediencies the attitudes
> and values which give Negro American life its sense of wholeness and
> which render it bearable and human and, when measured by our own terms,
> desirable.[14]

The pervasiveness of this phenomenon has been amply demonstrated by the radically different results that research pollsters and social scientists have gotten when using black rather than white investigators. During World War II, Memphis Negroes were asked, "Would Negroes be treated better or worse if the Japanese conquered the U.S.A.?" While 45 percent answered "worse" when the interviewer was white, only 25 percent did so when the inter-viewer was black. North Carolina Negroes in the early 1960's demonstrated higher educational aspirations, agreed more readily that there had to be changes "in the way our country is run," and were more prone to support student sit-ins when they were questioned by black interviewers. Of the Boston Ne-groes questioned during the same period, 87 percent were willing to agree that "the trouble with most white people is that they think they are better than other people" when questioned by other Negroes; only 66 percent ad-mitted this to whites. Studies made of black youths from two-year-olds to college students have confirmed these results.[15] All this bears out the truth of a song sung by generations of blacks:

> Got one mind for white folks to see,
> 'Nother for what I know is me;
> He don't know, he don't know my mind.

Unfortunately, this truth has not yet sufficiently penetrated the metho-dologies and perceptions of scholars who have too facilely summed up the attitudes and reactions of blacks. In *The Peculiar Institution,* the most im-portant and perceptive history of United States slavery yet written, Kenneth Stampp anticipated recent theories about the process of "infantilization" by which white masters attempted to produce a childlike race, but he did not commit the mistake of confusing the planters' ideal with reality. His study contains a wealth of suggestions about the private and *sub rosa* tactics used by slaves to resist the white man's design, maintain a sense of individual integrity and self-respect, and manifest a spirit of communal consciousness and solidarity with their fellow blacks.[16] Surprisingly few scholars have attempted this kind of analysis for the postslavery era.

For millions of Negroes in the decades after Emancipation, the normal outlets for protest were closed. They were denied the right of political expression and active demonstration. To understand their reaction to the system under which they lived it is necessary to broaden our definition of protest and resistance, to make it less restrictive and more realistic. This is particularly important because so much of the recent discussion has been concerned with the effects of American racial patterns upon Negro psychic and emotional development. Scholars have written about the psychic effects of the role that many blacks have had to assume among whites without having a full understanding of the roles Negroes have been able to play in black society. The assumption has been that the crucial roles for blacks have been the ones they have played before whites, but this must remain an untested hypothesis until the racial veil has been penetrated and the functions of such institutions as Negro churches and fraternal organizations have been understood. In these institutional enclaves blacks were able to assume many of the social, economic, and political roles denied them in the outside society. What effects these surrogates have had upon black psychic development and concepts of self cannot be understood until scholars drop their assumption that the white stage has been the central one for the development of Negro personality and study in a more open and detailed way the alternatives blacks have been able to construct for themselves.

Similarly, scholars have spoken too easily of Negro apathy and acquiescence without looking in any systematic way at the role spatial mobility has played for blacks. Precisely what has been the meaning of the migrations that have sent millions of Negroes from the South to the North and from rural to urban centers? How have Negroes perceived these demographic shifts? What effects have they had upon black social and psychic life? There have been equally superficial and incomplete discussions of the available peer group models upon which Negro youth could pattern their lives and aspirations. On the whole, such discussions have ignored the evidence of black folklore, black music, and black humor with their array of such heroes and models as tricksters, bad men, and signifiers, and the evidence of lower-class black culture in which entertainers, preachers, and underworld hustlers often occupy central positions.[17]

One can easily extend this list of omissions, but it should be evident

that, for all their contributions, too many studies of black history and society
have been written in a cultural vacuum, have ignored whole areas of black
life and culture, and have emphasized one stratum of Negro society to the
exclusion of the masses of blacks. Surely, this is too frail a framework upon
which to base hypotheses about the internal life of Negroes in the United
States. The remainder of this essay will use the example of early twentieth-
century black music to indicate the kind of evidence scholars must consult
before indulging in generalizations about Negroes—old or New.

Black Songs and Black Consciousness

In exasperation with a reporter who was questioning him about the nature
of the music he played, Big Bill Broonzy once remarked: "All music's gotta
be 'folk' music. I ain't never heard no horse sing a song." While his interpretation of folk music may have been too all-inclusive, Broonzy was reflecting the fact that for Negroes, probably more than for any other group in
the United States, music has been historically (and for large numbers has
remained) a *participant* activity rather than primarily a performer-audience
phenomenon. It is precisely this folk quality of Negro music that makes it
such a good medium for getting at the thought, spirit, and history of the
very segment of the Negro community that historians have rendered inarticulate through their neglect. This is evident in Muddy Waters' recollections
of his boyhood in Clarksdale, Mississippi, during the 1920's:

> I was just a boy and they put me to workin' right along side the men. I
> handled the plough, chopped cotton, did all of them things. Every man
> would be hollerin' but you don't pay that no mind. Yeah, course I'd holler
> too. You might call them blues but they was just made-up things. Like a
> feller be workin' or most likely some gal be workin' near and you want to
> say somethin' to 'em. So you holler it. Sing it. Or maybe to your mule or
> something or it's gettin' late and you wanna go home. I can't remember
> much of what I was singin' now 'ceptin' I do remember I was always
> singin', "I cain't be satisfied, I be all troubled in mind." Seems to me like
> I was always singin' that, because I was always singin' jest the way I felt,
> and maybe I didn't exactly *know* it, but I jest didn't like the way things
> were down there—in Mississippi.

This participant role was true not only of those who "hollered" in the fields,
sang in the churches, or picked a guitar at home, but also of those who went
out to listen and respond to professional entertainers. Norman Mason, a
trumpet player who backed up such classic blues singers as Ida Cox, Mamie
Smith, and Ma Rainey, has testified that he liked the blues

because it do express the feelings of people and when we used to play around through Mississippi in those cotton sections of the country we had the people *with* us! They hadn't much outlet for their enjoyment and they get together in those honkytonks and you should hear them. That's where they let out their suppressed desires, and the more suppressed they are the better the blues they put out, seems to me.[18]

What emerges from these statements—and they could be multiplied many times—is the important role music played in the lives of lower-class Negroes, both urban and rural.

Black songs were rarely completely formalized—handed down from generation to generation with no changes—or wholly spontaneous. Most often they were products of that folk process which has been called "communal re-creation," through which old songs are constantly reworked into essentially new entities.[19] The white sociologist and song collector Howard Odum, hearing the singing of a Negro road gang working in front of his Georgia home, promptly sat on a rock wall nearby in an effort to record the lyrics of their songs. When he finally made out the words, they were:

> White man settin' on wall,
> White man settin' on wall,
> White man settin' on wall all day long,
> Wastin' his time, wastin' his time.[20]

Utilizing a familiar structure and probably also a familiar tune, these black workers left themselves ample scope to improvise new words that fit their surroundings and their mood. An even better example of this process has been provided by the blues and jazz pianist Sam Price in relating an incident from his Texas boyhood:

> I'll never forget the first song I ever heard to remember. A man had been lynched near my home in a town called Robinson, Texas. And at that time we were living in Waco, Texas—my mother, brother and myself. And they made a parody of this song and the words were something like this:
>
> > I never have, and I never will
> > Pick no more cotton in Robinsonville,
> > Tell me how long will I have to wait,
> > Can I get you now or must I hesitate?[21]

The importance of this communal spontaneity is evident: the songs sung at work and at play constitute a record of events, impressions, and reactions which is rarely available through other sources.

To comprehend the importance of this record does not ensure that it will be read correctly. Despite their precocity in recognizing the centrality of music in black culture and their unremitting zeal in collecting that music, some of the most important students of early twentieth-century Negro folk music proved to be too deeply rooted in their own cultural milieu to comprehend the implications of much of what they had gathered. John Lomax, for instance, argued in a 1917 article that the prevailing mood of black songs "is one of introspection—self-pity is the theme that, perhaps above all others, dominates his singing," and printed lyrics like these:

> White folks go to college, niggers to de fiel';
> White folks learn to read an' write, niggers learn to steal.
> Well, it make no diff'ence how you make out yo' time,
> White man sho' to bring a nigger out behin'.

> Ain't it hard, ain't it hard,
> Ain't it hard to be a nigger, nigger, nigger?
> Ain't it hard, ain't it hard,
> Caze you can't git yo' money when it's due?

Or:

> Ought for ought an' figger for figger,
> All for white man an' nothin' for nigger.
> Nigger an' white man playin' seben-up, O my hon,
> Nigger win de money but 'fraid to pick it up, O my hon.

Yet, in spite of these songs and of his own perception of the introspective nature of Negro song, Lomax found the stereotypes of the past too much to overcome. Why blacks should sing songs of discontent, he concluded, "is difficult to say. There surely exists no merrier-hearted race than the negro, especially in his natural home, the warm climate of the South. The negro's loud laugh may sometimes speak the empty mind, but at the same time it reveals a nature upon which trouble and want sit but lightly."[22]

In their 1926 collection, *Negro Workaday Songs,* Howard Odum and Guy Johnson entitled one of their chapters "Just Songs to Help With Work" and characterized the songs presented as "songs for song's sake, expression for expression's sake, and 'hollerin' jes' to he'p me wid my work.' " Yet this chapter contains lyrics like these:

> I'm gonna buy me,
> Buy me a winchester rifle,
> Box o'balls,
> Lawd, Lawd, box o'balls.

> I'm gonna back my,
> Back myself in the mountains
> To play bad,
> Lawd, Lawd, to play bad.

Or this pick-and-shovel song for which the authors can find no "historical base" and in which they see little "sense":

> Well I can stan',
> Lookin' 'way over in Georgia,
> O-eh-he, Lawd, Lawd,
> She's burnin' down,
> Lawd, she's burnin' down.[23]

Perhaps the best example of this selective myopia can be found in one of the most valuable and scholarly collections of early twentieth-century black music, *American Negro Folk-Songs*. Its compiler, Newman I. White, concluded:

> In his songs I find him [the Negro] as I have found him elsewhere, a most naive and unanalytical-minded person, with a sensuous joy in his religion; thoughtless, careless, unidealistic, rather fond of boasting, predominantly cheerful, but able to derive considerable pleasure from a grouch; occasionally suspicious, charitably inclined toward the white man, and capable of a gorgeously humorous view of anything, particularly himself.

Professor White's view of Negroes was hardly original. What was new is that it was accompanied by a good number of songs like these:

> Some o' these mornings, and 'twon't be long,
> Capt'n gwine ter call me and I be gone.   (1915–1916)

> The times are hard and money is sca'ce;
> Soon as I sell my cotton and corn
> I am bound to leave this place.   (1915–1916)

> If a white man kills a negro, they hardly carry it to court,
> If a negro kills a white man, they hang him like a goat.   (1915–1916)

> The old bee makes de honey-comb,
> The young bee makes de honey;
> Colored folks plant de cotton and corn,
> And de white folks gits de money.   (1919)

> White man in the parlor reading latest news,
> Negro in the kitchen blacking Roosevelt's shoes.   (1915–1916)

> But God loves yo', yo' little black baby,
> Jes' de same as if yo' wuz white,
> God made yo', yo' little black baby,
> So I jes' says yo's all right.   (1915–1916)

White was scholarly enough to print these songs and others like them and thoughtful enough to feel the need to explain them, since they failed to fit his conclusions about black people. First, he discounted them quantitatively, arguing that "the very small number of such songs in my whole collection of nearly a thousand . . . is a matter of really primary significance." The impressive thing, of course, was not the small number of such songs (which were more numerous than White ever admitted) but the fact that in the repressive climate of the early twentieth century Negroes in the Deep South were willing to sing any of these songs openly. White himself must have realized this, for he constructed a more elaborate explanation in his theory of the "transcending of verbal meaning" in black songs. "It is very easy, in fact," he wrote, "to over-interpret all Negro folk-songs through forgetting that to the folk Negro the music, and not the words, is the important matter." [24] This is a particularly fascinating argument, coming as it did from a man who spent some ten years collecting the lyrics—not the music—of black songs and who, in the five hundred pages of his text, devoted only one seven-page appendix to "Specimens of Tunes." Newman White understood fully the importance of Negro folk lyrics; he resorted to the tortured logic and wishful thinking of arguments like verbal transcendence only when those lyrics threatened an image he needed to preserve.

Indeed, it is extremely doubtful that someone as familiar with black songs as Newman White could have failed to perceive that their most important element was the words, not the music. As Harold Courlander has argued for the blues—and his argument applies to the other basic forms of Negro song as well—"It is easy to overlook the reality that genuine blues in its natural setting is not primarily conceived as 'music' but as a verbalization of deeply felt personal meanings. It is a convention that this verbalization is sung." One finds this theme in the testimony of one Negro blues singer after another. As one of them put it:

> When you make a new blues and it says exactly what you got on your mind, you feel like it's pay day. Some blues, now, they get *towards* it, but if they don't quite get to what you got on your mind, you just got to keep on trying. There have been times when I sang till my throat was hoarse without really putting my difficulties in the song the way I felt them. Other times, it comes out just right on the first try. [25]

The concentration on content underlines the functional nature of most black music. This functionality stemmed from the fact that for black Americans, as for their African forebears, music was not primarily an art form but an integral part of life. One of the most important functions of black songs was the verbalization of personal and group feelings which had few, if any, other outlets. This too has been documented by many black singers.

Lil Son Jackson recalled the massive burden of economic and social injustice his sharecropper father labored under:

> That was the onliest way he could get relief from it, by singin' them blues. Just like me or anybody. I can get vexed up or somethin' or I have a sad feelin'; seems like to me that if I can sing, I feel better. But my father, he only just played at home and around. More or less at home is all I did know him to play. . . . They all played music, my father and mother too. . . . I never did take music to be a thing that I could make a livin' of; . . . I never did take interest enough in it to go to school and try to learn somethin' from the book, I more or less played what I felt.

"I tell you," Henry Townsend agreed,

> In most cases the way I feel, the song will come to you when you are really depressed you know. I mean, words'll come to you and you feel them and you decide you'll do something about it, so the thing that you do about it is more or less to put it in rhymes and words and make them come out. It gives you relief—it kinda helps somehow. I don't know—it kinda helps.[26]

If our understanding of the meaning of Negro folk songs has been hampered frequently by the predispositions of the pioneer analysts and collectors, it has been impeded as well by the nature of the songs themselves, which are often indirect and ambiguous. From the time Negroes first arrived in America, conditions have made it imperative for them to disguise their feelings from the white man and perhaps at times from themselves as well. As I have argued elsewhere, music has always provided one of the primary means for transcending the restrictions imposed by external, and even internal, censors. Through the use of innuendo, metaphor, and circumlocution, Negroes could utilize their songs as outlets for individual and communal release.[27]

The existence of double meaning in Negro folk songs has long been recognized. Howard Odum, for example, reflected upon the "paradoxes and contradictions" contained in the songs he collected, admitted that "the negro is very secretive," and spoke of "the resourcefulness and adaptability of the negro" and of "his hypocrisy and two-faced survival mechanisms."[28] The only instance in which this phenomenon was studied in any detail by the early twentieth-century collectors, however, focused upon sexual relations. In 1927 Guy Johnson pointed out that when black songs depict men stealing, cheating, and dying for a piece of their woman's jelly roll, angel food cake, or shortening bread, it is difficult to believe that these terms are meant to refer to food:

> Dupree was a bandit,
> He was brave an' bol',
> He stole that diamon' ring
> For some of Betty's jelly roll.
>
> Two little niggers layin' in bed,
> One turned over to the other an' said,
> "My baby loves short'nin, short'nin' bread,
> My baby loves short'nin' bread."

Johnson found that words like "cabbage," "keyhole," "cookie," and "cake" were frequently used as symbols for the female sexual organs, and it would be possible to add many similar metaphors to his list. Johnson never claimed that all double meanings in Negro music were of a sexual nature, and in a footnote he indicated: "There are, for example, many hidden references to the white man in the Negro's songs. This is an interesting field of research in which little has been done."[29] But it was doubtless easier for him and many of his colleagues to admit the existence of double meaning in sexual relations, since it merely confirmed their image of the low moral state of the Negro. They were much less ready to analyze double meaning that reflected lack of contentment or anything less than total adjustment. Once the door is opened, however, it is difficult to close again. Once the existence of *double-entendre* and veiled meaning is admitted in one area, it is hard to rule it out in others.

What precisely have Negroes meant in their twentieth-century religious music when they complained continuously, "Why doan de debbil let-a me be?" or asked, "What makes ole Satan hate me so?" and answered, "Cause he got me once an' let me go," or boasted, "Ole Satan thought he had me fast, / Broke his chain an' I'm free at last," or observed:

> Just let me tell you how this world is fixed:
> Satan has got it so full of tricks,
> You can go from place to place,
> Everybody's runnin' down the colored race.

In freedom, as in slavery, the Devil—over whom Negroes generally triumphed in their songs—often looked suspiciously like a surrogate for the white man. Similarly, while Negroes had long sung of "letters from the Lord" and "trains to glory," and while there can be no doubt that these phrases were frequently meant literally, during the early twentieth-century migration of blacks from the South to the North—which many Southern states desperately tried to stop—it is difficult to imagine that these metaphors did not assume contemporary connotations.

> Well, my mother got a letter, oh, yes;
> Well, she could not read it, oh, yes.
> What you reckon that letter said?
> That she didn't have long to stay here.
>
> Yes, I 'bleeged to leave this world,
> Yes, I 'bleeged to leave this world,
> Sister, I's 'bleeged to leave this world,
> For it's a hell to me.[30]

Nonreligious work songs and blues are a bit less of a dilemma, since they tend to be more direct and open, but this is by no means invariable. Even in as relatively formalized and popular a Negro work song as "John Henry," the meaning is by no means clear cut:

> This old hammer killed John Henry,
> But it can't kill me.
> Take this hammer, take it to the Captain,
> Tell him I'm gone, babe, tell him I'm gone.[31]

The possible meanings of the following lyrics are also intriguing:

> Niggers gettin' mo' like white fo'ks,
> Mo' like white fo'ks eve'y day.
> Niggers learnin' Greek an' Latin,
> Niggers wearin' silk an' satin,
> Niggers gettin' mo' like white fo'ks eve'y day.[32]

In 1917 John Lomax interpreted those lines as presenting "the cheerful side of improving social conditions." But they could as easily, and perhaps more meaningfully, be seen as an example of lower-class black satire and anger directed at those Negroes who were trying to become culturally "white." An even greater interpretive challenge is presented by these lyrics sung by a black Georgia worker:

> Ever see bear cat
> Turn to lion,
> Lawd, Lawd,
> Down in Georgia?
>
> My ol' bear cat,
> My ol' bear cat
> Turn to lion,
> Lawd, Lawd, Lawd.

> 'Fo' long, Lawd,
> Yes, 'fo' long, Lawd,
> I'll be back here,
> I'll be back here.[33]

The number of songs containing ambiguous metaphors and intriguing but obscure symbolism could be extended indefinitely. Still, as many of the lyrics quoted indicate, there are hollers, work songs, field songs, and blues whose meaning is really not subject to a great deal of interpretation. There are hundreds of songs from the first two decades of this century that make it unmistakably clear that Negro music has been a crucial, and perhaps central, vehicle for the expression of protest and discontent. There were constant complaints about the white "captain," about working conditions, about the unfairness of the sharecropping system. Sometimes these were expressed satirically:

> Reason I love my captain so,
> 'Cause I ast him for a dollah,
> Lawd, he give me fo'.

But often they were presented openly and baldly:

> Niggers plant the cotton,
> Niggers pick it out,
> White man pockets money,
> Niggers does without.[34]

During these years, blacks were still singing the words of a song first reported by Frederick Douglass during slavery:

> She sift de meal, she gimme de dust,
> She bake de bread, she gimme de crust,
> She eat de meat, she gimme de skin,
> An' dat's de way she tuck me in.[35]

There was often, one song admitted, "Plenty to eat, / Place to sleep," but "nothin' fer a feller, / Lawd, nothin' fer / A feller to keep."[36]

This sense of injustice, which certainly embodied no illusions about the American racial situation or the black man's place in it, was often accompanied by a great deal of anger, aggression, and self-pride:

> Well, if I had my weight in lime,
> I'd whip my captain till I went stone-blind.

> Well, you can't do me like you do po' Shine,
> You take Shine's money, but you can't take mine.[37]

Lines like "I wish my captain would go blind," "I didn't come here to be nobody's dog," "Ain't let nobody treat me dis way," "Ain't gonna be bossed aroun' no mo'," "Ain't gwine let you humbug me," "You call me dog, I don' ker," "I ain't gonna let nobody, / Nobody make a fool out o' me," were ubiquitous:

> If you don't like the way I work, jus' pay me off.
> I want to speak one luvin' word before I go:
> I know you think I'm pow'ful easy, but I ain't so sof';
> I can git another job an' be my boss.[38]

Often this anger took the form not of aggression so much as of refusing to play the game by the white man's rules: "Cap'n says, hurry, I say take my time," "Dere ain't no use in my workin' so hard," "When you think I'm workin', I ain't doin' a thing."[39]

> If you work all the week,
>   An' work all the time,
> White man sho to bring
>   Nigger out behin'.[40]

These lyrics are important because they are an assertion of a break with the idealized Puritan values and mores of white society. The "Bad Man" songs like "Stagolee" and "Dupree" ("I'm de bad nigger, / If you wants to know; . . . Shoot, nigger, / Shoot to kill") and the blues, especially in their depiction of sexual conduct, are similarly filled with assertions of independence from the cold, mocking world of bourgeois values and dicta that seemed so hypocritical.[41]

The same independence from the values of the larger society can be seen with regard to color. Certainly, Negro songs were often marked by the color preferences of white American society. What is more important, given the stereotype that most blacks during this period longed to be white, is that at least as often they were characterized by color pride. Negro troops in France during World War I were often heard singing: "It takes a long, tall, slim, black man to make a German lay his rifle down."[42] Again and again, black-skinned and brown-skinned women and men were held up as objects of desire and admiration:

> Some says yellow
> While others say brown,
> But for me I'll take the blackest in town.[43]

> A yellow girl I do despise,
> But a jut-black girl I can't denies.[44]

> Ain't crazy 'bout no high yellows, worried about no brown,
> Come to picking my choice, gimme
> The blackest man in town.[45]

> Some say, give me a high yaller,
> I say give me a teasin' brown,
> For it takes a teasin' brown,
> To satisfy my soul.[46]

Black songs of the early twentieth century could be accompanied by a deadening sense of fatalism and despair: "I didn't bring nuthin' in dis bright worl'; / Nuthin' I'll carry away," or "Trouble, trouble, / Been had it all my day; Believe to my soul / Trouble gonna kill me dead."[47] This mood, however, was often modified by the strong sense of change, freedom of movement, and mobility that pervaded these songs: "I jest come here to stay a little while," "Gwine whar' I never been befo'," "Oh, goin' down dat lonesome road, / An' I won't be treated this-a way," "I'm gonna row here few days longer, / Then, Lawd, I'm goin' on."[48] Frequently there seemed to be a new self-consciousness about movement and a need to distinguish it from mere running away. Thus in "John Henry" and similar work songs the request to "Take my hammer . . . to my captain, / Tell him I'm gone," was accompanied by this admonition:

> If he asks you was I running,
> Tell him no,
> Tell him no.
> Tell him I was going across the Blue Ridge Mountains
> Walking slow, yes, walking slow.[49]

Occasionally there was even a sense of the possibility of turning the tables on the whites:

> Well, I'm goin' to buy me a little railroad of my own,
> Ain't goin' to let nobody ride but de chocolate to de bone.
> Well, I'm goin' to buy me a hotel of my own,
> Ain't goin' to let nobody eat but de chocolate to de bone.[50]

Conclusion

The purpose of this essay is not to argue that Negro music has functioned primarily as a medium of protest. To state this would distort black music and black culture. Negroes have not spent all their time reacting to whites, and their songs are filled with comments on all aspects of life. But it would be an even greater distortion to assume that a people occupying the position that Negroes have in this society could produce a music as rich and varied as they have with few allusions to their situation or only slight indications of their reactions to the treatment they were accorded. While black music is not dominated by such reactions, it is a rich repository of them and offers a new window onto the lives and into the minds of a large segment of the black community that has been ignored because its members have not left behind the kind of sources that historians are used to working with.

To argue that music constituted a form of black protest does not mean that it necessarily led to any tangible and specific actions, but rather that it served as a mechanism by which Negroes could be relatively candid in a society that rarely accorded them that privilege, could communicate with other Negroes whom they would in no other way be able to reach, and could assert their own individuality, aspirations, and sense of being. Certainly, if nothing else, black music makes it difficult to believe that early twentieth-century Negroes internalized their situation so completely, accepted the values of the larger society so totally, or manifested so pervasive an apathy as we have been led to believe.

As it has been applied both implicitly and explicitly, then, the concept of the New Negro requires serious modification. As a historical phenomenon, of course, it retains great importance. For almost every generation of blacks since Emancipation, the idea of the New Negro, in all its varying forms, has been a crucial rallying cry and a source of great optimism and ego gratification. But its very ubiquity should make scholars wary of taking it too literally. It has had unquestionable utility as a vehicle for action, but as a means of historical understanding it has tended to obscure as much as it has revealed. And it will continue to do so until it is made to encompass not merely select groups of historically articulate Negroes but the entire spectrum of black society and all the realities of black culture.

7

Marcus Garvey and
the Politics of Revitalization

Although every piece in this volume was written in response to an invitation to deliver a lecture or contribute a paper to a journal or a book, this essay is the only one in which the precise subject was chosen by someone else. In 1980 I received a call from John Hope Franklin and August Meier, during which they told me that the volume on twentieth-century black leadership they were editing was close to completion but that the scholar commissioned to write an essay on Marcus Garvey had just dropped out. I agreed with their strong feeling that they had to find an alternate to write the essay. To publish such a volume without a piece on the most powerful and effective grass-roots nationalist leader in African-American history would inevitably look like a political statement. Therefore they needed a Garvey essay, and they needed one in the near future, *and* John Hope informed me (much to my surprise and I'm sure the surprise of my publishers) I was someone who could write quality stuff *quickly!*

Although I was not a Garvey scholar, my work in black folk culture had made his significance manifest, I was dissatisfied with the way many historians had treated him in the past, and I had read most of what existed in print on Garvey, which included much of his own work and other first-hand documents. In any case, there was then no accessible body of Garvey papers to consult—a vacuum which the multi-volume Garvey papers under the editorship of Robert A. Hill is happily filling. I would probably have had trouble saying no to John Hope and Augie, two historians I greatly admired, in any event but their request (all but the "write the essay *immediately*" part) intrigued me. I realized that I was being asked to do something I actually *wanted* to do: spend more time in Garvey's presence, learn more about him and his movement, and have the opportunity to think about the phenomenon of Garveyism in a more disciplined way. The result was published in John Hope Franklin and August Meier, eds., *Black Leaders of the Twentieth Century* (Urbana: University of Illinois Press, 1982).

> *The world has made being black a crime, ... I hope to make it a virtue.*
>
>   Marcus Garvey

In 1916, Marcus Garvey, a West Indian black without funds, influence, or substantial contacts, arrived in the United States for the first time. By the early 1920s he had built the largest and most influential Afro-American mass movement in American history. Before the decade ended, the movement he created and led, though it continued to exist both in the United States and abroad, was a weakened shadow of itself—internally divided and bereft of mass support. To understand the brief, dramatic, and profoundly significant career of Garvey and his Universal Negro Improvement Association (UNIA), one needs to understand the dynamic mix of personality and historical situation. Accordingly, this essay focuses upon the formative experiences of Garvey, the situation of American blacks when Garvey first arrived on American soil, and the interaction between the leader and the people he wanted to lead.

Marcus Mosiah Garvey, the eleventh child of Marcus and Sarah Garvey, was born in 1887 in St. Ann's Bay, a rural town on the north coast of Jamaica in the British West Indies. In a 1923 magazine article, Garvey shared his memories of his parents:

> My parents were black negroes. My father was a man of brilliant intellect and dashing courage. He was unafraid of consequences. He took human chances in the course of life, as most bold men do, and he failed at the close of his career. He once had a fortune; he died poor. My mother was a sober and conscientious Christian, too soft and good for the time in which she lived. She was the direct opposite of my father. He was severe, firm, determined, bold and strong, refusing to yield even to superior forces if he believed he was right. My mother, on the other hand, was always willing to return a smile for a blow, and ever ready to bestow charity upon her enemy. Of this strange combination I was born.

Garvey's account was corroborated by a white neighbor who testified that the elder Garvey, a master stonemason who took jobs only sporadically, preferring to lock himself in his room and read, "always acted as if he did not belong among the villagers; he was well read, and gave advice as a local lawyer. He was silent, stern. . . . He was 'Mr. Garvey' to every one, even to Sarah—his wife and children.'' Mrs. Garvey ''was just the opposite to him in every way. She was one of the most beautiful black women I have ever seen. . . . Her voice was gentle and caressing, her figure well shaped and erect. She was a regular Church-goer at the Wesleyan Methodist Church.''

Because nine of his siblings died in childhood, Garvey seems to have grown up close only to his older sister, Indiana. Among his other daily playmates were the nine children of the two white families that lived on the adjoining land. ''To me, at home in my early days,'' Garvey recalled, ''there was no difference between white and black.'' His closest friend, a white girl, ''knew no better than I did myself. We were two innocent fools who never dreamed of a race feeling and problem.'' Their innocence ended abruptly when Garvey's friend informed him that she was being sent away to school in Scotland and that she was instructed by her parents ''never to write or try to get in touch with me, for I was a 'nigger.' '' His friendship with white boys lasted a bit longer: ''We played cricket and baseball, ran races and rode bicycles together, took each other to the river and to the sea beach to learn to swim.'' At maturity, these associations, too, ended. ''I grew up then to see the difference between the races more and more. My school-mates as young men did not know or remember me any more. Then I realized that I had to make a fight for a place in the world.''

The young Garvey's fight was complicated by his father's growing stubbornness and reclusiveness, which damaged the family's financial position. At fourteen, Garvey left school to be apprenticed to his godfather, Mr. Burrowes, a printer. Though Garvey always felt insecure about his lack of formal education, this development was in many ways a happy one. At this small country printing establishment, Garvey was able to learn all facets of a trade that was to constitute one of his main means of communicating with those he wanted to influence. An added bonus was Burrowes's large library in which Garvey could continue to develop his interest in books. This experience only seems to have increased Garvey's resolve to succeed. As a schoolboy he had rebelled against those teachers who wanted to punish him physically: ''I simply refused to be whipped. I was not made to be whipped. It annoys me to be defeated.'' In the printing trade he learned that he had sufficient intelligence and experience to manage men: ''I was strong and manly, and I made them respect me. I developed a strong and forceful character.''

At the age of sixteen Garvey made the first of a series of moves that were to take him from the periphery to the center of events: he left his rural apprenticeship to take a position as a printer with his uncle in the city of Kingston. Here Garvey furthered his knowledge of the newspaper business. It was in Kingston, too, that Garvey became impressed with the power of oratory. Struck by the skill of the speakers he heard at barbershop forums and debates in local parks, Garvey set about learning the art with his characteristic energy. He went from church to church, absorbing the oratorical and platform styles of a variety of preachers. He would spend long hours alone in his room reciting poetry and passages from school readers and experimenting with different gestures. As his confidence grew, Garvey took an increasingly active role in the Saturday night discussion groups at Victoria Pier, where speakers debated and explored subjects of every sort. His acquaintances during these years were impressed by Garvey's enormous zeal. "He carried a pocket dictionary with him," one of them recalled, "and said he studied three or four words daily, and in his room he would write a paragraph or two using these words." Such energy led this teenager to rise to the position of foreman at one of Jamaica's largest printing establishments. But his ambitions extended beyond his own career. He helped to train black youth in elocution and arranged concerts and elocution contests for their edification. "He was always busy, planning and doing something for the underprivileged youth. Uplift work we called it," another early companion remembered. "I started to take an interest in the politics of my country," Garvey himself wrote of these years, "and then I saw the injustice done to my race because it was black, and I became dissatisfied on that account."

Garvey's dissatisfaction disrupted the orderly progress of his career. During the printers' strike of 1907, Garvey was the only foreman who took the side of the workers. Becoming a leading spokesman for their cause, Garvey found himself blacklisted once the strike failed. Though he was able to secure employment with the Government Printing Office, Garvey's mind was clearly on politics and the need for organization rather than on his vocation. In 1910 Garvey helped to found a political organization—the National Club—and created the *Watchman,* the first of his many newspapers. The failure of both ventures made evident the need for money to fund his political activities, and Garvey joined the stream of West Indian workers migrating to Central and South America in search of better opportunities. Thus, at the age of twenty-three, Garvey began a restless journey that was to keep him out of his native Jamaica for much of the remainder of his life.

In Costa Rica Garvey's uncle helped him secure a job as timekeeper on one of the United Fruit Company's banana plantations. Appalled at the conditions under which the West Indian migrants were forced to live and work, Garvey soon left the plantation and journeyed to Limón to protest to the British consul the treatment accorded those black British subjects. Met by an indifference that convinced him that black lives were simply of no consequence to white officials, Garvey tried more direct action by founding a paper, *La Nacionale,* which soon failed for lack of funds. Going next to Panama, Garvey was similarly disturbed by the condition of the West Indian workers on the Panama Canal. Again he protested, again he tried to establish a newspaper, *La Prensa,* and again he failed. In Ecuador, Nicaragua, Spanish Honduras, Colombia, and Venezuela the story was the same. Everywhere he traveled, Garvey was sickened by the exploitation of his people in the fields, mines, and cities. Returning to Jamaica in 1911, Garvey demanded that the governor take steps to protect overseas Jamaicans and was told—in a modern version of "Let them eat cake"—that if the Jamaicans disliked their treatment abroad they could always return home. If His Majesty's representatives proved indifferent, Garvey decided to see what might be done in England itself. Aided by his sister Indiana, who was working in England as a child's nurse, Garvey set out for London in 1912.

Garvey's two-year sojourn in England proved to be of great importance in shaping his future. Arriving in England with his plans still fluid and uncertain, he departed with a much clearer notion of what he wanted to accomplish. His own version of how this happened is a model of simplicity: "I read 'Up From Slavery,' by Booker T. Washington, and then my doom—if I may so call it—of being a race leader dawned upon me in London. . . . I asked, 'Where is the black man's Government?' 'Where is his King and his kingdom?' 'Where is his President, his country, and his ambassador, his army, his navy, his men of big affairs?' I could not find them, and then I declared, 'I will help to make them.' " Garvey's poetic rendition of his conversion to race leadership should not be taken literally. His decision was neither so simple nor so sudden; it had been in the making for years. A man of Garvey's temperament and upbringing had long chafed under Jamaica's tripartite racial system, which placed the island's 630,000 blacks under the 168,000 coloreds or mixed-bloods, with the 15,000 whites at the top of the racial pyramid. His years in London were important not merely for his reading of Washington—as crucial as this proved to be—but even more so for the blacks from all over the world he met and with whom he exchanged ideas. A British Consul General Report notes that "when in London, Garvey met a number of his own race from Africa and the West Indies . . . he heard form the lips of his countrymen and other coloured people about the sufferings of the darker races, and of their desire to unite for mutual understanding and protection."

Garvey and his movement have become so closely identified with the United States, where indeed they enjoyed their greatest success, that it is sometimes forgotten that Garvey grew up as a colonial in the British Empire and thus had most in common with the Africans and other West Indians who like himself had been living as part of a colonized majority in their own lands. Though he does not mention them in his scant autobiographical writings, there can be no doubt that Garvey was privy to the ideas and dreams of that group of black colonial writers and intellectuals who coalesced in

London around the *African Times and Orient Review* for which Garvey himself wrote. Within this circle, the young Garvey was exposed to ideas concerning race conservation, the preservation of group identity, anticolonialism, and African unity. It is not surprising, then, that when Garvey came to espouse the philosophy of Washington, it was with such significant additions as an emphasis on blackness and the glories of the black past and a determination to work for the redemption of Africa from foreign rule.

Before leaving England, Garvey articulated a new mission that coupled his sense of himself as a Jamaican with his growing identification with the entire black race. There would soon be a turning point in the history of the West Indies, he prophesied in the fall of 1913: "The people who inhabit that portion of the Western Hemisphere will be the instruments of uniting a scattered race who, before the close of many centuries, will found an Empire on which the sun shall shine as ceaselessly as it shines on the Empire of the North today." With this vision of himself and his fellow West Indians as the mechanism through which "the beloved and scattered millions" of the black diaspora would be united, Garvey found it impossible to remain any longer in London. "My brain was afire. There was a world of thought to conquer."

Garvey arrived home in Jamaica on July 15, 1914, and on the first of August—the anniversary of emancipation in the British West Indies—he established the Universal Negro Improvement and Conservation Association and African Communities' League, later shortened to the UNIA. The association's aims were stated in two parts. Those having to do with local conditions in Jamaica, which stressed the establishment of educational and industrial colleges, the elevation of the degraded to a "state of good citizenship," the promotion of commerce and industry, and the strengthening of "the bonds of brotherhood and unity among the races," could have been endorsed fully by Washington. The association's "General Objects" went a bit further and included such aims as the following: "To establish a Universal Confraternity among the race," "to promote the spirit of race pride and love," "to establish Commissionaries or Agencies in the principal countries of the world for the protection of all Negroes irrespective of nationality," "to conduct a world-wide commercial and industrial intercourse," and the vaguely worded "to strengthen the imperialism of independent African States."

If the goals of Garvey's new organization—with its bold motto: "ONE GOD! ONE AIM! ONE DESTINY!"—indicated the ways in which Garvey would supplement the goals of his mentor, Garvey's language in this period often remained pure Washingtonian. In his address to the first annual meeting of the UNIA in August 1915, Garvey stated that "the bulk of our people are in darkness and are really unfit for good society." Six months later he advised his fellow Jamaicans that Europeans were "longing to see the Negro do something for himself.'' Once the Negro raised himself to a higher state of civilization, ''all the other races would be glad to meet him on the plane of equality and comradeship. It is indeed unfair to demand equality when one of himself has done nothing to establish the right to equality.''

Garvey found it easier to proclaim the existence and aims of the UNIA than to get others, especially Jamaica's powerful middle class of coloreds, to share his vision of the destiny of West Indians and of the black race. Indeed, he found white government officials and clergy frequently more willing to help than were the affluent members of his own race. ''I was openly hated and persecuted by some of these colored men of the island who did not want to be classified as negroes, but as white. They hated me worse than poison. They opposed me at every step,'' Garvey recalled. It was not only his organization, but his very pretensions to leadership they opposed: ''I was a black man and therefore had absolutely no right to lead; in the opinion of the 'colored' element, leadership should have been in the hands of a yellow or a very light man.'' It was while he was suffering these shattering blows to his dreams that Garvey began, perhaps unconsciously, to explore other alternatives. If the Negro population of Jamaica was too divided and myopic to provide the leadership necessary to unite the world's blacks, Garvey would have to search elsewhere. Whether he came to this determination before or only after arriving in the United States is not clear. Nevertheless, it was during this crisis that Garvey wrote to Washington of his desire to travel to the United States to acquaint himself with America's black people. Washington's death in November 1915 deprived Garvey of the chance to meet the man who had influenced him so profoundly, but it did not alter his determination, or his need, to visit the United States. Before leaving Jamaica, Garvey wrote a final appeal to his fellow ''Afro-West Indians'':

> For God's sake, you men and women who have been keeping yourselves away from the people of your own African race, cease the ignorance; unite your hands and hearts with the people Afric, . . . Sons and daughters of Africa, I say to you arise, take on the toga of race pride, and throw off the brand of ignominy which has kept you back for so many centuries. Dash asunder the petty prejudices within your own fold; set at defiance the scornful designation of ''nigger'' uttered even by yourselves, and be a Negro in the light of the Pharaohs of Egypt, Simons of Cyrene, Hannibals of Carthage, L'Ouvertures and Dessalines of Haiti, Blydens, Barclays and Johnsons of Liberia, Lewises of Sierra Leone, and Douglasses and Du Boises of America, who have made, and are making history for the race.

In this mood, Garvey made his way to America.

Garvey had chosen precisely the right time for his American journey. The black population of the United States was in the midst of an experience that was to make it an ideal constituency for a man with Garvey's mission, energies, and oratorical abilities. To understand the ethos characterizing black America in the years following Garvey's arrival in March 1916, it is necessary to comprehend the impact of World War I on the dreams and expectations of many black Americans. Fifty years earlier blacks had emerged from the Civil War with hope in the American political process that, in the immediate aftermath of the war, produced three constitutional amendments and a host of Reconstruction reforms positively affecting the position of blacks within the system. "The Republican party is the deck," Frederick Douglass declared, "all else is the sea." The abandonment of the freedmen by the Republican party in the 1870s and 1880s abruptly ended the dream that Negro rights could be secured through conventional political behavior and gave rise to the view, advanced by some teachers and leaders, that no one had to be poor, that there was no need to fail, that the individual was the architect of his own fortune. Thus it is not surprising that with the blocking of political channels by federal indifference and southern disfranchisement, the new Negro leadership, epitomized by Washington, preached the possibilities of advancement through moral and economic development. Blacks must prove themselves worthy of freedom by developing their own capabilities. Tact, good manners, a resolute will, a tireless capacity for hard work ensured success for the individual and for the race, Washington insisted.

Although variations of this philosophy persisted long after 1918, World War I dealt it a blow from which it never fully recovered. With few exceptions, black Americans entered the armed forces with alacrity and served with enthusiasm and hope. Here was a perfect opportunity to prove their worth; a situation made to order for the Horatio Alger philosophy whose heroes had always proved themselves through inspired acts of heroism and devotion. The Texas Grand Master of the Negro Masons articulated the expectations of many when he announced: "We believe that our second emancipation will be the outcome of this war." This loyalty and hope were rewarded by segregating black troops; by subjecting them to untold indignities in training camps; by assigning them to labor battalions far out of proportion to their skills and intelligence; by warning the French not to fraternize with them lest they rape French women; by cautioning black troops at the end of the war not to expect in their homeland the kind of latitude they had enjoyed abroad.

Indeed, the America to which black troops returned was frighteningly familiar. Black soldiers were greeted not with gratitude but with fear. Ten returned soldiers were among the more than seventy blacks lynched in 1919; a far larger number were among those blacks assaulted in the year's twenty-five race riots. One veteran, returning from work during the Chicago race riot, was set upon by a white mob shouting, "There's a nigger! Let's get

him!'' ''The injustice of the whole thing overwhelmed me,'' he later testified. ''Had the ten months I spent in France been all in vain? Were those
little white crosses over the dead bodies of those dark-skinned boys lying in
Flanders field for naught? Was democracy merely a hollow sentiment?''

His question and his anger were reflected throughout black America.
Blacks had played the game by the rules and discovered that the rules simply
did not apply to them. ''We have been fighting the wrong fellow,'' a Negro
Masonic leader in California insisted. ''The low American, and not the German, is the brute who has ravished our women, lynched, flayed, burned and
massacred our men and women.'' Black people should practice the Christian
virtues, Bishop John Hurst maintained. ''If while exercising these virtues,
however, his assailants . . . persist in molesting him, let him do what self
respecting people should do—namely use his gun with effect and impose
respect.'' ''Let every Negro arm himself,'' the black New York *Commoner*
advised, ''and swear to die fighting in defense of his home, his rights and
his person.''

Implicit in all of these reactions was a heightened tendency to look
inward, to reach within the community for protection, understanding, and
sustenance. Not the least of the results of the great tension produced by the
demonstrated failure of the American success ethos for black Americans was
the impetus it gave to internal development and to searching within Afro-
American culture and looking to the black people themselves for those things
necessary to survival and the building of a meaningful dream. The anthropologist Anthony F. C. Wallace has argued that when a perceptible gap
arises between the images and expectations a culture has created within its
citizens and the realities of the culture, the resulting anxiety can often be
relieved only through the agency of what he has called a *revitalization movement:* ''a deliberate, organized conscious effort by members of a society to
construct a more satisfying culture,'' one that comes closer to their long-
standing dreams and expectations. The forms such movements take vary
from culture to culture. In the United States they have tended to stress the
revival of central cultural beliefs and values and the elimination of alien
influences. While the importance of such movements in the 1920s has been
emphasized for some time now, there has been less recognition of the extent
to which black America was characterized by them as well.

Garvey came to the United States prepared to preach the message of
revitalization to a people ready, often eager, to hear it. The time had come,
Garvey insisted, for blacks to stop emulating heroes of other races: ''We
must canonize our own saints, create our own martyrs, and elevate to positions of fame and honor black men and women who have made their distinct
contributions to our racial history.'' When Europe was inhabited by savages,
heathens, and pagans, he reminded his listeners, ''Africa was peopled with

a race of cultured black men, who were masters in art, science and literature; men who were cultured and refined; men, who, it was said, were like
the gods. . . . Black men, you were once great; you shall be great again."
He enjoined his audiences to "take down the pictures of white women from
your walls. Elevate your own women to that place of honour. . . . Mothers!
give your children dolls that look like them to play with and cuddle." God,
he insisted, "made no mistake when he made us black with kinky hair. . . .
We have outgrown slavery, but our minds are still enslaved to the thinking
of the Master Race. Now take these kinks out of your mind, instead of out
of your hair. You are capable of all that is common to men of other Races."
"We have a beautiful history," he thundered, "and we shall create another
one in the future." Over and over he insisted, "The faith we have is a faith
that will ultimately take us back to that ancient place, that ancient position
that we once occupied, when Ethiopia was in her glory."

In all of this Garvey articulated—more brilliantly than any other Afro-
American spokesman of the time—the doctrine of revitalization. In 1933
one of his supporters wrote that "Garvey sold the Negro to himself." This
theme has been picked up by a number of scholars so that one author writes
that "Garvey tried to restore to the black man the masculinity stolen from
him during the centuries of slavery," another that "Garvey put steel in the
spine of many Negroes . . . [and] helped to destroy their inferiority complex," and still another that "he stirred some two million Negroes to a
fierce race-consciousness which is still a compelling force in Negro life."
While there is validity in such observations, their total effect is to obscure
the substantial reservoir of pride, strength, and sense of history that existed
in the black folk throughout slavery and the years that followed. Blacks
certainly had hoped and worked to become part of the nation's economic
and political fabric, but they continued to retain a vivid sense of who and
what they were. Garvey did not create "race consciousness." How could
black men and women living in the racial situation that prevailed in the
United States in the early decades of the twentieth century not have been
race conscious? Indeed, Garvey was able to rise so suddenly and attract a
following so dramatically precisely because blacks retained a healthy consciousness of identity and community. What Garvey did was to provide a
political channel and a global perspective for that consciousness.

Before exploring the movement Garvey built, it is important to remember that he was not the only force for black revitalization in the 1920s. The
black writers of the Harlem Renaissance expressed revitalization in their
search for their African past. "I was a black man," lamented Langston
Hughes:

> But the white men came.
> And they drove me out of the forest.

> They took me away from the jungles.
> I lost my trees.
> I lost my silver moons.
> Now they've caged me
> In the circus of civilization.

They expressed it in their search for themselves. "What she needed to do now," Wallace Thurman wrote of one of his characters whose complexion ostracized her within the middle class, "was to accept her black skin as being real and unchangeable, to realize that certain things were, and would be, and with this in mind begin life new, always fighting, not so much for acceptance by other people, but for acceptance of herself." And, finally, they expressed it in their rediscovery of the black folk and their culture. Only among "the working girls and boys of the country," one of Claude McKay's characters in *Banjo* concludes, could one find cultural integrity: "that raw unconscious and the-devil-with-them-pride in being Negro that was his own natural birthright. . . . Down there the ideal skin was brown skin. Boys and girls were proud of their brown, sealskin brown, teasing brown, tantalizing brown, high-brown, low-brown, velvet brown, chocolate brown."

Among the black folk themselves one can see revitalization in a number of ways: in the continued revival of traditional black religious practices and their spread from the Holiness churches to the larger denominations; in the inclusion of traditional Afro-American musical forms in jazz and gospel music; and in the rise of the blues—an inward-looking music that insisted upon the meaningfulness of the daily yearnings, problems, and dreams of everyday black people. Garvey, then, for all of his uniqueness, was not an isolated force in the 1920s. His power and influence proceeded from his superb articulation of what many of his followers had long believed and acted upon in quiet dignity and strength: that blackness was nothing to apologize for; that black men and women shared a common proud heritage; and that the future was by no means hostage to white people. From the days of slavery, this had been the message of black Christianity in various forms, and it had been reiterated in myriad ways by the black folk in their songs, tales, proverbs, and anecdotes. The disillusioning difficult postwar years gave it added impetus. Like so many leaders, Garvey's influence was based upon not how far he was from, but how close he was to, the mass of the people to whom and for whom he tried to speak.

Garvey's initial activities in the United States were less those of organizing and politicking than of traveling and observing. He did deliver speeches in Harlem and elsewhere, but his main energies were devoted to learning about the conditions of American blacks. Washington was dead, but there was still much to be gained from trips to Tuskeegee Institute and other Afro-

American institutions in the thirty-eight states Garvey visited. Everywhere he went Garvey endeavored to meet black leaders, and with few exceptions he perceived in them the same qualities that characterized their Jamaican counterparts. What passed for race leadership in the United States, Garvey asserted, was little more than "treachery and treason of the worst kind," since anyone who wanted to lead had to first find some wealthy white benefactor "who will dictate to him what he should do in the leadership of the Negro race." Worse yet, Garvey was certain that the identical pettiness and self-hatred that plagued his race in Jamaica existed in the United States as well. Visiting W. E. B. Du Bois in the offices of the National Association for the Advancement of Colored People Garvey was "dumbfounded" to find that it was impossible to tell whether one was in a white office or that of a black protest organization. "There was no representation of the race there that any one could recognize. . . . you had to be as near white as possible, otherwise there was no place for you as stenographer, clerk or attendant in the office of the National Association for the Advancement of 'Colored' People." In America as in Jamaica, Garvey concluded, the race's leaders "had no program, but were mere opportunists who were living off their so-called leadership while the poor people were groping in the dark."

Convinced that he had found a leadership vacuum, Garvey in 1917 established the New York Division of the UNIA. Garvey later claimed that he had had no intention of shifting his center of operations to the United States and that he remained only when it became necessary for him to defeat the aims of local politicians who threatened to take over and pervert the purposes of the new organization. It is doubtful that Garvey needed this kind of inducement to stay in the United States. A man so perceptive and ambitious must have realized at once that Jamaica simply could not match the potential of America's large, diverse black population. Indeed, Garvey himself made this point just eight months after he arrived in the United States, calling the American Negro "the most progressive and the foremost unit in the expansive chain of scattered Ethiopia." Industrially, financially, educationally, and socially "the Negroes of both hemispheres have to defer to the American brother." Most crucially, he concluded, American blacks were far ahead of West Indians in "the spirit of self-consciousness and reliance." Garvey could not have failed to arrive at the corollary conclusion that the ideal place to build a movement for the unification of the world's blacks was not his native island, where he had recently failed so badly, but the United States. His "brief" visit was to last eleven years.

Garvey's ultimate intentions may be revealed as well by the fact that almost from the moment of his arrival he spoke as an integral part of the American black community. During the 1917 race riot in East St. Louis, Illinois, he denounced America's "continuous round of oppression" of black people who for three hundred years had "given their life blood" to help build the republic. His refusal to act or to speak like an alien visitor continued with his repeated opposition to black participation in World War I. Shortly after the armistice, as disillusioned black troops returned to America, Garvey warned that his people would not allow themselves to be exploited in this way again. "The first dying that is to be done by the black man in the future will be done to make himself free. And then when we are finished, if we have any charity to bestow, we may die for the white man. But as for me, I think I have stopped dying for him."

Statements like these, of course, matched the mood of many American blacks in those difficult postwar years and were responsible for increasing Garvey's popularity and his audience. "I am the equal of any white man; I want you to feel the same way," Garvey told his listeners. "No more fear," he thundered, "no more cringing, no more sycophantic begging and pleading." Blacks were demanding "that freedom that Victoria of England never gave; that liberty that Lincoln never meant; that freedom, that liberty that will see us men among men, that will make us a great and powerful people." Garvey's appeal was based not only upon his militance but also upon his sense of destiny and hope. "There is much to live for," he declared. "I see before me a picture of a redeemed Africa, with her dotted cities, with her beautiful civilization, with her millions of happy children, going to and fro. Why should I lose hope? . . . Lift up yourselves, men, take yourselves out of the mire and hitch your hopes to the stars; yes, rise as high as the very stars themselves. Let no man pull you down, let no man destroy your ambition, because . . . man is your brother; he is not your lord."

Words like these make it evident that if Garvey's rhetoric was revolutionary as racial doctrine, it was also appealingly familiar, steeped as it was in traditional nineteenth-century American ideology. Many of Garvey's widely circulated aphorisms could have been inserted into any American primer for schoolchildren: "Whatsoever man has done, man can do." "A man's bread and butter is only insured when he works for it." "If you have no confidence in self, you are twice defeated in the race of life." "[Man is] master of his own destiny, and architect of his own fate." No prophet of the American success ethos could have put these things better. Thus Garvey won an immediate audience not only because he preached the doctrine of revitalization at precisely the right time, but because he preached it in the right syllables. He used a tone and an ideological context that were instantly recognizable to those to whom traditional American ideology was still familiar. He was able to show his followers that the ideas they were raised on could lead to their own liberation.

When Garvey shouted out to his audiences, "Up, you mighty race!" he was not reciting totally new doctrine. Blacks had been enjoined to rise since they were emancipated. Garvey was appealing to a set of dreams and ideals that had long existed among American blacks. He was able to take Washington's philosophy and transform it from a doctrine geared to help one up the ladder of American mobility into a mechanism designed to increase the worldwide consciousness, unity, power, and autonomy of the race. He took a philosophy suffused with overtones of individualism and bent it to serve the purposes of the group.

Much of Garvey's labors were geared to instill a sense of responsibility in blacks for their place in the world. "Blame not God," he told his listeners, "blame not the white man for physical conditions for which we ourselves are responsible." The Creator intended humanity to be free. "That the Negro race became a race of slaves was not the fault of God Almighty . . . it was the fault of the race." "Sloth, neglect, indifference caused us to be slaves," he insisted. "Confidence, conviction, action will cause us to be free men to-day." He told the UNIA's Second International Convention in 1921: "If you want liberty you yourselves must strike the blow. If you must be free you must become so through your own effort, through your own initiative." Garvey was able to aim the Social Darwinist arguments that were so intertwined in his thought against the whites as well. If the latter really were convinced that the Negro was inferior, why did they find it necessary to hedge him in with laws enforcing his inferior state? The answer was obvious: whites feared black capabilities and talents, were afraid that blacks would outshine them. Give blacks a chance, Garvey taunted, and in fifty years "I will show you a nation of proud, refined and cultured black men and women, whose comeliness will outshine that of the age of Solomon." It was because Garvey did not expect whites to accept his challenge that he worked so hard to convince blacks they had to rise on their own.

The Negro, Garvey taught, was not at the bottom because he was held in contempt, he was held in contempt because he was at the bottom. Only when the race lifted itself up through its own initiative would it be in a position to demand respect. Many of his aphorisms were designed to illustrate that: "A race without authority and power, is a race without respect." "Don't be deceived; there is no justice but strength." "A race that is solely dependent upon another for its economic existence sooner or later dies." If power and autonomy were the goals, organization was the only viable means. One of the fundamental messages of Garvey's speeches, editorials, and articles was: organize as a race or perish as a race! He was convinced that "the greatest weapon used against the Negro is DISORGANIZATION." If Washington had lived, Garvey maintained, he would have had to change his program, for the New Negro needed a political voice as well as industrial opportunity. In the short run, political organization meant the creation of a strong and effective UNIA; ultimately, it entailed building an independent African nation powerful enough to protect black people everywhere.

Unlike most other black American political leaders of the period, Garvey understood the need to reach out with his message and his organization to the black people in general and not just the more educated classes. "The masses," he was convinced, "make the nation and the race." Certainly no other black spokesman was better equipped to affect the masses. Not only the content of Garvey's message, but the eloquence with which he propounded it, the skillful use he made of his weekly newspaper, and the spectacular pageantry that soon became characteristic of UNIA events were all designed to reach a maximum audience. In 1919 Garvey purchased an auditorium on 138th Street in Harlem, renamed it Liberty Hall, and held nightly meetings to bring his message to as many as 6,000 listeners at a time. In the next few years liberty halls appeared in such UNIA centers as Philadelphia, Pittsburgh, Cleveland, Detroit, Cincinnati, Chicago, and Los Angeles. On the platforms of these meeting halls, Garvey, whose wife described him as "calm, almost phlegmatic in conversation," was transformed into a charismatic speaker whose rich voice and dramatic gestures converted many of his listeners into followers. For all of his criticisms, Du Bois conceded that Garvey's "singular eloquence" made him "an extraordinary leader of men."

Those not within the reach of Garvey's voice were exposed to his message through the *Negro World,* which Garvey began in 1918 and which by the early 1920s had a weekly circulation of from 50,000 to 200,000. In order to communicate with blacks throughout the world, it carried columns in Spanish and French. That its readership did go beyond the United States is attested to by those colonial administrators who held it partially responsible for anti-white riots in 1919 in Jamaica, Trinidad, and British Honduras, by other authorities who banned it from their jurisdictions in the New World and Africa, and by Jomo Kenyatta, the future president of Kenya, who testified that "in 1921 Kenya nationalists, unable to read, would gather round a reader of Garvey's newspaper, the *Negro World,* and listen to an article two or three times. Then they would run various ways through the forest, carefully to repeat the whole, which they had memorised, to Africans hungry for some doctrine which lifted them from the servile consciousness in which Africans lived."

Garvey did not base his appeal exclusively upon his impressive oratorical and journalistic skills. Organization depended upon more than an audience; it required participants. To ensure the maximum number of participants, Garvey created a host of groups: an African Legion clad in blue military garb, Black Cross Nurses, uniformed marching bands, choristers, and various auxiliaries. The pageantry implicit in all of this was revealed during the UNIA's First International Convention in 1920. Spectators lined the streets of Harlem for miles to watch Garvey in military uniform and plumed hat lead his impressively arrayed followers marching under such banners as: "We Want a Black Civilization," "God and the Negro Shall Triumph," "Uncle Tom's Dead and Buried," "Africa Must be Free," and, at the head of the Woman's Auxiliary, "God Give Us Real Men!" The onlookers, according to Mrs. Garvey, "could not help but catch the spirit of the occasion; they clapped, waved flags and cheered themselves hoarse." Garvey, who was elected president general of the UNIA and provisional president of Africa, and who created numerous titles for his associates, seemed to have an insatiable appetite for ceremony. His wife described the court reception held during the convention of 1921:

> The Hall was transformed into a magnificent tropical setting, with lighting effects, appropriate music being played. Each Dignitary was timed to arrive according to his rank, and an anthem or appropriate music played until he was seated. . . . Young ladies were presented, and honours conferred on persons who had served the Race faithfully and well. Titles were: Kight Commander of the Nile, Distinguished Service Order of Ethiopia, and the Star of African Redemption. After the ceremonies, supper was served; guests were seated according to rank. Then followed the Grand Ball, with all the courtliness of training, natural gift for dancing and love of music.

Garvey's need to garb himself and his associates in the anachronistic trappings of aristocracy brought him enormous ridicule, especially from whites and the black middle class. He was "a clown strutting around in gaudy uniforms," a charlatan "who led big parades of ignorant people down the street selling pie in the sky." But there were other reactions as well, particularly from those groups Garvey was attempting to reach: "I remember as a lad in Cleveland, Ohio, during the hungry days of 1921, standing on Central Avenue, watching a parade one Sunday afternoon when thousands of Garvey Legionnaires, resplendent in their uniforms marched by. When Garvey rode by in his plumed hat, I got an emotional lift, which swept me up above the poverty and the prejudice by which my life was limited."

It seems to be indisputable that Garvey attracted millions of followers. It is more difficult to determine how many of them joined the UNIA. By the end of 1919, Garvey claimed two million members. Two years later he counted twice that number, and in June 1923 he announced that six million blacks were members of the UNIA. These figures reflected Garvey's hope and pride more than they did reality. Still, Garvey had much to be proud of. He had built not only the largest but the broadest mass movement in Afro-American history. The Communist party, surely no friend of Garvey's, was impressed by his success with the very elements the party itself had failed to enlist in substantial numbers: black workers and farmers. While it is not certain just how successful Garvey was outside the large northern cities, the organizational records of the UNIA indicate that the movement was not confined to these urban centers. By the mid-1920s the UNIA had established more than 700 branches in thirty-eight states in every section of the country including the Deep South. In addition, it had established more than 200 branches outside the United States, with the bulk of these clustering in the West Indies, Central America, and northern South America.

A clue to Garvey's unprecedented success in building a mass movement can be found in William L. Sherril's description of how he came to join the UNIA in Baltimore:

> One night on my way to a Show, I saw a huge crowd outside a Church, I went up and said, "what's going on in there?" A lady turned to me and said, "man alive, don't you know that Marcus Garvey is in there talking, yes, indeed, Garvey in person." "Shucks," I said, "I may as well see what he looks like." . . . I squeezed in, until I could get a good look at him; then suddenly he turned in my direction, and in a voice like thunder from Heaven he said, "men and women, what are you here for? To live unto yourself, until your body manures the earth, or to live God's Purpose to the fullest?" He continued to complete his thought in that compelling, yet pleading voice for nearly an hour. I stood there like one in a trance, every sentence ringing in my ears, and finding an echo in my heart. When I walked out of that Church, I was a different man—I knew my sacred obligations to my Creator, and my responsibilities to my fellow men, and so help me! I am still on the Garvey train.

Sherril, of course, was describing a conversion experience. For him, and presumably for many other members of the UNIA, Garvey's movement had deep religious overtones and significance.

Throughout the years of bondage American slaves had continued the African practice of drawing no clear line between the sacred and the secular, between the spiritual and the temporal world. This tendency remained strong in Afro-American culture in the years of freedom as well. Certainly it came to characterize the movement Garvey built and the style of leadership he created. One of Garvey's greatest assets was his comprehension of the importance of religion in black culture and his ability to incorporate so many of its elements in his movement.

It was not uncommon for Garvey's followers to refer to him as a Black Moses, a John the Baptist. Nor was it surprising, since Garvey himself invited such comparisons. He regularly employed a religious vocabulary, as in this speech he delivered in Liberty Hall in February 1921: "I wish I could convert the world of Negroes overnight to the tremendous possibilities of the Universal Negro Improvement Association. Let all the world know that this is the hour; this is the time for our salvation. Prayer alone will not save us; sentiment alone will not save us. We have to work and work and work if we are to be saved. . . . the time is now to preach the beatitude of bread and butter. I have contributed my bit to preaching this doctrine.'' More than this, Garvey dwelt endlessly on the suffering and betrayal of Jesus Christ, frequently casting himself in the role of Jesus. ''If Garvey dies,'' he told his followers, ''Garvey lives.'' ''Christ died to make men free,'' he wrote in 1923; ''I shall die to give courage and inspiration to my race.'' In his first message from Atlanta Prison in 1925, Garvey assumed the mantle of a full-fledged prophet assuring his fellow blacks: ''Would I not die a million deaths for you? Then why be sad? . . . I tell you the world shall hear from my principles even two thousand years hence. . . . Look for me in the whirlwind or the storm, look for me all around you, for with God's grace, I shall come.''

The religious quality of the UNIA was not confined to its leader's messianic style and rhetoric. Garvey utilized religion not merely to strengthen his own leadership, but to bolster the will and determination of those he wanted to lead. One of Garvey's favorite biblical texts was Psalms 68:31, which promised that ''princes shall come forth from Egypt; Ethiopia shall soon stretch forth her hand to God.'' But before Africa could be redeemed, black men and women had to redeem themselves from the errors they had learned through the white people's religion. In his 1922 Easter Sunday sermon Garvey called for a new resurrection: ''A resurrection from the lethargy of the past—the sleep of the past—from that feeling that made us accept the idea and opinion that God intended that we should occupy an inferior place in the world.'' No God, he insisted a year later, ''would create me a black man, to be a hewer of wood and a drawer of water. It is a lie! It is a damned lie.'' The God that blacks worshiped and adored created them the equals of all humanity and expected them to take control of their own destiny. God, Garvey taught, gave humans the gift of life and sovereignty over the earth, but He did not run an employment bureau; He did not dispense jobs to His children. He gave people the opportunities, the accomplishment was up to them.

Though Garvey taught of an impartial God who created all as equals, his anger at the way blacks had been treated led him at times to imply that suffering had rendered blacks more noble, more Christ-like than other races. ''The Cross,'' he wrote, ''is the property of the Negro in his religion because it was he who bore it.'' Although this dualism between universalism and particularism existed in Garvey's thought, he fell short of committing the error for which he condemned whites: advocating that God had a chosen race. In essence Garvey followed the spirit of the Old Testament itself and urged his fellow blacks to act not as a chosen but as a *choosing* people, a people with the same opportunities, the same possibilities, the same potential control over their destiny as every other people. Thus for Garvey religion was not an otherworldly affair; it taught ethical and practical principles that needed to be acted upon in this world: "I trust that you will so live today as to realize that you are masters of your own destiny, masters of your fate; if there is anything you want in this world it is for you to strike out with confidence and faith in self and reach for it, because God has created it for your happiness wheresover you may find it in nature."

Garvey was often ridiculed for picturing God as black. What he actually taught was more subtle and interesting. God, Garvey repeated over and over, had no color. However, since human beings were able to think of Him only in human terms, it was natural for them to conceive of God in their own physical shape. Whites, who had long done this themselves, had been successful in denying blacks the same privilege. It was now time "to see God through our own spectacles. . . . we shall worship Him through the spectacles of Ethiopia." "God is not white or black," he told a Cincinnati audience in 1921, "angels have no color, and they are not white peaches from Georgia. But if [whites] say that God is white, this organization says that God is black; if they are going to make the angels beautiful white peaches from Georgia, we are going to make them beautiful black peaches from Africa." Accordingly, the 1924 convention canonized Jesus Christ as a "Black Man of Sorrows," the Virgin Mary as a "Black Madonna," and resolved to idealize "God as a Holy Spirit, without physical form, but a Creature of imaginary semblance of the black race, being of like image and likeness."

James Weldon Johnson, who attended a number of UNIA meetings in New York's Liberty Hall, noted the elaborate liturgy and religious zeal he found there. Johnson's perceptions were quite accurate. The weekly meetings—generally held Sunday evenings—in liberty halls in New York and elsewhere closely resembled religious services. They were filled with the pomp and ceremony Garvey so loved and often featured processions of uniformed African Legionnaires or Black Cross Nurses. Hymns were sung, prayers recited, offerings received, just as in church. When Garvey was present, he delivered the major talk in his emotional, sermonizing style. When he was not, there would be a public reading of his front-page editorial in the week's *Negro World*. In addition, there would be talks by other UNIA leaders and sermons by clergy in attendance. And generally there were members of the clergy present, since a substantial number of black clergymen—Professor Randall Burkett has painstakingly identified more than 250—were active in the UNIA and helped to intensify the religious character already prominent in the movement.

Garvey worked hard to recruit clergy, hoping through them to reach their congregations. On occasion the strategy was more successful than Garvey could have hoped. At the 1924 convention, the Reverend R. H. Cosgrove of Natchez, Mississippi, reported that every one of the 500 members of his church was a member of the UNIA. Not surprisingly, those clergymen who became prominent in the UNIA tended to share Garvey's views and his militance. In 1923 the Reverend Thomas W. Anderson of the Second Baptist Church of Adrian, Michigan, told his Christmas Day audience that "the black man . . . must learn to fight; he must believe that God almighty . . . believes also in fighting." Blacks had to take charge of their own destiny. "If you don't have a bit of heaven here," he assured his audience, "don't worry, you won't have any hereafter."

The most important and influential of these ministers was the Episcopal priest George Alexander McGuire, who electrified the UNIA's first annual convention in 1920 by insisting that "the Uncle Tom nigger has got to go and his place must be taken . . . by a black man with a black heart." The element of revitalization was central to McGuire's appeal: "You must forget the white gods. Erase the white gods from your hearts. We must go back to the native church, to our own true God." The 1920 convention elected McGuire chaplain-general of the UNIA, and he quickly set about creating a *Universal Negro Ritual* and a *Universal Negro Catechism* intended to help reshape black religion. "O blessed Lord Jesus," read one of his suggested prayers, "Redeem Africa from the hands of those who exploit and ravish her. Renew her ancient glory, and grant that her oppressed and down-trodden children . . . may shortly be restored to their divine inheritance." In 1921 McGuire founded the African Orthodox Church and became its first bishop. Though there were many ties between the African Orthodox Church and the UNIA, Garvey neither endorsed nor joined McGuire's church for fear of alienating the many ministers and congregants of other denominations who were active in his movement, including such eclectic bands of non-Christian followers as black Jews and black Muslims. Whatever tensions existed between the two leaders, Garvey completely agreed with, and always acted upon, a principle McGuire enunciated at the 1924 convention: "Let it be understood, once and for all, that no constructive program for the Negro can be effective which underestimates the hold his religious institutions have upon him."

Garvey never made the mistake of underestimating the significance of religion. Nor did he commit the opposite error of focusing upon the spiritual to the neglect of the material needs of his people. From the beginning, fraternal sickness and death benefits were one of the features for which members were urged to pay their monthly 35-cent dues. Liberty halls served not only as scenes of inspirational public rituals but also as community centers sponsoring such social events as concerts, dances, and classes of various kinds. Notice boards held news of rooms or jobs. Liberty halls were sometimes converted into soup kitchens to feed the unemployed or into temporary dormitories for those without housing. "In the freezing winter days," Amy Jacques Garvey remembered, "stoves had to be kept going to accommodate the cold and homeless until they 'got on their feet' again."

Important as they were, Garvey considered such activities mere stopgaps. His organization was to function not as a welfare agency administering aid to the indigent, but as the center of a vast series of enterprises that would finally end black economic dependence. The Negro had for too long been a consumer, not a producer. "Let Edison turn off his electric light and we are in darkness in Liberty Hall in two minutes. The Negro is living on borrowed goods." In order to reverse this situation, Garvey established the Negro Factories Corporation in 1919 and offered "200,000 shares of common stock to the Negro race at par value of $5.00 per share." The ultimate object was to operate factories throughout the Western Hemisphere and Africa "to manufacture every marketable commodity." In New York City the corporation operated three grocery stores, two restaurants, a printing plant, a steam laundry, and a men's and women's manufacturing department that made the uniforms, hats, and shirts worn by members along with other items of clothing. In addition, the New York division owned several buildings, trucks, and the *Negro World*. Similar enterprises were operated or planned in other parts of the United States as well as in Central America and the West Indies. During the early 1920s, there were times when the UNIA and its allied corporations employed more than 1,000 blacks in the United States alone. The UNIA, Garvey pointed out to the white world, "employs thousands of black girls and black boys. Girls who could only be washer women in your homes, we made clerks and stenographers. . . . You will see from the start we tried to dignify our race." Here was a step toward Garvey's dream of a self-contained world of Negro producers, distributors, and consumers who could deal with or be independent of the rest of the world as necessity and circumstances dictated.

Garvey's attempts to lift the black world up economically were bedeviled by the very forces that Garvey decried: the difficulties of raising sufficient capital from an economically depressed and dependent group and the problems of dealing with white businessmen who were all too willing to exploit the economic disadvantages of blacks. Nothing demonstrated this more graphically than the failure of Garvey's most spectacular and significant economic activity: the Black Star Line that he created in June 1919 to operate a worldwide network of steamships. Within three months the Black Star Line had raised enough money through the sale of $5 stock certificates to purchase its first ship. Within a year the line had raised $610,000 and owned three ships. In spite of these initial successes, Garvey's dream of creating a great fleet of ships manned by black officers and men, so that "our race, too, would be respected in the mercantile and commercial world," was not to be. By the beginning of 1922, the Black Star Line was forced to suspend its operations, a victim of white businessmen who sold it decrepit vessels at inflated prices, of the inexperience and carelessness of Garvey and his chief associates, and of the dishonesty of some of its officers.

Economically, Garvey's venture into the maritime world left much to be desired. Its political capital, however, was considerable. Garvey pointed to the line as "the great attraction that brought to the Universal Negro Improvement Association millions of supporters." That attraction was manifest in the widespread sale of Black Star Line stock, which was limited to members of the Negro race. "I have sent twice to buy shares amounting to $125," one supporter wrote. "Now I am sending $35 for seven more shares. You might think I have money, but the truth, as I stated before, is that I have no money now. But if I'm to die of hunger it will be all right because I'm determined to do all that's in my power to better the conditions of my race." The child of another supporter recalled: "My mother was an intense Garveyite. She bought stock in it. . . . She lost money in its ventures and was disillusioned, but not in the principles involved. . . . The Back-to-Africa part was not important. Pride was. Negroes should have something of their own." The Black Star Line, the lawyer Henry Lincoln Johnson asserted, "was a loss in money but it was a gain in soul."

That gain was felt throughout the Western Hemisphere. Hugh Mulzac, a black ship's officer who sailed for Garvey on the *Yarmouth* in 1920, recorded the reception the ship received everywhere it docked. When it entered the harbor at Havana, "sympathizers flocked from all parts of the island toward the docks to greet the first ship they had ever seen entirely owned and operated by colored men. They came out in boats when we arrived, showering us with flowers and fruit . . . [we] were overrun with visitors from dawn until sunset." When the ship docked at Colon, "literally thousands of Panamanians swarmed the docks with baskets of fruit, vegetables and gifts. I was amazed that the *Yarmouth* had become a symbol for colored people of every land." In Costa Rica "we were accorded the welcome of conquering heroes. At Bocas del Toro thousands of peasants came down from the hills on horses, donkeys, and in makeshift carts . . . In the tumult that followed dancing broke out on the deck, great piles of fruit and flowers mounted on the hatch covers, and UNIA agents signed up hundreds of new members." In Philadelphia, Boston, and New York as well, there were spectacular receptions for the ship "with thousands joining the parades. Garvey made impassioned speeches, whipping the people into frenzied support of the association." The problem, Mulzac discovered, was that little or no distinction was being made between the commercial and symbolic functions of the voyage. There was no economic reason to be in many of these ports, and while the demonstrations were going on, hundreds of passengers aboard had to be fed and cared for, and hundreds of tons of coconuts were rotting in the hold. "It was," Mulzac concluded, "a helluva way to run a steamship."

The tension between the pragmatic and the symbolic was evident in other aspects of the Garvey movement as well. Garvey employed no symbol more frequently or more effectively than that of the African homeland. "Hail! United States of Africa!" he entitled a poem:

> The treason of the centuries is dead,
> All alien whites are forever gone;
> The glad home of Sheba is once more free.

Garvey embroidered this portrait of a free, independent African continent endlessly and argued for its necessity incessantly. "Show me the race or the nation without a flag, and I will show you a race of people without any pride," he proclaimed. Consequently, the convention of 1920 added to the "objects" of the UNIA the establishment of "a central nation for the race," created a red, black, and green flag for the African republic, and adopted a national anthem that began: "Ethiopia, thou land of our fathers, / Thou land where the gods loved to be."

The "brilliant, noble and grand" African past was a constant theme for Garvey in speech after speech, but he reminded his followers in 1923, "WE CANNOT LIVE BY THE PAST." The only "salvation for the Negro" was "through a free and independent Africa." Without that, blacks would be forever the exploited wards of other races, eternally incapable of demonstrating what they could accomplish. If the race remained a scattered, drifting remnant, "it will be only a question of time when the Negro will be as completely and complacently dead as the North American Indian, or the Australian Bushman." The question of independence was too crucial for Garvey to contemplate failure. African redemption, he prophesied, "is in the wind. It is coming. One day, like a storm, it will be here." He warned the white world: "We are coming 400,000,000 strong and we mean to retake every square inch of the 12,000,000 square miles of African territory belonging to us by right Divine."

Garvey utilized the idea of Africa to touch deeply many of the yearnings and needs of his people. He was preaching more than the redemption of Africa; he was preaching the redemption of the entire Negro people, the revitalization of the entire black race. Nevertheless, when Garvey cried out, "Wake up Ethiopia! Wake up Africa! Let us work towards the one glorious end of a free, redeemed and mighty nation," he was not being merely allegorical. He really did want to end white hegemony and substitute a black republic stretching, as he put it in one of his poems, "From Liberia's peaceful western coast / To the foaming Cape at the southern end." He did believe that so long as blacks lacked an autonomous, powerful nation of their own they would never be accorded their rights anywhere in the world. The diplomatic pressure an independent Africa could exert, for example, would be far more effective in protecting American Negroes than any anti-lynching bill.

Consequently, Garvey worked in every way he could for African independence, insisting that his goal was the exact counterpart of the Jewish yearning for a homeland in Palestine or the Irish desire for an independent Eire. He supported Senator Joseph France's plan to have the United States liquidate its allies' war debts in return for enough of their African territory to establish an independent nation for American Negroes. He petitioned the League of Nations to deliver the ex-German colonies in Africa to the custody of the UNIA. He negotiated with Liberia for a UNIA immigrant settlement on the Cavalla River in southern Liberia. This latter arrangement, scheduled to begin with 500 American families in 1924, failed on the eve of its birth due to a combination of British and French pressure to keep the deeply anticolonial Garveyites out of Africa and the growing fear of the elite Liberian governing class that an influx of American immigrants would ultimately threaten the Liberian status quo.

Garvey was deeply disappointed at his failure to win a settlement in Liberia, which he had envisioned as a beachhead from which Western Negroes could spread modern technical, scientific, and humanistic knowledge throughout the continent. There is no indication that Garvey ever worried about what effects the accelerated imposition of the body of Western knowledge would have upon indigenous African cultures. It is important to remember that Garvey's opposition to the West was political; he did not disdain Western culture, which he was, after all, part of. "Those of us who lead are well versed in Western civilization and are determined that the black man shall not be a creature of the past, but a full-fledged man of the present." In this respect, Garvey was never a cultural nationalist. He looked back to the glories of the African past, but even there he was proudest of those attributes that had contributed directly to the store of Western culture. He had little, if anything, to say about the glories of African religion or expressive art or social mores and patterns. These were not concerns of his, and he seems to have been willing to see them replaced as expeditiously as possible with their Western counterparts. It is not surprising, then, that one of the consistent "objects" of the UNIA was "to assist in civilizing the backward tribes of Africa."

In spite of Garvey's many activities concerning Africa, his widow insisted that "the term, back-to-Africa, was used and promoted by newspapers, Negro newspapers mostly, to ridicule Garvey. There was no back-to-Africa movement except in a spiritual sense.'' Mrs. Garvey was essentially correct. Garvey envisioned African independence as a gradual, long-term process and never seems to have advocated the massive return of blacks from the diaspora. Nevertheless, Garvey's vagueness and perhaps confusion about his plans, coupled with his tendency toward rhetorical excess, often gave a different impression. Thus, in 1921 he insisted that ''we are not preaching any doctrine to ask all the negroes of Harlem and of the United States to leave for Africa. The majority of us may remain here.'' But he also declared that when the pioneer mechanics and artisans had built the necessary railroads and institutions, ''The time will come for the command to be given, 'Come home!' '' The vision of the biblical exodus often informed his speeches: ''We shall gather together our children, our treasures and our loved ones, and, as the children of Israel, by the command of God, faced the promised land, so in time we shall also.''

Above all, it was his pessimism about the possibility of whites and blacks living in harmony that made him appear a champion of total repatriation. One of the salient messages emerging from his speeches and writings was his conviction that American blacks would never be accorded true equality. As the white population grew, blacks would be pushed out of the marketplace and become increasingly redundant economically. Nor could they look for protection to a government controlled by a white majority. He reminded those who believed that the black minority would win a share of the white majority's economic and political power that ''nothing of the kind has happened in all human history.'' So long as whites feared black competition, so long would there be 'not only prejudice, but riots, lynchings, burnings.'' The only solution was to provide an outlet for black energy and ambition where it would not threaten whites. The conclusion was obvious: ''The future of the Negro therefore, outside of Africa, spells ruin and disaster.''

If Garvey's distrust of whites and his desire to build a sense of black solidarity produced ambiguities in his attitudes regarding emigration to Africa, they created a consistent set of racial policies—too consistent, perhaps, for Garvey's own good. Garvey wanted to unite his people not only politically and economically but racially. ''I believe in a pure black race,'' he announced and argued that it was time to end ''the curse of many colors within the Negro race'' that slavery had produced; it was time to stop this ''wholesale bastardy'' and to create ''a race type and standard of our own.'' The UNIA, Garvey announced, ''is against miscegenation and race suicide. . . . It believes in the social and political physical separation of all peoples to the extent that they promote their own ideals and civilization.'' He assured the whites that blacks did not want racial amalgamation, and he pleaded with his people to be true to themselves: ''The Anglo-Saxon doesn't want to be a Japanese; the Japanese doesn't want to be a Negro. Then, in the name of God and all that is holy, why should we want to be somebody else?'' Garvey insisted that he was not attempting to exclude anyone. ''For once we will agree with the American white man, that one drop of Negro blood makes a man a Negro.'' In the UNIA ''100 per cent Negroes and even 1 per cent Negroes will stand together as one mighty whole.''

Garvey's zeal on the race issue led him to promote blackness wherever he could. He banned ads for skin lighteners and hair straighteners from his papers; he urged that children be given black dolls to play with and black role models to admire; he wrote odes to the beauty of black women: ''Black Queen of beauty, thou has given colour to the world, / Among other women thou art royal and the fairest.'' His zeal led him also into more dangerous waters. In the postwar years the black urge to revitalization clashed with such white revitalization movements as the Ku Klux Klan. These separate movements looked back with nostalgia on different heritages and forward with longing to distinct futures. Garvey, however, saw race policy as a means of bridging the gap. In 1922 Garvey met with leaders of the Klan in Atlanta to explain how close the UNIA and the KKK were on such matters as miscegenation and social equality. No other act of Garvey's brought him more criticism or cost him more support. Yet he refused to apologize for it. Compared with the ''farce, hypocrisy and lie'' typical of most whites, he welcomed the ''honesty of purpose'' of the Klan. ''They are better friends to my race, for telling us what they are, and what they mean, thereby giving us a chance to stir for ourselves.'' Potentially, he warned, ''every whiteman is a Klansman . . . and there is no use lying about it.''

It would be a mistake to see Garvey's attitudes toward the Klan as an aberration. They were deeply representative of Garvey's racial views and his abiding pessimism concerning the future of blacks in the United States. When President Warren G. Harding spoke out in 1921 ''against every suggestion of social equality,'' Garvey sent him a telegram of congratulations. Speaking in North Carolina in 1922, Garvey thanked southern whites for having ''lynched race pride into the Negro.'' In 1925 he forged an alliance with the Anglo-Saxon Clubs, invited their leader, John Powell, to speak in Liberty Hall, and announced: ''I unhesitatingly endorse the race purity idea of Mr. Powell and his organization.'' A year and a half before he died, Garvey endorsed the bill of the racist Mississippi Senator Theodore Bilbo for the repatriation of American Negroes to Africa and instructed all divisions of the UNIA to give it their ''undivided and wholehearted support.''

Garvey's racial ideology helped to determine his response to politics in general. In 1924 he answered a friendly overture from the Workers' party by stating: ''We belong to the Negro party, first, last and all the time.'' His fear of the racism of the white working class, combined with his lingering affection for Washingtonian self-help, gave his domestic politics a conservative cast. He was a consistent foe of the Communists, whom he branded "a group of lazy men and women who desire to level all initiative and intelligence and set a premium on stagnation." Communists and trade unionists, he warned, were "more dangerous to the Negro's welfare than any other group at present." He attributed the failure of modern government to individual selfishness and greed, which could be remedied by paying government officials enough to remove them from temptation and punishing them by death should they succumb anyway. He proposed to reform capitalism by limiting individual fortunes to one million dollars and preventing any corporation from controlling more than five million dollars. While reforms were necessary, Garvey hailed capitalism as "necessary to the progress of the world" and branded its opponents "enemies to human advancement." "The only convenient friend the Negro worker or laborer has, in America, at the present time, is the white capitalist," Garvey announced, since the capitalist's desire to maximize profits made him willing to use the cheapest available labor. Garvey urged the black worker to "keep his scale of wage a little lower than the whites until he is able to become, through proper leadership, his own employer."

One of Garvey's most remarkable achievements was the ease with which he bridged the cultural and political gulf between Jamaica and the United States and learned to comprehend and speak to the needs and aspirations of millions of American blacks. The areas in which he failed to make this transition sufficiently were ones in which he committed his most serious errors. Among these were those aspects of his racial ideology that led him to attempt to form a common front with white racists and that affected his relations with his fellow black leaders. Given the nature of many of his programs, it was inevitable that Garvey would make a number of potent enemies within the ranks of black intellectuals, editors, civil rights leaders, and political activists. His very attempt to articulate the feelings of the masses was bound to create some animus among a significant number of the educated and affluent. However inevitable some of this might have been, it cannot be attributed—as Garvey liked to do—wholly to his opponents. Not only Garvey's programs but his style and temperament helped to create the impossibly poor relations with other black leaders that constituted one of Garvey's greatest weaknesses and hampered his cause significantly.

Certainly Garvey was provoked. To give but two examples, Du Bois described him as "a little, fat black man, ugly, but with intelligent eyes and big head," who was "the most dangerous enemy of the Negro race in America and the world . . . either a lunatic or a traitor," and A. Philip Randolph's *Messenger* referred to him as "the supreme Negro Jamaican Jackass," a "monumental monkey," and an "unquestioned fool and ignoramus." Garvey bore more than a little responsibility for determining the tone of this debate and surely for setting its racial dimensions. He brought with him from Jamaica an abiding distrust of the light-skinned, middle-class Negroes who constituted so many of the leaders in America. The basis of his distrust was not only, or even primarily, their program but their class and color. He attacked Cyril Briggs, the light-complexioned leader of the militant African Blood Brotherhood, with which Garvey certainly might have forged an alliance, as a "white man." He criticized the "near-white" leaders of the NAACP, which Garvey delighted in calling the "National Association for the Advancement of Certain People." His favorite target was Du Bois, whom he branded a "lazy dependent mulatto" whose mixed Dutch, French, and Negro ancestry made him "a monstrosity" who "bewails every day the drop of Negro blood in his veins." The Negro press, "controlled by crafty and unscrupulous persons who have no love of race," was "the most venal, ignorant and corrupt of our time." Du Bois and his allies were planning the extinction of the black race through miscegenation and were thus "the greatest enemies the black people have in the world."

This unhappy, unproductive debate not only drained the energies of all involved and rendered impossible the kind of unified black community Garvey claimed he wanted, but also it ultimately undermined Garvey's leadership and the effectiveness of his organization. A number of black leaders and journalists with whom Garvey had been feuding mounted a campaign against Garvey's operation of the Black Star Line, alerting government officials to alleged illegalities. In January 1922 Garvey and three of his associates were arrested and in February indicted on twelve counts of fraudulent use of the mails to sell Black Star stocks. A prolonged delay in beginning the trial, during which Garvey was released on bail, annoyed his opponents and on January 15, 1923, eight prominent black men and women, including three editors, two NAACP officials, and three business people, wrote to the attorney general of the United States, denouncing Garvey as a demagogue who preached "distrust and hatred of all white people," and demanded that the attorney general "disband and extirpate" Garvey's "vicious movement" and speedily push the government's case against him. The trial began within four months. Though there was no evidence that Garvey was guilty of anything more than poor management, inexperience, and bad judgment in choosing some of his associates, he alone of the four defendants was found guilty and sentenced to five years in prison.

From New York City's Tombs Prison, which Garvey entered in the middle of June 1923, he asserted, "I am not here because I committed any crime against society or defrauded anyone, but because I have led the way to Africa's redemption." In September he was released on bail pending his appeal and enjoyed his last seventeen months of freedom in America. On

February 2, 1925, Garvey's appeal was denied, and six days later he entered Atlanta Penitentiary. In his many prison messages and editorials, Garvey was at his most prophetic and messianic: "If I die in Atlanta my work shall then only begin." Garvey was not destined to die in Atlanta. On November 18, 1927, President Calvin Coolidge commuted Garvey's sentence, which still had slightly more than two years to run. Early the next month, Garvey was deported as an undesirable alien. Hundreds of Garvey's followers gathered at the New Orleans pier to bid him farewell. "Be not dismayed," he told them. "Africa's sun is steadily and surely rising, and soon shall shed its rays around the world. I live and shall die for Africa redeemed. Steady yourselves and go forward!"

Despite Garvey's optimistic rhetoric and the considerable personal courage he exhibited during his prosecution and imprisonment, his incarceration and deportation separated him from the most powerful constituency he had and effectively destroyed his movement in the United States. Certainly it is true, as Amy Jacques Garvey has pointed out, that though Garvey was forced to leave America, "Garveyism remained." But it remained in severely diminished circumstances. In Garvey's absence its following declined drastically, and its leadership became hopelessly divided. At the time of Garvey's deportation, the UNIA was bankrupt with liabilities of over $200,000. The final ship in its fleet had been auctioned off for payment of debts; it had lost its liberty halls in New York and Pittsburgh as well as its New York office buildings and publishing plant. The UNIA continued to function, but its days of power and glory were behind it.

Garvey was to live more than twelve years in forced exile from the United States. They were years of characteristic energy and activity and of uncharacteristic isolation and futility. Making Jamaica his base of operations, Garvey edited several newspapers, hosted international conventions of the UNIA in 1929 and 1934, served three months in prison for contempt of court, was elected to the governing body of Kingston and its parish but was defeated in his bid for the Jamaican legislature, made an abortive attempt to organize a Jamaican People's party, and spent much time and energy feuding with his former UNIA colleagues in America and seeking financial support for his movement. Once again, Garvey was to find his native island too confining. On his way down, no less than on his way up, Garvey needed to be near the center of events.

In March 1935 Garvey took his magazine, the *Black Man*, which he had begun the year before, and moved permanently to London. When the colonial secretary in Jamaica warned British Military Intelligence that Garvey might relocate in London, the reply was: "he can do very little harm over here." That judgment proved to be correct. Garvey continued the patterns of the past: he edited his impressive magazine, he spoke in Hyde Park whenever the weather was fair and indoors wherever he could find a hall and an audience, but he seems not to have had meaningful interaction with London's black population, which had grown somewhat larger and more diverse since Garvey had lived there before World War I. Throughout these final years the major outlines of his philosophy remained familiar. He continued to be a proponent of racial separation, of success through individual and group initiative, and of African redemption. Nevertheless, he was no more predictable at the end of his life than he had been in the beginning. Even as he denounced Benito Mussolini for his rape of Ethiopia, he openly admired aspects of his regime and complained: "Mussolini copied fascism from me. . . . Mussolini and Hitler copied the program of the UNIA." Even as he championed the principles of liberty and the rights of oppressed peoples, he proved strangely indifferent to the plight of the Jews in Germany, charging that their troubles had "been brought on by themselves," because—of all reasons—"their particular method of living is inconsistent with the broader human principles that go to make all people homogeneous."

Garvey longed to return to the United States, if only for a visit, but was denied permission. He came as close as he could, spending three summers, from 1936 to 1938, in Toronto, where he held two regional UNIA conferences and his last international convention. Though the days of his own leadership were behind him, one of his final gestures was to establish a School of African Philosophy in Toronto to recruit and train prospective new leaders for the UNIA. In June 1939 his precarious financial situation forced him to suspend publication of the *Black Man*. For almost the first time since his youth, Garvey was without a journalistic voice. The last year of his life in London was lived in silent penury. In January 1940 he suffered a stroke that left him partially paralyzed, and on June 10, nine weeks short of his fifty-third birthday, he died.

Though he died in isolation, Garvey was not to be forgotten. Decades after his death, his name was still invoked, his ideas still discussed, his influence still felt. Garvey would not have been surprised; it was always his conviction that this would be so. Throughout his stormy, difficult life, Garvey had nurtured his vision of a proud, united black race and an independent Africa. He may not have always worked for it wisely or effectively, but he never ceased working for it and believing in it. In his "Appeal to Racial Pride," printed in the penultimate issue of the *Black Man,* Garvey closed with words that might well serve as his epitaph: "The end is not in our day but in our time we can make certain contribution toward it. . . . Let us not turn back, let us hold on, so that when the final history of man is to be written, there will not only be glory for others but there will be glory for us."

III

TOWARDS AN UNDERSTANDING OF POPULAR CULTURE

8

William Shakespeare and the American People: A Study in Cultural Transformation

In retrospect, nothing else I've written seems quite as "organic" as this essay. I certainly never planned an article on Shakespeare; it just grew out of a series of questions I had been asking myself since the period in which I had intensively researched black folk culture. It was in connection with that research that I read through a number of minstrel shows to comprehend how black culture had been depicted on the white stage. The fact that Shakespearean parody was one of the standard features of minstrelsy puzzled me considerably. Parody, to be effective, relies upon familiarity. The minstrels'

> All the world's a bar
> And all the men and women merely drinkers;
> They have their hiccups and their staggerings
>
> . . .

attained its humor from knowledge of the original soliloquy from *As You Like It,*

> All the world's a stage,
> And all the men and women merely players:
> They have their exits and their entrances
>
> . . .

which it was lampooning. For me, whose society considered Shakespeare emblematic of everything that made High Culture sacred and therefore inaccessible to the masses, the problem was: how could the extremely heterogenous audiences of minstrel shows have known enough to get the joke? That they obviously did was evident from the ubiquity of these parodies.

The assumptions of my own culture taught me to presume that since

Shakespeare was High Culture in my age he must have enjoyed the same status in nineteenth-century America. Yet the evidence of the minstrel shows seemed to belie this. Though the problem continued to haunt me, I did nothing about it. In this respect, too, I was being a true child of my culture: how could anyone lacking the erudition of the Shakespeare specialist be qualified to do research on one of the Great Minds, one of the Classic Writers of all time? Although cultural dispositions die hard, ultimately a trip to the Folger Shakespeare Library in Washington, D.C., where I found myself perfectly capable of handling the sources, and an invitation to participate in a Hungarian-American conference in Budapest on the relationship between high and low culture, broke the log jam and with the help and encouragement of a number of friends and colleagues I wrote the following essay which was published in *The American Historical Review,* 89 (February 1984).

The humor of a people affords important insights into the nature of their culture. Thus Mark Twain's treatment of Shakespeare in his novel *Huckleberry Finn* helps us place the Elizabethan playwright in nineteenth-century American culture. Shortly after the two rogues, who pass themselves off as a duke and a king, invade the raft of Huck and Jim, they decide to raise funds by performing scenes from Shakespeare's *Romeo and Juliet* and *Richard III*. That the presentation of Shakespeare in small Mississippi River towns could be conceived of as potentially lucrative tells us much about the position of Shakespeare in the nineteenth century. The specific nature of Twain's humor tells us even more. Realizing that they would need material for encores, the "duke" starts to teach the "king" Hamlet's soliloquy, which he recites from memory:

> To be, or not to be; that is the bare bodkin
> That makes calamity of so long life;
> For who would fardels bear, till Birnam Wood do come to Dunsinane,
> But that the fear of something after death Murders the innocent sleep,
> Great nature's second course,
> And makes us rather sling arrows of outrageous fortune
> Than fly to others that we know not of.[1]

Twain's humor relies on his audience's familiarity with *Hamlet* and its ability to recognize the duke's improbable coupling of lines from a variety of Shakespeare's plays. Twain was employing one of the most popular forms of humor in nineteenth-century America. Everywhere in the nation burlesques and parodies of Shakespeare constituted a prominent form of entertainment.

Hamlet was a favorite target in numerous travesties imported from England or crafted at home. Audiences roared at the sight of Hamlet dressed in fur cap and collar, snowshoes and mittens; they listened with amused surprise to his profanity when ordered by his father's ghost to "swear" and to his commanding Ophelia, "Get thee to a brewery"; they heard him recite his lines in black dialect or Irish brogue and sing his most famous soliloquy, "To be, or not to be," to the tune of "Three Blind Mice." In the 1820s the British comedian Charles Mathews visited what he called the "Nigger's (or Negroe's) theatre" in New York, where he heard "a black tragedian in the character of Hamlet" recite "To be, or not to be? That is the question; whether it is nobler in *de* mind to suffer, or tak' up arms against a sea of trouble, and by *opossum* end 'em." "No sooner was the word *opossum* out of his mouth," Mathews reported, "than the audience burst forth, in one general cry, '*Opossum! opossum! opossum!*' "—prompting the actor to come forward and sing the popular dialect song "Opossum up a Gum Tree." On the nineteenth-century American stage, audiences often heard Hamlet's lines intricately combined with those of a popular song:

> Oh! 'tis consummation
> Devoutly to be wished
> To end your heart-ache by a sleep,
> When likely to be dish'd.
> Shuffle off your mortal coil,
> Do just so,
> Wheel about, and turn about,
> And jump Jim Crow.[2]

No Shakespearean play was immune to this sort of mutilation. *Richard III*, the most popular Shakespearean play in the nineteenth century, was lampooned frequently in such versions as *Bad Dicky*. In one New York production starring first-rank Shakespearean actors, a stuttering, lisping Othello danced while Desdemona played the banjo and Iago, complete with Irish brogue, ended their revelries with a fire hose. Parodies could also embody a serious message. In Kenneth Bangs's version of *The Taming of the Shrew*, for example, Kate ended up in control, observing that, although "Shakespeare or Bacon, or whoever wrote the play . . . studied deeply the shrews of his day. . . , the modern shrew isn't built that way," while a chastened Petruchio concluded, "Sweet Katharine, of your remarks I recognize the force: / Don't strive to tame a woman as you would a horse." Serious or slapstick, the punning was endless. In one parody of the famous dagger scene, Macbeth continues to put off his insistent wife by asking, "Or is that dagger but a false Daguerreotype?" Luckily, Desdemona had no brother, or Othello "might look both black and blue," a character in *Othello* remarked, while one in *The Merchant of Venice* observed of Shylock, "This crafty Jew is full of *Jeux d'esprit!*" Throughout the century, the number of parodies with such titles as *Julius Sneezer, Roamy-E-Owe and Julie-Ate,* and *Desdemonum* was impressive.[3]

These full-fledged travesties reveal only part of the story. Nineteenth-century Shakespearean parody most frequently took the form of short skits, brief references, and satirical songs inserted into other modes of entertainment. In one of their routines, for example, the Bryants' Minstrels playfully referred to the famous observation in Act II of *Romeo and Juliet:*

> Adolphus Pompey is my name,
>> But that don't make no difference,
> For as Massa Wm. Shakespeare says,
>> A name's of no signiforance.

The minstrels loved to invoke Shakespeare as an authority: "you know what de Bird of Avon says 'bout 'De black scandal an' de foul faced reproach!'" And they constantly quoted him in appropriately garbled form: "Fust to dine own self be true, an' it must follow night an' day, dou den can be false to any man." The significance of this national penchant for parodying Shakespeare is clear: Shakespeare and his drama had become by the nineteenth century an integral part of American culture. It is difficult to take familiarities with that which is not already familiar; one cannot parody that which is not well known. The minstrels' characteristic conundrums would not have been funny to an audience lacking knowledge of Shakespeare's works:

> When was Desdemona like a ship?
> When she was Moored.[4]

It is not surprising that educated Americans in the eighteenth and nineteenth centuries knew their Shakespeare. What is more interesting is how widely Shakespeare was known to the public in general. In the last half of the eighteenth century, when the reading of Shakespeare's plays was still confined to a relatively small, educated elite, substantial numbers of Americans had the chance to see his plays performed. From the first documented American performance of a Shakespearean play in 1750 until the closing of the theaters in 1778 because of the American Revolution, Shakespeare emerged as the most popular playwright in the colonies. Fourteen or fifteen of his plays were presented at least one hundred and eighty—and one scholar has estimated perhaps as many as five hundred—times. Following the Revolution, Shakespeare retained his position as the most widely performed dramatist, with five more of his plays regularly performed in an increasing number of cities and towns.[5]

Not until the nineteenth century, however, did Shakespeare come into his own—presented and recognized almost everywhere in the country. In the cities of the Northeast and Southeast, Shakespeare's plays dominated the theater. During the 1810–11 season in Philadelphia, for example, Shakespearean plays accounted for twenty-two of eighty-eight performances. The following season lasted 108 nights, of which again one-quarter—27—were devoted to Shakespeare. From 1800 to 1835, Philadelphians had the opportunity to see twenty-one of Shakespeare's thirty-seven plays. The Philadelphia theater was not exceptional; one student of the American stage concluded that in cities on the Eastern Seaboard at least one-fifth of all plays offered in a season were likely to be by Shakespeare.[6] George Makepeace Towle, an American consul in England, returned to his own country just after the Civil War and remarked with some surprise, "Shakespearian dramas are more frequently played and more popular in America than in England." Shakespeare's dominance can be attested to by what Charles Shattuck has called "the westward flow of Shakespearean actors" from England to America. In the nineteenth century, one prominent English Shakespearean actor after another—George Frederick Cooke, Edmund Kean, Junius Brutus Booth, Charles and Fanny Kemble, Ellen Tree, William Charles Macready—sought the fame and financial rewards that awaited them in their tours of the United States.[7]

It is important to understand that their journey did not end with big cities or the Eastern Seaboard. According to John Bernard, the English actor and comedian who worked in the United States from 1797 to 1819, "If an actor were unemployed, want and shame were not before him: he had merely to visit some town in the interior where no theatre existed, but 'readings' were permitted; and giving a few recitations from Shakespeare and Sterne, his pockets in a night or two were amply replenished." During his travels through the United States in the 1830s, Tocqueville found Shakespeare in "the recesses of the forests of the New World. There is hardly a pioneer's hut that does not contain a few odd volumes of Shakespeare. I remember that I read the feudal drama of *Henry V* for the first time in a log cabin." [8] Five decades later, the German visitor Karl Knortz made a similar observation:

> There is, assuredly, no other country on the face of this earth in which Shakespeare and the Bible are held in such general high esteem as in America, the very country so much decried for its lust for money. If you were to enter an isolated log cabin in the Far West and even if its inhabitant

were to exhibit many of the traces of backwoods living, he will most likely
have one small room nicely furnished in which to spend his few leisure
hours and in which you will certainly find the Bible and in most cases also
some cheap edition of the works of the poet Shakespeare.[9]

Even if we discount the hyperbole evident in such accounts, they were far
from inventions. The ability of the illiterate Rocky Mountain scout Jim Bridger
to recite long passages from Shakespeare, which he had learned by hiring
someone to read the plays to him, and the formative influence that the plays
had upon young Abe Lincoln growing up in Salem, Illinois, became part of
the nation's folklore.[10] But if books had become a more important vehicle
for disseminating Shakespeare by the nineteenth century, the stage remained
the primary instrument. The theater, like the church, was one of the earliest
and most important cultural institutions established in frontier cities. And
almost everywhere the theater blossomed Shakespeare was a paramount force.
In his investigation of the theater in Louisville, Cincinnati, St. Louis, Detroit, and Lexington, Kentucky, from 1800 to 1840, Ralph Leslie Rusk concluded that Shakespeare's plays were performed more frequently than those
of any other author. In Mississippi between 1814 and the outbreak of the
Civil War, the towns of Natchez and Vicksburg, with only a few thousand
inhabitants each, put on at least one hundred and fifty performances of
Shakespeare featuring such British and American stars as Ellen Tree, Edwin
Forrest, Junius Brutus Booth, J. W. Walleck, Charles Kean, J. H. Hackett,
Josephine Clifton, and T. A. Cooper. Stars of this and lesser caliber made
their way into the interior by boat, along the Ohio and Mississippi rivers,
stopping at towns and cities on their way to New Orleans. Beginning in the
early 1830s, the rivers themselves became the site of Shakespearean productions, with floating theaters in the form first of flatboats and then steamboats
bringing drama to small river towns.[11]

By mid-century, Shakespeare was taken across the Great Plains and
over the Rocky Mountains and soon became a staple of theaters in the Far
West. During the decade following the arrival of the Forty-niners, at least
twenty-two of Shakespeare's plays were performed on California stages, with
Richard III retaining the predominance it had gained in the East and South.
In 1850 the Jenny Lind Theatre, seating two thousand, opened over a saloon
in San Francisco and was continuously crowded: "Miners . . . swarmed
from the gambling saloons and cheap fandango houses to see *Hamlet* and
Lear." In 1852 the British star Junius Brutus Booth and two of his sons
played *Hamlet, Macbeth, Othello,* and *Richard III* from the stage of the
Jenny Lind and packed the house for the two weeks of their stay. In 1856
Laura Keen brought San Franciscans not only old favorites but such relatively uncommon productions as *Coriolanus* and *A Midsummer Night's Dream.*

Along with such eminent stars from abroad, American actors like McKean Buchanan and James Stark kept the hunger for Shakespeare satisfied.[12]

But Shakespeare could not be confined to the major population centers in the Far West any more than he had been in the East. If miners could not always come to San Francisco to see theater, the theater came to them. Stark, Buchanan, Edwin Booth, and their peers performed on makeshift stages in mining camps around Sacramento and crossed the border into Nevada, where they brought characterizations of Hamlet, Iago, Macbeth, Kate, Lear, and Othello to miners in Virginia City, Silver City, Dayton, and Carson City. Walter M. Leman recalled the dearth of theaters in such California towns as Tod's Valley, Chip's Flat, Cherokee Flat, Rattlesnake, Mud Springs, Red Dog, Hangtown, Drytown, and Fiddletown, which he toured in the 1850s. In the Sierra town of Downieville, Leman performed *Richard III* on the second story of a cloth and paper house in a hall without a stage: "we had to improvise one out of the two billiard tables it contained, covering them with boards for that purpose." Such conditions were by no means confined to the West Coast. In earlier years, Leman had toured the Maine towns of Bangor, Belfast, Orono, and Oldtown, not one of which had a proper theater, necessitating the use of church vestries and other improvisations. In 1816 in Lexington, Kentucky, Noah Ludlow performed *The Taming of the Shrew, Othello,* and *The Merchant of Venice* in a room on the second floor of an old brewery, next door to a saloon, before an audience seated on backless, cushionless chairs. In the summer of 1833, Sol Smith's company performed in the dining room of a hotel in Tazewell, Alabama, "on a sort of landing-place or gallery about six feet long, and two and a half feet wide." His "heavy tragedian" Mr. Lyne attempted to recite the "Seven Ages of Man" from *As You Like It* while "Persons were passing from one room to the other continually and the performer was obliged to *move* whenever any one passed."[13]

Thus Shakespeare was by no means automatically treated with reverence. Nor was he accorded universal acclaim. In Davenport and neighboring areas of Eastern Iowa, where the theater flourished in both English and German, Shakespeare was seldom performed and then usually in the form of short scenes and soliloquies rather than entire plays. As more than one theater manager learned, producing Shakespeare did not necessarily result in profits. Theatrical lore often repeated the vow attributed to Robert L. Place that he would never again produce a play by Shakespeare "no matter how many more he wrote." But these and similar incidents were exceptions to the general rule: from the large and often opulent theaters of major cities to the makeshift stages in halls, saloons, and churches of small towns and mining camps, wherever there was an audience for the theater, there Shakespeare's plays were performed prominently and frequently. Shakespeare's popularity in frontier communities in all sections of the country may not fit Frederick Jackson Turner's image of the frontier as a crucible, melting civilization down into a new amalgam, but it does fit our knowledge of human beings and their need for the comfort of familiar things under the pressure of new circumstances and surroundings. James Fenimore Cooper had this familiarity in mind when he called Shakespeare "the great author of America" and insisted that Americans had "just as good a right" as Englishmen to claim Shakespeare as their countryman.[14]

Shakespeare's popularity can be determined not only by the frequency of Shakespearean productions and the size of the audiences for them but also by the nature of the productions and the manner in which they were presented. Shakespeare was performed not merely alongside popular entertainment as an elite supplement to it; Shakespeare was performed as an integral part of it. Shakespeare *was* popular entertainment in nineteenth-century America. The theater in the first half of the nineteenth century played the role that movies played in the first half of the twentieth: it was a kaleidoscopic, democratic institution presenting a widely varying bill of fare to all classes and socioeconomic groups.

During the first two-thirds of the nineteenth century, the play may have been the thing, but it was not the only thing. It was the centerpiece, the main attraction, but an entire evening generally consisted of a long play, an afterpiece (usually a farce), and a variety of between-act specialities. In the spring of 1839, a playbill advertising the appearance of William Evans Burton in *As You Like It* at Philadelphia's American Theatre announced, "Il Diavolo Antonio And His Sons, Antonio, Lorenzo, Augustus And Alphonzo will present a most magnificent display of position in the Science of Gymnastics, portraying some of the most grand and imposing groups from the ancient masters . . . to conclude with a grand Horizontal Pyramid." It was a characteristically full evening. In addition to gymnastics and Shakespeare, "Mr. Quayle (by Desire)" sang "The Swiss Drover Boy," La Petite Celeste danced "a New Grand Pas Seul," Miss Lee danced "La Cachuca," Quayle returned to sing "The Haunted Spring," Mr. Bowman told a "Yankee Story," and "the Whole" concluded "with *Ella Rosenberg* starring Mrs. Hield." [15]

Thus Shakespeare was presented amid a full range of contemporary entertainment. During the Mexican War, a New Orleans performance of *Richard III* was accompanied by "A NEW and ORIGINAL Patriotic Drama in 3 Acts, . . . (founded in part on events which have occurred during the Mexican War,) & called: Palo Alto! Or, Our Army on the Rio Grande! . . . TRIUMPH OF AMERICAN ARMS! Surrender of Gen. Vega to Capt. May! Grand Military Tableau!" It would be a mistake to conclude that Shakespeare was presented as the dry, staid ingredient in this exciting menu. On the contrary, Shakespearean plays were often announced as spectacles in their own right. In 1799 the citizens of Alexandria, Virginia, were promised the following in a production of *Macbeth:* "In Act 3d—A Regal Banquet in which the Ghost of Banquo appears. In Act 4th—A Solemn incantation & dance of Witches. In Act 5th—A grand Battle, with the defeat & death of Macbeth." At mid-century, a presentation of *Henry IV* in Philadelphia featured the "Army of Falstaff on the March! . . . Battlefield, Near Shrewsbury, Occupying the entire extent of the Stage, Alarms! Grand Battle! Single Combat! DEATH OF HOTSPUR! FINALE—Grand Tableau." [16]

Shakespeare's position as part and parcel of popular culture was reinforced by the willingness of Shakespearean actors to take part in the concluding farce. Thus Mr. Parsons followed such roles as Coriolanus, Othello, Macbeth, and Lear by playing Ralph Stackpole, "A Ring-Tailed Squealer & Rip-Staver from Salt River," in *Nick of the Woods.* Even Junius Brutus Booth followed his celebrated portrayal of Richard III with the role of Jerry Sneak in *The Mayor of Garrat.*[17] In the postbellum years Edward L. Davenport referred to this very ability and willingness to mix genres when he lamented the decline of his profession: "Why, I've played an act from *Hamlet,* one from *Black-Eyed Susan,* and sung 'A Yankee Ship and a Yankee Crew' and danced a hornpipe, and wound up with a 'nigger' part, all in one night. Is there any one you know of today who can do that?" [18] It is clear that, as much as Shakespearean roles were prized by actors, they were not exalted; they did not unfit one for other roles and other tasks; they were not elevated to a position above the culture in which they appeared. Most frequently, the final word of the evening was not Shakespeare's. *Hamlet* might be followed by *Fortune's Frolic, The Merchant of Venice* by *The Lottery Ticket, Richard III* by *The Green Mountain Boy, King Lear* by *Chaos Is Come Again* on one occasion and by *Love's Laughs at Locksmiths: or, The Guardian Outwitted* on another, and, in California, *Romeo and Juliet* by *Did You Ever Send Your Wife to San Jose?*.[19]

These afterpieces and *divertissements* most often are seen as having diluted or denigrated Shakespeare. I suggest that they may be understood more meaningfully as having *integrated* him into American culture. Shakespeare was presented as part of the same milieu inhabited by magicians, dancers, singers, acrobats, minstrels, and comics. He appeared on the same playbills and was advertised in the same spirit. This does not mean that theatergoers were unable to make distinctions between Shakespearean productions and the accompanying entertainment. Of course they were. Shakespeare, after all, was what most of them came to see. But it was a Shakespeare presented as part of the culture they enjoyed, a Shakespeare rendered familiar and intimate by virtue of his context.

In 1843 the curtain of the rebuilt St. Charles Theatre featured an arresting bit of symbolism: it depicted Shakespeare in a halo of light being borne aloft on the wings of the American eagle.[20] Shakespeare was not only domesticated; he was humanized. Henry Norman Hudson, the period's most popular Shakespearean lecturer, hailed Shakespeare as "the prodigy of our race" but also stressed his decency, his humility, his "true gentleness and lowliness of heart" and concluded that "he who looks the highest will always bow the lowest." [21] In his melodrama *Shakespeare in Love,* Richard Penn Smith pictured the poet not as an awesome symbol of culture but as a poor, worried, stumbling young man in love with a woman of whose feelings he is not yet certain. In the end, of course, he triumphs and proclaims his joy in words that identify him as a well-rounded human being to whom one can relate: "I am indeed happy. A poet, a lover, the husband of the woman I adore. What is there more for me to desire?" [22] Nineteenth-century America swallowed Shakespeare, digested him and his plays, and made them part of the cultural body. If Shakespeare originally came to America as *Culture* in the libraries of the educated, he existed in pre-Civil War America as *culture.* The nature of his reception by nineteenth-century audiences confirms this conclusion.

While he was performing in Natchez, Mississippi, in 1835, the Irish actor Tyrone Power observed people on the road hurrying to the theater. Their fine horses, ornate and often antique saddles, and picturesque clothing transported him back to Elizabethan England and "the palmy days of the Globe and Bear-garden." Power's insight was sound; there *were* significant similarities between the audiences of Shakespeare's own day and those he drew in America. One of Shakespeare's contemporaries commented that the theater was "frequented by all sorts of people old and younge, rich and poore, masters and servants, papists and puritans, wise men etc., churchmen and statesmen." The nineteenth-century American audience was equally heterogeneous. In both eras the various classes saw the same plays in the same theaters—though not necessarily from the same vantage point. Until mid-century, at least, American theaters generally had a tripartite seating arrangement: the pit (orchestra), the boxes, and the gallery (balcony). Although theater prices fell substantially from 1800 to 1850, seating arrangements continued to dovetail with class and economic divisions. In the boxes sat, as one spectator put it, "the dandies, and people of the first respectability and fashion." The gallery was inhabited largely by those—apprentices, servants, poor workingmen—who could not afford better seats or by those—Negroes and often prostitutes—who were not allowed to sit elsewhere. The pit was dominated by what were rather vaguely called the "middling classes"—a "mixed multitude" that some contemporaries praised as the "honest folks" or "the sterling part of the audience." [23]

All observers agreed that the nineteenth-century theater housed under one roof a microcosm of American society. This, the actor Joseph Jefferson maintained, was what made drama a more difficult art than painting, music, or writing, which "have a direct following, generally from a class whose taste and understanding are pretty evenly balanced,—whereas a theater is divided into three and sometimes four classes." Walt Whitman warmly recalled the Bowery Theatre around the year 1840, where he could look up to the first tier of boxes and see "the faces of the leading authors, poets, editors, of those times," while he sat in the pit surrounded by the "slang, wit, occasional shirt sleeves, and a picturesque freedom of looks and manners, with a rude good-nature and restless movement" of cartmen, butchers, firemen, and mechanics. Others spoke of the mixed audience with less enthusiasm. Washington Irving wrote a series of letters to the New York *Morning Chronicle* in 1802 and 1803 describing his theater experiences. The noise in the gallery he found "is somewhat similar to that which prevailed in Noah's Ark; for we have an imitation of the whistles and yells of every kind of animal." When the "gallery gods" were roused for one reason or another, "they commenced a discharge of apples, nuts & ginger-bread, on the heads of the honest folks in the pit." [24]

Little had changed by 1832 when the English visitor Frances Trollope attended the theater in several American cities. In Cincinnati she observed coatless men with their sleeves rolled up, incessantly spitting, reeking "of onions and whiskey." She enjoyed the Shakespeare but abhorred the "perpetual" noises: "the applause is expressed by cries and thumping with the feet, instead of clapping; and when a patriotic fit seized them, and 'Yankee Doodle' was called for, every man seemed to think his reputation as a citizen depended on the noise he made." Things were no better in Philadelphia and, if anything, worse in New York theaters, where she witnessed "a lady performing the most maternal office possible . . . and a general air of contempt for the decencies of life." [25] When he published his reminiscences in 1836, Tyrone Power tried to counter such accounts by praising the attentiveness and intelligence of his American audiences, but it appears that what differed was less the audience than Power's tolerance for it. For instance, in hailing the "degree of repose and gentility of demeanour" of the audience he performed for in New Orleans in 1835, he wrote:

> The least prolonged tumult of approbation even is stilled by a word to order: and when it is considered that here are assembled the wildest and rudest specimens of the Western population, men owning no control except the laws, and not viewing these over submissively, and who admit of no *arbiter elegantiarum* or standard of fine breeding, it confers infinite credit on their innate good feeling, and that sense of propriety which here forms the sole check on their naturally somewhat uproarious jollity.[26]

Evidence of this sort makes it clear that an understanding of the American theater in our own time is not adequate grounding for a comprehension of American theater in the nineteenth century. To envision nineteenth-century theater audiences correctly, one might do well to visit a contemporary sporting event in which the spectators not only are similarly heterogeneous but are also—in the manner of both the nineteenth century and the Elizabethan era—more than an audience; they are participants who can enter into the action on the field, who feel a sense of immediacy and at times even of control, who articulate their opinions and feelings vocally and unmistakably. Washington Irving wryly observed, "The good folks of the gallery have all the trouble of ordering the music." When the orchestra's selection displeased them, they stamped, hissed, roared, whistled, and groaned in cadence until the musicians played *"Moll in the wad, Tally ho the grinders,* and several other *airs* more suited to their tastes." The audience's vociferousness continued during the play itself, which was punctuated by expressions of disapproval in the form of hisses or groans and of approval in the form of applause, whistles, and stamping to the point that a Virginia editor felt called upon to remind his readers in 1829 that it was not "a duty to applaud at the conclusion of every sentence." A French reporter, attending a production of Shakespeare in California in 1851, was fascinated by the audience's enthusiasm: "the more they like a play, the louder they whistle, and when a San Francisco audience bursts into shrill whistles and savage yells, you may be sure they are in raptures of joy." Audiences frequently demanded—and got—instant encores from performers who particularly pleased them. "Perhaps," a New York editor wrote sarcastically in 1846, "we'll flatter Mr. Kean by making him take poison twice." [27]

Like the Elizabethans, a substantial portion of nineteenth-century American audiences knew their Shakespeare well. Sol Smith reported that in 1839, when he wanted to put on an evening of acts from various Shakespearean plays in St. Louis, he had "no difficulty in finding Hamlets, Shylocks and Richards in abundance, very glad of the opportunity to exhibit their hidden powers." Constance Rourke has shown that as far west as California, from miners' camps to the galleries of urban theaters, there were many who knew large parts of the plays by heart.[28] This knowledge easily became an instrument of control, as more than one hapless actor found out. In the winter of 1856 Hugh F. McDermott's depiction of Richard III did not meet the critical expectations of his Sacramento audience. During the early scenes of Act I "a few carrots timidly thrown, had made their appearance," but the full ardor of the audience was roused only when Richard's killing of Henry included a "thrust *a posteriori,* after Henry had fallen." Then, the Sacramento *Union* reported, "cabbages, carrots, pumpkins, potatoes, a wreath of vegetables, a sack of flour and one of soot, a dead goose, with other articles, simultaneously made their appearance upon the stage.'' The barrage woke the dead Henry, who fled followed by Richard, ''his head enveloped in a halo of vegetable glory.'' Pleas from the manager induced the audience to allow the play to go on—but not for long. Early in Act II, McDermott's ineptness brought forth first a storm of shouts and then a renewal of the vegetable shower accompanied this time by Chinese firecrackers. As poor Richard fled for the second time, ''a well directed pumpkin caused him to stagger; and with still truer aim, a potato relieved him of his cap, which was left, upon the field of glory, among the cabbages.'' [29]

Scenes like this account for the frequent assurance on playbills that ''proper officers are appointed who will rigidly enforce decorum.'' [30] Proper officers or not, such incidents were common enough to prompt a nineteenth-century gentleman to note in his diary, ''The egg as a vehicle of dramatic criticism came into early use in this Continent.'' [31] Nevertheless, the same California audiences capable of driving King Richard from the stage could pay homage to a performance they recognized as superior. Irish-born Matilda Heron's portrayal of Juliet on New Year's night 1854 ''so fascinated and entranced'' the ''walnut-cracking holiday audience,'' according to the San Francisco *Chronicle,* that ''they sat motionless and silent for some moments after the scene was done; and then suddenly recovering themselves from the thraldom under which they had been placed, they came down in a shower of applause that shook the house.'' [32]

These frenetic displays of approval and disapproval were signs of engagement in what was happening on the stage—an engagement that on occasion could blur the line between audience and actors. At a performance of *Richard III* with Junius Brutus Booth at New York's Bowery Theatre in December 1832, the holiday audience was so large that some three hundred people overflowed onto the stage and entered into the spirit of things, the New York *Mirror* reported. They examined Richard's royal regalia with interest, hefted his sword, and tried on his crown; they moved up to get a close look at the ghosts of King Henry, Lady Anne, and the children when these characters appeared on stage; they mingled with the soldiers during the battle of Bosworth Field and responded to the roll of drums and blast of trumpets by racing across the stage. When Richard and Richmond began their fight, the audience ''made a ring around the combatants to see fair play, and kept them at it for nearly a quarter of an hour by 'Shrewsbury's clock.' This was all done in perfect good humor, and with no intention to make a row.'' When Dan Rice came on to dance his famous Jim Crow, the on-stage audience made him repeat it some twenty times, ''and in the after-piece, where a supper-table [was] spread, some among the most hungry very leisurely helped themselves to the viands.'' [33] Frequently, members of the audience became so involved in the action on stage that they interfered in order to dispense charity to the sick and destitute, advice to the indecisive, and, as one man did during a Baltimore production of *Coriolanus* and another during a New York production of *Othello*, protection to someone involved in an unfair fight.[34]

These descriptions should make it clear how difficult it is to draw arbitrary lines between popular and folk culture. Here was professional entertainment containing numerous folkish elements, including a knowledgeable, participatory audience exerting important degrees of control. The integration of Shakespeare into the culture as a whole should bring into serious question our tendency to see culture on a vertical plane, neatly divided into a hierarchy of inclusive adjectival categories such as "high," "low," "pop," "mass," "folk," and the like. If the phenomenon of Shakespeare was not an aberration—and the diverse audiences for such art forms as Italian opera, such performers as singer Jenny Lind, and such writers as Longfellow, Dickens, and Mark Twain indicate it was not—then the study of Shakespeare's relationship to the American people helps reveal the existence of a shared public culture to which we have not paid enough attention. It has been obscured by the practice of employing such categories as "popular" aesthetically rather than literally. That is, the adjective "popular" has been utilized to describe not only those creations of expressive culture that actually had a large audience (which is the way I have tried to use it in this essay), but also, and often primarily, those that had questionable artistic merit. Thus, a banal play or a poorly written romantic novel has been categorized as popular culture, even if it had a tiny audience, while the recognized artistic attributes of a Shakespearean play have prevented it from being included in popular culture, regardless of its high degree of popularity. The use of such arbitrary and imprecise cultural categories has helped obscure the dynamic complexity of American culture in the nineteenth century.

Our difficulty also proceeds from the historical fallacy of reading the present into the past. By the middle of the twentieth century, Shakespearean drama did not occupy the place it had in the nineteenth century. As a Shakespearean scholar wrote in 1963, "the days when a Davenport and a Barry could open rival productions of *Hamlet* on the same night, as in 1875; when *Macbeth* could be seen at three different theatres in New York in 1849; when ten *Hamlets* could be produced in a single season, as in New York in 1857–58; . . . these days are unfortunately gone." [35] Although in the mid-twentieth century there was no more widely known, respected, or quoted dramatist in our culture than Shakespeare, the nature of his relationship to the American people had changed: he was no longer their familiar, no longer part of their culture, no longer at home in their theaters or on the movie and television screens that had become the twentieth-century equivalents of the

stage. If Shakespeare had been an integral part of mainstream culture in the
nineteenth century, in the twentieth he had become part of "polite" culture—an essential ingredient in a complex we call, significantly, "legitimate" theater. He had become the possession of the educated portions of
society who disseminated his plays for the enlightenment of the average folk
who were to swallow him not for their entertainment but for their education,
as a respite from—not as a normal part of—their usual cultural diet. Recalling his youthful experiences with Shakespeare, the columnist Gerald Nachman wrote in 1979 that in the schools of America "Shakespeare becomes
theatrical spinach: He's good for you. If you digest enough of his plays,
you'll grow up big and strong intellectually like teacher." The efforts of
such young producers and directors as Joseph Papp in the late 1950s and the
1960s to liberate Shakespeare from the genteel prison in which he had been
confined, to restore his plays to their original vitality, and to disseminate
them among what Papp called "a great dispossessed audience" is a testament to what had happened to Shakespearean drama since the mid-nineteenth
century.[36]

Signs of this transformation appear throughout the twentieth century. In
his 1957 treatise on how to organize community theaters, John Wray Young
warned, "Most organizations will find it difficult to please with the classics.
. . . Shakespeare, Ibsen, Chekhov, the Greeks, and the other masters are
hard to sell in the average community situation." Shakespeare had become
not only a hard-to-sell classic to average members of the community but
even an alienating force. In a 1929 episode of the popular comic strip
"Bringing Up Father," the neighborhood bartender, Dinty Moore, suddenly
goes "high hat" when he meets and courts a wealthy woman. The symbols
of his attempt to enter "society," which alienate him from his friends, are
his fancy clothing, his poodle dog, his horseback riding and golf, his pretentious language, *and* his reading of Shakespeare's *Romeo and Juliet,* which
so infuriates his friend Jiggs that he seizes the volume and throws it at
Moore.[37] In one of his wonderful monologues on politics, published in 1905,
George Washington Plunkitt, ward boss of the fifteenth assembly district in
New York City and one of the powers of Tammany Hall, admonished aspiring politicians:

If you're makin' speeches in a campaign, talk the language the people talk.
Don't try to show how the situation is by quoting Shakespeare. Shakespeare was all right in his way, but he didn't know anything about Fifteenth District politics. . . . go out and talk the language of the Fifteenth
to the people. I know it's an awful temptation, the hankerin' to show off
your learnin'. I've felt it myself, but I always resist it. I know the awful
consequences.[38]

For Plunkitt, and obviously for his constituents, Shakespeare symbolized "learning," irrelevant, impractical, pretentious—fit only for what Plunkitt called "the name-parted-in-the-middle aristocrats." Similarly, in her account of her life as a worker, Dorothy Richardson deplored the maudlin yellowback novels that dominated the reading habits of working women at the turn of the century and pleaded for the wide dissemination of better literature:

> Only, please, Mr. or Mrs. Philanthropist, don't let it be Shakespeare, or Ruskin, or Walter Pater. Philanthropists have tried before to reform degraded literary tastes with heroic treatment, and they have failed every time. That is sometimes the trouble with the college settlement folk. They forget that Shakespeare, and Ruskin, and all the rest of the really true and great literary crew, are infinite bores to every-day people.[39]

Culture is a process, not a fixed condition; it is the product of unremitting interaction between the past and the present. Thus, Shakespeare's relationship to the American people was always in flux, always changing. Still, it is possible to isolate a period during which the increasing separation of Shakespeare from "every-day people" becomes more evident. The American Theatre in San Francisco advised those attending its May 29, 1855, production of *A Midsummer Night's Dream* that "owing to the length of the play there will be NO FARCE." Similarly, in 1869 the Varieties Theatre in New Orleans announced in its playbill advertising Mrs. Scott Siddons in *As You Like It,* "In consequence of the length of this comedy, it will constitute the Evening's Entertainment." In following decades it became less and less necessary for theaters to issue such explanations. In 1873 the California Theatre in San Francisco advertised *Coriolanus* with no promise of a farce or between-act entertainment—and no apologies. This became true in city after city. There is no precise date, but everywhere in the United States during the final decades of the nineteenth century the same transformation was evidently taking place; Shakespeare was being divorced from the broader world of everyday culture. Gone were the entre-act diversions: the singers, jugglers, dancers, acrobats, orators. Gone, too, was the purple prose trumpeting the sensational events and pageantry that were part of the Shakespearean plays themselves. Those who wanted their Shakespeare had to take him alone, lured to his plays by stark playbills promising no frills or enhancements. In December 1890 Pittsburgh's Duquesne Theatre advertised productions of *The Merchant of Venice, Othello, Romeo and Juliet,* and *Julius Caesar* by announcing simply, "Engagement of Mr. Lawrence Barrett, supported by Miss Gale And a Competent Company of Players." Significantly, the frequent admonitions relating to audience behavior were now missing as well. By the early twentieth century, playbills of this type became the norm everywhere.[40] Once again, William Shakespeare had become *Culture*.

It is easier to describe this transformation than to explain it, since the transformation itself has clouded our vision of the past. So completely have twentieth-century Americans learned to accept as natural and timeless Shakespeare's status as an elite, classic dramatist, to whose plays the bulk of the populace do not or cannot relate, that we have found it difficult to comprehend nineteenth-century conceptions of Shakespeare. Too frequently, modern historians of the theater have spent less time and energy understanding Shakespeare's nineteenth-century popularity than in explaining it away. The formula is simple: how to account for the indisputable popularity of a great master in a frontier society with an "overwhelmingly uneducated" public. The consensus seems to be that Shakespeare was popular for all the wrong reasons: because of the afterpieces and *divertissements* that surrounded his plays; because the people wanted to see great actors who in turn insisted on performing Shakespeare to demonstrate their abilities; because his plays were presented in altered, simplified versions; because of his bombast, crudities, and sexual allusions rather than his poetry or sophistication; because of almost anything but his dramatic genius. "Shakespeare," we are told in a conclusion that would not be important if it were not so typical, "could communicate with the unsophisticated at the level of action and oratory while appealing to the small refined element at the level of dramatic and poetic artistry." [41]

Again and again, historians and critics have arbitrarily separated the "action and oratory" of Shakespeare's plays from the "dramatic and poetic artistry" with which they were, in reality, so intricately connected. We are asked to believe that the average member of the audience saw only violence, lewdness, and sensationalism in such plays as *Richard III, Hamlet, King Lear, Othello,* and *Macbeth* and was incapable of understanding the moral and ethical dilemmas, the generational strains between parents and children, the crude ambition of Richard III or Lady Macbeth, the haunting guilt of Macbeth, the paralyzing introspection and doubts of Hamlet, the envy of Iago, the insecurities of Othello. We have been asked to believe that such human conditions and situations were beyond the powers of most of the audience and touched only a "refined element" who understood the "subtleties of Shakespeare's art."

Certainly, the relationship of an audience to the object of its focus—be it a sermon, political speech, newspaper, musical composition, or play—is a complex one and constitutes a problem for the historian who would reconstruct it. But the problem cannot be resolved through the use of such ahistorical devices as dividing both the audience and the object into crude categories and then coming to conclusions that have more to do with the culture of the writer than that of the subject. In fact, the way to understand the popularity of Shakespeare is to enter into the spirit of the nineteenth century. Shakespeare was popular, first and foremost, because he was integrated into the culture and presented within its context. Nineteenth-century Americans were able to fit Shakespeare into their culture so easily because he *seemed* to fit—because so many of his values and tastes were, or at least appeared to be, close to their own, and were presented through figures that seemed real and came to matter to the audience. Shakespeare's characters, Henry Norman Hudson insisted, were so vivid, so alive, that they assumed the shape "of actual persons, so that we know them as well and remember them as distinctly as we do our most intimate friends." For the teenaged William Dean Howells, who memorized great chunks of Shakespeare while working as an apprentice printer in his father's newspaper office in the 1850s, the world of Shakespeare was one in which he felt as much "at home," as much like "a citizen," as he did in his small Ohio town.[42]

Both worlds enshrined the art of oratory. The same Americans who found diversion and pleasure in lengthy political debates, who sought joy and God in the sermons of church and camp meeting, who had, in short, a seemingly inexhaustible appetite for the spoken word, thrilled to Shakespeare's eloquence, memorized his soliloquies, delighted in his dialogues. Although nineteenth-century Americans stressed the importance of literacy and built an impressive system of public education, theirs remained an oral world in which the spoken word was central. In such a world, Shakespeare had no difficulty finding a place. Nor was Shakespearean oratory confined to the professional stage; it often was a part of life. Walt Whitman recalled that as a young man he rode in the Broadway omnibuses "declaiming some stormy passage from Julius Caesar or Richard" to passersby. In the 1850s Mark Twain worked as an apprentice to the pilot-master George Ealer on the steamboat *Pennsylvania:* "He would read Shakespeare to me; not just casually, but by the hour, when it was his watch, and I was steering. . . . He did not use the book, and did not need to; he knew his Shakespeare as well as Euclid ever knew his multiplication table." In Corpus Christi, Texas, in 1845, soldiers of the Fourth Infantry Regiment broke the monotony of waiting for the Mexican War to begin by staging plays, including a performance of *Othello* starring young Lieutenant Ulysses S. Grant as Desdemona. Many of Lincoln's aides and associates remembered his tendency to recite long, relevant passages from Shakespeare during the troubling days of the Civil War. Shakespeare was taught in nineteenth-century schools and colleges as declamation or rhetoric, not literature. For many youngsters Shakespeare was first encountered in schoolbooks as texts to be recited aloud and memorized. Through such means, Shakespearean phrases, aphorisms,

ideas, and language helped shape American speech and became so integral
a part of the nineteenth-century imagination that it is a futile exercise to
separate Americans' love of Shakespeare's oratory from their appreciation
for his subtle use of language.[43]

It was not merely Shakespeare's language but his style that recommended itself to nineteenth-century audiences. In a period when melodrama
became one of the mainstays of the American stage, Shakespearean plays
easily lent themselves to the melodramatic style. Shakespearean drama featured heroes and villains who communicated directly with the audience and
left little doubt about the nature of their character or their intentions. In a
series of asides during the opening scenes of the first act, Macbeth shares
his "horrible imaginings" and "vaulting ambition" with the audience (I.iii-
vii). Similarly, Iago confides to the audience "I hate the Moor," rehearses
his schemes of "double knavery" to betray both Cassio and Othello, and
confesses that his jealousy of Othello "Doth, like a poisonous mineral, gnaw
my inwards;/ And nothing can or shall content my soul/ Till I am evened
with him" (I.iii). As in melodrama, Shakespearean villains are aware not
only of their own evil but also of the goodness of their adversaries. Thus
Iago, even as he plots against Othello, admits that "The Moor—howbeit
that I endure him not—/ Is of a constant, loving, noble nature" (II.i).

Lines like these, which so easily fit the melodramatic mode, were delivered in appropriately melodramatic style. The actors who dominated the stage
during the first half of the nineteenth century were vigorous, tempestuous,
emotional. To describe these men, contemporaries reached for words like
"hurricane," "maelstrom," "avalanche," "earthquake," "monsoon," and
"whirlwind." Edmund Kean's acting, one of them noted, was "just on the
edge, sometimes quite over the edge of madness." It "blinded and stunned
the beholders, appalled the imagination, and chilled their blood." Walt
Whitman, who saw Junius Brutus Booth perform in the late 1830s, wrote of
him, "He illustrated Plato's rule that to the forming an artist of the very
highest rank a dash of insanity or what the world calls insanity is indispensable." [44] The first great American-born Shakespearean actor, Edwin Forrest,
carried this romantic tradition to its logical culmination. William Rounse-
ville Alger, who saw Forrest perform, described his portrayal of Lear after
Goneril rebuffs him:

His eyes flashed and faded and reflashed. He beat his breast as if not
knowing what he did. His hands clutched wildly at the air as though struggling with something invisible. Then, sinking on his knees, with upturned
look and hands straight outstretched towards his unnatural daughter, he
poured out, in frenzied tones of mingled shriek and sob, his withering
curse, half adjuration, half malediction.[45]

As in melodrama itself, language and style in American productions of Shakespeare were not utilized randomly; they were used to inculcate values, to express ideas and attitudes. For all of the complaints of such as Whitman that the feudal plays of Shakespeare were not altogether fitting for a democratic age, Shakespeare's attraction for nineteenth-century audiences was due in no small part to the fact that he was—or at least was taken to be—in tune with much of nineteenth-century American consciousness. From the beginning, Shakespeare's American admirers and promoters maintained that he was pre-eminently a *moral* playwright. To overcome the general prejudice against the theater in the eighteenth-century, Shakespeare's plays were frequently presented as "moral dialogues" or "moral lectures." For Thomas Jefferson, "A lively and lasting sense of filial duty is more effectually impressed on the mind of a son or daughter by reading *King Lear,* than by all the dry volumes of ethics and divinity that ever were written." For Abraham Lincoln, *Macbeth* stood as "the perfect illustration of the problems of tyranny and murder." And John Quincy Adams concluded, even as he was waging his heroic fight against the power of the slave South in the House of Representatives in 1836, that the moral of *Othello* was "that the intermarriage of black and white blood is a violation of the law of nature. *"That* is the lesson to be learned from the play." [46]

Regardless of specific interpretations, writers of nineteenth-century schoolbooks and readers seemed to have agreed with Henry Norman Hudson that Shakespeare's works provided "a far better school of virtuous discipline than half the moral and religious books which are now put into the hands of youth" and reprinted lines from Shakespeare not only to illustrate the art of declamation but also to disseminate moral values and patriotic principles. As late as 1870 the playbill of a New Orleans theater spelled out the meaning of *Twelfth Night:* "MORAL: In this play Shakespeare has finely penciled the portraits of Folly and Vanity in the persons of Aguecheek and Malvolio; and with a not less masterly hand, he has exhibited the weakness of the human mind when Love has usurped the place of Reason." The affinity between Shakespeare and the American people went beyond moral homilies; it extended to the basic ideological underpinnings of nineteenth-century America. When Cassius proclaimed that "The fault, dear Brutus, is not in our stars,/ But in ourselves, that we are underlings" (*Julius Caesar,* I.ii), and when Helena asserted that "Our remedies oft in ourselves do lie,/ Which we ascribe to heaven: the fated sky/ Gives us free scope" (*All's Well That Ends Well,* I.i), they articulated a belief that was central to the pervasive success ethos of the nineteenth century and that confirmed the developing American worldview. [47]

Whatever Shakespeare's own designs, philosophy, and concept of humanity were, his plays had meaning to a nation that placed the individual at the center of the universe and personalized the large questions of the day. The actor Joseph Jefferson held Shakespeare responsible for the star system that prevailed for so much of the nineteenth century since "his tragedies almost without exception contain one great character on whom the interest of the play turns, and upon whom the attention of the audience is centered." Shakespeare's characters—like the Davy Crocketts and Mike Finks that dominated American folklore and the Jacksons, Websters, Clays, and Calhouns who dominated American politics—were larger than life: their passions, appetites, and dilemmas were of epic proportions. Here were forceful, meaningful people who faced, on a larger scale, the same questions as those that filled the pages of schoolbooks: the duties of children and parents, husbands and wives, governed and governors to one another. In their lives the problems of jealousy, morality, and ambition were all writ large. However flawed some of Shakespeare's central figures were, they at least acted—even the indecisive Hamlet—and bore responsibility for their own fate. If they failed, they did so because ultimately they lacked sufficient inner control. Thus Othello was undone by his jealousy and gullibility, Coriolanus by his pride, Macbeth and Richard III by their ambition. All of them could be seen as the architects of their own fortunes, masters of their own fate. All of them, Hudson taught his audiences, "contain within themselves the reason why they are there and not elsewhere, why they are so and not otherwise." [48]

How important this quality of individual will was can be seen in the fate of Sophocles' *Oedipus* in nineteenth-century America. The play was introduced twice in the century to New York audiences and failed both times, largely because of its subject matter. The New York *Tribune*'s reaction, after *Oedipus* opened in January 1882, was typical: "King Oedipus certainly carries more woe to the square inch than anybody else that ever walked upon the stage. And it is woe of the very worst kind—without solace, and without hope." Sophocles seemed guilty of determinism—an ideological stance nineteenth-century Americans rejected out of hand. "The overmastering fates that broke men and women upon the wheel of torture that destiny might be fulfilled are far away from us, the gods that lived and cast deep shadows over men's lives are turned to stone," the New York *Herald*'s reviewer wrote. "The helpful human being—who pays his way through the world finds it hard to imagine the creature kicking helpless in the traps of the gods." Similarly, critics attacked the bloodshed and immorality in *Oedipus*. The New York *Mirror* denounced "a plot like this, crammed full of murder, suicide, self-mutilation, incest, and dark deeds of a similar character." [49] Shakespearean drama, of course, was no less laced through with gore. But, while this quality in Sophocles seemed to Americans to be an end in itself, Shakespeare's thought patterns were either close enough or were made to seem close enough so that the violence had a point, and that point appeared to buttress American values and confirm American expectations.

This ideological equation, this ability of Shakespeare to connect with Americans' underlying beliefs, is crucial to an understanding of his role in nineteenth-century America. Much has been made of the adaptations of Shakespeare as instruments that made him somehow more understandable to American audiences. Certainly, the adaptations did work this way—but not primarily, as has been so widely claimed, by vulgarizing or simplifying him to the point of utter distortion but rather by heightening those qualities in Shakespeare that American audiences were particularly drawn to. The liberties taken with Shakespeare in nineteenth-century America were often similar to liberties taken with folklore: Shakespeare was frequently seen as common property to be treated as the user saw fit. Thus many small changes were made for practical and moral reasons without much fanfare or fuss: minor roles were consolidated to create richer acting parts; speeches and scenes, considered overly long or extraneous, were shortened or omitted; sexual references were rendered more palatable by shifting such words as "whores" to "wenches" or "maidenheads" to "virtue"; contemporary sensibilities were catered to by making Juliet eighteen rather than thirteen or by softening some of Hamlet's angriest diatribes against Ophelia and his mother. Some of the alterations bordered on the spectacular, such as the flying, singing witches in *Macbeth* and the elaborate funeral procession that accompanied Juliet's body to the tomb of the Capulets in *Romeo and Juliet*. On the whole, such limited changes were made with respect for—and sensitivity to—Shakespeare's purposes.[50]

It is important to realize that, while some of the alterations were imported from England and others were made in America, none were adopted indiscriminately. Of the many drastically revised editions of Shakespeare that originated in England, only three held sway in the United States during the nineteenth century: David Garrick's *Catharine and Petruchio* (1756), Nahum Tate's revision of *King Lear* (1681), and Colley Cibber's revision of *Richard III* (1700). For our purposes, the first is the least significant, since it was largely a three-act condensation of *The Taming of the Shrew*, which retained the basic thrust of Shakespeare's original and won considerable popularity as an afterpiece. If brevity was the chief virtue of Garrick's *Catharine and Petruchio*, the attractions of Cibber's *Richard* and Tate's *Lear* were more complex and suggest that those alterations of Shakespeare that became most prevalent in the United States were those that best fit the values and ideology of the period and the people.

For most of the nineteenth century Colley Cibber's *Richard III* held sway everywhere.[51] Cibber's revision, by cutting one-third of the lines, eliminating half of the characters, adding scenes from other Shakespearean plays and from Cibber's own pen, succeeded in muting the ambiguities of the original and focusing all of the evil in the person of Richard. Thus, although Cibber retained Shakespeare's essential plot and much of his poetry, he refashioned the play in such a way that, while his work was done in the England of 1700, it could have been written a hundred years later in the United States, so closely did it agree with American sensibilities concerning the centrality of the individual, the dichotomy between good and evil, and the importance of personal responsibility. Richmond's speech over the body of the vanquished Richard mirrored perfectly America's moral sense and melodramatic taste:

> Farewel, Richard, and from thy dreadful end
> May future Kings from Tyranny be warn'd;
> Had thy aspiring Soul but stir'd in Vertue
> With half the Spirit it has dar'd in Evil,
> How might thy Fame have grac'd our English Annals:
> But as thou art, how fair a Page thou'st blotted.

If Cibber added lines making clear the fate of villains, he was no less explicit concerning the destiny of heroes. After defeating Richard, Richmond is informed that "the Queen and fair Elizabeth,/ Her beauteous Daughter, some few miles off, are/ On their way to Gratulate your Victory." His reply must have warmed America's melodramatic heart as much as it confirmed its ideological underpinnings: "Ay, there indeed my toil's rewarded." [52]

Tate's altered *King Lear,* like Cibber's *Richard III,* virtually displaced Shakespeare's own version for almost two centuries. Tate, who distorted Shakespeare far more than Cibber did, devised a happy ending for what was one of the most tragic of all of Shakespeare's plays: he created a love affair between Edgar and Cordelia and allowed Cordelia and Lear to live. Although there were certainly critics of this fundamental alteration, it proved popular with theatergoers. When in 1826 James H. Hackett chided his fellow actor Edmund Kean about his choice of Tate's ending rather than Shakespeare's, Kean replied that he had attempted to restore the original, "but when I had ascertained that a large majority of the public—whom we live to please, and must please to be popular—liked Tate better than Shakespeare, I fell back upon his corruption; though in my soul I was ashamed of the prevailing taste, and of my professional condition that required me to minister unto it." [53] Still, many Americans defended the Tate version on ideological grounds. "The moral's now more complete," wrote a contemporary, "for although Goneril, Regan, and Edmond were deservedly punished for their crimes, yet Lear and Cordelia were killed without reason and without fault. But now they survive their enemies and virtue is crowned with happiness." [54] That virtue be "crowned with happiness" was essential to

the beliefs of nineteenth-century Americans. Thus audiences had the pleasure of having their expectations confirmed when Edgar concludes the play
by declaiming to "Divine Cordelia":

> Thy bright Example shall convince the World
> (Whatever Storms of Fortune are decreed)
> That Truth and Vertue shall at last succeed.[55]

The profound and longstanding nineteenth-century American experience with
Shakespeare, then, was neither accidental nor aberrant. It was based upon
the language and eloquence, the artistry and humor, the excitement and action, the moral sense and worldview that Americans found in Shakespearean
drama. The more firmly based Shakespeare was in nineteenth-century culture, of course, the more difficult it is to understand why he lost so much
of his audience so quickly.

A complete explanation would require a separate research project of its own,
but it is appropriate here to probe tentatively into the factors underlying
Shakespeare's transformation. Some of these were intricately connected to
the internal history of the theater. So long as the theater was under attack
on moral grounds, as it was in the eighteenth and early nineteenth centuries,
Shakespeare, because of his immense reputation, could be presented more
easily and could be used to help make the theater itself legitimate. Shakespearean drama also lent itself to the prevalent star system. Only the existence of a small repertory of well-known plays, in which Shakespeare's
were central, made it feasible for the towering stars of England and America
to travel throughout the United States acting with resident stock companies
wherever they went. The relative dearth of native dramatists and the relative
scarcity of competing forms of theatrical entertainment also figured in
Shakespeare's popularity. As these conditions were altered, Shakespeare's
popularity and centrality were affected. As important as factors peculiar to
the theater were, the theater did not exist in a vacuum; it was an integral
part of American culture—of interest to the historian precisely because it so
frequently and so accurately indicated the conditions surrounding it. A fuller
explanation must therefore be sought in the larger culture itself.[56]

   Among the salient cultural changes at the turn of the century were those
in language and rhetorical style. The oratorical mode, which so dominated
the nineteenth century and which helped make Shakespeare popular, hardly
survived into the twentieth century. No longer did Americans tolerate speeches
of several hours' duration. No longer was their attention riveted upon such
political debates as that between Webster and Hayne in 1830, which con-
sumed several days. It is true that in the closing years of the century William
Jennings Bryan could still rise to national political leadership through his

superb oratorical skills, but it is equally true that he lived to see himself become an anachronism, the bearer of a style redolent of an earlier culture. The surprisingly rapid decline of oratory as a force in national life has not received the study it deserves, but certainly it was affected by the influx of millions of non-English-speaking people. The more than one thousand foreign-language newspapers and magazines published in the United States by 1910 testify graphically to the existence of a substantial group for whom Shakespeare, at least in his original language, was less familiar and less accessible.[57] These immigrant folk helped constitute a ready audience for the rise of the more visual entertainments such as baseball, boxing, vaudeville, burlesque, and especially the new silent movies, which could be enjoyed by a larger and often more marginal audience less steeped in the language and the culture.

If what Reuel Denney called the "deverbalization of the forum" weakened Shakespeare among some segments of the population, the parallel growth of literacy among other groups also undermined some of the props that had sustained Shakespeare's popularity. Literacy encroached upon the pervasive oral culture that had created in nineteenth-century America an audience more comfortable with listening than with reading. Thus the generations of people accustomed to hearing and reciting things out loud—the generations for whom oral recitation of the King James version of the Bible could well have formed a bridge to the English of Shakespeare—were being depleted as America entered a new century.[58]

These language-related changes were accompanied by changes in taste and style. John Higham has argued that from the 1860s through the 1880s romantic idealism declined in the United States.[59] The melodramatic mode, to which Shakespeare lent himself so well and in which he was performed so frequently, went into a related decline. Edwin Booth, the most influential Shakespearean actor in America during the closing decades of the nineteenth century, played his roles in a less ferocious, more subtle and intellectualized fashion than his father and most of the other leading actors of the first half of the century had. When asked how his acting compared to his father's, Booth replied simply, "I think I must be somewhat quieter." The younger Booth's quietness became the paradigm.[60] The visceral, thunderous style fell into such disfavor that by 1920 the critic Francis Hackett not only berated John Barrymore for his emotional portrayal of Richard III but also took Shakespeare himself to task for the "unsophisticated" manner in which he had crafted the play—the play that nineteenth-century audiences had enjoyed above all others: "the plot, the psychology, the history, seem to me infantile. . . . Are we led to understand Richard? No, only to moralize over him. Thus platitude makes cowards of us all." [61]

These gradual and decisive changes in language, style, and taste are important but by themselves do not constitute a totally satisfying explanation for the diminished popularity of Shakespeare. As important as changes in language were, they did not prevent the development of radio as a central entertainment medium at the beginning of the 1920s or the emergence of talking movies at the end of that decade. Nor was there anything inherent in the new popular media that necessarily relegated Shakespeare to a smaller, elite audience; on the contrary, he was quite well suited to the new forms of presentation that came to dominance. His comedies had an abundance of slapstick and contrived happy endings, his tragedies and historical plays had more than their share of action. Most importantly, having written for a stage devoid of scenery, Shakespeare could and did incorporate as much spatial mobility as he desired into his plays—twenty-five scene changes in *Macbeth,* one of his shortest plays, and forty-two in *Antony and Cleopatra,* where the action gravitated from Alexandria to such locales as Rome, Messina, Athens, and Syria. This fluidity—which caused innumerable problems for the stagecraft of the nineteenth century—was particularly appropriate to the movies, which could visually reproduce whatever Shakespeare had in mind, and to radio, which, like the Elizabethan stage itself, could rely upon the imagination of its audience. That these new media did not take full advantage of so recently a popular source of entertainment as Shakespearean drama demands further explanation.[62]

Shakespeare did not, of course, disappear from American culture after the turn of the century; he was transformed from a playwright for the general public into one for a specific audience. This metamorphosis from popular culture to polite culture, from entertainment to erudition, from the property of "Everyman" to the possession of a more elite circle needs to be seen with the perspective of other transformations that took place in nineteenth-century America.

At the beginning of the century, as we have seen, the theater was a microcosm; it housed both the entire spectrum of the population and the complete range of entertainment from tragedy to farce, juggling to ballet, opera to minstrelsy. The theater drew all ranks of people to one place where they constituted what Erving Goffman has called a "focused gathering"—a set of people who relate to one another through the medium of a common activity. The term is useful in reminding us that, in the theater, people not only sat under one roof, they interacted. In this sense, the theater in the first half of the nineteenth century constituted a microcosm of still another sort: a microcosm of the relations between the various socioeconomic groups in America. The descriptions of such observers as Washington Irving and Mrs. Trollope make it clear that those relations were beset by tensions and conflicts. Even so convinced a democrat as Whitman complained by 1847 that the New York theaters were becoming " 'low' places where vulgarity (not only on the stage, but in front of it) is in the ascendant, and bad-taste carries the day with hardly a pleasant point to mitigate its coarseness." Whitman excepted only the Park Theatre "because the audiences there are always intelligent, and there is a dash of superiority thrown over the Performances." Earlier in the century the Park Theatre had received the patronage of the entire public; by the 1830s it had become more exclusive, while the Bowery, Chatham, and other theaters became the preserves of gallery gods and groundlings. This development was not exclusive to New York. "I have discovered that the *people* are with *us,*" Tyrone Power reported from Baltimore in 1833, since the Front Theatre, at which he was performing, drew "the sturdy democracy of the good city," while its rival, the Holiday Theatre, was "considered the aristocratic house." [63]

Not only was there an increasing segregation of audiences but ultimately of actors and styles as well. On a winter evening in 1863, George William Curtis, the editor of *Harper's,* took a "rustic friend" to two New York theaters. First they went to see Edwin Forrest at Niblo's Gardens. "It was crammed with people. All the seats were full, and the aisles, and the steps. And the people sat upon the stairs that ascend to the second tier, and they hung upon the balustrade, and they peeped over shoulders and between heads." Forrest's acting, Curtis wrote, was "a boundless exaggeration of all the traditional conventions of the stage." Still he conceded that Forrest "move[d] his world nightly. . . . There were a great many young women around us crying. . . . They were not refined nor intellectual women. They were, perhaps, rather coarse. But they cried good hearty tears." After one act his friend whispered, "I have had as much as I can hold," and they went up the street to the Winter Garden, where Edwin Booth was portraying Iago. "The difference of the spectacle was striking. The house was comfortably full, not crowded. The air of the audience was that of refined attention rather than of eager interest. Plainly it was a more cultivated and intellectual audience." And just as plainly they were seeing a very different type of acting. "Pale, thin, intellectual, with long black hair and dark eyes, Shakespeare's Iago was perhaps never more articulately represented . . . ; all that we saw of Booth was admirable." [64]

In 1810 John Howard Payne complained, "The judicious few are very few indeed. They are always to be found in a Theatre, like flowers in a desert, but they are nowhere sufficiently numerous to *fill* one." By the second half of the century this was evidently no longer the case. Separate theaters, often called *legitimate* theaters, catering to the "judicious," appeared in city after city, leaving the other theaters to those whom Payne called "the idle, profligate, and vulgar." [65] The psychologist Robert Somer has shown the connections between space and status and has argued that "society compensates for blurred social distinctions by clear spatial ones.'' Such scholars as Burton J. Bledstein and William R. Taylor have noted the Victorian urge to structure or rationalize space.[66] As the traditional spatial distinctions among pit, gallery, and boxes within the theater were undermined by the aggressive behavior of audiences caught up in the egalitarian exhuberance of the period and freed in the atmosphere of the theater from many of the demands of normative behavior, this urge gradually led to the creation of separate theaters catering to distinct audiences and shattered for good the phenomenon of theater as a social microcosm of the entire society.

This dramatic split in the American theater was part of more important bifurcations that were taking place in American culture and society. How closely the theater registered societal dissonance can be seen in the audiences' volatile reaction to anything they considered condescending behavior, out of keeping with a democratic society. The tension created by hierarchical seating arrangements helps explain the periodic rain of objects that the gallery unleashed upon those in more privileged parts of the theater. When Washington Irving was ''saluted aside [his] head with a rotten pippen'' and rose to shake his cane at the gallery gods, he was restrained by a man behind him who warned that this would bring down upon him the full wrath of the people; the only course of action, he was advised, was to ''sit down quietly and bend your back to it.'' [67]

English actors, who were *ipso facto* suspected of aristocratic leanings, had to tread with particular caution. Edmund Kean failed to do so in 1821 when he cancelled his performance of *Richard III* in Boston because only twenty people were in the audience. The next day's papers denounced him for insulting and dishonoring the American people and suggested that he be taken ''by the nose, and dragged . . . before the curtain to make his excuses for his conduct.'' Four years later, when Kean returned to Boston, he attempted to make those excuses, but it was too late. The all-male audience that packed the theater and overflowed onto the streets allowed him neither to perform *Richard III* nor to ''apologize for [his] indiscretions.'' A barrage of nuts, foodstuffs, and bottles of odorous drugs drove him weeping from the stage and the theater, after which the anti-Keanites in the pit and gallery turned on his supporters in the boxes and did grievous damage to the theater. Kean performed in Philadelphia, New York, and Charleston but precipitated another riot in Baltimore and finally left the country for good.[68]

In 1834 the Irishman Tyrone Power committed exactly the same error—he cancelled a performance in Albany, New York, when the audience numbered less than ten—and found that even his outspoken democratic sympathies could not save him from a similar fate. When he next performed two days later, he reported, ''the house was filled with men, and everything foreboded a violent outbreak. . . . On my appearance the din was mighty deafening; . . . every invention for making the voice of humanity bestial was present and in full use. The boxes I observed to be occupied by well-dressed men, who generally either remained neutral, or by signs sought that I should be heard.'' Upon the intervention of the manager, Power was allowed to explain himself, after which "the row was resumed with added fierceness: not a word of either play or farce was heard.'' [69]

The full extent of class feeling and divisions existing in egalitarian America was revealed on a bloody Thursday in May 1849 at and around the Astor Place Opera House in New York City. The immediate catalyst was a longstanding feud between two leading actors, the Englishman William Charles Macready and the American Edwin Forrest, who had become symbols of antithetical values. Forrest's vigorous acting style, his militant love of his country, his outspoken belief in its citizenry, and his frequent articulation of the possibilities of self-improvement and social mobility endeared him to the American people, while Macready's cerebral acting style, his aristocratic demeanor, and his identification with the wealthy gentry made him appear Forrest's diametric opposite. On May 7, Macready and Forrest appeared against one another in separate productions of *Macbeth*. Forrest's performance was a triumph; Macready's was never heard—he was silenced by a storm of boos and cries of "Down with the codfish aristocracy,'' which drowned out appeals for order from those in the boxes, and by an avalanche of eggs, apples, potatoes, lemons, and, ultimately, chairs hurled from the gallery, which forced him to leave the stage in the third act.

Macready was now prepared to leave the country as well, but he was dissuaded by persons of "highest respectability,'' including Washington Irving and Herman Melville, who urged him not to encourage the mob by giving in to it and assured him "that the good sense and respect for order prevailing in this community will sustain you.'' Eighteen hundred people filled the Astor Place Opera House on the evening of May 10, with some ten thousand more on the streets outside. Assisted by the quick arrest of the most voluble opponents inside the theater, Macready completed his performance of *Macbeth,* but only under great duress. Those outside—stirred by orators' shouts of "Burn the damned den of the aristocracy!'' and "You can't go in there without . . . kid gloves and a white vest, damn 'em!''—bombarded the theater with paving stones, attempted to storm the entrances, and were stopped only after detachments of militia fired point blank into the crowd. In the end at least twenty-two people were killed, and over one hundred and fifty were wounded or injured.[70]

If the eighty-six men arrested were at all typical, the crowd had been composed of workingmen—coopers, printers, butchers, carpenters, servants, sailmakers, machinists, clerks, masons, bakers, plumbers, laborers—whose feelings were probably reflected in a speech given at a rally the next day: "Fellow citizens, for what—for whom was this murder committed? . . . To please the aristocracy of the city, at the expense of the lives of unoffending citizens . . . , to revenge the aristocrats of this city against the working classes." Although such observers as the New York *Tribune* saw the riot as the "absurd and incredible" result of a petty quarrel, the role of class was not ignored. The *Home Journal* viewed the riot as a protest against "aristocratizing the pit" in such new and exclusive theaters as the Astor Place Opera House and warned that in the future the republic's rich would have to "be mindful where its luxuries offend." The New York *Herald* asserted that the riot had introduced a "new aspect in the minds of many, . . . nothing short of a controversy and collision between those who have been styled the 'exclusives,' or 'upper ten,' and the great popular masses." The New York correspondent for the Philadelphia *Public Ledger* lamented a few days after the riot, "It leaves behind a feeling to which this community has hitherto been a stranger—an opposition of classes—the rich and poor . . . , a feeling that there is now in our country, in New York City, what every good patriot hitherto has considered it his duty to deny—*a high and a low class.*" [71]

The purpose of acting, Shakespeare had Hamlet say in his charge to the players, "was and is, to hold, as 'twere, the mirror up to nature; to show virtue her own feature, scorn her own image, and the very age and body of time his form and pressure" (III.ii). The functions of the nineteenth-century American stage were even broader. As a central institution, the theater not only mirrored the sweep of events in the larger society but presented an arena in which those events could unfold. The Astor Place Riot was both an indication of and a catalyst for the cultural changes that came to characterize the United States at the end of the century. Theater no longer functioned as a cultural form that embodied all classes within a shared public space, nor did Shakespeare much longer remain the common property of all Americans. The changes were not cataclysmic; they were gradual and took place in rough stages: physical or spatial bifurcation, with different socioeconomic groups becoming associated with different theaters in large urban centers, was followed inevitably by the stylistic bifurcation described by George William Curtis and ultimately culminated in a content bifurcation, which saw a growing chasm between "serious" and "popular" culture.

Increasingly in the second half of the nineteenth century, as public life became everywhere more fragmented, the concept of culture took on hierarchical connotations along the lines of Matthew Arnold's definition—"the best that has been thought and known in the world . . . , the study and pursuit of perfection." Looking back on "the disgraceful scenes of the Astor Place Riot" some thirty years later, Henry James pronounced it a manifestation of the "instinctive hostility of barbarism to culture."[72] This practice of distinguishing "culture" from lesser forms of expression became so common that by 1915 Van Wyck Brooks found it necessary to incorporate the terms "highbrow" and "lowbrow" to express the chasm between which "there is no community, no genial middle ground." "What side of American life is not touched by this antithesis?" Brooks asked. "What explanation of American life is more central or more illuminating?"[73] Walt Whitman understood the drift of events as early as 1871. "We find ourselves abruptly in close quarters with the enemy," he charged in *Democratic Vistas,* with "this word Culture, or what it has come to represent." "Refinement and delicatesse," he warned, "threaten to eat us up, like a cancer." Whitman insisted that culture should not be "restricted by conditions ineligible to the masses," should not be created "for a single class alone, or for the parlors or lecture-rooms," and placed his hopes for the creation of a classless, democratic culture in the leadership of the new "middling" groups— "men and women with occupations, well-off owners of houses and acres, and with cash in the bank."[74]

The groups to which Whitman turned were neither willing nor able to fulfill his expectations. The emergence of new middle and upper-middle classes, created by rapid industrialization in the nineteenth century, seems to have accelerated rather than inhibited the growing distinctions between elite and mass culture. When, in the waning years of the century, Thorstein Veblen constructed his concept of conspicuous consumption, he included not only the obvious material possessions but also "immaterial" goods— "the knowledge of dead languages and the occult sciences; of correct spelling; of syntax and prosody; of the various forms of domestic music . . . ; of the latest proprieties of dress, furniture, and equipage"; of the ancient "classics"—all of which constituted a conspicuous culture that helped confer legitimacy on the newly emergent groups.[75] "Culture" became something refined, ideal, removed from and elevated above the mundane events of everyday life. This helps explain the vogue during this period of manuals of etiquette, of private libraries and rare books, of European art and music displayed and performed in ornate—often neoclassical—museums and concert halls.[76]

It also helps explain the transformation of Shakespeare, who fit the new cultural equation so well. His plays had survived the test of time and were therefore immortal; his language was archaic and therefore too complex for ordinary people; his poetry was sublime and therefore elevating—especially if his plays could be seen in a theater and a style of one's own choice, devoid of constant reminders that they contained earthier elements and more universal appeals as well. The point is not that there was a conspiracy to remove Shakespeare from the American people but that a cultural develop-

ment occurred which produced the same result—a result that was com-
pounded by the fact that during these years American entertainment was
shaped by many of the same forces of consolidation and centralization that
molded other businesses.[77]

If the managers of the new theater chains and huge booking agencies
approached their tasks with a hierarchical concept of culture, with the conviction that an unbridgeable gulf separated the tastes and predilections of the
various socioeconomic groups, and with the belief that Shakespeare was
"highbrow" culture, then we have isolated another decisive factor in his
transformation.

The transformation of Shakespeare is important precisely because it was
not unique. It was part of a larger transformation that Richard Sennett has
argued characterized Western European culture after the eighteenth century,
in which public culture fractured into a series of discrete private cultures
that had less and less to do with one another. The audience that had been
heterogenous, interactive, and participatory became homogeneous, atomized, and passive—in Sennett's phrase, "a spectator rather than a witness."[78] When George Makepeace Towle was rediscovering his native land
shortly after the Civil War, opera was still part of the public domain. "*Lu-
cretia Borgia* and *Faust, The Barber of Seville* and *Don Giovanni,* are
everywhere popular," he wrote in 1870; "you may hear their airs in the
drawing rooms and concert halls, as well as whistled by the street boys and
ground out on the hand organs." In the twentieth century, such scenes became increasingly rare as grand opera joined Shakespeare in the elevated
circles of elite culture.[79]

The journey could lead in the opposite direction as well. From 1840 to
1900, chromolithography—the process by which original paintings were reproduced lithographically in color and sold in the millions to all segments
of the population—was one of the most familiar art forms in the nation. It
was hailed as a vehicle for bringing art "within the reach of all classes of
society" and praised as "art republicanized and naturalized in America."
These very characteristics made chromolithography anathema to E. L. Godkin of *The Nation* and the genteel group for whom he spoke. To Godkin,
chromolithography symbolized the packaged "pseudo-culture" that "diffused through the community a kind of smattering of all sorts of knowledge" and gave people the false confidence of being "cultured." "A society of ignoramuses who know they are ignoramuses, might lead to a tolerably
happy and useful existence," he wrote, "but a society of ignoramuses each
of whom thinks he is a Solon, would be an approach to Bedlam let loose.
. . . The result is a kind of mental and moral chaos." Godkin's view prevailed. By the 1890s the term "chromo" had come to mean "ugly" or
"offensive." Thus, while at the Philadelphia Centennial Exposition in 1876

chromolithographs were exhibited as "Fine Arts" along with sculpture, painting, and engravings, seventeen years later at Chicago's Columbian Exposition of 1893 they were classified as, and exhibited with, "Industrial" or "Commercial" arts. Indeed, the Columbian Exposition itself, with its sharp physical division between the Midway, containing common entertainments, and the Court of Honor or White City, containing monumental classic architecture, stood as a fitting symbol of the bifurcated culture that had come to characterize the United States.[80]

This is not to suggest the existence of an idyllic era when the American people experienced a cultural unity devoid of tensions. In the nineteenth-century folk paintings of Edward Hicks, the wolf and the lamb, the lion and the fatling, the leopard and the kid might occupy the same territory in harmony, but reality was more complex—as Hicks and his countrymen well knew. Still, America in the first half of the nineteenth century did experience greater cultural sharing in the sense that cultural lines were more fluid, cultural spaces less rigidly subdivided than they were to become. Certainly, what I have called a shared public culture did not disappear with the nineteenth century. Twentieth-century Americans, especially in the palaces they built to the movies and in their sporting arenas, continued to share public space and public culture. But with a difference. Cultural space became more sharply defined, more circumscribed, and less fluid than it had been. Americans might sit together to watch the same films and athletic contests, but those who also desired to experience "legitimate" theater or hear "serious" music went to segregated temples devoted to "high" or "classical" art. Cultural lines are generally porous, and there were important exceptions— Toscanini was featured on commercial radio and television, and Shakespeare's works were offered on the movie screen. But these were conscious exceptions to what normally prevailed. The cultural fare that was actively and regularly shared by all segments of the population belonged to the lower rungs of the cultural hierarchy.

As we gradually come to the realization that Fred Astaire was one of this century's fine dancers, Louis Armstrong one of its important musicians, Charlie Chaplin one of its acute social commentators, we must remember that they could be shared by all of the people only when they were devalued as "popular" art, only when they were rendered nonthreatening by being relegated to the nether regions of the cultural complex. By the twentieth century, art could not have it both ways: no longer could it simultaneously enjoy high cultural status and mass popularity. Shakespeare is a prime example. He retained his lofty position only by being limited and confined to audiences whose space was no longer shared with, and whose sensibilities were no longer violated by, the bulk of the populace.

9

Jazz and American Culture

In early 1987 Willard B. Gatewood, Jr., president of the Southern Historical Association, and Ed Harrell, chairman of its Program Committee, were kind enough to invite me to give the opening night address at the Association's annual meeting in New Orleans in November. They wanted me to speak on any aspect of jazz history that interested me, and they lured me with the promise that my paper would not be followed by the customary critiques of commentators but by "a one hour complimentary cocktail reception" and a performance by the Preservation Hall Jazz Band. In spite of these enticements, I was hesitant to accept. The invitation came at an extremely busy time; I was struggling to complete my book, *Highbrow/Lowbrow*, which I had promised to send in final form to the publisher that coming summer. I ultimately agreed for two reasons: The moment they told me what they wanted, I knew exactly what I would speak on—the relationship of jazz to the new hierarchical concept of Culture that made its appearance in the United States at the turn of the century.

I was dealing with this cultural phenomenon in the book I was finishing, and the idea of fitting jazz into the larger cultural framework intrigued me. More crucially, I was loathe to do anything to discourage or undermine those of my colleagues who were striving to take seriously such aspects of American culture as jazz which had suffered neglect at the hands of historians for so long. The notion of having jazz as the centerpiece of the opening night session delighted me. The enormous amount of pressured work my decision cost me was more than compensated for by the large, enthusiastic group of historians who gathered in the Clarion Hotel on the night of November 11, and by the warm—and wet—reception and wonderful music that followed. As a friend commented at the time, "This *is* a lot better than criticism!" Inevitably, of course, the criticism came anyway—abundantly and helpfully—before a slightly expanded version of the paper was published in the *Journal of American Folklore,* 102 (January–March 1989).

❖•❖

The increasing scholarly interest in jazz symbolizes what I trust is an ongoing reversal of a long-standing neglect by historians and their colleagues in many other disciplines of a central element in American culture. The neglect, of course, has not been an aberration on the part of academics. In neglecting or ignoring jazz, scholars have merely reflected the values and predispositions of the larger society in which they operated. But even this simple statement belies the true complexity of the problem: American society has done far more than merely neglect jazz; it has pigeonholed it, stereotyped it, denigrated it, distorted its meaning and its character. The nature and significance of the type of attention our society has paid to jazz reveal a great deal about our culture.

Anthropologically, perhaps, my title—Jazz *and* American Culture—doesn't make a great deal of sense since Jazz is an integral part of American culture. But it is not culture in the anthropological sense that I'm dealing with here, since in fact that's not what culture meant to the society at the time jazz came upon the scene as a recognizable entity. When jazz became an identifiable form of music to the larger society, it was held to be something quite distinct from *Culture* as that term was then understood. It is the dialectic between the two—between jazz and Culture—that forms the subject of this article.

One can debate at great length the specific origins of the music we have come to know as jazz: *when* it first appeared, *where* it first appeared, *how* it was diffused, *what* its relationships to other forms of American music were. For my purposes, it is sufficient to observe that roughly during those decades that spanned either side of the year 1900, that period we call the Turn of the Century, a music or musics that came to be known as jazz appeared in and were quickly diffused throughout the United States at the same time that a phenomenon known as Culture (with a capital C) made its appearance.

America emerged from the 19th century with most of the cultural structures that have become familiar to us in place, or in the process of being put into place. Adjectival categories were created to box and identify expressive culture: High, Low, Highbrow, Lowbrow, Popular. Though these terms lacked, and continue to lack, any genuine precision, they were utilized with some consistency though always with a degree of confusion since the terms themselves were confusing and deceptive. That is, Popular Culture, in spite of its name, did not have to be truly *popular* in order to win the title. It merely had to be considered to be of little worth aesthetically, for that became the chief criterion: the cultural categories that became fixed around the turn of the century were aesthetic and judgmental rather than descriptive terms. So pervasive did this system of adjectival boxes become, that from the early years of this century, if one used the word "culture" by itself, it was *assumed* to carry the adjective "high" with it. The notion of culture was lifted out of the surrounding world into the universe of gentility. The word "culture" became equated with the word "refinement" which in fact was precisely the definition it carried in the single-word definition pocket dictionaries popular at the turn of the century.[1]

Thus at approximately the same time, two new words—or more accurately, two older words with new meanings—came into general usage. Their dual appearance is significant because the two—Culture and Jazz—helped to define one another. That is, they served as convenient polar points, as antitheses. One could understand what Culture was by looking at the characteristics of jazz and reversing them.

Jazz was, or at least seemed to be, the new product of a new age; Culture was, or at least seemed to be, traditional—the creation of centuries.

Jazz was raucous, discordant; Culture was harmonious, embodying order and reason.

Jazz was accessible, spontaneous; Culture was exclusive, complex, available only through hard study and training.

Jazz was openly an *interactive,* participatory music in which the audience played an important role, to the extent that the line between audience and performers was often obscured. Culture built those lines painstakingly, establishing boundaries that relegated the audience to a primarily passive role, listening to, or looking at the creations of true artists. Culture increased the gap between the creator and the audience, jazz narrowed that gap. Jazz was frequently played in the midst of noisy, hand-clapping, foot-stomping, dancing and gyrating audiences. Those who came to witness Culture in art museums, symphonic halls, opera houses, learned what Richard Sennett has called "Silence in the face of Art."[2]

If jazz didn't obliterate the line between composer and performer, at the very least it rendered that line hazy. Culture upheld the differentiation between the composer and the performer and insisted that the performer take no liberties with the work of the creator who in Culture assumed a central, often a sacred, position. Jazz was a performer's art; Culture a composer's art.

Jazz seemed uniquely American, an artistic form that, if Frederick Jackson Turner and his followers had only known it, might have reinforced their notions of indigenous American development and divergence from the Old World. Culture was Eurocentric—convinced that the best and noblest were the products of the Old World which the United States had to learn to emulate.

These two very different entities were expressions of radically divergent impulses in America. Culture was the product of that side of ourselves that craved order, stability, definition. It was the expression of a colonial side of ourselves that we have not done nearly enough to understand. I am convinced that we would know ourselves better if we understood our past more firmly as the history of a people who attained political and economic independence long before we attained cultural independence. Culturally we remained, to a much larger extent than we have yet recognized, a colonized people attempting to define itself in the shadow of the former imperial power. Jazz was an expression of that other side of ourselves that strove to recognize the positive aspects of our newness and our heterogeneity; that learned to be comfortable with the fact that a significant part of our heritage derived from Africa and other non-European sources; and that recognized in the various syncretized cultures that became so characteristic of the United States not an embarrassing weakness but a dynamic source of strength.

It is impossible, then, to understand the place jazz occupied in America—at least until the years after World War II—without understanding that its emergence as a distinct music in the larger culture paralleled the emergence of a hierarchized concept of Culture with its many neat but never precisely defined adjectival boxes and categories.

In the *Edinburgh Review* in 1820 the Reverend Sydney Smith asked a question that was to haunt a substantial number of influential Americans for the remainder of the 19th century: "In the four quarters of the globe, who reads an American book? or goes to an American play? or looks at an American picture or statue?"[3] Who, Smith was demanding, paid any attention to American culture at all? The question was quickly converted into an even more tortured query: *was* there an American culture worth paying attention to in the first place? As the century progressed an impressive number of Americans asked themselves some version of this question.

In his 1879 biography of Nathaniel Hawthorne, Henry James created his famous litany of American cultural deficiencies which read in part: "no cathedrals, nor abbeys, nor little Norman churches; no great Universities nor public schools—no Oxford, nor Eton, nor Harrow; no literature, no novels, no museums, no pictures." Americans, James concluded, had "the elements of modern man with *culture* quite left out."[4]

Culture was quite left out because it required standards and authority of a kind that was difficult to find in a country with America's leveling, practical tendencies. The real peril America faced, *The Outlook* declared in 1893, was not a dearth of art but the acceptance of inferior standards. "We are in danger of exalting the average man, and rejoicing in . . . mediocrity."[5]

Increasingly, in the closing decades of the 19th century the concept of culture took on hierarchical connotations along the lines of Matthew Arnold's definition of culture—"the best that has been thought and known in the world."[6] This practice of distinguishing "culture" from lesser forms of expression became so common that by 1915 Van Wyck Brooks concluded that between the highbrow and the lowbrow "there is no community, no genial middle ground."[7]

The new concept of Culture that became powerful in these years took its inspiration and its standards from Europe as the young Charles Ives discovered when he attempted to inject American idioms into his Second Symphony, which he completed in 1901 or 1902. "Some of the themes in this symphony suggest Gospel Hymns and Steve Foster," Ives noted. "Some nice people, whenever they hear the words 'Gospel Hymns' or 'Stephen Foster,' say 'Mercy Me,!' and a little high-brow smile creeps over their brow—'Can't you get something better than that in a symphony?' "[8]

So little did the arbiters of musical taste think of their own country's contributions that in 1884 when the critic Richard Grant White was invited to write a history of American music, he refused for lack of an American music to write about. American psalmbook-makers and singing-school teachers were, White declared, "about as much in place in the history of musical art as a critical discussion of the whooping of Indians would be."[9]

There were some who began to see in American and, particularly, Afro-American folk music evidence of an indigenous American musical tradition. After hearing the Jubilee Singers in 1897, Mark Twain wrote a friend, "I think that in the Jubilees and their songs America has produced the perfectest flower of the ages; and I wish it were a foreign product, so that she would worship it and lavish money on it and go properly crazy over it."[10] The most famous of these voices was that of the Czech composer Antonín Dvořák who was teaching and composing in the United States when he made his striking statement in 1893:

> I am now satisfied that the future music of this country must be founded upon what are called the negro melodies. This must be the real foundation of any serious and original school of composition to be developed in the United States.[11]

These notions flew too directly in the face of the comfortable evolutionary predispositions of the day which simply ruled out the possibility that those at the top of society had anything to learn from the "plantation melodies" of Afro-Americans firmly ensconced in "the lowest strata of society." In the 1890s the Boston critic William Apthorp declared that such compositions as Dvořák's *New World Symphony* and Edward MacDowell's *Indian Suite* were futile attempts "to make civilized music by civilized methods out of essentially barbaric material," resulting in "a mere apotheosis of ugliness, distorted forms, and barbarous expression."[12]

These were the voices that prevailed. John Philip Sousa, America's preeminent bandmaster at the turn of the century, complained of the "artistic snobbery" that had plagued his career. "Notwithstanding the credo of musical snobs," he asserted, " 'popular' does not necessarily mean 'vulgar' or 'ephemeral.' " To touch "the public heart" required inspiration and the "stamp of genius." "Many an immortal tune has been born in the stable or the cottonfield. *Turkey in the Straw* is a magic melody; anyone should be proud of having written it, but, for musical high-brows, I suppose the thing is declassée. It came not from a European composer but from an unknown negro minstrel."[13] The stamp of European approval remained the *sine qua non* for true culture. "Either we do not believe in our own opinions, or we feel that we do not know enough to make them," *Putnam's Magazine* complained. "How long will it be," it asked wistfully, "before London applauds *because* New York approves?"[14] Thomas Wentworth Higginson agreed. The discussion over whether the United States had a distinct culture would cease, he insisted, "When Europe comes to America for culture, instead of America's thronging to Europe."[15]

The primary obstacle to the emergence of a worthy American music, Frederick Nast asserted in 1881, "lies in the diverse character of our population. . . . American music can not be expected until the present discordant elements are merged into a homogeneous people."[16] It was obvious under whose auspices the "merger" was to take place. In 1898 Sidney Lanier argued that it was time for Americans to move back "into the presence of the Fathers" by adding the study of Old English to that of Greek and Latin, and by reading not just Homer but Beowulf. "Our literature needs Anglo-Saxon iron; there is no ruddiness in its cheeks, and everywhere a clear lack of the red corpuscles."[17] American society, Henry Adams observed in his autobiography, "offered the profile of a long, straggling caravan, stretching loosely towards the prairies, its few score of leaders far in advance and its millions of immigrants, negroes, and Indians far in the rear, somewhere in archaic time."[18]

It should hardly surprise us that such attitudes informed the adjectival categories created in the late 19th and early 20th centuries to define types of culture. "Highbrow," first used in the 1880s to describe intellectual or aesthetic superiority, and "lowbrow," first used shortly after 1900 to mean someone or something neither "highly intellectual" or "aesthetically refined," were not new terms; they were derived from the phrenological terms "highbrowed" and "lowbrowed" which were prominently featured in the 19th-century practice of determining intelligence and racial types by measuring cranial shapes and capacities. A familiar illustration of the period depicted the distinctions between the lowbrowed Ape and the increasingly higher brows of the "Human Idiot," the "Bushman," the "Uncultivated," the "Improved," the "Civilized," the "Enlightened," and, finally, the "Caucasian," with the highest brow of all. The categorization did not end this broadly, of course, for within the Caucasian circle there were distinctions to be made: the closer to Western and Northern Europe a people came, the higher their brows extended. From the time of their formulation, such cultural categories as Highbrow and Lowbrow were openly associated with and designed to preserve, nurture, and extend the cultural history and values of a particular group of peoples in a specific historical context.[19]

It was into this world of rapidly accelerating cultural hierarchy that jazz was born or at least in which it became a widely diffused music. In 1918 the *New Orleans Times—Picayune* described the "many mansions in the houses of the muses." There was the "great assembly hall of melody" where "most of us take our seats," while a smaller number pass on to the "inner sanctuaries of harmony" where "nearly all the truly great music is enjoyed." Finally, there was still one more apartment

> down in the basement, a kind of servants' hall of rhythm. It is there we hear the hum of the Indian dance, the throb of the Oriental tambourines and kettledrums, the clatter of the clogs, the click of Slavic heels, the thumpty-tumpty of the negro banjo, and, in fact, the native dances of the world.

Rhythm, though often associated with melody and harmony, "is not necessarily music," the *Times-Picayune* instructed its readers. Indeed, when rhythm took such forms as ragtime or jazz it constituted an "atrocity in polite society, and . . . we should make it a point of civic honor to suppress it. Its musical value is nil, and its possibilities of harm are great."[20]

This was the paradigmatic response the upholders of "Culture" accorded jazz in the decades in which it was establishing itself as a familiar form of American music. As early as 1901 the American Federation of Musicians ordered their members to refrain from playing ragtime: "The musicians know what is good, and if the people don't, we will have to teach them."[21] On a January Sunday in 1922 the Reverend Dr. Percy Stickney Grant used his pulpit in New York's Episcopal Church of the Ascension on Fifth Avenue to advise his parishioners that jazz "is retrogression. It is going to the African jungle for our music. It is a savage crash and bang."[22] Jazz, the *New York Times* editorialized in 1924, is to real music exactly what most of the "new poetry," so-called, is to real poetry. Both are without the structure and form essential to music and poetry alike, and both are the products, not of innovators, but of incompetents. . . . Jazz, especially when it depends much on that ghastly instrument, the saxophone, offends people with musical taste already formed, and it prevents the formation of musical taste by others.[23]

The *Times* returned to the subject again and again insisting that jazz "is merely a return to the humming, hand-clapping, or tomtom beating of savages."[24]

A writer in *Collier's* dismissed jazz as "trash" played on "lowbrow instruments."[25] Once America regained its soul, Rabbi Stephen Wise proclaimed, jazz "will be relegated to the dark and scarlet haunts whence it came and whither unwept it will return."[26] Condemnation by analogy became a favorite sport. Jazz, various critics insisted, bore the same relationship to classical music as a limerick did to poetry, or a farmhouse to a cathedral, or a burlesque show to legitimate drama.[27] Jazz was attacked not only for returning civilized people to the jungles of barbarism but also for expressing the mechanistic sterility of modern urban life. Jazz, the composer and teacher Daniel Gregory Mason charged, "is so perfectly adapted to robots that the one could be deduced from the other. Jazz is thus the exact musical reflection of modern capitalistic industrialism."[28] H. L. Mencken put it more succinctly when he described jazz as the "sound of riveting."[29]

The denigration of jazz was not confined to white critics. Jazz music and musicians bordered too closely upon the racial stereotypes of rhythmic, pulsating, uninhibited blacks for many race leaders. Maude Cuney-Hare, the music editor of *The Crisis,* criticized the "common combination of unlovely tones and suggestive lyrics" that characterized much of jazz. "Music should sound, not screech; Music should cry, not howl; Music should weep, not bawl; Music should implore, not whine."[30] The advice that Dave Peyton, the music critic for the politically militant *Chicago Defender,* gave to aspiring pianists was to "put two or three hours a day on your scale work, [and] stay away from jazz music." Peyton complained consistently that "Heretofore our orchestras have confined themselves to hot jazzy tunes" too exclusively and that in general blacks remained too firmly within their own musical universe:

We have played music as we think it should be played without trying to find out if we are playing it correctly. So few of us have the time to visit the grand symphony orchestras, the de luxe picture houses and other places where things musically are done correctly.[31]

Lucien H. White, the music critic for the Harlem paper, *New York Age,* excoriated jazz as music "producing a conglomerate mixture of dissonances, with a swing and a lilt appealing only to the lover of sensuous and debasing emotions." White joined forces with the National Association of Negro Musicians, Hampton Institute's journal *The Southern Workman,* and many prominent blacks in attacking those who played jazz versions of the old spirituals. A Jewish musician who dared to transform the Hebrew's despairing cry *Eli, Eli* into a jazz number "would be cast out by his people as unorthodox and unclean," White charged. So should it be with black musicians who transgressed "upon the outpourings of the racial heart when it was wrung and torn with sorrow and distress."[32] There was comparable anger on the part of whites when jazz musicians utilized themes from classical composers. Frank Damrosch was typical in denouncing the "outrage on beautiful music" perpetrated by jazz musicians who were guilty of "stealing phrases from the classic composers and vulgarizing them."[33] Jazz musicians, a critic warned, had better "keep their dirty paws off their betters."[34] Throughout the early history of jazz, its practitioners were treated consistently as low-caste defilers of the clean and sacred classic music of both the white and the black societies they inhabited.

Not all the reactions to jazz were necessarily negative. In 1924 Leopold Stokowski, the conductor of the Philadelphia Orchestra, attributed the "new vitality" of jazz to black musicians: "They have an open mind, and unbiased outlook. They are not hampered by traditions or conventions, and with their new ideas, their constant experiments, they are causing new blood to flow in the veins of music."[35] A number of critics praised jazz as a perfect idiom for articulating personal feelings. In one of the first books devoted exclusively to jazz, Henry Osgood called it "a protest against . . . the monotony of life . . . an attempt at individual expression."[36] Interestingly, jazz was also lauded for being a form of *national* expression. "No matter what is said about it," the *Literary Digest* proclaimed, "jazz is a native product. . . . Jazz is completely American."[37] In his influential *The Seven Lively Arts,* Gilbert Seldes called jazz "our characteristic expression," which appeared to agree with those who felt it was "about the only native music worth listening to in America," and, with the mixed admiration and condescension characteristic of the time, praised black Americans for articulating and keeping alive "something which underlies a great deal of America—our independence, our carelessness, our frankness, and gaiety."[38]

There was no real contradiction between these apparently divergent sets of views. In fact, jazz was often praised for possessing precisely those characteristics that made it anathema to those who condemned it: it was praised *and* criticized for being innovative and breaking with tradition. It was praised *and* criticized for being a form of culture expressing the id, the repressed or suppressed feelings of the individual, rather than submitting to the organized discipline of the superego which enforced the attitudes and values of the bourgeois culture. It was praised *and* criticized for breaking out of the tight circle of obeisance to Eurocentric cultural forms and giving expression to indigenous American attitudes articulated through indigenous American creative structures. It was, in short, praised *and* criticized for being almost completely out of phase with the period's concept of Culture.

It was this quality of course that made jazz one of those houses of refuge in the 1920s for individuals who felt alienated from the central culture. We have come to understand the importance of such actual and symbolic cultural oases as Paris and Greenwich Village for those who sought relief from the overwhelming sense of Civilization in the post–World War I years. We need to continue to develop our understanding of the ways in which Afro-American culture, and especially jazz, served as a crucial alternative as well.

As I have argued elsewhere, many of those who found jazz and blues stimulating and attractive in the 1920s and 1930s did so because these musical forms seemed to promise them greater freedom of expression, both artistically and personally. This was especially true of young people who Louis Armstrong observed were among the most numerous and avid followers of the bands he played with. In the early 1920s, a group of young whites who were born or raised in and around Chicago and who were to become well-known jazz musicians—Benny Goodman, Bud Freeman, Dave Tough, Eddie Condon, Milton ''Mezz'' Mezzrow, Gene Krupa, Muggsy Spanier, Jimmy McPartland, Frank Teschemacher, Joe Sullivan, George Wettling— were stunned by the music of such black jazzmen as Joe Oliver, Jimmie Noone, Johnny and Baby Dodds, and Louis Armstrong, all of whom were then playing in clubs on Chicago's South Side. These white youngsters spoke about jazz, Condon recalled, ''as if it were a new religion just come from Jerusalem.''[39]

The analogy was not far fetched: in their autobiographies these musicians often described what amounted to conversion experiences. In 1924 Eddie Condon, Jimmy McPartland, and Bud Freeman dropped in to a club where Joe Oliver's band was playing: ''Oliver lifted his horn and the first blast of Canal Street Blues hit me,'' Condon has written.

> It was hypnosis at first hearing. Everyone was playing what he wanted to play and it was all mixed together as if someone had planned it with a set of micrometer calipers; notes I had never heard were peeling off the edges and dropping through the middle; there was a tone from the trumpets like warm rain on a cold day. Freeman and McPartland and I were immobilized; the music poured into us like daylight running down a dark hole.[40]

From these encounters the young white musicians absorbed a new means of expressing their musical individuality. But it was more than musical individuality; it was also the cultural freedom, the ability to be and express themselves—which they associated with jazz—that many of these young musicians found attractive. World War I was over, Hoagy Carmichael recalled, but the rebellion against "the accepted, the proper and the old" was just beginning. "And for us jazz articulated. . . . It said what we wanted to say."[41]

This view was not confined to jazz musicians. Jazz, Sigmund Spaeth wrote in 1928, "is a distortion of the conventional, a revolt against tradition, a deliberate twisting of established formulas."[42] The vogue of jazz, Alain Locke insisted,

> should be regarded as the symptom of a profound cultural unrest and change, first a reaction from Puritan repressions and then an escape from the tensions and monotonies of a machine-ridden, extroverted form of civilization.[43]

For younger black musicians, especially those whose careers began in the late 1930s and 1940s, jazz performed many of the same functions. "Jazz has always been a music of integration," the saxophonist Sonny Rollins commented some years later.

> Jazz was not just a music; it was a social force in this country, and it was talking about freedom and people enjoying things for what they are and not having to worry about whether they were supposed to be white, black, and all this stuff. Jazz has always been the music that had this kind of spirit.[44]

For black musicians jazz also provided a sense of power and control, a sense of meaning and direction, in a world that often seemed anarchic. In his autobiography Sidney Bechet thought about the ups and downs of his life and concluded: "The onliest thing I've ever been sure of how it was going is the music; that's something a man can make himself if he has the feeling."[45] In the 1930s a young William Dixon looked around his neighborhood and concluded that even in Harlem whites were everywhere in control: "it did seem, to a little boy, that these white people *really* owned everything. But that wasn't entirely true. They didn't own the music that I heard played."[46]

The striking thing about jazz is the extent to which it symbolized revolt wherever it became established. In Denmark, according to Erik Wiedemann, "From 1933 on advocating jazz became part of the anti-fascist culture-radical movement."[47] Marshall Stearns, after lecturing at the Zagreb Conservatory of Music in 1956, reported that the Yugoslav students and faculty agreed that "jazz symbolized an element of unconscious protest which cut through the pretenses of tradition and authority."[48] As recently as March 1987, two leaders of the Jazz Section of the Czech Musicians' Union were sentenced to jail for "unauthorized" activities. Karel Srp, who was not released until January 1988, was forced to spend 20 days in solitary confinement in a cell whose floor was covered with excrement.[49] Thus the phenomenon of jazz as a potent and potentially dangerous form of alternative culture became well established throughout the world.

But the primary impact jazz had was not as a form of revolt; it was as a style of music, a medium of culture. That this music which was characterized as vulgar at best and as harmful trash at worst by the Guardians of Culture and that for a long time was appreciated largely by those on the margins of American society; that this form of music which seemed so firmly ensconced on the American cultural periphery, should become the most widely identifiable and emulated symbol of American culture throughout the world by the mid-20th century is one of the more arresting paradoxes of modern American history. For so many decades the Keepers of the Flame had predicted that when Europe took an interest in our expressive arts as well as in our machine shops, that when Europe looked to the United States for culture as well as for technology, then and only then would we know we had truly arrived as an equal entity. And, as they hoped, Europe ultimately did come to America for culture—and the culture they came for was jazz.

"It required the stubbornness of Europeans," the Frenchman Phillipe Adler wrote in 1976, "to convince America that she had . . . given birth to one of the most dazzling arts of the twentieth century."[50] This is not to say that there was universal acceptance of jazz across the Atlantic. Many of the responses were familiar: in England in the 1920s Harold Spender worried that music in the United States might be "submerged by the aboriginal music of the negro."[51] In France the poet Georges Duhamel dismissed jazz as "a triumph of barbaric folly."[52]

Nevertheless, jazz was accorded a more positive critical reception in Europe during those early years than it was in its own country. "Jazz is a philosophy of the world, and therefore to be taken seriously," the German critic George Barthelme wrote in a Cologne newspaper in 1919. "Jazz is the expression of a *Kultur* epoch. . . . Jazz is a musical revelation, a religion, a philosophy of the world, just like Expressionism and Impressionism."[53] Jazz, the Austrian musician Ernst Krenek, maintained, "has revived the art of improvisation to an extent unknown by serious musicians since . . . the contrapuntal extemporization of the fifteenth century."[54] In France Hughes Panassié placed the jazz band on a higher plane than the symphony orchestra for while the latter "functions only as a transmitter," the musicians in jazz "are *creators,* as well."[55]

In the United States, the types of jazz that were most easily and widely accepted initially were the filtered and hybridized versions that created less cultural dissonance. Listening to Paul Whiteman's jazz band in 1926 Edmund Wilson complained of the extent to which Whiteman had "refined and disciplined his orchestra" and thus reduced the music he was playing "to an abstract pattern."[56] The degree to which blacks could be left out of this musical equation was stunning. In the mid-1920s the composer John Alden Carpenter praised jazz as "the first art innovation originating in America to be accepted seriously in Europe," and predicted that "the musical historian of the year 2,000 A.D. will find the birthday of American music and that of Irving Berlin to have been the same."[57] After hearing the black pianist Earl Hines perform, Paul Whiteman went up to him and commented wistfully: "If you were only white."[58] For all her dislike of jazz, Maude Cuney-Hare disliked preemption even more. "Just as the white minstrels blackened their faces and made use of the Negro idiom," she complained in the 1930s, "so have white orchestral players today usurped the Negro in Jazz entertainment."[59]

But here too the preemption was limited by the fact that jazz was not for long an exclusively *American* affair. Eric Hobsbawm has written of the "extraordinary expansion" of jazz "which has practically no cultural parallel for speed and scope except the early expansion of Mohammedanism."[60] By the mid-20th century jazz was no longer exclusively American any more than classical music was exclusively European. Americans found that one of the results of creating a truly international culture is that you lose control over the criteria of judgment and categorization. The recognition that black musicians received throughout the world had its effect in their own country as well.

If André Levinson's declaration in the *Theatre Arts Monthly* in 1927 that "jazz is henceforth admitted into the hierarchy of the arts" was premature, and it was, it certainly understood the direction American culture was taking.[61] Transitions are by definition almost impossible to identify with precision; they are most often gradual and cumulative. As early as 1925 the great apostle of classical music, the *Times'* critic, W. J. Henderson, admitted that jazz was the only original American music not based on European models, which explained why Europe had stretched out its arms not toward the American composers of art music but to ragtime and jazz.[62] Though there were others who perceived what Henderson did, I would argue that for most Americans the decisive transitional moment was not until after World War II when the cultural significance of jazz could no longer be denied. The highly successful tours of musicians like Dizzy Gillespie, Benny Goodman, and Louis Armstrong through Asia, the Middle East, and Africa, as well as

Europe, brought national attention to the stature of jazz music, *American jazz* music, *Afro-American* jazz music, throughout the world.

It did not take the State Department long to understand that the visit of a musician like Gillespie to Pakistan stimulated interest not only in jazz but in American culture in general.[63] "United States Has Secret Sonic Weapon— Jazz," a *New York Times* headline proclaimed in 1955, and its subhead added: "Europe Falls Captive as Crowds Riot to Hear Dixieland." What most surprised the *Times* reporter was not that jazz was popular but that it was taken so seriously. The European approach, he noted, "is what most Americans would call a 'long-haired approach.' They like to contemplate it, dissect it, take it apart to see what makes it what it is." He was informed by one European fan that jazz contained a tension between musical discipline and individual expression which "comes close to symbolizing the conditions under which people of the atomic age live." Jazz, he was told in Switzerland, "is not just an art. It is a way of life." To his own surprise the reporter concluded that "American jazz has now become a universal language."[64] The accumulation of these experiences ultimately made it common for national magazines to say matter-of-factly, as *Newsweek* did in 1973: "The U.S. wouldn't have an art form to call its own without jazz."[65]

All of this recognition did not mean the total extinction of the easy responses of the past which had either denigrated jazz or explained its accomplishments away. Amidst the tributes there was still condescension. In his *Music in American Life* Jacques Barzun could state that jazz "is our one contribution to music that Europe knows about and honors us for," even as he ranked it with "sports and philately as the realm of the self-made expert," spoke darkly of its characteristic "repetition and the excitement that precedes narcosis," and concluded that "jazz is more symptom and pastime than unperishable utterance."[66] Nor had Americans fully outgrown the convenient racial explanations for jazz that denied blacks any credit for hard work, application, or talent in acquiring musical skills which were generally attributed to genes rather than genius. As late as 1974 a man of Virgil Thomson's stature could marvel at black music's ability to incorporate every imaginable form of music: "European classical composition, Anglo-Saxon folklore, Hispanic dance meters, hymns, jungle drums, the German lied, Italian opera, all are foods for the insatiable black hunger," he wrote, and then, whether he intended to or not, he nullified his tribute by observing: "As if inside all U.S. blacks there were, and just maybe there really is, some ancient and African enzyme, voracious for digesting whatever it encounters in the way of sound."[67]

To say that by our time jazz has become part of that entity we call art is only part of the truth. Jazz in fact is one of those forces that have helped to transform our sense of art and culture. In the early 1930s the Englishman Constant Lambert argued that jazz was the first music "to bridge the gap between highbrow and lowbrow successfully."[68] One could go further and perceive jazz as a music that in fact bridged the gap between all of the categories that divided culture; a music that found its way through the fences we use to separate genres of expressive culture from one another. When Duke Ellington predicted that "Soon it'll all be just music; you won't have to say whether it's jazz or not, just whether you like it," he was articulating a feeling with deep roots in the jazz community.[69] "There is no point in talking about different kinds of jazz," Charlie Parker told a reporter. "The most important thing for us is to have our efforts accepted as music." When he was asked about the differences between jazz and European "art" music, Parker's answer was characteristic: "There is no boundary line to art."[70] "We never labeled the music," the drummer Kenny Clarke told an interviewer. "It was just modern music. . . . We wouldn't call it anything, really, just music."[71] In his memoirs, Dizzy Gillespie was willing to recognize only two categories of music: "there's only good and bad."[72]

From the beginning jazz musicians refused to limit themselves; they reached out to embrace the themes, the techniques, the idioms of any music they found appealing and they did so with a minimum of fuss or comment. As early as the second decade of this century, the stride pianist James P. Johnson, who was to have a major influence upon Fats Waller and Duke Ellington, was paying little attention to the boundary lines: "From listening to classical piano records and concerts . . . I would learn concert effects and build them into blues and rags. . . . When playing a heavy stomp, I'd soften it right down, then I'd make an abrupt change like I heard Beethoven do in a sonata."[73] When the pianist Earl Hines discussed the formative influences upon his music, he included both the Baptist church and Chopin.[74] When Gil Evans was asked if the *Sketches of Spain* score he wrote for Miles Davis, which was influenced by the Spanish composers Joaquin Rodrigo and Manuel de Falla, was classical or jazz music, he responded: "That's a merchandiser's problem, not mine."[75] When Miles Davis was asked the same question, he responded similarly: "It's music."[76]

None of this is to suggest that jazz musicians merely wanted to blend into the larger pool of musicians. They understood they had something special to contribute to the musical world. When the drummer Max Roach enrolled in the Manhattan School of Music and the trumpeter Kenny Dorham entered New York University, they were both told that they approached their instruments incorrectly. Roach understood that this was a reflection of the differences between jazz and classical music. Conservatories taught brass players a sonority meant to allow them to blend with other instruments while jazz musicians learned to seek a distinctive voice geared to the fact that in jazz individual interpretation is far more central than in classical music.[77] This is precisely what Benny Goodman was trying to express when he discussed his double life as a jazz musician and a classical clarinetist. "Expression," he maintained, was the great difference between the two kinds of music: "The greatest exponents of jazz are those with the most originality in ideas plus the technique to express them. In classical music . . . the musician must try and see into the composer's mind and play the way he believes the composer meant the piece to be played."[78] Mezz Mezzrow said the same thing less politely: "to us . . . a guy composed *as* he played, the creating and performing took place at the same time—and we kept thinking what a drag it must be for any musician with spirit to have to sit in on a symphonic assembly-line."[79]

For black musicians especially, jazz was also a form of communal expression. Even as formally trained a musician as John Lewis of the Modern Jazz Quartet could insist, "We have to keep going back to the goldmine. I mean the folk music, the blues and things that are related to it."[80] When the contemporary composer John Cage criticized jazz music for relying too heavily on emotions, the pianist Cecil Taylor refused to listen:

> He doesn't have the right to make any comment about jazz, nor would Stravinsky . . . I've spent years in school learning about European music and its traditions, but these cats don't know a thing about Harlem except that it's there. . . . They never subject themselves to, like, what are Louis Armstrong's criteria for beauty, and until they do that, then I'm not interested in what they have to say. Because they simply don't recognize the criteria.[81]

In their refusal to be governed by the categorical orthodoxies that prevailed, in their unwillingness to make absolute distinctions between the vernacular and classical traditions, in their insistence that they were just attempting to play *music* and just wanted to be accepted as musicians, in their determination to utilize the *entire* Western tradition, as well as other cultural traditions, jazz musicians were revolutionizing not only music but also the concept of culture. No one has put this better, again and again, than Duke Ellington, as he did in 1957 when he attempted to explain the impact that the Shakespeare Theatre in Stratford, Ontario, had upon his composition *Such Sweet Thunder,* a title he took from *A Midsummer Night's Dream:* "I never heard so musical a discord, such sweet thunder" [IV, 1]:

> I have a great sympathy with Shakespeare because it seems to me that strong similarities can be established between a jazz performance and the production of a Shakespeare play—similarities between the producers, the artists, and the audiences.

> There is an increasing interrelationship between the adherents to art forms in various fields. . . . It is becoming increasingly difficult to decide where jazz starts or where it stops, where Tin Pan Alley begins and jazz ends, or even where the borderline lies between classical music and jazz. . . . I suspect that if Shakespeare were alive today, he might be a jazz fan himself—he'd appreciate the combination of team spirit and informality, of academic knowledge and humor.[82]

Ellington's outlook can help us to find our way amidst and through the cultural boxes and categories and fences with which we have so unnecessarily burdened ourselves. To understand what Americans since the turn of the century thought of jazz is crucial if we are to understand how they reacted to it or how the music and its practitioners were treated. But if we are to comprehend American culture, we can no longer afford to assume jazz really *was* what many Americans thought it was. We have to make that empathetic leap and allow ourselves to see jazz as an integral vibrant part of American culture throughout this century; to realize that before even the most prescient Europeans and long before any appreciable number of Americans thought of jazz as an indigenous American contribution to the culture of the world, jazz was precisely that. Jazz tells us much about what was original and dynamic in American culture even as it reveals to what extent our culture, or more correctly, our cultural attitudes had not yet weaned themselves from the old colonial patterns of the past. Jazz has much to tell us about our history and, indeed, much to tell us about ourselves if only we have the wisdom and the skill to listen to it and learn from it.

10

Progress and Nostalgia: The Self Image of the Nineteen Twenties

I wrote this essay at the University of East Anglia in Norwich, England, where I was a visiting professor during the academic year, 1967–68. When I was completing my study of William Jennings Bryan—*Defender of the Faith: William Jennings Bryan, the Last Decade, 1915–1925* (1965)—I worried about the fact that I had not done enough to test my thesis that Bryan embodied the concerns and attitudes of his constitutency in the South and West. At the time I wrote that book I simply didn't know enough about how to search for mass attitudes. I did treat the responses of Bryan's constituencies to such movements as Fundamentalism, the Ku Klux Klan, and Prohibition, but I didn't go any further. Once the book was completed, I began to explore other possibilities in my teaching by extending my inquiry to the popular and mass culture that became so important after World War I. Shortly after I arrived in Norwich, I was asked to give a number of public lectures in England and on the Continent. For material for these lectures I turned to the wide spectrum of cultural materials I had been using in my Berkeley courses.

This essay, which reflects my first hesitant attempts to utilize popular culture to augment and test some of the arguments I had made in my study of Bryan, is based upon one of the public lectures I gave during my year abroad. I had never before tested these materials outside the classroom, and I was encouraged by the interested responses of audiences both in England and Germany. I was also emboldened to use these materials more openly by my growing conviction that until historians supplemented the ubiquitous printed record with the materials of folk and popular culture, they would never be able to recover the voices of those who had been rendered historically inarticulate because they were not adequately represented by printed sources or at least by the *kinds* of printed sources traditionally used by American historians.

One of my colleagues at East Anglia, the novelist and critic Malcolm Bradbury, was in the audience when I spoke on the culture of the 1920s, and he offered to include the piece in a collection he was editing. It was one of the very first of my essays accepted for publication and appeared in Malcolm Bradbury and David Palmer eds., *The American Novel and the Nineteen Twenties* (London: Edward Arnold, 1971).

❖❖❖

I

Americans have always been comfortable with the idea of progress. The belief that inevitable change brought with it inevitable advancement and betterment fitted easily with, and was reinforced by, the stress on the individual, the belief in human perfectibility, the relative rootlessness and lack of tradition, the unparalleled mobility, the indefatigable optimism, the sense of uniqueness and destiny that has characterized so much of America's history. "Democratic nations," Tocqueville wrote, taking the United States as his model, "care but little for what has been, but they are haunted by visions of what will be; in this direction their unbounded imagination grows and dilates beyond all measure." Evidence of the validity of Tocqueville's observation abounds everywhere from Jefferson's assertion, "The creator has made the earth for the living, not the dead," to Senator Orville Platt's jubilant announcement in the last decade of the nineteenth century, "We live in a new creation. Literally, the old things have passed away and all things have become new. Human society is full of creators." When Emerson proclaimed that the one fundamental split in society was between the Party of the Past and the Party of the Future, the Party of Memory and the Party of Hope, and described himself as "an endless seeker, with no past at my back," he seemed to be speaking for his countrymen in general.

Only recently have scholars come to the realization that the ode to progress, no matter how eloquently composed, was not alone in the land; it was accompanied by a cry of longing for what had been.[1] The compulsion to peer forward was paralleled by an urge to look backward to a more pristine, more comfortable, more familiar time. Nostalgia is beginning to be recognized as an historical force no less prevalent and perhaps no less important than the idea of progress. Nor were its roots dissimilar. The imagery which pictured nineteenth-century Americans as latter-day Adams in an Edenic "Garden of the World," may have allowed them to visualize themselves as free to rise, favoured as they were by a perfect and completely open environment and untrammelled by the taint of original sin or the heritage of the past, but it also confronted them with the dilemma of whether the roads from Eden could lead anywhere but down. Richard Hofstadter has captured this dilemma perfectly in his ironic comment that "the United States was the only country in the world that began with perfection and aspired to progress." Thomas Jefferson served as a paradigm of this dilemma when he assured his country of its destined power and influence at the same time that he urged it to retain its purity and simplicity by remaining a nation of agrarians.

The central paradox of American history, then, has been a belief in progress coupled with a dread of change; an urge towards the inevitable future combined with a longing for the irretrievable past; a deeply ingrained belief in America's unfolding destiny and a haunting conviction that the nation was in a state of decline. This duality has been marked throughout most of America's history but seldom has it been more central than during the decade after the First World War. The force of nostalgia was manifest in the nineteen twenties in three related but distinct forms: a national movement to restore to America a former purity, cohesiveness and national purpose which had been diluted by the introduction of "alien" elements and ideologies; a cultural schism which saw a large segment of the population alienated from modernity and longing to return, at least symbolically, to a golden past; and a profound ambivalence towards the future which affected the actions and rhetoric of even some of the most fervid apostles of the "New Era."

II

The nineteen twenties were ushered in by the failure of a prophecy—specifically, Woodrow Wilson's prophetic assurance to his countrymen that he was leading "this great peaceful people into war" in order to foster the world-wide adoption of American democratic principles and forms: "for democracy, for the right of those who submit to authority to have a voice in their own Governments, for the rights and liberties of small nations, for a universal dominion of right." To enlist the American people fully in this cause, German ideology was converted into the very antithesis of everything America stood for. Prussian militarism had to be contained to ensure the principle of self-determination of all peoples; German materialism had to be defeated if the principles of Christianity which the United States represented were to have any chance of universal application. "This war," a member of the Committee of Public Information wrote to George Creel, "is being fought in the minds of great masses of people as truly as it is being fought on the battle fields of Europe."

How seriously this missionary impulse was taken is illustrated by the American reaction to the February Revolution in Russia. The United States was the first nation to extend diplomatic recognition to Kerensky's provisional government for, as Wilson put it, the overthrow of Czarist autocracy in Russia now gave America "a fit partner of a League of Honor." From the beginning the United States viewed the Russian Revolution through the prism of American ideology. "It was the American flag that has brought about the peaceable revolution in Russia," the *Des Moines Register* concluded on 23 March 1917, "and it is the American flag that will bring about the revolution in Germany, peaceable or violent, for that revolution is bound to come. It is American ideals that dominate the world." When Russian determination to fight the war faltered in the Spring of 1917, the United States sent a commission headed by Elihu Root to reassure the provisional government and strengthen its will. After some time spent in travelling through Russia, Root wired Wilson: "We have found here an infant class in the art of being free containing 170 million people and they need to be supplied with kindergarten material. . . . ."

The October Revolution which established Lenin and Trotsky in power, and the Versailles Treaty which indicated that the war aims of the Allies were not in concord with those of Wilson, left the messianic prophecies of the United States everywhere in ruins. The resulting disappointment supposedly impelled a disillusioned American people to turn inward, to abandon their former dreams, to forsake idealism for hedonism. "Feeling cheated," Lloyd Morris has written: "the war generation was cynical rather than revolutionary. It was tired of Great Causes. . . . It wanted slices of the national cake. There resulted the general decision to be amused."

In fact, the immediate aftermath of the First World War exhibited the opposite tendencies. Americans did not abandon their old verities and values but reasserted them with renewed vigour. The psychologist Leon Festinger and his associates, in their study of prophetic movements, concluded that while there are limits beyond which belief will not withstand disconfirmation, the introduction of contrary evidence often serves not to destroy the belief but rather to strengthen the conviction and enthusiasm of the believers. The dissonance resulting from the clash of a belief-system and facts which tend to discredit it produces anxiety which can be reduced in one of three ways: by discarding the disconfirmed belief; by blinding oneself to the fact that the prophecy has not been fulfilled; by reconfirming the belief and increasing proselytizing in the hope that "if more and more people can be persuaded that the system of belief is correct, then clearly it must be correct."[2]

Although Americans exhibited all three tendencies during the nineteen twenties, the latter two, and especially the third, constituted by far the most prevalent responses. With respect to Russia, for instance, there was little disposition to recognize that Americans had misinterpreted the direction and meaning of the revolutions of 1917. At first the Bolshevik regime was seen as merely a passing phase in the Russian drive to adopt American ideals. George Kennan predicted that the new regime would fail because it violated "certain fundamental economic laws," and for two years after the October Revolution the *New York Times* repeatedly (ninety-one times in all) reported that the Bolsheviks were on the brink of defeat. While Wilson joined England and France in an abortive attempt to bring down the new government by sending troops to Siberia, his ultimate response was to deny the existence of the Bolsheviks by withholding recognition; a refusal which the United States persisted in until Franklin Roosevelt took office in 1933.

On the domestic front, too, the defeat of American predictions about the effects of the First World War resulted in a nationwide tendency to reassert the viability and meaning of the very principles and beliefs upon which the failed prophecy had been erected. The full significance of the Red Scare of 1919 cannot be grasped unless it is perceived as an attempt to restate traditional American values, to reconfirm long-standing American images, to purify the nation and call it back to its historic mission by ridding it of intruding ideologies and groups. Stanley Coben, utilizing the anthropological theories of Anthony F. C. Wallace, has likened the Red Scare to a "revitalization movement" (other examples of which were the American Indian Ghost Dance cults of the late nineteenth century and the Boxer movement in China from 1898 to 1900), which under the spur of intensive social disruption attempts to relieve anxiety by reviving central cultural beliefs and values and eliminating alien influences.[3]

The emphasis upon revivification was omnipresent in the early postwar years: in the national repudiation of every possible form of radicalism; in the reaction against strikes and unionization; in the race riots of 1919 which struck out against the changed image and status of black Americans; in Warren Harding's assurance to his countrymen that theirs was a time for "not heroics but healing; not nostrums but normalcy; not revolution but restoration." A substantial portion of the nation faced the new decade not in excited anticipation of what might be or in stubborn satisfaction with what was, but with a nostalgic yearning for what had been. Americans continued to have grandiose hopes for the future, but increasingly their dreams were moulded upon the patterns of the past.

Nowhere was this clearer than in the national attitude toward immigration and acculturation. A heterogeneous conglomeration of peoples, Americans above all other nationalities have had to strive for a sense of national identity and speculate endlessly about the process by which the diverse national and ethnic groups emigrating to the United States became American. The most familiar concept, of course, was that of the melting pot which Crèvecoeur spoke of as early as the seventeen eighties when he wrote, "Here individuals of all nations are melted into a new race of men," and which Frederick Jackson Turner was still celebrating at the end of the nineteenth century when he concluded that "In the crucible of the frontier the immigrants were Americanized, liberated, and fused into a mixed race, English in neither nationality nor characteristics.'' ''America is God's crucible,'' the hero of the 1908 play *The Melting Pot* exclaimed, ''. . . A fig for your feuds and vendettas! Germans and Frenchmen, Irishmen and Englishmen, Jews and Russians—into the Crucible with you all! God is making the American.''

The concept of the melting pot was a unique and difficult base upon which to build a sense of identity, since it posited an ever-changing American image dependent entirely upon the ethnic components that were ''melted'' down. Indeed, for many Americans the concept was too difficult and, as Milton Gordon has shown, the melting pot was continually confronted by a counter concept—the idea of Anglo-conformity. If immigrants to the United States could not accommodate themselves to the nation's character, ''moral, political and physical,'' John Quincy Adams wrote in 1818, ''the Atlantic is always open to them to return to the land of their nativity and their fathers. To one thing they must make up their minds, or they will be disappointed in every expectation of happiness as Americans. They must cast off the European skin, never to resume it.'' ''Our task,'' an educator asserted one hundred years later, ''is to . . . assimilate and amalgamate these people as a part of our American race, and to implant in their children, so far as it can be done, the Anglo-Saxon conception of righteousness, law and order, and popular government. . . .''[4]

A number of reformers during the Progressive Era took the melting pot idea one step further in complexity by arguing for ''cultural pluralism.'' The United States, they maintained, should become a ''democracy of nationalities,'' a ''nation of nations,'' in which every ethnic group retained many of its identifying characteristics, each living in harmony with the others. While this concept may have come closer to describing the reality of the acculturation process than either of the others, it never took strong hold of the American imagination. The First World War not only made it difficult for ideas like cultural pluralism to take root; it led to the rejection of the melting pot itself. Profoundly disturbed by the sight of German- and Irish-Americans openly calling for the victory of the Central Powers and immigrants from the subject peoples of the Austrian Empire along with English- and French-Americans siding with the Allies, large numbers of Americans, from the President down, reacted against what were popularly called ''hyphenated Americans.'' ''When the Klan first appeared,'' its Imperial Wizard Hiram Wesley Evans recalled, ''the nation was in the confusion of sudden awakening from the lovely dream of the melting pot. . . . [Nordic Americans] decided that even the crossing of salt water did not dim a single spot on a leopard; that an alien usually remains an alien no matter what is done to him. . . . They decided that the melting pot was a ghastly failure. . . .''

For all his hyperbole, Evans reflected the national mood. In the Americanization movement with its emphasis upon "One country, one language, one flag," and in the immigration acts of 1921 and 1924 with their national origins formula which reversed the tide of immigration from southern and eastern Europe and Asia in favour of the more familiar northern European countries, this mood was made explicit. Americans in the postwar era were turning away from the idea of the melting pot with its dynamic, future-oriented concept of national identity and embracing the notion of Anglo-conformity which looked to the past and took as its model the early Anglo-American. If the term "melting pot" remained in use, it came to symbolize less and less a crucible which boiled *down* differences into a new composite identity and more and more one which boiled *out* differences into the image of the old American. To be sure, the melting pot concept had been attacked periodically in the nativist movements of the nineteenth century, but not until the nineteen twenties was the reaction strong enough to legislate it out of existence. In their immigration policies, as in so much else, Americans during the nineteen twenties exhibited a national urge to turn backwards in an effort to recapture the images and meaning of their country's youth.

III

It would, of course, be an egregious misreading of the nineteen twenties to maintain that it was *primarily* a backward-looking decade. The "New Era" deserved its title in many respects. The impact of the new technology, of the automobile, of mass production and consumption, of the radio, the movies and other forms of mass media, of modernist religious teachings in the churches, of the enhanced political and cultural influence of large cities, of the greater emphasis upon science in the schools which now reached far greater portions of the population than ever before in American history, of new moral codes and standards, was very real and constituted what Walter Lippmann called the "acids of modernity" which were eating into and transforming the entire society.

Historians in emphasizing these developments to the exclusion of all else, however, have been in danger of ignoring the tone and aspirations of a large part of the United States. As I have argued elsewhere at greater length, the tendency to see the nineteen twenties as an age of materialism in which the American people turned their backs upon idealism and reform does not accurately describe a decade which was marked by furious struggles waged over prohibition, religion, the rights of Catholics and Jews, the very nature of the morality and ethos that would define and guide Americans in the years to come. If the term "idealism" is used to define not merely those movements of which historians approve but any movement that puts forward a set of principles about which people feel strongly enough to band together and fight for, then idealism and crusading zeal were still very much alive throughout the decade.[5]

The millions of Americans who joined or at least sympathized with the Ku Klux Klan and fundamentalist movements and who fought for the enforcement of prohibition were an indication that a substantial part of the population greeted the new forces of the nineteen twenties with a sense of loss, frustration and antipathy. They were as alienated from the ethos and developments of the age as the bitterest members of the Lost Generation. They attempted to reverse the trends dominating modern America and return to the moral and ethical code of the past. They longed for the *Gemeinschaft,* the community, which they had been brought up to believe was central to America. They constituted one half of a pervasive sectional and cultural schism that disrupted the prewar progressive coalition, prevented the resurgence of a new political and economic reform movement, rendered the Democratic Party almost impotent, and prevented the nineteen twenties from ever becoming the materialistic, hedonistic age it has been pictured as.

The United States with its heterogeneity, individualism, mobility and success ethic may never have furnished fertile soil for the growth of a true *Gemeinschaft* culture characterized by permanence, intimacy and binding tradition. But the rural, small-town cultures of nineteenth-century America, which Robert Wiebe has called "island communities," at least approached this ideal in principle if not always in fact. The insularity of these communities was first seriously disturbed by the nationalizing tendencies of the expanding industrial economy after the Civil War. This threat to the independence and integrity of small-town America helped give rise to the reform movements of the late nineteenth and early twentieth centuries which Richard Hofstadter has characterized as efforts "to realize familiar and traditional ideals under novel circumstances." By the early decades of the twentieth century the threat had expanded inevitably to the social and cultural spheres. The further Americans were carried from their version of the *Gemeinschaft* the more ideal it seemed to become.

In 1925 a woman in Muncie, Indiana, recalled that

> In the nineties we were all much more together. People brought chairs and cushions out of the house and sat on the lawn evenings. We rolled out a strip of carpet and put cushions on the porch steps to take care of the unlimited overflow of neighbors that dropped by. We'd sit out so all evening. The younger couples perhaps would wander off for half an hour to get a soda but come back to join in the informal singing or listen while somebody strummed a mandolin or guitar.

By the twenties the citizens of Muncie were besieged by newspaper and magazine advertisements urging them to buy automobiles and "Increase Your

Weekend Touring Radius." "A man who works six days a week," a banker was quoted in one such ad, "and spends the seventh on his own doorstep certainly will not pick up the extra dimes in the great thoroughfares of life." On 4 July 1891, a Muncie merchant noted in his diary: "The town full of people—grand parade with representatives of different trades, an ox roasted whole, four bands, fire-works, races, greased pig, dancing all day, etc." On 4 July 1925, Robert and Helen Lynd found Muncie deserted; its inhabitants had taken to the road.

The automobile was only the most visible and dramatic symbol of the new forces that were eroding traditional standards and modes of action in religion, morality, familial patterns, life styles. The changes left large numbers of Americans bewildered and alienated. Unlike the writers and artists of the Lost Generation they could not escape to Europe or to bohemian enclaves within the United States. Instead they attempted to contain the forces reshaping America through a series of movements which, unlike the Red Scare and anti-immigration movements, were regional rather than national in character. It is important to understand that the cultural regionalism exemplified by prohibition, fundamentalism and the Klan was psychic and not purely geographic in character. All three movements had supporters in large cities as well as in small towns and rural communities, but it would be a mistake to deduce from this that they were therefore urban as well as rural in tone and purpose. The large numbers of urban migrants from rural, small-town America faced a difficult, often impossible, cultural adjustment which left them bereft of identity. They, perhaps even more than those who remained behind, craved a lost sense of community and longed for a reassertion of the old moral values. Though they were technically urbanites—inhabitants of the *Gesellschaft*—they were psychically attuned to the cultures from which they had emigrated. They supported prohibition, fundamentalism and the Klan precisely because these movements promised a real or symbolic flight from the new America back to the familiar confines of the old.

The fate of the prohibition experiment provides an excellent example. Prohibition came into being as a movement during the reform ethos of Jacksonian America and retained its reformist overtones right down to the nineteen twenties. It won the support of a large segment of the nation's progressives and was passed in the form of a constitutional amendment during the Progressive Era itself by reformers who could see nothing more reactionary in deciding that man for his own good must not drink alcoholic beverages than in ruling that he must not eat impure beef or work in dangerous and unhealthy surroundings. "Those who labour for prohibition," William Jennings Bryan declared, "are helping to create conditions which will bring the highest good to the greatest number without any injustice to any, for it is not injustice to any man to refuse him permission to enrich himself by injuring his fellowmen.'' To dismiss prohibition as simply a reform that failed is to miss the importance of what occurred to it during the twenties. As an *institutional* reform its impact was significant. In spite of lax and inefficient enforcement, the consumption of alcohol during the nineteen twenties was from 30 to 50 percent lower than it had been during the period 1911–1915. If this was not reflected in the image of the nineteen twenties it was because prohibition had the greatest impact upon the beer-drinking working classes and was least effective among the wealthier professional classes who could afford bootleg liquor and who set much of the tone and style of the decade. Nevertheless, sharply decreased rates of arrests for drunkenness, hospitalization for alcoholism and the incidence of such diseases as cirrhosis of the liver, all attest to the relative effectiveness of the reform.

Prohibition failed in the twenties not because it was institutionally impossible but because it was more than an institutional reform. It was in addition, as Joseph Gusfield has argued so convincingly, a ''symbolic reform'' which gave recognition and legitimacy to the norms and values of rural, Protestant America. It existed as a national symbol of the work habits and morality of the old America; it clearly told every immigrant and every urbanite what it meant to be an American; it attempted to make the American Protestant ideal of the good life national by enshrining it in law. ''The hope of perpetuating our liberties,'' an advocate of prohibition maintained, ''is to help the foreigners correct any demoralizing custom, and through self-restraint assimilate American ideals.'' This cultural imperialism, perhaps even more than the material effects of the reform, infuriated the urban, industrial, immigrant populations who constituted the chief opponents of prohibition. As the decade progressed, prohibition was transformed from a complex reform movement into an essentially cultural crusade which cut through the lines of reform. Increasingly it lost many of its reformist supporters and forged natural alliances with the multitude of other movements which had as their aim the nostalgic reassertion of a fading life style.[6]

The very defensiveness of these movements in the face of the new developments of the twenties forced them into an aggressive posture. Their fears and aspirations were evident in the rhetoric of the Klan's leader, Hiram Wesley Evans, who lamented in 1926 that ''the Nordic American today is a stranger in large parts of the land his fathers gave him.'' Traditional Americans, Evans complained, were beset by confusion and hesitancy ''in sharp contrast to the clear, straightforward purposes of our earlier years.'' They were plagued by futility in religion and a general moral breakdown: ''The sacredness of our Sabbath, of our homes, of chastity, and finally even of our right to teach our own children in our own schools fundamental facts and truths were torn away from us. Those who maintained the old standards did so only in the face of constant ridicule.'' Robert Moats Miller has argued that the Klan of the twenties was a genuine counterrevolutionary movement. Certainly, under Evans's leadership it sought to combat and defeat the entire host of evils threatening its countrymen. The Klan, Evans warned, would be satisfied with no less than ''a return of power into the hands of the everyday, not highly cultured, not overly intellectualized, but entirely unspoiled and not de-Americanized average citizen of the old stock.''

In the final analysis, however, the movements for which Evans spoke were less counterrevolutionary than defensive; movements on the run which were struggling vainly to stave off the erosion of their cultures and life style— but not at the price of giving up all of the advantages of modernity. It is this that explains why they were so often content with the symbols rather than the substance of power. By the middle of the decade the fundamentalists had begun to stem the tide of the modernist advance within the churches and, through local pressure and intimidation, had made serious inroads upon the teaching of evolution in the schools. But this was not enough. They demanded such statewide laws as the Tennessee Anti-Evolution Act of 1925 not because they really desired to overturn modern education in the states and the nation, but because they craved the comfort of statutory symbols which would settle the question of whose version of the good society was legitimate. The Governor of Tennessee recognized this when, after signing the bill into law, he told the legislature: ''After a careful examination, I can find nothing of consequence in the books now being taught in our schools with which this bill will interfere in the slightest manner. Probably the law will never be applied.'' All that the framers of the bill intended, he insisted, was to lodge ''a distinct protest against an irreligious tendency to exalt so-called science, and deny the Bible in some schools and quarters. . . .''

The extent to which symbols became paramount was manifest in the trauma and fear induced by Al Smith's campaign for the Presidency in 1928. It was not Smith's political programme which in many respects met the economic needs of rural, small-town America better than that of the Republican Party, nor even his Catholicism which activated these feelings, but his urban background, his appeal to the polyglot populations of the big cities, his very speech, dress and manner. Al Smith, the Anti-Saloon League's journal observed, ''is different from any candidate of either party within the knowledge of the present generation. . . . He is not in harmony with the principles of our forefathers.'' The southern Democratic editor George Fort Milton warned that Smith's primary appeal would be to the aliens, the Negroes, the Catholics, the Jews, ''who feel that the older America, the America of the Anglo-Saxon stock, is a hateful thing which must be overturned and humiliated,'' and called upon ''the Old America, the America of Jackson and of Lincoln and Wilson'' to ''rise up in wrath'' and defeat them.

Although the nationalizing and standardizing forces of large-scale industry and the mass-media were more deeply entrenched in the Republican Party of Herbert Hoover, Smith's defeat was greeted with widespread rejoicing. America, the *St. Paul Pioneer Press* announced jubilantly,

> is not yet dominated by its great cities. Control of its destinies still remains in the small communities and rural regions, with their traditional conservatism and solid virtues. . . . Main Street is still the principal thoroughfare of the nation.

IV

Had nostalgia in the nineteen twenties been confined to the national tendency to reassert traditional values and images following the failed prophecies of the First World War and to the past-orientated movements of the culturally alienated, it could be treated as an important force but one still on the periphery of a decade that seemed so dedicated to and enamoured of change. The most pervasive manifestation of nostalgia in the twenties, however, took the form of the ambivalence I discussed at the outset of this essay. In 1914 Walter Lippmann wrote of Woodrow Wilson's "inner contradiction": "He knows that there is a new world demanding new methods, but he dreams of an older world. He is torn between the two. It is a very deep conflict in him between what he knows and what he feels." This inner contradiction ran like a thread throughout the decade.

No one has seen this more perceptively or illustrated it more brilliantly than John William Ward in his study of the reaction to Charles Lindbergh's flight across the Atlantic in 1927. Lindbergh had not been the first to conquer the Atlantic. Almost ten years before his flight a British dirigible had crossed the ocean and in 1919 two planes, one manned by a crew of five and the other with two aboard, repeated the feat. But Lindbergh did it *alone*. ". . . no kingly plane for him," an American bard rhapsodized. "No endless data, comrades, moneyed chums; / No boards, no councils, no directors grim— / He plans ALONE . . . and takes luck as it comes." In a technological age of growing organization, complexity and facelessness, Lindbergh symbolized the self-sufficient individual of the past. Compared with Robinson Crusoe, Daniel Boone, Davy Crockett, he was a reminder of America's own uncomplicated beginnings; a product not of the city but of the farm, not of schools and formal training but of individual initiative and self-contained genius.

There was, of course, something jarring in all this. Lindbergh had not been alone. He was enveloped in a plane which was the product of the city, of technology, of organization. In spite of their odes to individualism, Americans really never lost sight of this. Lindbergh himself recognized it when he paid tribute to the industries that had created his plane and entitled the volume describing his flight, *We*. President Coolidge proudly pointed out that over one hundred companies had furnished material and services in the plane's construction. Thus on the other side Lindbergh's flight was recognized as the triumph of modernity. As another American poet put it: "All day I felt the pull / Of the Steel Miracle." In these two reactions Ward has documented one of the basic tensions in American life. The crucial point is that this tension was not merely present in the antithetical reactions of different groups but *within* the responses of the same groups and individuals. Americans were still torn between the past and the future, the individual and society.[7]

It is difficult to find any aspect of American culture in the twenties that did not exhibit this tension. Motion pictures, which came into their own as a popular art form during the decade with 100,000,000 people attending 20,000 theatres weekly by 1926, seem on the surface to have been one long celebration of the new woman, the new morality, the new youth, the new consumption patterns that marked postwar America. Films with such titles as *Forbidden Fruit, Flapper Wives, Week-end Wives, Parlor, Bedroom and Bath, Madness of Youth, Children of Divorce, Modern Maidens, Dancing Mothers, Love Mart* were advertised as featuring "Brilliant men, beautiful jazz babies, champagne baths, midnight revels, petting parties in the purple dawn, all ending in one terrific smashing climax that makes you gasp." The reality fell short of the promises. As uninhibited as they might have been, the movies of the twenties rarely failed to conclude without a justification of the moral standards of the past. Flappers and "It" girls married at the end of the film and entered a life of middle-class respectability. Faithless husbands and wives mended their ways and returned to patient, forgiving mates. The new woman may have been depicted as tough but, as David Robinson has put it, their toughness was used to protect their purity, not to dispose of it. The widespread popular revulsion against the excesses of the first wave of postwar movies forced Hollywood to resort to the cliché of the happy and moral ending; a standard which never marked European movies to the same extent and which made them seem, to movie critics at least, less artificial and more realistic.[8]

The career of Cecil B. DeMille is instructive. After attempting to make the bathroom and bedroom national shrines in his series of postwar sexual comedies, DeMille turned to the public for suggestions for new films. Impressed by the number of requests for religious themes, DeMille hit upon a new formula in his widely popular films, *The Ten Commandments* (1923) and *The King of Kings* (1927). Sex and orgies were still prominent but they were now placed within a religious framework with a moral message. "Better than any other director of the era," Arthur Knight has written of De-

Mille, "he seems to have apprehended a basic duality in his audiences—on the one hand their tremendous eagerness to see what they considered sinful and taboo, and on the other, the fact that they could enjoy sin only if they were able to preserve their own sense of righteous respectability in the process." This was the result not of hypocrisy but of the kind of tension manifest in the response to Lindbergh. Just as Americans could accept the fruits of modern technology only if they could assure themselves that the potency of the individual was enhanced in the process, so they could enjoy the freedom of the new morality only by surrounding it by the verities of the past.

The continued popularity of the comedy film throughout the twenties provided an outlet for the disquiet the decade produced in many Americans. Charlie Chaplin, Buster Keaton, Harold Lloyd, the Keystone Kops, did not celebrate the new age, they satirized it; they did not worship order and stability, they emphasized surrealistic anarchy and mayhem; they did not deify the products of a consumer society, they destroyed them with wilful abandon; they did not bow down to the image and manners of the new middle classes, they parodied them with hilarious accuracy. They focussed not on the strong but on the weak, not on the confident man on the make but on the bewildered man whose direction and goals were uncertain.

Even more indicative of the difficulty Americans had in embracing the new was the increased popularity of the Western film, which reached its classic stage in the twenties. The West continued to be a place of regeneration. In *The Mollycoddle* (1920), a young man brought up amid the decadence and over-civilization of France returned to his native West and regained the latent virility which enabled him to throw off his effete manners and emerge as a hero. Above all, the West continued to be the centre of virtue and morality. The Western heroes of the nineteen twenties—Tom Mix, Buck Jones, Hoot Gibson—were strong, clean-living, uncomplicated men who needed the help of neither institutions nor technology in defeating darkly clad villains and urban scoundrels. They were living embodiments of the innocence, freedom and morality which Americans identified with and longed to regain if only vicariously.

The desire to escape from the complexity of their own time led American moviegoers back beyond the history of their own West. In the immensely popular films of Douglas Fairbanks—*The Mark of Zorro* (1920), *The Three Musketeers* (1921), *Robin Hood* (1922), *The Thief of Bagdad* (1923–24), *Don Q., Son of Zorro* (1925), *The Black Pirate* (1926), *The Gaucho* (1927), *The Iron Mask* (1929)—and in the desert epics of Rudolph Valentino, Americans were transported to a world in which moral issues were clearly delineated and the ability of the individual to influence his own destiny was undiluted by modernity. This search for simplicity accounts also for the surprising success of such anthropological documentary films as *Na-*

nook of the North (1922) and *Moana* (1926) as well as the literary vogue of
Harlem and the fascination with Negro folklore throughout the decade. In
these re-creations of Arctic Eskimos, South Sea Islanders, urban and rural
blacks, Americans of the twenties were able simultaneously to feel superior
to those who lacked the benefits of modern technology and to envy them for
their sense of community, their lack of inhibitions, their closer contact with
their environment and with themselves.

During the nineteen twenties the newspaper comic strip, like the movies, became a regular feature of American popular culture with tens of millions of readers daily by 1924. Like the movies, too, the comic strip had its
anarchic side. *Mutt and Jeff, Bringing Up Father, Abie the Agent, Barney
Google, Moon Mullins, Krazy Kat* laughed at propriety, order, romantic
love, the sanctity of money and position. It was through the medium of
nostalgia rather than satire, however, that the strips had their greatest impact. "If historians of the next century were to rely upon the comic strip,"
Stephen Becker has written, "they would conclude that we were a peaceful
lot of ruminant burghers from 1920 to 1929, with only occasional flashes of
inspired insanity, and that our social conflicts and national crises were settled by family conferences at the dinner table." *The Gumps* and *Gasoline
Alley,* which first appeared in 1917 and 1919 respectively, were typical of
an entire genre of family-centred comic strips which constituted one of the
most popular forms of mass culture in the nineteen twenties. The characters
inhabiting these strips were distinguished primarily by their lack of distinction: decent, plain-looking, dependable, unexciting, independent but
community-oriented people who were destined to live out their lives among
neighbours just like themselves. Their very normality, the strips seemed to
be saying, made them worth celebrating and emulating. Their virtues were
those of the old America and when they strayed from these (for as normal
people they had foibles) they were brought to account sharply.

A striking feature of the comic strips of the nineteen twenties was their
almost total lack of heroic figures. The central males in *Toots and Casper,
Tillie the Toiler, Betty, Fritzi Ritz,* and ultimately *Blondie,* were ineffectual,
usually diminutive men whose entire lives revolved around the statuesque,
beautiful women for whom the strips were named. It was from their wives
or sweethearts (e.g., their present or potential families) that they derived
meaning and purpose. The financial tycoon Daddy Warbucks of *Little Orphan Annie* was one of the decade's few prototypes of the incredibly powerful heroes who were to proliferate in the comic strips of the Great Depression. But in spite of the great wealth of her capitalist benefactor, Annie's
triumphs in situation after situation were due, more often than not, to her
own inner qualities and the innocence, goodness and old-fashioned virtues
of the average people who were always on hand to help her. The comic

strips of the nineteen twenties, with their quiet resignation, their emphasis upon steadiness, their celebration of the average, might appear to have been incongruous additions to newspapers whose front pages heralded the new, advertised the spectacular achievements of uncommon men, and called for endless change and progress. But they were a necessary addition, for they comprised the other half of the cultural equation that characterized the United States throughout the decade.[9]

V

This web of ambivalence must be unravelled in order to reveal the meaning of any aspect of American culture in the twenties. Serious artists and musicians attempted to come to terms with modern forms of painting and music at the same time that they were returning to the themes and sources of an earlier America: the art of the Shakers, the Indians and the colonial primitives, in painting; the tribal chants of the Indians, the spirituals of black slaves, the songs of cowboys and the Anglo-American folk, in music. Ernest Hemingway spoke for many members of his literary generation when he recalled that avant-garde Paris was a good place in which to think and write about his native Michigan. During the twenties Americans found it far easier to come to terms with the new if it could be surrounded somehow by the aura of the old.

In their accounts of the "galloping materialism" of the nineteen twenties, historians have made much of the secularization of American religion during the decade and the penchant Americans had for incorporating within the religious message the vulgarizations of American business rhetoric and ideology. The advertising executive Bruce Barton in his best-selling *The Man Nobody Knows* (1925) transformed Jesus into a twentieth-century hustler, "the most popular dinner guest in Jerusalem," who "picked up twelve men from the bottom ranks of business and forged them into an organization that conquered the world." Comparisons like these were ubiquitous but the reasons for them may not be quite as simple as we have assumed. It is entirely possible that modern businessmen were led to this rhetoric not out of supreme confidence in their standards and vocation but, on the contrary, because they were defensive and needed the ideals of Christ to justify and sell themselves to the American people. After announcing his aphorism, "The business of America is business," President Coolidge was quick to add this strained and obviously defensive analogy: "The man who builds a factory builds a temple, the man who works there worships there, and to each is due not scorn and blame but reverence and praise." "Would Isaiah be writing more Bibles if he were here today," Henry Ford asked, and answered self-consciously, "He would probably be gaining experience; living down in the shops among workingmen; working over a set of blueprints; . . . There is no reason why a prophet should not be an engineer instead of a preacher.''

Statements like these, when placed beside the rhetoric of businessmen who more often than not sounded like figures out of nineteenth-century McGuffey Readers or Horatio Alger novels, indicate the need American business spokesmen still had for some noble purpose which stretched beyond mere material reward; they continually manifested the inability to accept the practices of modern business and technology purely in terms of practicality and efficiency. When Henry Ford declared, ''I am more interested in people than I am in profits. . . . I don't give a hang for money as such, only as it helps me to help people with it,'' and when Herbert Hoover studded his speeches and writings with such words as ''salvation,'' ''devotion,'' ''service,'' ''dedication,'' ''liberty,'' ''vision,'' ''courage,'' ''faith,'' they were not derided by a cynical, materialistic generation but enshrined as two of the chief icons of America's business civilization. The production techniques of American business in the twenties may have been new, but the images used to justify them were old and hallowed.

To stress the force of nostalgia and the presence of ambivalence is not to deny the realities of change. The desire to have things both ways—to accept the fruits of progress without relinquishing the fundamentals of the old order—explains many of the tensions in American life, but it has never led to complete paralysis. In spite of the persistent lag between actuality and perception, there has been a gradual acceptance of changes and a reordering of desires, expectations and action throughout American history. Americans in the twenties, as before and since, tended to turn to the past in their ideology and rhetoric more than in their actions. Still, the existence of this dualism between a past and future orientation is important for if it has not prevented action it has certainly impeded and shaped it. ''The health of a people,'' Alfred North Whitehead has observed, ''depends largely on their ability to question their inherited symbols in light of contemporary actualities, to keep them fluid, vibrant, and responsive.'' The nineteen twenties had begun with the failure of President Wilson's prophecy concerning the First World War. They were to end with the failure of President Hoover's prophecy that the United States was on the threshold of abolishing poverty and ensuring the promises of the American dream to all its citizens. The confused and ambivalent symbols and images with which the American people emerged from the nineteen twenties made it all the more difficult and painful for them to cope with the material and psychic traumas that lay before them.

11

American Culture and
the Great Depression

In the Fall of 1984, I was a member of an American Studies delegation invited by the Chinese Ministry of Education to visit universities and government institutes in China to determine the state of their study and teaching of the United States and to suggest what American scholars might do to further those endeavors in the Chinese academic world. During that absorbing journey I came to know Kai Erikson, a professor of sociology at Yale University, who talked with me about a two-part series, "Reflections on America," he was publishing in *The Yale Review,* which he edited, and to which he asked me to contribute a piece reflecting on American life during the Great Depression.

Though I was born five days before Franklin Roosevelt was inaugurated and have some youthful impressions of the closing years of the Depression, Kai was clearly asking me to contribute scholarly, not personal, reflections. As a *scholar,* my Depression experiences really began only when I came to Berkeley to teach in 1962. In my first year I was asked to teach a large lecture course on the United States from 1929 to the present. Fifteen weeks— forty-five lectures—on America *since* 1929; a period of only thirty-three years duration! I was overwhelmed; nothing in my undergraduate studies at The City College of New York or my graduate studies at Columbia University had prepared me to teach those years in such detail. Indeed, though a few of my teachers, like William Leuchtenburg, occasionally ventured beyond the Great Depression, that was rare. Nor had American historians in general yet written much about those years. Thus in the first few years of my lecture course, my students found me spending what must have seemed to them an inordinate amount of time on the 1930s, with which I felt much more familiar, as a historian, than the rest of the period. Although my early lectures tended to be political and institutional, I quickly became fascinated with and engaged in understanding thirties' culture and began to experiment with ways of presenting that culture—especially in its popular and mass manifestations—to my students.

While I had not yet published anything on the Depression when Kai spoke with me, it was my intention—and still is—to someday write a book on American culture and the Great Depression. Thus, utilizing materials from my class lectures, from a lecture on Depression culture I had given in varied formats at several museums and universities, and from a paper I was preparing for the 1985 annual meeting of the American Folklore Society, I took this opportunity to articulate in print some of my still tentative overviews concerning Americans and their culture during the Great Depression.

After this essay was published in *The Yale Review,* 74 (Winter 1985), I went on to write a number of other pieces on Depression culture, three of which are included in this volume and follow the present essay. In re-reading the four Depression pieces for this collection, I found that I obviously had liked my ways of putting things so well I occasionally used them more than once in essays which were written over a series of years, published separately, and not originally intended to be read consecutively. Borrowing from oneself is not one of the cardinal sins; Mozart and many of his colleagues did it repeatedly. But in my case, I fear, the repetitions don't bring quite the same pleasures. Thus I have left this first essay as it was originally written and have tried to remove as many redundancies as practical from the three essays that follow it.

> Say, my mind's going back to 19 and 29.
> Say, my mind's going back to 19 and 29.
> Say, I lose my job, and I didn't have one more dime.

When he recorded these words in 1974, the bluesman K. C. Douglas was in good company. America's mind has seldom strayed too far from that year of trauma and the decade of depression that followed it. Every economic setback since the Second World War has brought inevitable comparisons with, and pervasive fears of, a return to the conditions that prevailed during the Great Depression. The thirties have become one of the most essential criteria by which we measure our well-being and security. But their significance transcends this. That almost half a century after the Depression ended Americans still sing about it, write and read about it, make and watch movies depicting it, pay fascinated attention to the iconographic gallery created by contemporary photographers, attend to the testimony of its survivors, revive its music, its drama, and its fashions, attests to the profound impact the Depression has had upon our culture and our imaginations.

It is ironic, then, that we still know so little about the culture of a decade that has made such a lasting imprint upon us, and that so much of what we do know is so overwhelmingly political and institutional. Until relatively recently, we have spoken and written as if the political culture of the 1930s represented all of American culture; as if Franklin Roosevelt and his advisers spoke for the vast majority of Americans; as if one could understand the impact of the Depression upon American consciousness by comprehending the reform impulse of the 1930s. Until we begin to explore more fully than we have the varied cultural dimensions of the Depression decade, we will continue to have more questions than answers.

One of the most important and interesting questions that continues to disturb us plagued contemporaries as well. "I do not know why there isn't more revolutionary spirit developing," the social worker Lillian Wald mused in 1931. Nor do we know all these years later. "The amazing thing," Sherwood Anderson observed, "is that there is so little bitterness," and we continue to share his amazement. "Our vegetable garden is coming along well and we are less worried about revolution than we used to be," the *New Yorker* commented in 1932 when conditions were close to their nadir. "People are in a sad but not a rebellious mood."

There were some, like Chicago's mayor Anton Cermak, who seriously predicted revolution if conditions did not improve rapidly. And there were others who echoed the impatience of New York's Fiorello LaGuardia: "We are either going to have child labor laws, old age pensions, and unemployment insurance in this country, or we are going to have chaos and disorder, and something worse. There is something peculiar about human beings. They just simply refuse to go hungry. And you can't preach loyalty on an empty stomach."

There is abundant evidence that Cermak and LaGuardia were correct: had there been no eventual social and economic reform of significance, there would have been upheaval of some kind. "I am going to feed my children," a Kentucky miner told an investigating committee. "I am going to kill, murder, rob for my children because I won't let my children starve. . . . If you put a man into poverty then you send him down to Hell and sin. Believe me, it would not take much for me to go down and steal a good square meal." Early in the New Deal, a Michigan villager told a federal official:

> I don't believe you realize how bad things were getting before this set-up started. . . . They all said that if things got any worse and something didn't happen pretty soon, they'd go down Main Street and crash the windows and take what they needed. They wouldn't pick on the little stores. They'd go after the big stores first. . . . No man is going to let his wife and children starve to death.

Even as the New Deal reform began to expand in 1935, the bluesman Carl
Martin sang:

> Everybody's crying: "Let's have a New Deal,"
> 'Cause I've got to make a living,
> If I have to rob and steal.

Nevertheless, it would be a mistake to convert such testimony into descriptions of the national mood. No matter how completely one may agree
with those who predicted upheaval if reform did not come, the remarkable
thing about the American people before reform did come was not their action but their inaction, not their demands but their passivity, not their revolutionary spirit but their traditionalism.

Probably no people is ever really prepared for major economic crisis.
But it would be difficult to find a nation as unprepared as the United States
was in 1929. To be sure, there were significant groups—regional, occupational, ethnic—that had not shared in the abundance of twentieth-century
industrial America. For many black Americans the Depression merely intensified an unjust economic situation that had long been prevalent. "De rag-
gedy man see de hahd time, . . . When his money is gone," black workers
in the South sang during the 1930s. "Now you an' me see de hahd time,
. . . Sence we wuz bawn." Nevertheless, as a people, Americans had not
experienced a major protracted economic crisis since the 1890s.

The shock caused by the Depression stemmed not alone from lack of
experience. It came also—and perhaps largely—from ideology and expectations. The American people, of course, did not enter the Depression as a
tabula rasa; they entered it with ideals, values, and hopes—and one must
understand how these interacted with the events of the 1930s. Belief in secular progress had been traditional with Americans at least since the era of
the Enlightenment and continued to exert great influence throughout the early
decades of the twentieth century—especially in its material form. It is because the prophecy of inevitable progress had become so intricately equated
with material growth and material expansion that the Depression had a particularly profound emotional and psychological impact. In one prolonged
blow a large part of the expectations of the American people seemed to have
been stripped away.

Americans had been living in what they had assured themselves was a
supremely rational and progressive society. Suddenly they found themselves
inhabiting a land whose cruel incongruities and ironies could no longer be
ignored. Everywhere there was want and yet everywhere there was plenty.
People were hungry and crops rotted in the field. Children went without
clothes while clothing factories closed down and cotton crops were being
destroyed to keep them off the market. Americans were bewildered by the

rapidity of events and what appeared to be the completeness of the destruction of their plans, their expectations, their certainties. Not only were they
suddenly transformed from recipients of the ever-increasing fruits of a golden
land into victims of malevolent forces, but these forces appeared to be almost anonymous and unidentifiable. It was, in those early years, hard to
know either where to turn or whom to blame. In *The Grapes of Wrath*, John
Steinbeck captured the pervasive bewilderment, the sense of impotent anger,
that characterized so much of Depression America. Squatting in the door-
ways of their cabins, his Oklahoma tenant farmers watch tractors sent by
the bank push down the fences and houses which had demarcated the land
they and their fathers before them had farmed. An outraged tenant approaches the tractor driver and engages him in the following dialogue:

> "[This house] is mine. I built it. You bump it down—I'll be in the window
> with a rifle. You even come too close and I'll pot you like a rabbit."
>
> "It's not me. There's nothing I can do. I'll lose my job if I don't do
> it. And look—suppose you kill me? They'll just hang you, but long before
> you're hung there'll be another guy on the tractor, and he'll bump the
> house down. You're not killing the right guy."
>
> "That's so," the tenant said. "Who gave you orders? I'll go after
> him. He's the one to kill."
>
> "You're wrong. He got his orders from the bank. The bank told him,
> 'Clear those people out or it's your job.' "
>
> "Well, there's a president of the bank. There's a board of directors.
> I'll fill up the magazine of the rifle and go into the bank."
>
> The driver said, "Fellow was telling me the bank gets orders from the
> East. The orders were, 'Make the land show profit or we'll close you up.' "
>
> "But where does it stop? Who can we shoot? I don't aim to starve to
> death before I kill the man that's starving me."
>
> "I don't know. Maybe there's nobody to shoot. Maybe the thing isn't
> men at all . . ."

The more than one million men and women drifting through the country on
foot and in freight cars were an appropriate symbol of the mood of the
people at large. Even their protests often had no readily identifiable ends.
There was a good deal of anger without meaningful focus, a good deal of
movement without direction.

Very much related to the factor of trauma in explaining the mood of the
American people in the early years of the Depression was that of fear. In
answering her own question as to why there was so little revolutionary spirit
in the country, Lillian Wald wrote: "People are so glad to be kept above
the starving line that the fear of losing that may be at the bottom." A number of scholars have argued that the borderline of economic and social ca-

tastrophe does not constitute the optimal environment for radical activity. "The abjectly poor, and all those persons whose energies are entirely absorbed by the struggle for daily sustenance, are conservative because they cannot afford the effort of taking thought for the day after to-morrow," Thorstein Veblen wrote in the wake of the Depression of 1893. And Eric Hoffer has maintained: "The intensified struggle for existence is a static rather than a dynamic influence." This proposition—that the struggle for sustenance and the search for personal security so dominated the lives of many Americans that they had little time to worry about larger issues—needs further testing and exploration. It is certainly true that such early Depression expressions of agrarian dissent as the Cow War and the Farm Holiday Movement were strongest in western Iowa, eastern Nebraska, and southern Minnesota, where land values were high and income well above average, and much less prevalent in areas with low land values and high rates of tenancy. It is equally true that when too many people were scrambling for too few jobs it was difficult to build a sense of group solidarity—a sense which American workers have rarely had in any case.

We do not yet understand enough about the unemployed in the United States. Contemporary studies of unemployment in Europe found that the hate and envy of the unemployed often focused upon an unexpected object: not the employer but the employed. The world, according to an unemployed man in Poland, was divided into only two groups: those with jobs and those without. Fear and insecurity helped to dissolve or weaken many of the bonds that had existed among workers. "The unemployed," two students of the situation in Austria and Poland in the early 1930s concluded, "are a mass only numerically, not socially."

This proposition, too, needs testing for the United States. But we also need to understand what it meant for those who were employed to know that if they lost the job they had they were unlikely to find other work. In 1939, Anna Novak spoke of her experiences in the Chicago meat-packing houses when she had begun to work there eight years earlier:

> We used to have to buy the foremen presents, you know. On all the holidays, Christmas, Easter, Holy Week, Good Friday, you'd see the men coming to work with hip pockets bulging and take the foremen off in corners, handing over their half pints. They sure would lay for you if you forgot their whiskey, too. Your job wasn't worth much if you didn't observe the holiday "customs." The women had to bring 'em bottles, just the same as the men. You could get along swell if you let the boss slap you on the behind and feel you up. God, I hate that stuff, you don't know! I'd rather work *any* place but in the stockyards just for that reason alone. I tried to get out a couple of times. Went to work for Container Corp. [Box

factory near the yards.] Used to swing a hammer on those big wooden
boxes. Look at my hands, now. [Her hands are misshapen; blunted, thick-
ened fingers and calloused at every joint.] My husband wouldn't let me
keep on there, it got to be too much for me to handle. I had to have work
so I went back to the yards.

It was not unusual testimony. "In '34 they had me going like a clock 10
and 12 hours a day. I used to get home so tired I'd just sit down at the table
and cry like a baby," Mary Siporin remembered in the closing years of the
decade. "I mean there's a conditioning here by the Depression," a garbage
worker told interviewers, many years later. "I'm what I call a security cat.
I don't dare switch [jobs]. 'Cause I got too much whiskers on it, seniority."

The testimony of both the employed and unemployed in the early phases
of the Depression helps us to comprehend just how important the element
of fear and the desire for security were to the Depression generation. When
the sociologists Robert and Helen Lynd revisited "Middletown"—Muncie,
Indiana—in 1935, they found a community "scarred by fear." In the decades following the Second World War, the tendency to look back nostal-
gically upon the thirties as a time of commitment, crusading, and reform
has led us to lose sight of so mundane a concern as security. To be sure,
the quest for security could be channeled into the area of reform, as it was
under the New Deal, whose most enduring and popular reforms dealt with
such matters as unemployment insurance and old-age pensions. One might
argue as well that the hunger for security was even more important than a
sense of class solidarity in leading millions of workers to support the CIO
in the late 1930s. But in the bleak early years of the Depression, when
America's economic situation and prospects were at their worst, this quest
for security, this concern with one's own fortunes and needs, can help to
explain the initial inaction of the American people.

Just how personal the search for security was in the early thirties can
be seen in American advertising. Under a drawing of a couple lost in a dark
forest of imposing trees, a pharmaceutical company declared: "The past few
years have been years of worry. Fears have walked abroad. Nerves have
been harassed as never before." Though the trend had begun earlier, and
was certainly prominent during the 1920s, the emphasis on the fear of personal failure and the desire for a sense of personal security intensified and
became one of the dominant motifs in Depression-decade advertising. Magazine ads in the early 1930s were filled with pictures of anxious men and
women plagued by lack of sleep, lack of confidence, lack of financial means,
lack of foresight and planning; beset by the scourge of halitosis, flawed skin,
yellow teeth, bad English, caffeine addiction; worried by every fear imaginable. The Hartford Fire Insurance Company warned, "Modern life, with

all its ease and sophistication, is still afflicted by the monsters of disaster. Always they are ready and waiting to wipe out the savings of years or to impose upon you unexpected and disastrous financial obligations." "ARE YOU GUARDING YOUR CHILD?" Phillips' Milk of Magnesia wanted to know. "IS A MOTHER'S LOVE ENOUGH?" Johnson & Johnson wondered, while warning that "even some bandages that are plainly marked "sterilized" on the package are not worthy of your trust . . . dirty fingers may have touched them . . . destroyed their cleanliness." A host of advertisers emphasized that "in times like these," "when jobs are hard to get—hard to hold," when "the man who is sick—or half-sick—is soon outstripped by competition," nobody could afford to "miss a single day" due to colds, constipation, sore muscles, or aching backs.

In the insecure, disaster-prone world of American advertising, relief was just around the corner. "Irritable. Nervous. Jumpy. He knows it himself, but doesn't know why. What a pity someone doesn't tell him—*before he cracks!*" Happily, General Foods was there to point its finger at the coffee habit and its cure: drinking Postum. Jobs could be kept, lovers won, social acceptance assured by bathing with Lifebuoy Soap, shaving with Gillette Razor Blades, drinking Ovaltine, using Listerine Mouth Wash. And always, the security that seemed so elusive could be assured. Bankers Life warned against the man who was "Kind to His WIFE but Cruel to His WIDOW," and stressed how unnecessary such behavior was since "Security is such a precious thing to a woman . . . such an easy thing for a man to give." "Securely yours," an automobile ad boasted, "here is a picture of security— the security to seek for your family, the security that is theirs on the highway too, in a body by Fisher."

If security was in fact more difficult to obtain in the real world, the world of the ads was not one of unremitting fantasy; it mirrored—and intensified—one of the decade's most persistent and profound concerns. Indeed, the overt assurance that security was within reach if only individuals took the proper initiative was often belied by the dominant visual images of the ads. The somber tones, the dark shadows, the anxious faces, the haunted looks that pervaded so much of American advertising were a testament to the anxieties, fears, and despair that haunted so many Americans as the Great Crash of 1929 settled into the Great Depression of the 1930s.

If we left our explanation of the mood of the American people during the initial stages of the Great Depression at this—the result of shock and fear— we would have explained a good deal. But we would be overlooking the most interesting and possibly the most important element: the tendency to internalize the responsibility for one's position which often led to feelings of shame.

Americans had long been taught that human beings were ultimately responsible for themselves; that they were the architects of their own fortunes, the masters of their own fate; that material success was a sign of virtue, and failure a sign of personal worthlessness; that poverty was not merely unfortunate, but somehow disreputable, even sinful; that unemployment was an indication of indolence and failure. Despite all of the objective evidence that the American people were victims of external circumstances largely beyond their control, substantial numbers of them had so internalized the traditional sense of personal responsibility for such conditions as unemployment and poverty, that while on the one hand they might reject Herbert Hoover for not giving them adequate help, on the other they felt a deep sense of shame for being in such a dependent position.

Though the *New Yorker* was hardly a representative journal, it was speaking for more than its usual constituency when it asserted in 1932: "It has always seemed to us difficult to be a rebel in this country where there is nothing to rebel against except one's own stupidity." Following an automobile tour of the country, Sherwood Anderson was almost incredulous at the attitudes of the people he met. Hitchhiker after hitchhiker he picked up on the road apologized to him, a total stranger, for being down and out. "It is a very queer thing but the truth is that we Americans, who talk so proudly of our individuality and of our independence, are always going about explaining ourselves." The reason for this, he concluded, is that "We Americans have all been taught, from childhood, that it is a sort of moral obligation for each of us to rise, to get up in the world. . . . Progress. Progress. That was the cry." He invited his readers to test his theory for themselves:

> . . . the next time you are on the road pick up one of the Americans now down and out. Talk to him in a friendly way. See how quickly he begins to explain himself, to apologize. It may be that he has nothing to do with the circumstances that have put him where he is but just the same he feels guilty. He does not blame his civilization. He feels that in some way he is not a good American because he has not risen above his fellows.
>
> There is the wheat farmer who for a few years was a prosperous farmer. Now he is down and out. He is old and knows he cannot get work. He was going to live with some of his dead wife's relatives and was ashamed. He needed little encouragement from me to begin explaining himself. Although he had worked hard all his life, raising food for people to eat, he was in no way indignant about what his civilization had done to him. He should have been smarter, shrewder, should have taken more advantage of other men. "It's my own fault," he said, "I was not smart enough."

As if to document Anderson's observations, A. S. Johnson, a migrant farmer from Arkansas living in a Farm Security Administration Camp in Yuba City,

California, in 1940, reflected on his own experiences: "Our sorrows and trials and tribulations are brought on by ourselves, more than anybody. Mine has. I'm ajudging everybody from myself." When one of his interviewers asked him why he thought his troubles were his own fault, he responded: "It's because I didn't do like I should've done. I didn't look ahead strong enough to see. I'll tell you my great trouble, boys, and you'll find it that-a-way along through life. You take some people and they'll never know what a dollar's worth. . . . I've made good money. Just about as good a money as most men that work for wages. But it's, I guess, come easy and go easy. I didn't save it." This internalization of responsibility was common. The following letter to Eleanor Roosevelt from a woman in Aurelia, Iowa, was typical of a substantial number of the millions of letters written to the Roosevelts during the Depression:

> Dear Mrs. Rosevelt:
>
> I am coming to you for help please do not think this does not cause a great feeling of shame to me to have to ask for old clothing. I am a Luthern Sunday school teacher. We are very poor. I know we must not let our clothes keep us from church (neither do I), but some times I feel so badly when I see all the others dressed so nice. I don't care for swell clothes, But you know one feels awful in old clothes worn shiney and thread bare. I think your clothes would fit me by your picture. Please do not think me unworthy. I am so badly in need of a summer coat and under things and dresses. oh don't think that it is not with a effort I ask you to please send me anything you may have on hand in that line which you do not care to wear yourself. Not a great lot only a few please. I never thot the time would come when I would find it nessary to do this oh please help me. May god bless you and Mr. Rosevelt. If you think me unworthy don't send anything. But think! think! hard put yourself in my place. we mothers always put what little we have to spend on our children. I to am a mother. I haven't had a new coat in 16 years so please don't think me unworthy I do not wish my children to feel ashamed. regardless of what you do please do not put my name and letter up for people to laugh at.

The sentiment in the final line was repeated in letter after letter: "My one request is, to please keep this correspondence confidential." "I would not wish at the cost of my life that any one should know I wrote you this letter." "I am sorry I cannot give you my name as I do not want publicity." "It is So EmbarreSing to Sign my full name I will Just give my initials."

The shame in so much of this testimony was often accompanied by a strong sense of dignity. Mr. Johnson of Yuba City made it clear that his material failures had not made him lose a sense of his own worth. "I've raised two mighty fine boys and a mighty fine girl. I don't figger my life's wasted. Here's how it is. A man that wastes his life is a man that goes through with everything in the world he has ever made or ever had and leaves no representatives behind. That's the way I've got it figured. Well I've got three parties—we have—to represent us . . . and I've not lived for nothing. No! I haven't lived for nothing.'' But if the pervasive sense of internalized responsibility did not necessarily eliminate feelings of self-esteem, it did seem to mitigate expressions of overt anger or indignation.

The common feelings of shame were exacerbated by the tensions that joblessness and poverty created within families. ''One of the most common things—and it certainly happened to me—was this feeling of your father's failure,'' the son of an unemployed carpenter testified. ''Sure things were tough, but why should I be the kid who had to put a piece of cardboard into the sole of my shoe to go to school? . . . It was simply this feeling of regret that somehow he hadn't done better. . . . There was conflict in the home. . . . Children develop doubts about their parents. They leave home early, out of necessity.'' Dr. Nathan Ackerman, a psychiatrist who did field work in 1937 among Pennsylvania miners who had been unemployed from two to five years, was impressed by the ''internal distress'' the men felt:

> They hung around street corners and in groups. They gave each other sol-
> ace. They were loath to go home because they were indicted, as if it were
> their fault for being unemployed. A jobless man was a lazy good-for-nothing.
> The women punished the men for not bringing home the bacon, by with-
> holding themselves sexually. By belittling and emasculating the men, un-
> dermining their paternal authority, turning to the eldest son. Making the
> eldest son the man of the family. These men suffered from depression.
> They felt despised, they were ashamed of themselves.

The propensity many Americans had to internalize the blame for what had happened to them during the early years of the Depression was intensi-fied by the statements and writings of many of their leaders and guides. If during periods of prosperity people did not practice the habits of thrift and prudence, if they gambled away their savings, John E. Edgerton, president of the National Association of Manufacturers, asked in 1930, ''Is our eco-nomic system or government or industry to blame? What system or govern-ment can keep people from being fools?'' In March 1931, at a time when he was only employing 32 percent of his workers full time, Henry Ford declared, ''The average man won't really do a day's work unless he is caught and cannot get out of it. There is plenty to do, if people would do it.'' Roger Babson's 1932 book, *Cheer Up!*, was typical of many manuals of the time in attributing the Depression to ''the dishonesty, inefficiency, and gen-eral carelessness which develop during good times.'' The good news was that if financial crisis was due to individual failings, it could be cured by "moral character," by the application of "courage, confidence, and conquest." His approach was typified by his word to the wives:

> Do not forget that your acquiescences and folly helped to push your husband over the edge, and that the present hard times furnishes you with an opportunity to redeem yourself by helping him to keep up the courage and energy to rebuild. . . . Now is the hour to rectify your mistake and his by an enthusiastic, energetic activity, a stout heart and a word of good cheer.

Throughout the country newspapers argued that economic crises were merely a question of attitude and if only people would stop hoarding their money, good times would return. "The whole depression business is largely mental," a Muncie, Indiana, newspaper editorialized in June 1930. "If tomorrow morning everybody should wake up with a resolve to unwind the red yarn that is wound about his old leather purse, and then would carry his resolve into effect, by August first, at the latest, the whole country could join in singing, 'Happy Days Are Here Again.' "

Attitudes like these, which were no strangers to the Hoover administration, help explain the constant attempt to restore "confidence" as if it were the individual rather than the system that had broken down. "Ninety percent of our difficulty in depressions," President Hoover asserted, "is caused by fear." Even Franklin Roosevelt kept this line of reasoning alive in the famous aphorism from his first inaugural address, "The only thing we have to fear is fear itself."

Once again, American advertising reflected one of the dominant moods of these early Depression years. "In the final analysis, we are responsible for our own defeats and our own victories," a 1932 ad from International Correspondence Schools advised. "It's Time for Action!" the businessman in an Addressograph-Multigraph ad vowed. "I'm one of thousands of business men who have been sitting tight, waiting for business to return to normal. . . . Now I'm tired of waiting for a miracle to happen. I'm going to do something about it—*myself.* I've determined that my salvation lies in my own hands." A Ford Motor Company ad asserted in 1932, "Being unemployed does not need to mean being out of work. There may be work even though one may not be hired to do it. In the last analysis independence means self-dependence." The Hammermill Paper Company warned in 1932, "For many, the present salary cuts will be permanent," but not "for the man who *refuses* to stay down." In June 1932, Hamilton Watches advised those graduating to "be thankful they are graduating in a TOUGH YEAR!" and pitied the graduates of the past "who had missed the moulding lessons" of early struggle "by graduating into a too soft and ready world!"

Although many of these attitudes softened and altered as the crisis persisted, popular culture throughout the Depression decade remained a central vehicle for the dissemination and perpetuation of those traditional values that emphasized personal responsibility for one's position in the world. A case in point was Margaret Mitchell's *Gone with the Wind*. Published in June 1936, the novel sold a million copies by the end of the year. It dominated all fiction sales for two years and became the basis of the decade's most spectacular movie. We often employ such imprecise and unhelpful terms as "escapism" to explain phenomena like *Gone with the Wind*. Even if the American people were seeking to "escape" their plight, however, the real question is why they chose this particular vehicle to do it; why, in the midst of the nation's worst economic crisis, so many Americans should have been so deeply attracted to a novel about the Civil War. There is no single explanation, but we would be committing a serious error if we did not attempt to understand the extent to which Americans were attracted to those cultural expressions which helped them, or at least appeared to help them, comprehend their own world. The real significance of *Gone with the Wind*, then, was not escape—it probably provided no more of that than most expressive culture does—but reaffirmation. Looking beneath the surface of the novel, it is clear that it depicted a world not really far removed from the America of the 1930s: a world which at the beginning of the novel was bursting with hope and promise, as the America of the 1920s with its promise of unprecedented and unending prosperity had been; a world governed by order and reason, as the world of the 1920s had seemed to be to so many Americans; a world which suddenly disintegrated into the chaos and unreason of civil war, as the world of the 1920s had suddenly disintegrated into the chaos and unreason of economic crisis. Through the novel's more than a thousand pages, Scarlett O'Hara emerges as the individual who refuses to give in to these irrational processes. She survives the war, the siege of Atlanta, the destruction of her society. She grows and matures, rebuilds her plantation, and, although on the very last page she loses her man, Rhett Butler, she remains unbowed:

> With the spirit of her people who would not know defeat, even when it stared them in the face, she raised her chin. She could get Rhett back. She knew she could. There had never been a man she couldn't get, once she set her mind upon him.
>
> "I'll think of it tomorrow . . . I can stand it then. Tomorrow, I'll think of some way to get him back. After all, tomorrow is another day."

In the culture of the 1930s, the calamities of the past could become didactic mechanisms for illustrating the ways in which people might triumph over adversity, rediscovering in the process those enduring values they had lost sight of in better times. The most profitable film of 1936, *San Francisco,* which reenacted the 1906 earthquake, provides another example. Mary Black (Jeanette MacDonald), a minister's daughter, migrates from her small town to pursue her singing career. In San Francisco she meets Blackie Moran (Clark Gable), a gambler and proprietor of a Barbary Coast saloon, who does everything he can to convert her to his life style, attempting to divert her career from the opera to the world of popular entertainment, even insisting that she appear publicly in a skimpy costume. Having alienated her through his insensitivity and obstinacy, Moran discovers the extent of his true feelings only during the earthquake. Searching for her everywhere amid the ruins of San Francisco, the transformed saloon keeper has even attained enough humility to sink to his knees in prayer when he finally finds her. His priorities sorted out, Moran is reunited with his love and together they join a crowd of refugees singing "The Battle Hymn of the Republic," as they descend from the surrounding hills to rebuild the stricken city, over which the image of modern San Francisco is superimposed. The analogies are clear: the individual could rise above disaster—be it civil war, earthquake, or depression—in pursuit of redemption, a theme that penetrated much of Depression culture.

Radio proved to be as important a vehicle for this message as the movies. The humorist Will Rogers, whose casual wit and rustic manner made him something of a folk hero, frequently used his extremely popular weekly radio show to discuss the economic crisis. In the fall of 1931, he warned his listeners that they had better stop wasting energy on peripheral issues. "What does Prohibition amount to your neighbor's children, if they're not eating? Food, not drink, is our problem today." The *only* issue, he insisted, was a more equal division of the nation's wealth. "All the feed is going into one manger and the stock on the other side of the stall ain't getting a thing. . . . We got it, but we don't know how to split it up." "The working classes didn't bring this on," he advised his audience. "It was the big boys."

Yet even in the midst of his iconoclasm, Rogers's major thrust was to reiterate traditional ideals in a manner that led him in the final analysis to attribute the nation's plight to the failure of the individual. He warned the nation that the "cuckoo times" of the late 1920s would never return, and a good thing too since it was during those "lunatic" years that Americans had forsaken the work ethic and learned the profligate ways that brought them to their present plight. "The trouble with America is it's just muscle-bound from holding the steering wheel. The only place we're callused from work is the bottom of our driving toe." It was in this context that Rogers enunciated his famous aphorism: "We are the first nation in the history of the world to go to the poorhouse in an automobile." We had been so preoccupied with frivolities and games, with "getting radios and bathtubs and facial creams, and straight eights, that we forgot to see if we had any bacon or beans.'' There was only one way to relieve unemployment:

> and that's for everybody to go to work. *Where?* Why right where you are. Look around, you will see a lot of things to do: weeds to cut, fences to be fixed, lawns to be mowed, filling stations to be robbed, gangsters to be catered to. There is a million little odds and ends right under your eye that an idle man can turn his hand to every day. 'Course he won't get paid for it, but he won't get paid for not doing it. My theory is that it will keep him in practice in case something does show. You can keep practicing so that work won't be a novelty when it does come.

Attitudes like these were reiterated every evening from 7 to 7:15 P.M., when some forty million Americans tuned in to the adventures of *Amos 'n' Andy,* the early Depression's most popular radio show—so popular that movie theaters interrupted their films to broadcast it. Combining the techniques of nineteenth-century blackface minstrelsy with the values of that century's success and work ethics, the show's white creators portrayed the adventures of two black migrants from rural Georgia in Chicago and then in New York. The industrious, idealistic, sensible Amos would save his friend Andy from his own indolence, credulity, and pomposity again and again, articulating those lessons that Andy should, but rarely did, learn from the experience. ''My papa used to tell me dat yo' ain't never goin' git nuthin' dat yo' don't work fo'. Dis heah thing o' bein' on Easy Street might be alright—I don't know—but I always remember whut he say: if I ever git anything, I goin' have to work fo' it.'' Tempted by Andy and Kingfish to invest the $500 he has saved for his marriage in a scheme that would double it, Amos first writes his fiancée for advice. Her answer, the Kingfish ruefully reports, is ''dat he made his money de hard way, an' dat was de best way to make sure he was goin' make some more.'' Amos retained not only his values but his optimism. ''Times like dese does a lot o' good,'' he assured his friends, '' 'cause when dis is over, which is bound to be, an' good times come back again, people like us dat is livin' today is goin' learn a lesson an' dey goin' know whut a rainy day means . . . so maybe after all, dis was a good thing to bring people back to deyre senses an' sort a remind ev'body dat de sky AIN'T de limit.''

Amos's philosophy of hard work and faith was echoed in a myriad of ways in the culture of the period. In 1933 Walt Disney won the first of his Academy Awards for *The Three Little Pigs,* an immensely popular cartoon which emphasized, in song and story, that only those who worked diligently could keep the wolf from their door. While his brothers cavorted about and consequently built insubstantial houses, which the wolf easily blew down, the eldest pig applied himself, sermonizing in song:

> I build my house of stones.
> I build my house of bricks.
> I have no chance to sing and dance,
> For work and play don't mix.

The Three Little Pigs, according to the *New York Times,* was shown at more theaters during the year than any other film. The critic Lewis Jacobs reported that the film's theme song, ''Who's Afraid of the Big Bad Wolf?'' became ''a national anthem overnight.'' In 1934, Disney won another Academy Award for *The Tortoise and the Hare,* which, along with his widely popular *The Grasshopper and the Ant,* continued to reaffirm such traditional values as self-reliance and perseverance.

In 1937 the nation's press turned the death of John D. Rockefeller into a ceremonial occasion for the reiteration of these very values. They reprinted dozens of such Rockefeller aphorisms as ''Work! Persevere! Be Honest! Save!'' ''Live within your means.'' ''You won't have a happy life if you don't work.'' Rockefeller's life, the Charlotte *Observer* declared, was an example of what ''the simple virtues of thrift and frugality and saving will accomplish'' and a symbol of the ''unlimited possibilities'' offered every American citizen. ''A tragedy for America if this system and this spirit and this encouragement offered by democracy should perish from the face of the earth!''

The historian's natural propensity to periodize—to divide the years under consideration into neat, distinct, meaningful segments—has to be held in check when dealing with a period as short as a decade. It may be true that the values I have been dealing with were stronger at the beginning than at the end of the thirties, and that the decade of deflated economic activity and hopes inevitably took its toll and produced, or at least expedited, changed attitudes and expectations. The fact remains that throughout the decade of the Depression, one can find traditional attitudes towards the individual, society, work, and mobility expressed with great conviction in a wide variety of cultural genres by virtually all segments of the population. It is equally true, however, that the expressive culture of the decade constitutes a vital indicator of the subtle but important ways in which these values were undergoing alteration.

We must resist the temptation, therefore, to argue that the decade of the 1930s was *either* one thing *or* another, or to divide it into two periods: the first a time of conservatism, the second a time of innovation and change. The mistaken urge of a number of scholars to impose symmetry and order on Roosevelt's dynamic but confused, often contradictory, and always eclectic reform efforts by dividing them into a First and Second New Deal should not be extended to the realm of expressive culture. Rather, we must try to comprehend the Great Depression as a complex, ambivalent, disorderly period which gave witness to the force of cultural continuity even as it manifested signs of deep cultural change. It is to this latter development that I would now like to turn.

Americans, of course, have been both producers and consumers. Traditionally, however, they were more comfortable conceiving of themselves as producers and organizing around their production functions in such groups as the National Association of Manufacturers, the American Federation of Labor, or the American Medical Association. It is not surprising that the development of a mass consumption economy, which W. W. Rostow has argued was in place by the 1920s, brought inevitable changes in cultural attitudes. Thus by our own time, Americans are more prone to identify themselves as consumers and much easier to organize on this basis than at any other point in their history. While this fundamental shift (which has important implications for our understanding of what happened to traditional American attitudes toward success and the individual) took place not suddenly but cumulatively, as all such changes do, the Great Depression unquestionably expedited it.

In the politics of the 1930s the consumer was called, with reason, the "forgotten man." But in the expressive culture of the decade, we can find crucial indications of the alterations taking place. The sociologist Leo Lowenthal was one of the first observers to begin to delineate the contours of this change. As early as 1944, he called attention to what he termed a shift from producer to consumer consciousness. Comparing the biographies in popular magazines of the early twentieth century with those appearing at the end of the Great Depression, Lowenthal found that the businessmen and politicians who dominated the popular biographies of the early period had given way by 1940 to subjects from the area of popular entertainment. The earlier figures, whom Lowenthal called the "Idols of Production," belonged to vocations that tended to serve society's basic needs, while those of the later period, the "Idols of Consumption," were directly or indirectly related to the sphere of leisure time. The purpose of the earlier biographies was didactic; they held forth examples of success that presumably could be imitated and they concentrated on the process by which their subjects had attained success. This no longer was the purpose of the later biographies whose subjects' rise seemed to be more attributable to being in the right place at the right time, or knowing the right people, or having the right looks or athletic prowess, than to any rational social pattern of upward mobility which could be emulated by eager readers. The emphasis of these later biographies was no longer how their subjects rose to success but what they did with it, how they "spent" it once they had earned it, what effects it had upon their private lives and their patterns of consumption.

Again, it is crucial to remember that we are not dealing with an either/ or phenomenon. As this essay has tried to demonstrate, there was much greater retention of traditional production values than the specific sources Lowenthal examined indicated. Still, Lowenthal's pioneering research and hypotheses are important in enhancing our understanding of the effects of the Depression upon popular consciousness. Evidences of the transition Lowenthal wrote of existed throughout the culture. Though the popular success literature of the period continued to urge readers to improve themselves, it paid unprecedented attention to questions of consumption and the use of leisure, placed more emphasis upon the present than the future, and no longer focused as strongly upon the deferral of gratification, which had been so essential to the traditional success ethic.

In *Life Begins at Forty,* which was either first or second on the best-seller lists in 1933 and 1934, Walter Pitkin asserted that "AMERICANS DIE YOUNG LARGELY BECAUSE THEY NEVER START LIVING" and denounced "our silly dollar-chasing and our greasy grind of factory and our stupid philosophies of life" which led to exhaustion. Considering that people spent "most of their time and energy in making a living," should we be surprised "that so few of us know how to live?" It was time, he urged his fellow citizens, to carry out "successfully the dominant desires of the moment." Marjorie Hillis, in her best-selling *Orchids on Your Budget* (1937), urged her readers to "get more fun out of living" because "we might die tomorrow." Money, she argued, "should be invested in happiness" since "that drab and old-fashioned virtue," savings, "has never been really enjoyed by anyone except the very penurious and Mr. Coolidge." Coolidge and the virtues he "both preached and embodied—industry, thrift, personal integrity," Paul Hutchinson asserted in *Reader's Digest* in 1933, "are under such scrutiny as they have never been subjected to in the past. They must change—they *are* changing—because Western civilization itself is changing." A good plan, Harold Reilly asserted in the same magazine four years later, "is to forget yesterday, ignore tomorrow, live today." A similar spirit was reflected in such other best-selling manuals of the decade as Edmund Jacobson's *You Must Relax,* Dorothea Brande's *Wake Up and Live!,* and Lin Yutang's *The Importance of Living.*

The ads of the thirties often reflected the trend towards consumption mobility which was to become so important in the decades after the Second World War. Thus in a 1937 ad for Packard, a young boy is pictured leaning against a white picket fence, looking at something wistfully:

Years ago, a little freckle-faced boy watched with envy as a magnificent new motor car went by. To that boy it was more than a motor car, it was a symbol of a way of life: it was an emblem of success. And as his longing eyes followed the disappearing car I promised him that some day he too would own a Packard. Yes, I was that boy. And today I'm keeping the promise I made to myself some 25 years ago.

Consumption values had by no means become dominant in the 1930s. The decade's most popular success manual, Dale Carnegie's *How to Win Friends and Influence People*—which sold 729,000 copies in 1937 and over ten million in the next twenty-five years—was as preoccupied as ever with traditional concerns over occupational mobility, but in a way which further indicated the changes Americans were experiencing. Carnegie told the story of interviewing Roosevelt's Postmaster General, James Farley, and asking him the secret of his success. "He said, 'Hard work,' and I said, 'Don't be funny.' " Success, Carnegie insisted, was not the result of hard work or technical knowledge; it was due to "skill in human engineering—to personality and the ability to lead people." To teach his multitude of readers the requisite skills, Carnegie offered six rules for making people like you, twelve rules for winning people to your way of thinking, nine rules for changing people without giving offense or arousing resentment, seven rules for making your home life happier. For making other people like you, Carnegie suggested the following strategies: "Smile." "Remember that a man's name is to him the sweetest and most important sound in any language." "Be a good listener." "Make the other person feel important." For winning people to your way of thinking, he advised: "The only way to get the best of an argument is to avoid it." "Never tell a man he is wrong." "Let the other man do a great deal of the talking." "Let the other man feel that the idea is his."

Dale Carnegie's aims did not differ significantly from those of the nineteenth-century industrialist Andrew Carnegie, but his means would have thoroughly alienated that apostle of success and individualism. The latter-day Carnegie's formulas were those of manipulation, of adjustment, of interpersonal relations. They were formulas more appropriate to the rise of the organizational man than to the rise of the traditional rugged individualist. His great success was a testament to the fact that the old success formulas no longer appealed to a population which had finally become conscious of the implications of the institutionalized, bureaucratized world in which it functioned.

It is hardly surprising that American attitudes towards the success ethos and towards institutions were reflected in the gangster film—which enjoyed its greatest popularity in the early Depression years—since crime had become an avenue of mobility, especially for marginal Americans. According to the historian Mark Haller, of the 108 directors of the Chicago underworld in 1930, 30 percent were of Italian descent, 29 percent were of Irish descent, 20 percent were Jewish, and 12 percent were black; "not a single leader was recorded as native white of native born stock." That at least some criminals saw their rise in terms of traditional success formulas is made clear by Alvin Karpis, a "public enemy" from Topeka, Kansas, who denied J. Edgar Hoover's charge that he was a "hoodlum." You could succeed in his line of work, Karpis insisted, only "if you were a dedicated stickup man, if you worked hard, if you were determined to keep going in the face of all obstacles, and if you were smart in the choice of your partners and associates."

Like Karpis, the film gangsters portrayed by such actors as Edward G. Robinson and James Cagney were caricatures of the traditional Alger hero. They also rose to success through diligence and application, but only by denying the values that Alger had affirmed. They attained temporary eminence and power, but their ultimate reward was invariably violent death. It would be a mistake to attribute these endings primarily to the censorship Hollywood was subject to, since the folk songs and tales about gangster heroes that remained so popular throughout the thirties ended in precisely the same way.

The classic gangster film was not merely about the individual but about organization. "We're gonna get organized," the boss in *Scarface* (1932) proclaims. "Running beer ain't a nickel game any more. It's a business and I'm gonna run it like a business!" As Robert Warshow has pointed out, it is when the gangster is apart from his organization, when he is alone, that he is most vulnerable. *Scarface* begins with the death of the old boss, Big Louie, after the last of his henchmen have gone home, and it ends with the death of the new boss, Tony Camonte, alone with his sister and cut off from his mob by a police siege. "You can't go away," he begs his mortally wounded sister. "I'll be all alone. You can't leave me here all alone. . . . I'm no good by myself." Whatever truth emerged at his death, on his way up, Camonte felt and acted like a self-sustaining individual. Forming his fingers in the shape of a pistol and silently mouthing the word "bang," he tells his henchman the "only law" he follows: "Do it first! Do it yourself! And keep on doin' it!" He enjoys looking out of his apartment window at a huge Cook's Tours advertising sign featuring a revolving globe under which large neon letters proclaim: "THE WORLD IS YOURS." "Someday," Camonte vows, "I look at that sign and say: 'O.K. She's mine!' " The last shot of the movie focuses upon that sign blinking its mocking message high above the prostrate form of the dead gangster on the city streets below. Caesar Enrico Bandello, the central figure of *Little Caesar* (1930), suffers a similar fate. No other film gangster was modeled more closely on the traditional success figure. So self-absorbed is he that he can't believe his own demise. "Mother of Mercy, . . . is this the end of Rico?" he gasps as he dies beneath a billboard advertising the success of his old comrade who has forsaken a career in crime for one as a professional dancer.

Surely it is not too much to argue that these films, and the many others like them, were about more than the death of a gangster. They were, on a number of levels, concerned with the demise of a tradition now shrouded in ambivalence and doubt, just as the gangster hero of *Public Enemy* (1931)—who was killed when he disobeyed the instructions of his boss and rashly confronted his rivals on his own—is returned to his family shrouded from head to toe in bandages, a mummified symbol of a time now gone.

Movie fan magazines, whose readership seems to have been largely female, provide another example of the ambivalence which surrounded the success ethos in the Depression. On the surface, the tradition appeared to be intact. *Photoplay* magazine illustrated its conviction that physical beauty was an act not of nature but of the will, through numerous conversion stories. Joan Crawford, who began with many physical defects, became a glamorous star through "a cold, hard will to work and succeed." In twelve months Eleanor Powell "transformed herself from sheer ugliness into actual radiant beauty." No matter what your problems, *Photoplay* sermonized, "you can—and you *must*—be attractive. Being attractive depends upon your personality. . . . *Be* somebody." Beneath the surface, however, was the reality that most women, regardless of their efforts, could never become Joan Crawford. This tension was relieved in a simple formula: success brought unhappiness. Margaret Sullivan paid a terrible price for her fame: "unhappiness, deathly unhappiness, mental depression, and nervous torture." Movie stars missed the simple real pleasures of life. "Concentration on work can anesthetize a woman's natural reactions," *Photoplay* concluded. "You always have to make a choice in a situation like this. Husband or career. Home and anonymity or success, money, fame."

Such films as *Cleopatra* (1934), *Mary of Scotland* (1936), and *Elizabeth the Queen* (1939) came to the same conclusion. Refusing to betray the man she loves in order to save the throne she worked so hard to win, Cleopatra proclaims, "I'm no longer a queen. I'm a woman!" "Look well for love, look well, and not finding it, give nothing," a dying Cleopatra proclaims. "But if blessed with Cleopatra's fortune, give all!" The story of Queen Mary begins with a resolute woman determined to be queen, and ends with a softer being who finds fulfillment in her womanhood. "Let me live or die at your side," she tells her husband. "I'm your wife. I love you. . . . What's my throne? I'd put a torch to it for any one of the days I've had with you." As she condemns her lover Essex to death, Queen Elizabeth tells him that she has learned from him "that no one can be trusted, a lover least of all. I will remember that." "Take care, your Majesty," Essex responds, "lest that be all you ever have to remember." Choosing her throne over her man, the queen is left to wail, "I'm old! I'm old! With you I could have been young again."

For the gangster, success ended in death; for the professional woman it ended in unfulfillment; for many others it ended in the realization that success no longer meant merely the mastery of oneself but of the institutions that characterized the new society. This helps explain the widespread popularity of private detective novels and movies in the Great Depression. The private detective appeared to be much wiser and far more effective than the regular policemen because he was free, as they were not, to bypass institutional constraints and emulate the procedures of the criminal. Forced to operate within the law, the police were pictured as inefficient and incapable of coping with their adversaries.

This growing perception that it was less and less possible to achieve traditional ends through the existing system helped to give birth to a new folk figure in the late Depression years. In 1938, Superman made his first appearance in *Action Comics* and became the prototype of a host of heroes who were to become prominent in American culture. Jules Feiffer, the cartoonist and playwright, who was an avid young reader of comics in the 1930s, has left us a fine recollection of Superman's emergence:

> The problem in pre-super days was that, with few exceptions, heroes were not very interesting. . . . Villains, whatever fate befell them in the obligatory last panel, were infinitely better equipped than those silly, hapless heroes. Not only comics, but life taught us that. Those of us raised in ghetto neighborhoods were being asked to believe that crime didn't pay? . . . Nice guys finished last; landlords, first. Villains . . . were miles ahead. It was not to be believed that any ordinary human could combat them. More was required. Someone with a call. When *Superman* at last appeared, he brought with him the deep satisfaction of all underground truths: our reaction was less, "How original!" than, "But, of course!"

Superman was important because his alter ego, his fake identity, Clark Kent, was a caricature of what individuals had become in an organized, depersonalized world: faceless, impotent, frustrated. Kent could transform himself by taking off his clothes; the rest of the society could react through the world of the mass media.

Fantasies, of course, were not new to the 1930s, but the nature of the prevailing fantasies is revealing. Superman had existed before in American culture. The super heroes of the mid-nineteenth century were concerned with overcoming the environment. Real people might have to struggle with the vastness of nature in America; their super fantasies, like the folk figures Mike Fink and Davy Crockett, did not: they could cross rivers in a single stride, uproot trees with a single yank, conquer wild animals with their bare hands. One hundred years later, the concern had shifted from the environment to the bureaucracy, from nature to society. The people of the 1930s might be confined by institutions, might have to respond to them and through them, but they could relieve their tensions and express their feelings through their super projections. Thus though Superman and his clones functioned with the consent of the law, they operated outside it. Nowhere is it recorded that Superman stopped for a search warrant before breaking down walls to capture the criminals. The popularity of Superman symbolized public unrest with the institutions and bureaucracies that more and more shaped the contours of everyday life.

Faced with a marked dissonance between the social goals they had been taught to work for and the inadequate means society provided for attaining those goals, Americans found a necessary outlet for their anguish in the dynamic humor of the Great Depression, which in fact proved to be one of the most creative periods of humor in our history. The distrust of institutions, the sense that the world no longer worked as it was supposed to, that the old verities and certainties no longer held sway, was expressed in one of the decade's most ubiquitous forms of humor: the humor of irrationality. In their popular radio program, *Easy Aces,* which was broadcast three times a week, Jane and Goodman Ace made frequent use of this form of wit, as in the following dialogue from the 1932–1933 season:

JANE: I wish we would go to Los Angeles for our vacation this summer.

ACE: All right—anything you say—

JANE: That's what you said last summer—you said we would go to Los Angeles and we didn't go any place.

ACE: No, no, last summer we didn't go to Europe. It was the summer before we didn't go to Los Angeles. It gets monotonous not going to the same place every year. Let's not go up to Lake Louise, around Banff—mighty pretty country around there, they tell me.

JANE: No, I like Los Angeles.

ACE: All right—then we won't go to Los Angeles—have it your way—and let's plan on not going about the last two weeks in August—that'll be about the most inconvenient time for me to get away. How does that strike you?

One could be certain of nothing in the humor of the thirties. In one of their most famous routines, Abbot endeavors to prove to Costello that he is not there: "Are you in St. Louis? "No." "Are you in Chicago?" "Of course not." "Well, if you're not in St. Louis and you're not in Chicago, you must be somewhere else." "Ye-es." "Well, then, if you're somewhere else, you're not here." No one demonstrated the illogic of logic, the fragility of certainty, more surely than the Marx Brothers, in whose madcap anarchy one gets a glimpse of the decade's travail. Even before the full advent of the Depression, Groucho was tilting his lance at the economic system. Confronted by his employees demanding their wages in *The Cocoanuts* (1929), he asks if they want to be wage slaves and when they reply in the negative, he cries out, "No, of course not! Well, what makes wage slaves? Wages! I want you to be free. . . . Be free, my friends, one for all and all for me and me for you and three for five and six for a quarter." The surrealism increased with the deepening crisis. "Pick a number from one to ten," Groucho instructs Chico in *Duck Soup* (1933). "Eleven," replies Chico. "Right," declares Groucho. In *Animal Crackers* (1930), Groucho is quick to agree when a pompous conservative observes that "The nickel is not worth what it used to be ten years ago":

> I'll go further than that. . . . Do you know what this country needs today? A seven-cent nickel. Yes sirree, we've been using five-cent nickels in this country since 1492 and that's pretty near a hundred years daylight saving. Now why not give the seven-cent nickel a chance? If that works out, next year we could have an eight-cent nickel. Think what that would mean. You could go to a news stand, buy a three-cent newspaper and get the same nickel back again. One nickel carefully used would last a family a lifetime!

The thirties' assault on American truisms took place on all levels of humor. "A penny saved," Ogden Nash observed, "is—impossible." James Thurber revised another American proverb in his fable, "The Shrike and the Chipmunks," in which Mrs. Chipmunk forces her husband out of bed, insisting: "You can't be healthy if you lie in bed all day and never get any exercise." She takes him for a walk during which they are caught and killed by a shrike. *"Moral: Early to rise and early to bed makes a male healthy and wealthy and dead."* W. C. Fields added to the confusion by commenting, "Any man who hates dogs and children can't be all bad." And Mae West boasted, in her version of the well-known children's rhyme, "When I'm good I'm very, very good, but when I'm bad I'm better."

In 1937, *Gone with the Wind* was the year's best-selling work of fiction while *How to Win Friends and Influence People* headed the nonfiction lists. A decade in which a book heralding the virtues of the past as a model for the present, and one which taught the techniques of adjustment necessary for the conquest of the future, could be *simultaneously* the most popular books, is not an easy decade to sum up. That, of course, has been one of the points of this essay. The attempt to answer one question—why did the American people react as they did in the early years of the Great Depression?—has led us into a complex world of conflicting urges: a world that looked to the past even as it began to assume the contours of the future; a world in which a crisis in values accompanied the crisis in the economy; a world of special interest to historians because the normal process of cumulative and barely perceptible change was expedited and made more visible by the presence of prolonged crisis.

The purpose of this essay has been to scratch the surface of that world and to suggest that however central politics was to the Depression decade, it needs to be seen in the total context of Depression culture. There can be no attempt to understand the Great Depression and its effect upon our own society without attempting to understand the reactions and attitudes of the American people, and there can be no understanding of the American people without a serious attempt to understand the everyday culture they were exposed to and interacted with.

12

Hollywood's Washington: Film Images of National Politics During the Great Depression

During the academic years 1981–1983, I was fortunate enough to be a Fellow of the Smithsonian Institution, first at the National Museum of American History and then at the Woodrow Wilson International Center for Scholars. Thus for two years I lived in close proximity to the incomparable source materials in the libraries, archives, and museums of Washington, D.C. I was by then increasingly involved in the research into nineteenth-century American culture that formed the basis of my study *Highbrow/Lowbrow*. But I also found time to dig into the rich cultural materials from the 1930s held by the Motion Pictures, Broadcasting, and Recorded Sound Division of the Library of Congress. I spent day after day watching films, reading radio scripts and listening to tapes of radio programs. When I returned to Berkeley in the fall of 1983, I incorporated many of these materials into my lecture course, as the preceding essay indicates.

It was during this period of intense research that I also came to realize just how complex the films of the Depression were. Though they have, too frequently and too easily, been characterized as "escapist," in fact they seemed to me so deeply grounded in the realities and intricacies of the Depression that they offered scholars a rich array of insights into a uniquely wide range of the social, cultural, and political issues, problems, and attitudes involving and characterizing American society and its people throughout the decade. When in the spring of 1983 I was invited to give a paper on some aspect of the film of the Great Depression at the 1984 annual meeting of the Organization of American Historians, I decided to focus on and attempt to comprehend how Hollywood had responded to and reflected the politics of the Great Depression. An expanded version of the paper was

originally published in *Prospects: An Annual of American Cultural Studies*
X (1986), and is reprinted here with revisions.

In her recollections of the 1930s, Louise Tanner helped to create an image
that has stayed with us despite a number of studies that should have dis-
solved it by now. Thirties movies were, she insisted,

> a flop as a source of Communist propaganda. Some studios—notably War-
> ner brothers—tried to bring Father to grips with social reality. But most of
> the cinemoguls agreed with Louis B. Mayer that Dad got all the social
> significance he needed at home. The script writers of Hollywood might
> take the Spanish Civil War to heart but they were more concerned with a
> public that preferred Carole Lombard doing secretarial work in a penthouse
> with a white telephone. Father sitting there in the dark forgot his own
> plight as he watched the gods and goddesses of the screen sweeping down
> staircases into dining rooms with a footman behind every chair. Depression
> movies portrayed an America devoid of economic conflict.[1]

Tanner was typical in seeing Hollywood as primarily "escapist" and in
arguing that when politics did intrude upon this apolitical norm it was invariably the politics of the Far Left. If we have been taught to associate any
color with the 1930s, it has been *red:* the "Red Decade" was filled with
left-wing activity and filled as well with Republicans and businessmen—
solid, respectable burghers, who feared the specter of imminent communist
takeover. The films of the Great Depression constitute an important corrective to some of these standard images in reminding us that there were other
fears and other threats stalking the land in the 1930s. The fear of fascism
and, indeed, the appeal of fascism, have not yet been dealt with adequately
by historians of the Depression. It is ironic that in a decade when fascism
was the leading political force in Europe, we have had so little analysis of
it as a potential force in the United States.

Ronald Reagan's recent remark coupling fascism and the New Deal would
have seemed far less strange in the 1930s themselves.[2] There were those
who saw the New Deal as a first step toward not communism but fascism.
A month before Roosevelt's inauguration, Norman Thomas returned from a
trip to the Middle West and spoke of "a distinct trend toward an American
brand of fascist dictatorship and toward war." "Something is happening to
America," E. Francis Brown asserted in *Current History* in the summer of
1933. "Ahead we cannot see, but signs there are which bear out the conten-
tion of the Italian newspaper, the *Giornale d'Italia,* that America is 'on the
road to fascism.' " By the end of the year, Harold Loeb and Selden Rod-

man warned that "certain features of the program of the present Democratic administration in Washington have all the economic earmarks of fascism." Magazine readers in the early years of the New Deal commonly came across articles entitled, "Roosevelt—Dictator?" "Fascism and the New Deal," "America Drifts Toward Fascism," "The Great Fascist Plot," "Is America Ripe for Fascism?" "Must American Go Fascist?" "Will America Go Fascist?" "Need the New Deal Be Fascist?" Most critics generally agreed with Norman Thomas that FDR did not have the temperament of a fascist dictator, but the machinery he was establishing—especially the National Recovery Administration, with its implicit union of industry and government—constituted the basic threat along with Roosevelt's failure to make sufficient inroads upon the economic and social crisis.[3]

In the mid-1930s a number of books dealt with this specter of emergent fascism. Raymond Gram Swing, in *Forerunners of American Fascism* (1935), argued that two of the preconditions for fascism—the impoverishment of the middle class and large-scale unemployment—already existed; the third—paralysis of government—was rapidly developing, and the fourth—the threat of a strong communist movement—was being fabricated by a conservative press. Building upon these conditions, Swing fashioned a believable scenario for the repetition of the Italian and German experiences in the United States:

> So the condition in this country today is that the New Deal is not doing what it needed to do. . . . And in the country there is the rise of great popular unrest and dissatisfaction. . . . This dissatisfaction will continue to rise. And as it rises the demagogues rise with it. And as they gain momentum, and their following increases, they will be recognized as the coming force in politics. And then the holders of economic power will begin to pay attention to them. And then we may expect to see repeated here the pattern of Germany and Italy, the coalition between the radicals [the demagogues] and the conservatives in the name of national unity. Then we shall be told that the trouble with America is that we have too much liberty, too much individualism . . . and that our Salvation lies in all pulling together, and particularly in bending our wills to the will of the leader. And a good many people will be ready to throw away their liberties as they toss up their hats. We shall then be told that it is un-American to oppose and to criticize. We shall be told that the unequal distribution of economic power is part of the American tradition, just as we are already told that it is against the spirit of the Constitution to advocate economic democracy.[4]

Later in the year, the most popular of the books dealing with American fascism—Sinclair Lewis's *It Can't Happen Here*—was published. The "it" of course was fascism and the purpose of the book was to show how easily "it" could be made to fit into American life and politics. Thus Lewis wrote of his fascist leader, Berzelius Windrip: "He could dramatize his assertion that he was neither a Nazi or a Fascist but a Democrat—a homespun Jeffersonian-Lincolnian-Clevelandian-Wilsonian Democrat . . . the while he innocently presented as his own warm-hearted Democratic inventions, every anti-libertarian, anti-Semitic madness of Europe."[5]

The novel's able depiction of the Americanization of fascism convinced Hallie Flannagan that it should be mounted as a play by her Federal Theater Project. "When dictatorship comes to threaten a democracy," Flannagan warned, "it comes in an apparently harmless guise, with parades and promises; but . . . when such dictatorship arrives, the promises are not kept and the parade grounds become encampments." *It Can't Happen Here* opened on October 27, 1936, in twenty-two separate productions in eighteen cities, including an English and a Yiddish version in New York City, another Yiddish version in Los Angeles, a Spanish version in Tampa, and a black version in Seattle.[6]

Several months before the play opened, Lawrence Dennis, in *The Coming American Fascism,* joined the chorus predicting the actual possibility of a fascist takeover in the United States. The difference was that Dennis, himself a fascist, welcomed the imminent revolution. The alternatives to moribund liberal capitalism, he insisted, were fascism or communism. Dennis had no doubt which the American people would choose. Communism would mean the total destruction and reorganization of the present system, while fascism would utilize the existing structure and offer Americans a middle-class rather than a proletarian revolution. "Fascism regards private property rights, private initiative, and the free market . . . as useful institutions." Americans were completely prepared for fascism, Dennis boasted. Advanced technology had already created all the apparatus necessary for total indoctrination while "our national corporations and social organizations have unified and nationalized us into the most standardized people on earth." "Angry and frustrated men with a will to power," Dennis predicted, would utilize all the catchwords of the present system to create "an American fascist party, called by another name, of course."[7]

This focus upon the promise, or threat, of fascism, which fascinated so many writers by the middle of the thirties, had been a constant preoccupation of Hollywood since the beginning of the decade and was to remain a subject to which films continued to pay close attention until America's entry into World War II. Political films of the early 1930s, whether realistic or melodramatically implausible, most often contained graphic accounts of the nation's plight and vulnerability. In *Washington Masquerade,* released during the summer of 1932, Lionel Barrymore played Jeff Keane, newly elected reform senator from Kansas, who does battle on the floor of the Senate with the political servants of the nation's power and light monopolies. He rises to remind the senior senator from his state, who had just called government ownership of public utilities "communistic," that

> The Almighty Hand . . . placed all the ingredients for the creation of power and light at the disposal of mankind. This land belongs to its millions of people! . . . if we, here in Washington, blinded by old formulas, if we haven't learned the lesson that every wind has carried in these last three tragic years, a hundred million people in this country have learned it. They've been forced to learn it! With the tears streaming down their cheeks, and their families famished—in the land where there's more than plenty! It's my solemn belief that a hundred million people are making up their minds that the things that belong to them and to nobody else, have been taken out of their hands and have been given back to them again at heartbreaking and impossible prices! [8]

Two weeks before Roosevelt's election, Hollywood depicted the crisis more graphically and began to search for a more explicit solution. *Washington Merry-Go-Round* was "Dedicated to those public servants in Washington who despite the hidden malignant force which operates to defeat the principles of representative government are serving their country sincerely and well." Again we have a newly elected reform congressman, Button Gwinnett Brown, a descendant of a signer of the Declaration of Independence, who discovers a Washington his ancestor would have wept to see: a city populated by weak, venal congressmen; cynical, manipulative lobbyists; unemployed men and women who no longer have faith in themselves—a city dominated, according to a press release for the film, by an "invisible power that leads, bleeds and squeezes the people of the country!" [9] Presiding over this sad mix is the master lobbyist Norton—a surname given to political evildoers in at least three separate films during the decade—who makes his own intentions clear: "Never in the history of this country has there been a greater opportunity for a strong man. Italy has her Mussolini, Russia her Stalin. Such a man will rise in America too. A man not afraid to break the law."

Several weeks after Roosevelt's inauguration, William Randolph Hearst's Cosmopolitan Studios, in conjunction with MGM, released *Gabriel Over the White House,* the movies' most searing indictment of conditions and most frightening prescription for action yet. Whether or not the film echoed "the very heart-cry of the nation," as one ad promised, it certainly echoed the misery of the nation. [10] On the day after his inauguration, President Judd Hammond is confronted by an angry reporter with the following litany:

> Starvation and want are everywhere. . . . Farmers burn corn and wheat. Food is thrown away into the sea while men and women are begging for bread. Men are freezing without coats while cotton rots in the fields. Thousands of homeless—millions of vacant homes. . . . What does the new administration say to . . . this tale of misery and horror—of lost hope—of broken faith—of the collapse of the American democracy?

Looking like Warren Harding and sounding like Herbert Hoover, President Hammond rests his case on traditional platitudes and faith: ''America will weather this depression as she has weathered other depressions. . . . Through the spirit of Valley Forge—the spirit of Gettysburg . . . and the spirit of the Argonne. The American people have risen before—and they will rise again.''

This gray bureaucrat is transformed not through a rational process of reform or education, but by means of a miracle. Driving his own car recklessly, the president crashes, suffers a severe concussion, and is pronounced ''beyond any human help.'' At this point, the curtains near his deathbed rustle, the spirit of Gabriel presumably enters his body, and the leader is reborn in one of the numerous scenes in which Depression Hollywood resolved a crisis through the process of redemption. The rejuvenated President does more than merely survive; he engages in what can only be called an orgy of action. Proclaiming ''As President of these United States my first duty is to the people!,'' he uses surplus food to feed the hungry; he dispenses aid to the farmers; he enlists the unemployed in an Army of Constructions ''subject to military discipline'' until a revived industry can reabsorb them; he prevents the foreclosure of mortgages until workmen can go back to work; he protects the people's bank accounts; he repeals ''that cesspool'' Prohibition; he ends crime by summarily arresting all racketeers, trying them by military court-martial, and shooting them; he invites representatives of all foreign nations to a disarmament conference on an American battleship, demonstrates the awesome might of American air power, and bullies them into disarming and paying their debts.

And he accomplishes all of this *alone,* forcing his formally dominant Cabinet to bend to his will or resign and coercing Congress into declaring a State of National Emergency and according him ''full responsibility for the government.'' Accused by a senator of subverting ''the government of our fathers,'' he responds: ''I believe in democracy as Washington, Jefferson and Lincoln believed in democracy, and if what I plan to do in the name of the people makes me a dictator, then it is a dictatorship based on Jefferson's definition of democracy—a 'government for the greatest good of the greatest number.' '' Collapsing as he uses Lincoln's quill pen to sign the universal disarmament accord, he dies while being assured by his lover that he has proven himself "one of the greatest men who ever lived."

The film's most striking characteristic is the extent to which it antici- pated Lewis's novel and made the coming of dictatorship plausible within an American context. Equally significant was the popularity of the film and the relative calm with which it was received. Walter Lippmann dismissed it as "the infantile world of irresistible wishes. . . . A dramatization of Mr. Hearst's editorials," The *New Republic* denounced it as "a half-hearted plea for fascism," and *The Nation* accused it of attempting to "convert innocent American movie audiences to a policy of fascist dictatorship in this coun- try." However, most observers saw nothing sinister in its message. The *New York Times'* reviewer summarized its plot as the story of "an earnest and conscientious President who tackles the problems of unemployment, crime and the foreign debts something after the fashion of a Lincoln." The *Chicago Tribune* hailed it as one of the "six best movies of the windy month" and advised its readers: "Don't miss this one!" The *San Francisco Chronicle* praised it as the story of "a President [who] suddenly becomes a reformer of government and puts the United States on a prosperous basis." *The Commonweal* hailed the film's advocacy of the summary court-martial and execution of criminals as "the only possible defense of society against a menace worse than revolution itself. In humanity, justice and decency, there cannot be two sides to such questions." The *Hollywood Reporter* hoped that the film would "put an end to the great problems that confront our nation today by showing . . . how a President of the United States handled the situation and the marvelous results he attained." [11]

It was precisely this casual acceptance that helped to create so much of the nervousness that pervaded the decade. Critic Bruce Bliven commented that the audience at performances of *Gabriel Over the White House* "cheers loudly both the promise of jobs for the unemployed and the threat of a big navy. It is as enthusiastic over the abandonment of democracy as it is over reverential mouthings about Lincoln." If the film had appeared under dif- ferent conditions, Bliven concluded, "with, for example, Mr. Hoover re- elected and the depression suddenly much worse, it might even have had serious political consequences." [12]

Bliven should have been better prepared for this reaction since it had characterized the response to Roosevelt's first Inaugural as well. Although that address has been most frequently remembered for Roosevelt's assurance that the nation had nothing to fear but fear itself, in fact the new president spent much of his time stressing just how monumental the problems were: "Values have shrunken to fantastic levels; taxes have risen; our ability to pay has fallen; government of all kinds is faced by serious curtailment of income; the means of exchange are frozen in the currents of trade; the withered leaves of industrial enterprise lie on every side; farmers find no markets for their produce; the savings of many years in thousands of families are gone. More important, a host of unemployed citizens face the grim problem of existence and an equally great number toil with little return.'' When he was not focusing upon what he called ''the dark realities of the moment,'' he was concerned with the need for ''a unity of duty hitherto evoked only in time of armed strife'' and for the need to ''move as a trained and loyal army willing to sacrifice for the good of a common discipline.'' He hoped that the normal balance of executive and legislative authority would be ''wholly adequate to meet the unprecedented task before us.'' Should it not be, ''I shall not evade the clear course of duty that will then confront me. I shall ask the Congress for the one remaining instrument to meet the crisis—broad Executive power that would be given to me if we were in fact invaded by a foreign foe.'' The people of the United States, he concluded, ''have asked for discipline and direction under leadership. They have made me the present instrument of their wishes. In the spirit of the gift I take it.'' [13]

Eleanor Roosevelt found her husband's inauguration a ''little terrifying . . . because when Franklin got to that part of his speech when he said it might become necessary for him to assume powers ordinarily granted to a president in war time, he received his biggest demonstration.'' [14] She could hardly have taken much comfort from the reaction of the nation's newspapers. Under such headlines as ''FOR DICTATORSHIP IF NECESSARY,'' and ''BROAD POWER SOUGHT IF CONGRESS DELAYS,'' the press widely reported the President's warnings, noted the applause with which they had been greeted, quoted such officials as Representative Black of New York who praised the President's courageous willingness ''to assume the entire burden of the complex problem himself,'' and generally refrained from showing any marked signs of concern or dismay. [15]

There were other disconcerting signs as well, from Al Smith's desire to see the government become ''a tyrant, a despot, a real monarch,'' as it had during World War I when it ''took our Constitution, wrapped it up and laid it on the shelf and left it there until it was over,'' to Republican Governor Alfred M. Landon's conclusion that ''Even the iron hand of a national dictator is in preference to a paralytic stroke,'' to the confession of the business magazine *Barron's* that ''Sometimes openly and at other times secretly, we have been longing to see the superman emerge. The question whether Mr. Roosevelt properly belongs in that category is not now answerable; the point is that for the moment he acts like one.'' *Barron's* realized that dictatorship was contrary to the spirit of American institutions. ''And yet—well, a genial and lighthearted dictator might be a relief from the pompous futility of such a congress as we have recently had. . . . Only, let our semi-dictator smile upon us as he semi-dictates." [16]

Though this kind of enthusiasm for authoritarianism seemed to diminish, especially as Hitler's regime became more overtly brutal, it never receded completely. In King Vidor's *Our Daily Bread,* released a year and a half after Roosevelt's inauguration, a group of unemployed people take refuge on an abandoned farm and attempt to establish a viable community based on simple barter, subsistence farming, and self-government. Someone suggests they turn to socialism for their governmental model and another voice suggests democracy, but a Swedish immigrant carries the day with his logic: "We got a big job here and we need a big boss." The business journal *Fortune* agreed. It devoted its July 1934 issue to praising Italian fascism and wondering whether "Fascism is achieving in a few years or decades such a conquest of the spirit of man as Christianity achieved only in ten centuries." Though it proclaimed itself "non-Fascist," *Fortune* concluded that "the good journalist must recognize in Fascism certain ancient virtues of the race, whether or not they happen to be momentarily fashionable in his own country. Among these are Discipline, Duty, Courage, Glory, Sacrifice." [17]

On the surface, the films of the 1930s were far less disposed than *Our Daily Bread* to grasp the naked hand of authority. More typically, they seemed to lend their energies to warning against, rather than calling for, the emergence of the big boss. In late 1934, just two weeks after General Smedley Butler startled a congressional committee with the assertion that he had been approached to lead a fascist putsch, Walter Wanger, who was convinced that the public was "eager . . . for themes that dare to grapple with real problems," released *The President Vanishes,* which was advertised as containing "revelations of the forces behind the operations of the nation." [18] These forces are identified as a group of power brokers—a banker, politician, newspaper publisher, judge, oil man, and master lobbyist—who are described by the lobbyist's cynical wife as "the government of the United States. They don't hold any office but things happen because *they* want them to happen." They use their resources and their hold on the mass media to promote a war to maximize their profits and recoup the loans they made to Europe in World War I. They search for a slogan which like those of the past—REMEMBER THE ALAMO, REMEMBER THE *MAINE,* KEEP THE WORLD SAFE FOR DEMOCRACY—will stampede the people into war. Finding their motto—SAVE AMERICA'S HONOR—they manipulate public opinion, undermine the president—"America . . . a great country without a leader. We need a man!"—and finance a paramilitary group, the Gray Shirts, who give a slightly modified fascist salute as they bark out the password, "Union!" "Today we number millions," their leader Lincoln Lee tells them. "Tomorrow we will encompass the earth. He who stands in our way must be destroyed. That goes for brother and sister and rulers in high places." The *New Republic,* which had been convinced that movies "getting after such sacred trumpery in earnest could not be made," was awed by the manner in which this film, despite its many oversimplifications, pinpointed those elements in the society which "will work in just about this way, ostensibly for God and actually for profits, with all this ballyhoo of press and radio." Audiences, the *New York Daily News* found, responded with enthusiasm to the film's message, frequently breaking into spontaneous applause.[19]

By the end of the decade, in *Confessions of a Nazi Spy* (1939), the threat to the American form of government had become both external and internal. A German-financed German-American Nazi movement waged a campaign against what its leader called "the chaos that breeds in democracy and racial equality" and worked for the day when the United States would become "*Unser Amerika*—Our America," a nation free to solve its problems without the restraints imposed by the Constitution or the Bill of Rights. What was under attack was not just a nation, the prosecutor tells the jury during the spy trial which ends the film, "America is not simply one of the remaining democracies. America *is* democracy. A democracy that has a God-given inspiration of free men determined to defend forever the liberty which we have inherited."

On the eve of America's entry into World War II, *Meet John Doe* introduced the American people to D. B. Norton, a fabulously wealthy media baron with his own private army and his own distinctive ambitions. "These are daring times," he tells a group of businessmen, labor leaders, and political bosses. "We're coming to a new order of things. There's too much talk been going on in this country. Too many concessions have been made. What the American people need is an iron hand. Discipline!" In one of the most affecting scenes in the film, Norton's disillusioned and slightly drunk editor, Connell, who has just learned of his employer's intention to become dictator, tells John Doe of his feelings for the American system: "I'm a sucker for this country. I'm a sucker for the *Star Spangled Banner* and I'm a sucker for this country. I *like* what we got here. I like it. A guy can say what he wants and do what he wants without having a bayonet shoved through his belly. . . . And we don't want anyone coming around changing it, do we? No sir! And when they do I get mad. I get boilin' mad. . . . I get mad for a guy named Washington and a guy named Jefferson and Lincoln. Lighthouses, John. Lighthouses in a foggy world."

On the whole, then, Depression Hollywood came to the defense of the traditional American democratic system in the face of rising authoritarianism, but its defense was ridden through by a recurrent streak of pessimism and doubt. From the beginning of the decade, Hollywood evinced a pervasive ambivalence concerning the American people, who were constantly referred to as the core and hope of the state but who were depicted again and again as weak, fickle, confused sheep who could be frightened, manipulated, and controlled. This tendency can be seen as early as *American Madness* (1932) which combined eloquent praise of the people with brilliant scenes of frenzied mobs succumbing to rumors and storming the banks. President Hammond in *Gabriel Over the White House* refers to the people as "the roots of the nation," claims that he exists "only by the will of the people," and yet speaks of the need "to arouse the stupid, lazy people of the United States" and chooses to rule them without their consent. President Stanley in *The President Vanishes* asserts, "I have faith in the American people"; yet he lies and schemes "to bring the American people back to their senses." In film after film, hardened politicians understand and exploit the weaknesses of the public they ostensibly serve.

In *The Phantom President* (1932), a smooth-talking, charismatic medicine-show doctor takes the place of the dull presidential candidate he physically resembles, prescribes a medicine of thirteen herbs that will cure the country, and is elected by gullible voters. The identical theme is reiterated on the local political level in *The Dark Horse* (1932). A gubernatorial candidate, Zachary Hicks ("Hicks, The Man from the Sticks"), who is characterized as "so dumb that every time he opens his mouth he subtracts from the sum total of human knowledge," is a certain loser until his campaign is taken over by a manager who teaches him to answer every question, "Yes—and again—no," and to plagiarize from the speeches of Abraham Lincoln. The film ends with Hicks's triumph and the political sharpster's departure to manage an equally insipid candidate in another state. In *Thanks a Million* (1935), a cynical political manager dumps his party's uninspiring gubernatorial candidate in favor of an apolitical crooner who is elected by charming the people with his quips and songs. In *The President Vanishes,* the special interest groups are so successful in fomenting the war spirit among the people that the President arranges to have himself kidnapped to take the electorate's mind off war. "Three days ago the people were crying for war," a newspaper publisher observes. "Now they're crying for just one thing— their President." In almost every politically focused Depression film from *Washington Merry-Go-Round* (1932) to *Meet John Doe* (1941), public opinion is portrayed as equally mindless and volatile, succumbing to the last persuasive voice it is exposed to. "We've been fed baloney so long we're getting used to it," a citizen in the latter film laments.

In addition to their other faults, the people are frequently portrayed as blindly self-interested. Everyone constantly comes to Washington "to get something. Why doesn't someone come to *give* something?'' a congressman asks the Bonus Marchers in *Washington Merry-Go-Round.* ''Why don't you help the government instead of hindering it? . . . You call yourselves *ex*-servicemen, why don't you call yourselves *service*-men!'' This attempt to arouse the people to go beyond their own immediate interests and act for the general welfare was common in Depression movies. The gangster film *Scarface* (1932) began with the challenge: ''This picture is an indictment of gang rule in America and of the callous indifference of the government to this constantly increasing menace to our safety and our liberty. . . . The government is your government. What are *You* going to do about it?''

Hollywood's tendency to place responsibility for the nation's plight upon the people themselves was accompanied by a tendency to view the people as unable or at least unlikely to free themselves from their own narrow concerns. John Doe's (and Frank Capra's) alter ego, the hobo known as ''The Colonel,'' refers to this when he defines one of his favorite terms—''Heelots'':

> a lot of heels. They begin creeping up on ya, trying to sell you somethin'.
> They got long claws and they get a stranglehold on ya. And you squirm
> and you duck and you holler and you try to push them away, but you
> haven't got a chance. They gotchya! First thing you know, you own things.
> . . . You're not the free and happy guy you used to be. You gotta have
> money to pay for all those things. So you go after what the other fella's
> got. And there you are: you're a heelot yourself.

Ambivalence toward the people was paralleled by an ambivalence concerning politics. This took the form of a deep suspicion of politicians and the political process. One John Doe club in a small town refuses to let the mayor join, explaining: ''You know how politicians are!'' Indeed, if Hollywood audiences didn't know, they soon learned as they watched a parade of greedy, short-sighted politicians in movies depicting national and local politics. There were exceptions, such as *The Man Who Dared* (1933), the biography of Mayor Anton Cermak of Chicago who was killed by a bullet intended for President-elect Roosevelt, and who in the film turns to Roosevelt and whispers with his dying breath: ''I'm glad it was me and not you.''[20] This positive image was more than matched by such films as *The Night Mayor* (1932), based on the life of New York's playboy mayor, Jimmy Walker, whom Roosevelt forced to resign, or *The Great McGinty* (1940), which depicted the rise of a politician who began as a bum voting thirty-eight times in one municipal election and rose through the ranks to become alderman, mayor, and governor only to fall when he attempted in one brief flash of honesty to buck the machine and help the poor. ''This is the story,'' the film's introduction tells us, of a man who ''was dishonest all his life except one crazy minute. . . . [and] had to get out of the country.'' Mc-Ginty's moment of honesty was rare; most Hollywood politicians were not that imaginative. Closer to the mark was *The Phantom President,* in which the vision of a senator's smug face dissolves into the image of a horse's ass.

The *Washington Post* reviewer who took Capra to task for making every politician in *Mr. Smith Goes to Washington,* save the hero himself, ''a moving force of dishonesty, thievery, treachery and corruption,'' could have extended his charge to virtually every other film dealing with politics. The Columbia Pictures press release for *Washington Merry-Go-Round* boasted that its congressman hero ''alone among his associates seems to want to give anything to the government. The rest, almost without exception, are looking for everything they can get out of it.''[21]

Paradoxically, this deep suspicion of politics and politicians was linked with a constant appeal for greater political direction. The clergyman praying for the safe return of the kidnapped president in *The President Vanishes,* speaks of how desperately the American people need their leader: ''He preached the precious gospel of peace. In our frenzied greed we struck him down. Oh God, restore him to us so that he may lead us in the paths of righteousness.'' This paradox often resolved itself through a demand for leaders who would rise above politics, who would be greater than the system, above petty argumentation, ordinary concerns, sordid selfish interests. Such figures came closest to realization in the divinely inspired President Judd Hammond of *Gabriel Over the White House* or Capra's simple creations, Jefferson Smith and John Doe, whose innocence and goodness allow them to transcend the system.

In thirties' movies, as well as in many other aspects of Depression culture, there was a tendency to utilize patriotic symbolism, especially that of the Civil War, and to take heart from the examples of extraordinary individuals—Abraham Lincoln being a favorite—who were clothed in a quasi-religious aura. How pervasive the Lincoln image could be is manifest in *Gabriel Over the White House,* in which President Hammond uses Lincoln's quill pen to sign the disarmament accords, has a bust of Lincoln in his office, takes inspiration from hearing his followers sing ''The Battle Hymn of the Republic,'' and uses the following Lincolnesque rhetoric to address the Bonus Army:

> It is not fitting for citizens of America to come on weary feet to seek their President. It is rather for their President to seek them out, and to bring to them freely the last full measure of protection and health. And so I come to you.[22]

This spiritual elevation of the leader could easily have the effect of diminishing his followers. At the close of *The President Vanishes,* a grateful President Stanley offers that small band of followers who stood by him anything they want. Val the grocery boy asks only that he be given a photo of his leader signed "to my faithful subject." When the First Lady protests, "You're not a subject. This is a Republic!" Val counters, "I know all that but that's what I want," and assures Stanley in a worshipful tone, "Anything you want is okay with me, Mr. President."

Ambivalent feelings about the people and the politicians often helped lead to a quiet but pervasive sense of despair concerning the future of both the individual and democracy. This despair can be seen in how often those who champion the cause of the people and the cause of democracy are forced to go beyond the democratic method, are forced to lie to and manipulate the people for their own good. This dilemma is at the core of Hollywood's Washington; indeed, it helps to define it. In *Washington Merry-Go-Round* and *Mr. Smith Goes to Washington,* the attempts of two freshman congressmen to reform the system by working through it have disastrous results. Representative Brown is thrown out of the House by a bogus electoral recount staged by the local political machine in his state, and Senator Smith's reputation and political future are almost destroyed by the machine-ruled press of his home state. Both are forced to go beyond politics to save the people from their own democratic political system. In *Gabriel Over the White House,* the newly inspired President Hammond can protect the people from the rigors of the economic disaster only by abandoning the system entirely and ruling without it. In *The President Vanishes,* the only way in which the decent President Stanley can prevent the nation from being stampeded into war by the special interests is to stage his own kidnapping and blame it on the Gray Shirts, whose leader he has murdered. He can find no way of utilizing the system itself in order to save it. He must ape the methods of the interests he is fighting; he must deceive a gullible public for its own good; he must break the law in order to uphold it.

In *Meet John Doe,* the answer to the crisis of the Great Depression resides not in the government but in the John Doe clubs that blossom all over the nation, in which local people dedicate themselves to helping each other. Still, it is clearly implied that without the media-manufactured symbol of the great and good quintessential American John Doe, the clubs would crumble and the people would be incapable of sustaining their local efforts. Thus, even in those many movies which do not openly advocate authoritarian rule, which in fact combat it, the thrust is toward the importance of the leader. Contrasted with the venal politicians, greedy lobbyists, and the confused, easily led public, a figure such as President Stanley is wise, patient, and good. Although the means he employs are illegal and immoral, he is vindicated because he uses them for the greater good.

This disturbing picture of leadership in a democracy is paralleled by the equally disturbing focus upon the need for vigilante action; not only is it necessary for the leader to go beyond the system, but the people too must take matters into their own hands. *This Day and Age* (1933) has become the symbol of this focus. A group of high school students, disgusted by the failure of the courts to convict the murderer of a local shopkeeper and a fellow student, take matters into their own hands. They kidnap the murderer, try him in a dark, deserted brickyard where hundreds of frenetic students conduct what one of them calls "a court of justice if not of law as you understand it." "We haven't got time for rules of evidence," they inform him as they obtain his confession by lowering him into a pit filled with rats. To the tune of the Revolution's "Yankee Doodle Dandy" and other traditional American songs, they ride him on a rail back to town where they invade the home of the judge who originally freed the murderer and force him to hear the confession. A relieved judge and sheriff praise the "heroic" boys and retrospectively legitimate their methods by deputizing the boys. Newspaper ads invited the public to "SEE . . . COURAGEOUS YOUTH . . . throwing off the yoke of oppression as their forefathers did before them. . . . 5000 torches light the heavens . . . 10,000 glowing faces flame with eagerness, determination, and undying courage . . . as civilization goes on trial." Cecil B. De Mille, the ads promised, "shows us where we're heading." [23]

This Day and Age was the most egregious and most effective portrayal of the need for citizens to take the law into their own hands, but it was by no means unique; it represented a popular genre—especially in the early years of the Depression. *Song of the Eagle* (1933) told the story of Prohibition through the saga of the Hoffman family, who build a brewery, lose it during Prohibition, and attempt to begin again when the Eighteenth Amendment is repealed, only to be terrorized by gangsters who destroy their trucks and raid their customers. Young Bill Hoffman looks for relief not to the law but to his wartime buddies whom he enlists to "fight fire with fire" as they successfully adopt the gangsters' own methods to save the brewery. Paramount Studios boasted that the film depicted the situation that would confront the nation as soon as alcohol was legalized again. The film offered, one ad promised, "a decisive solution to the problem confronting every American citizen." "This is your country," another ad announced. "Are you going to save it?" [24]

Certainly, Hollywood was perfectly capable of advocating legal means of redressing wrongs. In *Young Mr. Lincoln* (1939), the hero defends two clients against a lynch mob with his folksy wisdom: "Trouble is when men start takin' the law into their own hands, they're just as apt in all the confusion and fun to start hangin' somebody who's not a murderer as somebody who is. Then the next thing you know they're hangin' one another just for

fun. . . . We seem to lose our heads in times like this. We do things together that we'd be mighty ashamed to do by ourselves." This antivigilante
tone characterized a number of films produced in the second half of the
1930s: *Fury* (1936), *The Legion of Terror* (1936), *Black Legion* (1936),
They Won't Forget (1937), and *Mountain Justice* (1937).

However, in the early 1930s most political films emphasized the need
for forms of extraordinary action. In *Washington Merry-Go-Round,* the master lobbyist Norton cannot be controlled by official Washington, which he
dominates, but only by a group of ex-soldiers (led by the deposed Representative Brown) who kidnap him, force him to confess, and then give him a
gun with which to commit suicide. In *Gabriel Over the White House,* a
military judge tells the gangster he is sentencing to death that "we have in
the White House a man who has enabled us to cut the red tape of legal
procedures and get back to first principles. An eye for an eye, Nick Dia-
mond! A tooth for a tooth! A life for a life!"

This need to continually go beyond the system helped to create the
mood of bleak pessimism that characterized so many of these films. Always
implicit in them was the message that the system no longer worked, no
longer could contain the powerful forces that everywhere beset it, no longer
could be responsive to the people it ostensibly served. The satirical political
films of the Depression reflected the identical theme. In his extremely popular *Million Dollar Legs* (1932), W. C. Fields portrayed the president of
Klopstockia, who is forced by his country's political process to win his
office anew each morning in an Indian-wrestling match. He attends cabinet
meetings toting a gun and wearing brass knuckles, while those around him
engage in meaningless intrigues against him. A year later, the Marx Brothers went even further in depicting the meaninglessness of government. In
Duck Soup (1933), Rufus T. Firefly (Groucho Marx) becomes President of
Freedonia and makes it clear from the beginning that he will be corrupt since
corruption is an inherent part of authority. Upon taking office he sings:

> The last man nearly ruined this place,
> He didn't know what to do with it.
> If you think this country's bad off now,
> Just wait till I get through with it.

He irresponsibly steers the nation toward war and when peace threatens, he
cries out: "But there must be a war—I've paid a month's rent on the battlefield." Nothing has meaning: not country, not war, not patriotism. At the
film's climax, with Freedonia triumphant, Margaret Dumont begins to sing
the national anthem and the Marx Brothers pelt her with apples.

Political films were not alone in communicating this message. It pervaded the crime films and G-men films of the decade. When the gangster

Tony Camonte in *Scarface* refers happily to the "Writ of Hocus Pocus" that so often rescues him from the police, he is articulating something very much on Hollywood's mind in the 1930s: the system of justice has been taken over by sinister forces. All too frequently it was gangsters and corrupt politicians rather than honest citizens who benefited from constitutional legalities and the courts. And in back of the gangsters in film after film were respectable bankers and businessmen. "This is a business," a gangster says in *You Can't Get Away With Murder* (1939). "Don't you think those Wall Street guys got their hands in everybody's pocket?" Racketeers, a crusading publisher in *Bullets or Ballots* (1936) testifies, "have the American public pretty well whipped. . . . [They] laugh at your laws, they make a joke of your courts. They rule by the fear of their bullets. They must be smashed by the power of your ballots." The need to root out lawlessness through the system was the ostensible message of this film. Its effective message was articulated by an aroused police commissioner, who tells the gang boss whose premises he is searching without a warrant, "Go get your restraining orders and injunctions and anything else you need. The police used to waste a lot of time getting them trying to stop you. From now on we act first. We'll let you waste *your* time getting 'em. Maybe you can stop us."

So long as the police operated within the law, so long would they be incapable of coping with their adversaries. This was the premise of the entire popular genre of private-eye movies and books. The private detective's advantage over the regular police was his freedom from institutionalized legal constraints. The distinction between him and the criminals he fought resided not in the methods employed but the end for which each labored. The means, a desperate Hollywood seemed to be saying, were less important than the ends. If there was in the 1930s a growing consciousness of the centrality of institutions, it was accompanied by a good deal of anger and discontent, by much awareness of the fact that the system no longer operated as it had been designed to. This distrust of modern institutions, this sense that the world no longer functioned as it was supposed to, that the old verities and certainties no longer held sway, formed the bridge of continuity between aspects of 1930s culture and the bleak *film noir* mood of the 1940s.[25]

Depression films help us to perceive continuity in still another area. Few contemporary historians would portray the 1920s without dealing with the cultural politics that were so central to the decade. For some time now we have understood the 1920s as a period of cultural conflict—a period of dissonance between the traditional ideals and the new patterns of modern living, between small-town ways and the new urban presence, between the long-standing model of what an American was and the new realities of what Americans were actually becoming. Similarly, it would be difficult to find serious students of the 1950s who would fail to focus upon the emergence or reemergence of the politics of culture in that decade in order to understand such phenomena as McCarthyism or the American reactions to the Cold War. Indeed, one cannot understand contemporary America and the phenomenon of Ronald Reagan without some comprehension of these cultural tensions.

If these cultural forces were so important in the 1920s and reemerged after World War II as central aspects of the political landscape, what happened to them during the Great Depression? Our notion of the 1930s has for too long ignored this central question. Our preoccupation with the issues of politics and the economy in the thirties and the war in the forties has beguiled us into believing that the salient cultural issues disappeared. We have chosen to highlight those parts of the Depression that had to do with the New Deal—with reformation, progress, and the ongoing emergence of the new society and economy. Insofar as we have recognized the existence of cultural dissonance in the Depression, we have confined it to such peripheral groups as the Midwestern Regionalists, who filled their paintings with nostalgia for a faded Arcadia, or the Southern Agrarians with their endless lament for a lost world, their angry tirade against urban culture and urban peoples, and their resistance to what Alan Tate called ''that all-destroying abstraction, America.'' [26]

The films of the 1930s remind us that similar laments could be found in the mass culture of the Great Depression. A significant number of the decade's films were concerned with restoration, as if something had been removed from American life. Senator Jeff Keane in *Washington Masquerade* refers to a group of corrupt politicians and lobbyists, who had tempted him to forgo his crusade for reform, as ''men like you—men who prowl into . . . people's houses right beneath their breasts where their hearts beat. And for what? So that you can take this land that Washington gave us and make it your own and laugh at us!'' Referring to the special interests, Representative Button Gwinnett Brown in *Washington Merry-Go-Round* charges, ''They've made a scrap of paper out of the Declaration of Independence, they've made a joke out of the Constitution.'' ''We're going to have law and order again,'' he tells the lobbyist Norton. ''The people are not going to stop until they get their government back.''

Our Daily Bread, King Vidor's story of a group of Depression victims who find refuge on an abandoned farm, gets to the heart of Hollywood's restoration theme. On the farm they learn that, as one of them puts it, the earth ''makes you feel safe, confident. . . . It's like a mother.'' Going back to the land helps them discover themselves and sort out their priorities. The snake in the garden is an urban woman who corrupts the community's simple, earthy leader and convinces him to go to the city with her. ''Don't think back, baby,'' she tells him. ''Think ahead!'' Throughout the films of the Depression it was the city, as the representative of modernity, that corrupted the traditional dream and fouled the promise of America; the city that spawned the amoral men and fallen women of the gangster films; the city that formed the backdrop for the glittering but empty antics of the glamorous men and women of the decade's screwball comedies.

Hollywood's Washington became a symbol of the forces and developments that had derailed America from its destiny and led it astray. Into the nation's capital, troop a group of starry-eyed reformers from small-town America who quickly become the dupes or victims of the sordid, cynical urban businessmen, journalists, politicians, and lobbyists. Senator Jeff Keane is attracted to a beautiful, sophisticated woman, secretly in the employ of corrupt interests, and led to abandon his ideals and desert the people who elected him; Representative Button Gwinnett Brown is deprived of the office to which he was rightly elected; Senator Jefferson Smith is pilloried, mocked, and almost destroyed; President Craig Stanley is dragged to the brink of impeachment for daring to champion the traditional pacifism of the American people against the avarice of hungry capitalists; the idealistic James Pomeroy in *Breach of Promise* (1932) sees his campaign for the U.S. Senate disrupted by blackmail inspired by a rural woman who became a "wild girl" in the city.

The full dimensions of this cultural conflict are revealed in the works of the Depression's best-known and most widely admired creator of film: Frank Capra.[27] Although Capra did not treat the nation's capital until *Mr. Smith Goes to Washington* in 1939, he dealt with national issues from the very beginning of the Great Depression. In *American Madness* (1932), the first American film to depict the banking crisis in any detail, Capra told the story of Tom Dixon, a banker who championed the average depositor in a manner that buttressed traditional values. "Let's get the right kind of security," he tells his directors. "Not stocks and bonds that zigzag up and down. Not collateral on paper but character. *Character!* It's the only thing you can bank on and it's the only thing that'll pull this country out of the doldrums."

In *American Madness* we get the first clear statement of the dichotomy that runs through so much of Capra's mature work and so many of Hollywood's films in general: the dichotomy between a real and a fantasy society. The camera lovingly shows us the workings of a large modern urban bank, but this documentary realism is belied by the bank president who tells us that he personally reviews each and every loan application and, most fantastic of all, that "most of the depositors I know personally. I've seen them grow up in the community. I knew their fathers and mothers before them." Materially, Capra depicted a modern urban bank; spiritually and ideologically he gave us a nineteenth-century small-town bank. The combination reveals the great dissonance that existed between Capra's ideals and the situation he and other Americans were facing in the 1930s: they brought nineteenth-century small-town values and expectations to bear on a crisis involving twentieth-century modern bureaucracies. This portrait of an idealistic banker, who first loses his faith in the people as he watches them succumb to rumors and stage a run on his bank and then regains his faith when the mob suddenly listens to those who remind it of how he had helped them when they needed him, lacks only one of the ingredients that came to characterize Capra's quintessential Depression films: the overt struggle between small-town and big-city values. This Capra added in his Depression trilogy: *Mr. Deeds Goes to Town* (1936), *Mr. Smith Goes to Washington* (1939), and *Meet John Doe* (1941).

In each of these films Capra focused upon a small-town hero who came, like a lamb to the slaughter, into the midst of the sharpsters and hucksters of the big city, suffered profound humiliation and disillusionment, and survived to convert the heroine and the cynical newspapermen whom Capra used to symbolize urban values. In *Mr. Smith Goes to Washington*, Capra has his hero Jefferson Smith say, "great principles don't get lost once they come to light." That is precisely the function of the Capra hero: he brings great principles to light, he unites traditional ideals and action. It was no accident that the name of Capra's first hero in this vein, Longfellow Deeds, was a combination of the nineteenth-century poet/thinker, Longfellow, and the man of action, of deeds—the man who, as Patrick Gerster has pointed out, is *deeded* the American tradition and clarifies its meaning for others.[28] Thus when the hard-boiled newspaper reporter Babe Bennett, whose name symbolizes just how much urban Americans have to learn from their small-town countrymen, escorts Deeds to Grant's Tomb and remarks that most people find it a letdown, Deeds responds, "Oh, that depends on what they see," and proceeds to become her teacher by sharing his vision with her:

> I see a small Ohio farm boy becoming a great soldier. I see thousands of marching men. I see General Lee with a broken heart surrendering. And I can see the beginning of a new nation like Abraham Lincoln said. And I can see that Ohio boy being inaugurated as president. Things like that can only happen in a country like America.

In *Mr. Smith Goes to Washington*, Capra once again married the image of the thinker, the idealist, the nineteenth-century giver of tradition—Jefferson—with Everyman—Smith. Jefferson Smith, the head of the Boy Rangers in, and the newly appointed U. S. Senator from, a western state, is in effect a grown-up Boy Scout—the idealized image of what we had all been in our youth, of what America had been in its youth—come to Washington. In this film, as in the others, we have Capra's classic double conversion: first, Smith's worldly-wise assistant Saunders and her coterie of newspaper cynics are converted by the innocence and wisdom of Smith and then they help to restore his faith when the corruption and lack of ideals he finds in Washington depress him severely. It is only after she comes to appreciate Smith that Saunders is able to reveal her own small-town origins and her long-hidden first name, Clarissa—a traditional piece of herself that she had learned to repress in the atmosphere of the nation's modern urban capital.

Babe Bennett and Clarissa Saunders, like their counterpart, Anne Mitchell, in *Meet John Doe,* are drawn back to the small-town innocence and unpretentiousness they—and America—have somewhere lost. They had been, as Babe puts it, "too busy being smart alecks. Too busy in a crazy competition for nothing." But with the help of unspoiled individuals like Deeds, Smith, and Doe, whom America presumably still had in abundance, they could redeem themselves. And this is precisely what so many of Capra's—and Hollywood's—Depression films are about: redemption. As Leonard Quart has observed, Capra was not concerned with the politics of social restructuring or revolution but with the politics of conversion and moral regeneration.[29] If the films of the early Depression flirted with the need for social change and authority, Capra's political films dealt with the need for a return to the basics of American tradition. At the heart of his later films, Capra has written,

> was the rebellious cry of the individual against being trampled into an ort
> by massiveness—mass production, mass thought, mass education, mass
> politics, mass wealth, mass conformity . . . a growing resentment against
> being compartmentalized.

In a 1972 interview, Capra put his message more succinctly: "you dirty bastards, get off our necks!"[30]

It is important to understand that there is something deeper going on in Capra's films than the mere recitation of past virtues. Capra is struggling to understand how traditional American values and means could be made to work in contemporary America. Thus Capra progressively enlarges the scope of his canvas. While Tom Dixon faces a conservative board of bank directors and a frightened group of depositors, Deeds faces urban snobbery, cynicism, and petty larceny, Smith faces the entrenched power of the United States Senate, and John Doe faces the massive power of a media baron determined to become a fascist dictator. Capra kept expanding his investigation and less and less could he find satisfactory or believable ways out of the dilemma in which his representative traditional American man found himself. In film after film the villain becomes increasingly invulnerable to attack; you can stymie him and thwart some of his specific goals, but you cannot permanently defeat him, for in the end he has the power. This is graphically demonstrated at the end of *Meet John Doe* when D. B. Norton silences the hero at a political convention by cutting off the microphone—that is, by literally keeping the source of power in his own hands.

This telling scene reminds us that Capra focused on not only the values of traditional small-town America but also its chief means of communication: oral culture. His heroes invariably function through the spoken word while many of his urban villains—cynical newspaper reporters and snobbish literary types—are people of the written word. It is when they are shorn of their ability to speak directly with the people that Capra's heroes are at the nadir of their political influence: Tom Dixon unable to speak the truth effectively in the midst of a riotous run on his bank; Longfellow Deeds prevented by a severe personal depression from speaking in his own behalf at his insanity trial; Jefferson Smith threatened with silence by the rules of the Senate; John Doe attempting to address his followers through a dead mike.[31]

It was this dilemma—this futile search for ways in which to make the means and ends of traditional America effective again—that made it so difficult for Capra to find appropriate endings for his political films. Capra filmed five different endings for his final Depression film, *Meet John Doe,* in one of which, Gary Cooper, portraying a frustrated, impotent Doe unable to expose the fascist ambitions of D. B. Norton, plunges to his death from the city hall on Christmas Eve. Capra has testified that he did not dare to use this ending. "You just don't kill Gary Cooper. It's a hell of a powerful ending, but you just can't kill Gary Cooper."[32] Of course, it was not Gary Cooper that Capra was afraid of killing; it was a dream, a hope, an ideal that he did not dare portray as dead. If Capra could not allow Doe to destroy himself, neither could he allow him to triumph. The film ends with Doe being led away from his intended suicide perch by a small band of people who harbor the improbable dream of rebuilding the network of John Doe Clubs that Norton had wrecked.

Capra's difficulties with *Meet John Doe* were not unique; he had difficulty finding endings for all his political films. The reason was not aesthetic; it was that the logical endings, the effective endings that flowed organically from all of the facts and details that Capra gave his audiences, were not those endings Capra wanted. In life, Tom Dixon would have lost control of his bank or, at the very least, lost his faith in the people; in life, Longfellow Deeds would have been committed to an insane asylum or, at the very least, lost control of his millions; in life, Jefferson Smith would have been expelled from the Senate or, at the very least, been beaten into impotent quiescence; in life, John Doe would have jumped to his death or, at the very least, faded into obscurity.

The crisis of the Great Depression challenged the rationality of the American system and Frank Capra responded by reasserting his faith in traditional values and verities. But in spite of his aggressive optimism and his comedic style, his response, like Hollywood's in general, was increasingly ridden through with ambiguities and a brooding pessimism. Hollywood films were far more prone to expose than to prescribe. Many of the films I have been discussing were quite successful in portraying the difficulties and the irrationalities of the American governmental system but they refrained from drawing the logical conclusions from the material they themselves supplied. Instead they tended to impose formulaic endings, which often bordered on the miraculous. Nothing Jefferson Smith did, for example, was sufficient to overcome the machinations of the lobbyists and machine politicians in the U.S. Senate. Victory comes only when the corrupt senior senator from his state has an unlikely bout of conscience and suddenly confesses. There were, as we have seen, other cultural responses to the breakdown of the traditional system: the response of the Marx Brothers or W. C. Fields; of Superman or the Hardboiled Detective; of those Hollywood filmmakers who flirted with authoritarianism and direct vigilante action. But such responses entailed a loss of innocence. Capra, and many of his Hollywood colleagues, insisted upon victory *plus* innocence—on traditional ideals and traditional heroes winning on their own terms.

There is a hubris which makes critics and scholars prone to believe that only they are privileged to see the kinds of cultural tensions, incongruities, and ambivalences I have been discussing and to write as if contemporary audiences somehow could not or would not see these things. It is important for us to investigate seriously the possibility—for which I believe much evidence exists—that, culturally, people can have their cake and eat it too; the possibility that a substantial number of Americans understood that the implied endings of many of the films they saw were closer to reality than the imposed endings; the possibility that audiences were able to learn from the main thrust of the films they saw even while they derived comfort and pleasure from the formulaic endings.

Capra's films help us to perceive another truth about Hollywood's Washington. No matter how close Capra's message may have been to that of the Regionalist painters or the Agrarian writers, he himself was very different. While they were native-born Midwesterners or Southerners, Capra had been born in a village on the outskirts of Palermo, Sicily, and brought up in an immigrant neighborhood in Los Angeles, the son of poor, illiterate parents. Capra is an important reminder that the reiteration of the traditional American creed emanated not just from defensive old-stock Americans but often issued in its most dynamic and aggressive form from converts to Americanism. This dynamism was reflected in the comment of a Hollywood producer shortly after he saw a preview of *Mr. Smith Goes to Washington* in 1939: "The great thing about that picture is that it makes America exciting."[33] Stephen Handzo has referred to the remarkable talent that "the Sicilian-born, slum-raised'' Capra had ''for evoking the hopes and dreams of Middle America.''[34] But Capra was not unique. Cultural historians have yet to investigate the impact of the presence of so many first- and second-generation Americans among the producers, directors, actors, writers, and studio heads in Hollywood and the reciprocal cultural relationship they had with the larger population.

It would be misleading to pretend that Hollywood's Washington was invariably serious. In *Thanks a Million* (1935), the American people sing of the complexities of their new government:

> They started up the NRA to keep the big bad wolf away
> Then FDR began to be a headache to the GOP
> Now that codes are everywhere we've got initials in our hair
> The farmer's IOU's O.K. since Congress formed the AAA
> The CCC chops down a tree and sells it pronto FOB . . .
> The RFC and NHA led millions to the AAA
> The AAA has crops it cuts and all of us are going nuts!

The film's hero croons his optimistic campaign speech:

> I'm sitting high on a hilltop
> Tossing all my troubles to the moon
> Where the breeze seems to say don't you worry
> Things are bound to pick up pretty soon.[35]

In *Stand Up and Cheer* (1934), the President appoints a Secretary of Amusement ''whose duty it shall be to amuse and entertain the people—to make them forget their troubles.'' With his budget of one hundred million dollars, the new secretary launches a ''Smile Campaign'' which soon has the American people singing in the streets:

LABORER: I'm laughing and I've got nothing to laugh about
             So if I can laugh, sing, dance, and shout—brother so can
             you!
WASHWOMAN: I'm laughing, with a dozen kids I have to feed
             So if I can laugh while I'm in need, sister so can you!
FARMER: I'm laughing and there's a mortgage around my neck
             So if I can plow and sing, by heck, neighbor so can you!

Persevering against special interests that want the economic crisis to continue, the Department of Amusement finally is able to announce the joyous news that the Depression is over:

> Can't you see the writing that's on every wall?
> The worst is over—here comes the clover—

> We're out of the red!
> We're out of the red!
> We're out of the red!
> We're out of the red![36]

In spite of this reiteration, the crisis was to last long beyond 1934 and Hollywood continued to reflect its political ramifications, continued both to mirror and to influence prevailing attitudes and ideologies. The writer John Clellon Holmes, who was a young and avid moviegoer in the 1930s, has observed, "We learned so much from the movies, and the lessons were so painless, that I, for one, still associate certain films with the dawning of certain ideas." He was never able to forget the actor Edward Arnold's portrayal of the fascistic D. B. Norton in *Meet John Doe*. "Edward Arnold's reptilian eyes behind his pince-nez will always signify for me the desperate lust for power out of which the powerlessness of modern life produces totalitarians. . . . In the years that followed, when I became attracted to, and then involved with, and finally disaffected from, party politics, the memory of this film (and others like it) had an influence on my decisions and aversions that is incalculable."

Scholars need to pay more attention to this ongoing conversation between Hollywood and its audiences. We need to investigate seriously Holmes's assertion that "the movies of the thirties constitute, for my generation, nothing less than a kind of Jungian collective unconscious, a decade of coming attractions out of which some of the truths of our maturity have been formed."[37]

13

The Historian and the Icon: Photography and the History of the American People in the 1930s and 1940s

This essay, like a number of others in this volume, outgrew my original intentions or, in this case at least, my original assignment. While I was working in the Library of Congress searching for illustrations for my book *Highbrow/Lowbrow*, two friends, Carl Fleischhauer of the Library's American Folklife Center and Beverly Brannan of its Prints and Photographs Division, told me of an exhibit and book they were planning. They intended to focus on the photographs of Roy Stryker's renowned photographic section, which had operated under the auspices of three different agencies of the federal government—the Resettlement Administration (RA) from 1935 to 1937, the Farm Security Administration (FSA) from 1937 to 1942, and the Office of War Information (OWI) from 1942 to 1943. They wanted to approach those photographs not as a sequence of celebrated "hit" photographs but as integral parts of a series the photographer was assigned to take on cotton pickers or migrant workers or urban poverty or Americans celebrating the Fourth of July. Carl and Beverly were convinced that, when seen alongside other photographs taken on the same subject at the same time by the same photographer, the photographs would assume more meaning than when seen as isolated shots.

I liked the conception a lot and agreed to write a background essay for the book that would accompany the Library of Congress exhibition. When they wondered which historian might write on photography itself, I recommended Alan Trachtenberg of Yale University. As it turned out, Trachtenberg and I became involved in the entire project from selecting photographs to attending planning sessions to editing the texts that accompany the photographs. I had never before worked on a historical project centering on photography, and I found the experience remarkably enjoyable and edifying. Indeed, I learned enough about photography from working with Beverly, Carl, and Alan that when it came time to write my "background" piece I couldn't quite bring it off. I tried to concentrate exclusively on the historical context, but the photographs kept intruding.

After several honest attempts to do what I had been asked to do, I allowed the photographs and their photographers to take center stage and informed Beverly and Carl that they were going to have *two* essays on photography. Once I stopped fighting the urge to focus on photography, I spent a wonderful summer reading books and articles, studying photographs, and writing about a subject I had never considered before in a concentrated way.

The experience of writing something I hadn't *intended* to write is no longer novel to me, but it remains a largely mysterious and puzzling phenomenon. While hard work and thoughtful work remain prerequisites, parts of the essay almost seemed to write themselves, or at least to structure themselves. The only useful thing I can tell students about this process is that when it happens they shouldn't fight it but go with it. One of the joys of writing is to surprise yourself, occasionally at least. This essay certainly accomplished that. It was originally published in Carl Fleischhauer and Beverly W. Brannan, eds., *Documenting America, 1935–1943* (Berkeley: University of California Press, 1988), and is reprinted here with several additional photographs and a number of substantial textual changes. When I speak of "this volume" in the essay, I am referring, of course, to *Documenting America*.

> *We are practical beings, each of us with limited functions and duties to perform. Each is bound to feel intensely the importance of his own duties and the significance of the situations that call these forth. But this feeling is in each of us a vital secret, for sympathy with which we vainly look to others. The others are too much absorbed in their own vital secrets to take an interest in ours. Hence the stupidity and injustice of our opinions, so far as they deal with the significance of alien lives. Hence the falsity of our judgments, so far as they presume to decide in an absolute way on the value of other persons' conditions or ideals.*

> William James, "On a Certain
> Blindness in Human Beings"[1]

One of the more elusive and difficult historical truths is that even in the midst of disaster life goes on and human beings find ways not merely of adapting to the forces that buffet them but often of rising above their circumstances and participating actively in the shaping of their lives. Only relatively recently have historians begun to comprehend the implications of Ralph Ellison's important questions concerning the history of Afro-Americans in the United States: "Can a people . . . live and develop for over three hundred years simply by *reacting?* Are American Negroes simply the creation of white men, or have they at least helped to create themselves out of what they found around them? Men have made a way of life in caves and upon cliffs, why cannot Negroes have made a life upon the horns of the white man's dilemma?"[2] Even amid the extreme conditions of the Holocaust's concentration camps, human beings clung to life, to each other, to those creative acts that made it possible to preserve some semblance of their culture, their dignity, their sanity.

To say these things is not to minimize the importance or the impact of such phenomena as slavery, persecution, and economic travail. It is simply to assert that human beings are not wholly molded by their immediate experiences; they are the bearers of a culture which is not static and unbending but continually in a state of process, perennially the product of interaction between the past and the present. From the rarified perspective of power and decision making, which historians tend to chronicle and analyze most frequently, it is perhaps too easy to forget that all people, not just the movers and the shakers, bring something complex and enduring to their experiences and that they retain the capacity of affecting events as well as being affected by them, of changing the present as well as being changed by it, of acting as well as being acted upon.

The suffering of Depression America never approached the prolonged anguish of centuries of slavery or the intense horrors of the Holocaust, but that has not prevented us from searching for perfect victims during the 1930s as well as on the plantations and in the concentration camps. The images are familiar: Dorothea Lange's "Migrant Mother" (figure 6), one of the most widely reproduced and familiar photographs in our history, with its gaunt, haunted—and haunting—central figure and its frightened, helpless children, immediately captured the imagination of the Depression generation and has come to represent that generation to its descendants.[3] This appears to have been the sixth and final photograph Lange took of Florence Thompson and several of her daughters on a rainy March afternoon in 1936. In an earlier photograph in the series (figure 4), Lange utilized not only people but things—a battered trunk and an empty pie plate—to symbolize homelessness and poverty.[4] Many of the other widely reproduced photographs by Lange and her colleagues were similar to "Migrant Mother" in subject matter and intent. For all of the undeniable power of these images, William Stott has commented upon how little of these people we actually see: "They

Figures 1–6: *Migrant Mother.* These six images of thirty-two-year-old Florence Thompson and her children were made by Dorothea Lange in a migrant labor camp in Nipomo, California, March 1936.

Figure 1

Figure 2

Figure 3

Figure 4

Figure 5

Figure 6

come to us only in images meant to break our heart. They come helpless, guiltless as children and, though helpless, yet still unvanquished by the implacable wrath of nature—flood, drought and the indifference of their society. They come, Pare Lorentz said, 'group after group of wretched human beings, starkly asking for so little, and wondering what they will get.' Never are they vicious, never depraved, never responsible for their misery. And this, of course, was intentional.''[5]

Although images like these were and are among the best-known representations of the Depression, for some students of the thirties the very existence of other images, the very fact that the Resettlement Administration (RA) and Farm Security Administration (FSA) photographers did not adhere inexorably to the victimization model, is troubling. Maurice Berger, the curator of a recent exhibit of RA and FSA photographs at the Hunter College Art Gallery in New York City, for example, is uncomfortable with Arthur Rothstein's photo of a farmhand in Goldendale, Washington, in 1936 or Lange's photo of the wife and children of a tobacco sharecropper in Person County, North Carolina, in July 1939 (figures 7, 8). Utilizing the technique of shooting from below, "an angle that traditionally signifies stature and esteem," Rothstein, Berger charges, created a "metaphor of stability . . . a respect for hard labor and the dignity of toil." Lange's photo "similarly ignores the devastation [of the Depression]. Not only do the robust mother and son smile, but the children appear clean, well-fed, and neatly dressed." Images like this result in "weakening the effect of the depictions of abject poverty, racial unrest, crime, disease, and despair." The photos that most commend themselves to Berger are those of the faceless and the helpless. In his "Farmer sampling wheat in Central Ohio, Summer 1938" (figure 9), Ben Shahn "shoots the filthy and ragged farmer from above (a common device in his FSA work), short-circuiting metaphors of dignity. Bent over and completely anonymous, the farmer is captured from a perspective that underlines his position on the economic ladder." John Vachon's "Sick child, Aliquippa, Pennsylvania, January 1941" (figure 10) is even more effective: "Nestled in a heap of rags, old clothing and filth, the girl is too ill to respond to the photographer's intrusion; in the midst of detritus and decay, she lies unprotected. The viewer is left gasping at the utter desperation and perilousness of her condition. 'I cannot help her,' one thinks, 'but neither can she help herself.' . . . It is through trauma that the unstaged photograph manipulates most effectively.''[6]

Photographic images, like statistics, do not lie, but like statistics the truths they communicate are elusive and incomplete. The statistical chaos that prevailed in the early years of the Depression concerning such fundamental matters as the number of men and women out of work confused contemporaries and continues to frustrate historians. As late as 1936 Roo-

Figure 7: Farmhand near Goldendale, Washington, July 1936. Arthur Rothstein.

Figure 8: The wife and children of a tobacco sharecropper on their front porch, Person County, North Carolina, July 1939. Dorothea Lange.

Figure 9: Farmer sampling wheat in Central Ohio, Summer 1938. Ben Shahn.

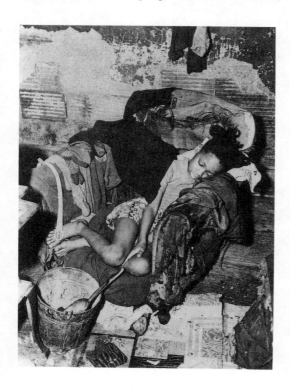

Figure 10: Sick child, Aliquippa, Pennsylvania, January 1941. John Vachon.

sevelt's chief welfare adviser, Harry Hopkins, conceded that his information on unemployment was not "adequate," and whether there were eight million or eleven million jobless depended on whose figures were consulted. Rather than being used as tools for understanding the nature of the economic devastation, unemployment figures became partisan weapons, manipulated to protect or assault political leaders, to defend or alter national and local policies. President Hoover ruthlessly slashed the latest unemployment figures that reached his desk, eliminating those workers he decided were only temporarily jobless and those he deemed not seriously bent on finding work. Hoover was a classic example of how ideology can mold facts to fit expectations. In the midst of figures that told of growing unemployment, privation, and the inability of local governments and agencies to cope with the crisis, Hoover could tell a delegation that came to him in June 1930 requesting immediate expansion of federally sponsored public works, "Gentlemen, you have come sixty days too late. The depression is over." He could insist incessantly that "our people have been protected from hunger and cold" and that "nobody is actually starving." He could proclaim that "the hoboes, for example, are better fed than they have ever been." And he could maintain, even years later, that the ubiquitous apple sellers who had quickly become a feature of city street corners represented not the unemployed but rather those who had "left their jobs for the more profitable one of selling apples."[7]

To this day, estimates of the number of unemployed during the Depression's nadir in 1933 differ, ranging from thirteen to sixteen million, though statistics provided by the Bureau of Labor Statistics and the Committee on Economic Security make it clear that by March of that year at least one out of every four American workers was jobless and that only about one-quarter of those were receiving any relief, most of it grossly inadequate. But even these stark facts tell us too little. By 1933 the practice euphemistically referred to as work-sharing was widespread as employer after employer converted their workers into part-time employees. Thus while unemployment may have been the most widely dreaded condition, it was only the most extreme of the problems American workers faced. We may never know precisely how many of those who were working during the Depression had their hours—and pay—drastically reduced, but these figures indicating the number of full-time workers employed by the United States Steel Corporation are instructive:

1929: 224,980
1930: 211,055
1931: 56,619
1932: 18,938

On April 1, 1933, United States Steel employed not one full-time worker.[8]

By themselves statistics can never tell us enough; they have to be accompanied by other kinds of materials to assume their full meaning. We have focused so completely on the plight of the unemployed that we have forgotten the often desperate situation of the three out of four workers who still had employment of some sort. What did it mean to work in the midst of a severe economic crisis when losing one's job could mean disaster? How did this threat affect one's behavior and orientation? In 1939 Anna Novak remembered that when she worked at the Chicago meat-packing houses in 1931 both men and women had to secure their jobs by bringing the foremen bottles of whiskey on all the holidays. "Your job wasn't worth much if you didn't observe the holiday 'customs.' " Women had an additional price to pay: "You could get along swell if you let the boss slap you on the behind and feel you up. God, I hate that stuff, you don't know!" She attempted to find other work but ultimately was forced to return to the world of the stock-yards.[9] It was not unusual testimony. Workers found themselves bound to accept the conditions that prevailed at their place of work. In spite of being driven "like a clock 10 and 12 hours a day" and returning home "so tired I'd just sit down at the table and cry like a baby," Mary Siporin had no alternative but to cling to her job. A garbage worker testified that he was so conditioned by the desperate need for security during the Depression that even many years later, "I don't dare switch [jobs]."[10] Even this testimony gives us an incomplete picture; it does not explain the thousands of workers in the rubber, automobile, and steel industries who jeopardized everything in 1936 and 1937 to strike for their right to help determine the conditions of their employment. For some workers, at least, the route to greater security seemed to be not through accommodation and resignation but through militancy and organization.

Thus while the dreary statistics of unemployment, suicide, malnutrition, and sickness are central to any understanding of the time, they, together with the haunting photographic images of blasted farms, faces, and hopes, leave us unprepared for other truths of life in the Great Depression. Following a lecture in which I mentioned the tens of millions of Americans who attended movies weekly in the 1930s, a student confessed that he had had no inkling that people continued to do such "normal" things. He knew that films were made during the thirties, but the images of that decade, struck so deeply into his consciousness, made it difficult for him to accept the fact that people actually could break away from their suffering long enough to attend and respond to movies. Similarly, we are not prepared to see the symbolic victims we have become familiar with do anything but appear appropriately despairing, to suffer—with admirable dignity perhaps—but to suffer nonetheless. Life, and human beings, however, are rarely that one-dimensional. The first two pictures Lange took of the Thompson family, although aesthetically less arresting than the final two, embody truths no less important. Here, in the midst of the starkest poverty, we see smiling children and a dreamy adolescent (figures 1 and 2).

Truths crowd out truths; realities impinge on realities; images confuse as well as enlighten, interfere as well as communicate, clash as well as complement. Neither in photographs nor in life is reality composed of a series of either/or images. In their account of three sharecropper families, *Let Us Now Praise Famous Men* (1941), James Agee and Walker Evans included many photos of the Burroughs family,* including their widely reproduced shot of an unshaven, tired, anxious Floyd Burroughs in a tattered work shirt (figure 11). They chose not to use a picture that Floyd Burroughs had requested they take of him, his arms thrown confidently around the shoulders of his smiling wife and sister-in-law, with his children posed in front, everyone looking clean and contented in their best clothing (figure 12). It was a classic family pose but not one congenial to the purposes of the book from which it was excluded. As William Stott has put it, "This George Gudger needs no one's pity"; nor did his family, which showed their ability to be "this clean without running water or sanitary facilities, this decently dressed on little money, this self-respecting in economic servitude, this gentle despite their hardships."[11] The fact that Burroughs, who seems to have had no objections to the other photographs that were taken, wanted himself and his family pictured in this light as well, is an important part of the reality of the thirties that we can ignore only at great cost to our understanding of the self-images and the aspirations of people like the Burroughs.[12]

That the photographs from Stryker's section are filled with these tensions and ambiguities is a clue to their essential soundness as guides for the historian. The argument that only those photographs that depict unrelieved suffering and exploitation can be trusted as accurate portrayals and have anything to say to us has at its core a concept which ultimately subverts the struggle for historical understanding: the notion that things must be one way or the other, and therefore that it is impossible to maintain any semblance of dignity or self-worth or independence in the face of poverty and exploitation. If photographs tell us that people do have this capacity, we must deny our eyes and convince ourselves that we are examining manipulated icons. If our ears tell us that even in the midst of desolation people can sing songs of transcendence and joy, we must insist that such songs are mere anodynes in the mouths of deluded singers. The urge, whether conscious or

---

*Following the mode of the period, Agee and Evans changed the names of the families they depicted in their book. Thus the Burroughs family was renamed the Gudgers, and Floyd Burroughs became George Gudger.

Figure 11: Floyd Burroughs (George Gudger), Hale County, Alabama, 1936. Walker Evans.

Figure 12: The Burroughs family (the Gudgers and Emma), Hale County, Alabama, 1936. Walker Evans.

not, to deprive people without power of any determination over their destiny, of any pleasure in their lives, of any dignity in their existence, knows no single part of the political spectrum; it affects radicals and reactionaries, liberals and conservatives, alike. The only culture the poor are supposed to have is the culture of poverty: worn faces and torn clothing, dirty skin and dead eyes, ramshackle shelters and disorganized lives. Any forms of contentment or self-respect, even cleanliness itself, have no place in this totality.

It is hardly a new position. This is what the psychologist Bruno Bettelheim had in mind when he argued that the German concentration camps infantilized their victims, whose wills became almost totally linked with those of their "significant others"—the guards/gods. It is the plantation universe sketched by the historian Stanley Elkins and populated with black slaves whose condition turned them into "Sambos" with no wills of their own and a fantasy life "limited to catfish and watermelons."[13] Here we have a closed universe whose inhabitants act according to a predetermined script. The poor and the weak, who were treated like ciphers by the more powerful during their lives, would hardly be surprised to find themselves being treated like ciphers by scholars long after their deaths. But both they and we deserve better. Historians have the same obligations to their dead subjects that anthropologists have to their living ones. They must recognize their humanity, search for their points of view, respect their complexity. The dictum that "God is in the details" has particular relevance for historians. It is precisely the details that these photographs help us to recover.

This volume is filled with truths that have been too often crowded out, realities that have been too easily blurred, images that have been too frequently lost by the simple repetition of a single dimension, by the sustained search for the ideal. The photograph is beguiling because it seems to be the quintessential objective document—reality in black and white—and thus makes a greater claim on our credulity than other types of documents. We know that newspaper reports, magazine articles, autobiographies, congressional testimony, and political speeches are all imperfect sources, deeply affected by the views and circumstances of the reporters, writers, and politicians who create them. We have even begun to learn the truth of the old saw that while figures may not lie, liars figure, and thus that even hard statistics, so solid and reliable in appearance, have to be subjected to the most rigorous of tests. But what of photographic records? While we may dismiss ideal types, we continue, sometimes in spite of ourselves, to search for ideal sources, and what could recommend themselves better than photographic records, which appear to come to us not as the figments of someone's imagination but as the objective artifacts of demonstrable reality? The truth, of course, as Halla Beloff has written, is that "like the computer, the camera is an instrument of human intelligence.''[14] Consequently, the images it creates are also the products of human intelligence, like all of the other sources historians utilize, and the photograph has to be read with the same care and thoughtfulness we have learned to apply to written sources. With photographs, as with other types of historical materials, a simple change in context can drastically alter the meaning of an "objective" image. This is well demonstrated by what occurred when the figure of the plantation owner in Dorothea Lange's "Plantation owner, Clarksdale, Mississippi, June 1936" (figure 13) was used by itself two years later in Archibald MacLeish's book *The Land of the Free* (1938), accompanied by a page of MacLeish's verse (figure 14).

That MacLeish could use the white man for purposes that seem quite divergent from those implicit in the original photograph underlines the essential ambiguity present in Lange's picture to begin with: it captured the image of a man who exemplified the exploitative, racist, undemocratic features of southern plantation life even while he also doubtless represented many of the qualities that built the type of individualistic freedom that has characterized America throughout so much of its history. It is not that Lange and MacLeish necessarily distorted the image they were utilizing but that they had their hooks into different aspects of that image. The importance of photography as a source is precisely this: it can freeze conflicting realities, ambiguities, paradoxes, so that we can see them, examine them, recognize the larger, more complex, and often less palatable truths they direct us to.

Photographs, then, are a source that needs to be interpreted and supplemented by other evidence. They are incomplete, as historical sources always are. They have been collected and filtered through other hands, as historical sources always have been. They are filled with contradictions and paradoxes, as the most valuable historical sources frequently are. In short, they behave much like other sources historians depend on. What differs is less the uniqueness of photographic materials than our tendency to see photographs as more "real" than other sources and our relative inexperience in using them historically. We have to learn the truth of Alan Sekula's observation that "the photograph, as it stands alone, presents merely the *possibility* of meaning."[15]

As creators, the photographers represented in this volume helped to mold the period in which they lived, but we must remember that they were the creatures as well as the creators of their culture and never stood wholly apart from it. They were not coolly detached observers making disinterested portraits of a people apart; they were members of a society representing a culture to itself. They were, to a greater degree than they could have been aware, taking pictures of themselves as well as of their fellow Americans. This of course makes their work particularly valuable as a source for under-

Figure 13: Plantation owner, Clarksdale, Mississippi, June 1936. Dorothea Lange.

We told ourselves we were free because we were free.

We were free because we were that kind.

We were Americans.

All you needed for freedom was being American.
All you needed for freedom was grit in your craw

And the gall to get out on a limb and crow before sunup.

Those that hadn't it hadn't it.

"Have the elder races halted?

Do they droop and end their lessons wearied over there beyond the seas?

We take up the task eternal and the burden and the lesson —

Pioneers Q Pioneers."

We told ourselves we were free because we said so.

We were free because of the Battle of Bunker Hill
And the constitution adopted at Philadelphia

Figure 14: From Archibald MacLeish, *Land of the Free*.

standing their era but should also caution us to remember the fragility of their images and the need to supplement them.

The veteran photographer Ansel Adams complained to Roy Stryker, "What you've got are not photographers. They're a bunch of sociologists with cameras."[16] Though Adams might have said this of many groups of photographers, his insight helps us to understand both the strengths and weaknesses of these photographs as historical sources. For such influential sociologists of the period as Robert S. and Helen Merrell Lynd, Muncie, Indiana, was "Middletown" and its inhabitants nameless, ideal Middle Americans living and working in the prototypical Middle American setting. We learn to know them not as individuals but as representations. Similarly, from the photographers of the 1930s we have inherited the images of people with precious little additional information. Again, we come to know them as types: migrant farmers, sharecroppers, hoboes, unemployed men, desperate mothers, ragged children. In the captions to the photographs in this volume few names of those pictured are given because the photographers simply failed to supply them or provide other essential data concerning the people they were photographing. Dorothea Lange never inquired after the name of the woman whose image she made immortal (we know her as Florence Thompson because of researchers who later sought her out and interviewed her); never noted the names of the four daughters pictured in the series; never sought to learn the whereabouts of Thompson's other three children or her husband; and, so far as we can tell, never wondered where Florence Thompson had been or where she hoped to go. "I did not ask her name or her history," Lange noted simply, as if this was the most reasonable possible action. Lange and most of her fellow photographers not only failed to record such elementary information as the names and backgrounds of their subjects, they rarely thought to collect such facts in the first place. They generally did not conceive of these details as necessary in accomplishing their goals. In Florence Thompson and her daughters Lange knew she had found precisely the ideal image she was searching for. When she completed her six shots, she slipped into her car and drove off. "I did not approach the tents and shelters of other stranded pea-pickers," she later noted. "It was not necessary; I knew I had recorded the essence of my assignment."[17]

The photographers were not unique. The writers employed by the Federal Writers' Project of the Works Progress Administration (WPA), who left us a monumental collection of interviews with a wide spectrum of Americans, did collect and record their subjects' names and asked them questions that frequently elicited many of the details of their subjects' lives. But they too were specifically interested in those they interviewed as types: former slaves, stockyard workers, members of the maritime union, riders of the rails, traveling salesmen, and those details that did not directly bear upon such categories were usually neither elicited nor preserved. Sylvia Diner, a WPA interviewer collecting folk songs and lore from Yugoslavian immigrants in New York City in 1938, was annoyed when her subjects insisted upon interrupting the interviews to discuss the German conquest of Czechoslovakia, a fate which they feared lay in store for their homeland as well. The singing of folk songs ended abruptly in the Sekulich home when the oldest daughter turned on the radio and the family gathered round it to hear the latest news. "The historic ballads of long ago were obliterated in the heat of current events," Diner complained. Although she praised "the analytical powers and keen concern of these supposedly simple, backward people," the details of their political views went essentially unrecorded since they deviated from her immediate conception of the group she was interviewing.[18] Similarly, the folklorists of the period collected songs, stories, jokes, anecdotes, proverbs from people whose individual names, histories, and circumstances they recorded so rarely or so incompletely that today we too often have the folklore without the folk, whose identities have become blurred by time—indeed, were *allowed* to become blurred by time—through the methods the folklorists of the period employed.

But there is a positive side to this as well; it was precisely from the photographers' attempts to picture their subjects not as individuals but as components of a larger context that at least part of the triumph of their photographs as historical documents derives. The demand for documentation, the hunger for authenticity, the urge to share in the experiences of others were widespread throughout the thirties. In this respect the FSA photographs were part of a much larger world of documentary expression that included the movie newsreels, radio news programs, the Federal Theatre's documentary plays called "Living Newspapers," the WPA's *American Guide* series which produced geographical and cultural road maps for every state and major city as well as a host of interesting byways, the blossoming of photojournalism in *Life* and *Look* magazines, and such quasi-documentary expression as radio soap operas. William Stott has made the interesting point that while the Hoover administration was continually embarrassed by the documentary approach, the New Deal "institutionalized documentary; it made the weapon that undermined the establishment part of the establishment."[19]

The historian Irving Bernstein recently observed that "the anguish of the American people during hard times demanded a pictorial record."[20] While Bernstein has probably summed up the initial motives of many of the FSA photographers accurately, they accomplished far more than the depiction of American anguish; they created a record of American life. The photographers may have set about documenting the immediate impact of the severe economic depression, but they succeeded in creating a remarkable portrait of their countrymen's resiliency and culture. In these photographs, as in such other sources as the many oral interviews that were recorded during and after the 1930s, the more than fifteen million letters people wrote to President and Mrs. Roosevelt, and the rich folklore that was collected, we are made witness to a complex blend of despair and faith, dependency and self-sufficiency, degradation and dignity, suffering and joy.

It is difficult to take exception to a statement made by Bob Aden, who was the subject of a John Vachon photograph in 1942: "I'm sure the experience of the Depression—what we went through—established patterns and habits that all of us have carried through for the rest of our lives. For example, I could never stand to buy anything on time; I had to have the money to pay for it. The first time I bought an appliance on time, it scared me to death."[21] The effects of the Depression and the war that followed it were deep and enduring. But, as these photographs indicate, while few escaped the tumultuous events that surrounded them, they were not the mere mute products of those events; in a number of important ways, their lives often transcended their immediate experiences. What scholars are too prone to dismiss as the "trivia" of life are revealed by these sources to be often integral parts of life's essence. Ella Watson's world (figures 15, 16, 17; see also figures 1, 2 in essay 14) was crucially affected by the conditions of her employment; by the actions of governments, federal and local; by the racial mores and prejudices of her fellow Americans. But her world was not confined entirely by these perimeters; it included her relationships with her family, her friends, her church. It did not begin and end with the hours during which she wielded her mop in government offices; it was richer and more complex, embodying other dimensions. Whatever his original intentions, Gordon Parks's accomplishment was to afford us a glimpse of a hard life lived with a greater degree of dignity and strength, containing more variety and choice and telling us more about an entire culture, than he may have initially realized.

The process of visual documentation was by no means simple, and the photographers' own needs and perceptions often become almost indelibly intermeshed with those of their subjects. Depression Americans, living through one of the greatest crises in their history, were prone to look back upon the past, and particularly the folk past, as a symbol of a simpler, cleaner, less problem-ridden time when individuals still commanded their own destinies and shaped their own universe to a greater extent than was any longer possible. This urge to look back, which certainly was present in the nineteenth century, became particularly noticeable after the trauma of the First World War. In the 1920s popular culture was laced through with an emphasis on the self-sufficient heroes of such bygone eras as the Old West, when good

Figure 15: Ella Watson, Washington, D.C., 1942, cleaning a government office at night. Gordon Parks.

Figure 16: Ella Watson, right, and her adopted daughter. Gordon Parks.

Figure 17: Ella Watson receiving a blessing and anointment from Reverend Smith at St. Martin's Spiritual Church. A second exposure depicts another celebrant receiving a rose from Reverend Gassaway. Gordon Parks.

and bad supposedly were distinguished with ease and human beings had the capacity to alter their environment. This urge led as well to an appreciation of the self-contained folk in what were conceived of as primitive societies and explains the surprising popularity of such documentary films as Robert Flaherty's *Nanook of the North* (1922), which depicted the hard but integrated and meaningful life of an Eskimo group, and the vogue of Black Harlem, where people were portrayed as still expressing their repressed urges and experiencing life more fully on their own terms. There was, of course, another side to this romantic urge: if the "primitive" were envied, they were also pitied and depicted as excluded from the wondrous fruits of modernity.

This ambivalent yearning to combine the innocence and clarity of the past with the sophistication and technological complexity of the present can be discerned throughout modern American culture but was particularly strong in the 1930s, when composers like Aaron Copland and George Gershwin, Hollywood directors like King Vidor and Frank Capra, and artists like Grant Wood and Thomas Hart Benton turned to the folk past and the small town in their search for the American Way.[22] This trend helps to explain why industrial strikes featured rural folk songs and singers, why Americans were so taken with films like Capra's *Mr. Deeds Goes to Town* (1936), *Mr. Smith Goes to Washington* (1939), and *Meet John Doe* (1941) which sought to probe the fate of small-town values in modern urban America, and why the photographers in Stryker's section spent far more time and energy recording agrarian and small-town America than industrial and urban America.* It is in this context that we should understand such series as "Tenant Farmers" (see, for example, figures 18, 19), in which Arthur Rothstein seems to be indulging in nostalgia for the self-sufficiency and simplicity of the Afro-American culture of Gee's Bend, Alabama, even while he reveals the bare poverty and almost total lack of modern conveniences that characterized the lives of these tenant farmers. This is not to say that in "Tenant Farmers" we are viewing Rothstein's fantasies rather than a black southern community in the 1930s, but that in order to understand the particular form Rothstein supplied for the substance he photographed we need to comprehend more fully the intellectual prism through which he observed that community.

It might be argued that because these photographs begin only in 1935 and stretch well into the war, it is hardly surprising that they show normal pursuits, since conditions were so much improved. It is true that in the summer of 1935 the United States economy entered its first really impressive expansion since the Depression had begun, with employment in manufacturing increasing from 7.2 million in July 1935 to 9.1 million two years later. For the entire economy there were some four million more jobs in 1937 than there had been in 1935. Despite these heartening improvements, more than seven and a half million workers remained unemployed in 1937, substantial numbers of homeless men and women continued to roam the country, and hundreds of thousands of dispossessed farmers made the trek to California in search of work and land. America had hardly reached Nirvana. Nevertheless, President Roosevelt, who was urged by such conservative advisers as Secretary of the Treasury Henry Morgenthau to declare the New Deal completed, and who was himself perennially troubled by the unbalanced budget and the federal government's increasing role in the economy, used the undeniable improvements to rationalize a cutback in federal spending, including relief. The results were, or at least should have been, predictable. In October 1937 America experienced a severe collapse reminiscent of the one eight years earlier, causing income, production, and consumption to fall and unemployment to rise to well over ten million—almost one in every five

---

*Only about 25 percent of the photographs in the FSA-OWI Collection depict subjects in towns of fifty thousand or more inhabitants. Most of the urban photographs were made in 1942 and 1943 (Nicholas Natanson, *Urban Representation in the RA-FSA-OWI File, 1935–43;* unpublished report in *Documenting America, 1935–1943,* project records, Supplementary Archives, Prints and Photographs Division, Library of Congress).

Figure 18: Willie S. Pettway, Gee's Bend, Alabama, 1937. Arthur Rothstein.

Figure 19: Bucket and gourd, Gee's Bend, Alabama, 1937. Arthur Rothstein.

American workers—by 1938. Unemployment was to remain critically high until America's entry into World War II: almost nine and half million in 1939, over eight million in 1940, and, on the eve of Pearl Harbor, despite the stimulus that defense spending and the Lend-Lease Act (1941) had given the economy, five and a half million workers—almost one out of ten—were without jobs.[23]

World War II ended unemployment and led President Roosevelt to spend money and to centralize economic decisions to an extent he had not been willing to attempt in peacetime. But though the coming of war helped to ease the economic problems, it replaced them with the difficulties, trauma, and crises endemic to war, so that the context in which all of the photographs included here were taken remained an America beset by crisis. It was, moreover, an America not particularly confident of the future. In 1979 John Cockle, who had been photographed by John Vachon in May 1942 when Cockle was a student at the University of Nebraska, declared, "One big difference between us and people in school now is that most now have a pretty good feeling that when they get through there will be a demand for their services. That was not at all true in the late thirties, early forties. We knew we were going into the service—that was clear even before the United States was in the war. But when we got out, what then?" During the war itself 79 percent of the soldiers questioned were convinced it would be difficult for veterans to secure good jobs after the war, while 56 percent anticipated a widespread depression when the war ended and they reentered civilian society.[24]

Earlier I attempted to demonstrate that when viewed as a concise series, even so small a number of images as those Dorothea Lange took of the Thompsons supplies more dimensions and the possibility of a deeper reading than the single photo that has been most widely reproduced. This is truer still of the larger series from which we have made extensive selections that help to reveal both how the agency photographers worked and how the American people lived in the midst of America's most searing economic crisis and the early years of the war that succeeded it. Looking back on his collection from the vantage point of old age, Roy Stryker observed that "the work we did can be appreciated only when the collection is considered as a whole. The total volume, and it's a staggering volume, has a richness and distinction that simply cannot be drawn from the individual pictures themselves."[25] Though it is obviously impossible for all but a relatively few to view the collection as a whole, its significance is far better represented by the series presented here than by the single images previously available.

A number of contemporaries pointed out the difficulty of seeing the Depression with the naked eye. Caroline Bird commented that "you could feel the Depression deepen but you could not look out of the window and

see it. Men who lost their jobs dropped out of sight. They were quiet, and
you had to know just when and where to find them. . . . It took a knowing
eye—or the eye of poverty itself—to understand or even to observe some of
the action.''[26] This helps to underscore the importance of the FSA-OWI
photographs and the reason why the images that appear to have had the
greatest contemporary impact were those that concentrated upon the Depression's ravages. For the historian there is another kind of invisibility: the
difficulty of perceiving those aspects of Depression life that were not the
immediate result of privation and upheaval. The series featured in this volume help to penetrate both kinds of invisibility.

Americans suffered, materially and psychically, during the years of the
Great Depression to an extent which we still do not fully fathom, and continued to suffer in ways even less clear to us during the war. But they also
continued, as people always must, the business of living. They ate and they
laughed, they loved and they fought, they worried and they hoped, they
created and reared children, they worked and they played, they dressed and
shopped and ate and bathed and watched movies and ball games and each
other; they filled their days, as we fill ours, with the essentials of everyday
living. It is true, certainly, that they did these things in the context not just
of change—which is the context of all historical action—but of rapid, visible
change. During these years people learned to look to institutions, especially
to the federal government, in ways that their ancestors and they themselves
just a few decades earlier would never have expected. As important as this
truth is, as central as this development was, we cannot begin and end our
portrait of the American people by focusing all of our attention on the New
Deal or FDR or the breadlines. We need, desperately, to enter the movie
palace and the ballpark, the workplace and the living room, the neighborhood and the church, the stores and the streets, the farmhouse and the fields.

These photographs help us begin this process, but we will be able to
learn from them only if we study them with the understanding that as familiar as the people in them might appear, they were citizens of another decade,
privy to another consciousness through which they saw and understood reality. What Warren Susman has said of moving-picture images applies to still
photographs as well: they ''may contain disguised or unconscious assumptions and perceptions, clues to issues and concerns often fundamental to the
filmmakers, but not obvious because we fail in our effort to see as they saw,
feel as they felt.''[27] Thus we must adopt an anthropological vision and pre-
pare ourselves for the possibility that these people whose lives we are sharing for the moment are not necessarily earlier versions of ourselves whom
we can know just by knowing ourselves. It is much safer to approach the
people who inhabit these pages as different from ourselves, as people whose
lives and thoughts we have to strive to understand in however flawed a

manner. To attempt to capture *their* way of doing things, *their* consciousness, *their* worldview, is the stuff of history, the quest that gives historians purpose and meaning. The photographs that fill this volume help us do that, help us to comprehend a part of America we have heretofore neglected.

Any account of the period's culture must be expansive enough to include crosscurrents, ambiguities, tensions. A culture that made both *The Grapes of Wrath* and *Gone with the Wind* best-selling novels and critically acclaimed and widely attended motion pictures, was clearly not a culture monolithically fixated on either confronting or evading the central problems of the period. On the surface, John Steinbeck's *The Grapes of Wrath* and Margaret Mitchell's *Gone with the Wind* seem to be symbols of different cultural urges. The former, by graphically and sympathetically depicting the plight of Dust Bowl migrants, helped to compel Americans to confront one of the nation's salient problems, while the latter, by transporting Americans back to the Civil War era seen from a blatantly and romantically Southern perspective, ostensibly helped them forget such pressing realities. This simple dichotomy ignores the fact that, as different as they were, both of these novels—and films—sprang from the same ideological matrix and shared visions of the future. Both had at their core the conviction that the individual could surmount the difficulties of the present and that societal regeneration was possible. "We ain't gonna die out," Ma Joad declares toward the close of Steinbeck's book. "People is goin' on—changin' a little, maybe, but goin' right on.''* *Gone with the Wind* ends on a more individual but no less optimistic note with Scarlett O'Hara refusing to accept the finality of Rhett Butler's decision to leave her.

With its graphic depictions of the horrors of war, *Gone with the Wind*, like *The Grapes of Wrath,* did not deny the harshness of the world it depicted. Nevertheless, again like *The Grapes of Wrath,* its central thrust was to affirm traditional American values and optimism.[28] Both of these novels and films were part of a redemptive genre that included, for example, the highly popular and critically acclaimed film *Stagecoach* (1939) which pictured the individual redemptions of an outlaw, a prostitute, and an alcoholic doctor thrown together on a flight for life through Indian territory.[29]

In the culture of the 1930s past calamities could become didactic mechanisms for illustrating the ways in which people might triumph over adversity, rediscovering in the process those enduring values they had lost sight of in better times. *San Francisco,* the most profitable film of 1936, depicted the transformation of a hard-bitten saloonkeeper who only through the trauma of the 1906 earthquake is able to sort out his priorities and discover his true

---

*The film adaptation of the novel closes with Ma Joad asserting even more confidently, "We're the people that live. They can't wipe us out. They can't lick us. We'll go on forever, Pa, cause we're the people."

feelings for a woman he had formerly maltreated, even attaining enough humility to sink to his knees in prayer when he finally finds her unharmed by the disaster.

These notions of individual and societal survival and regeneration were endemic to the culture of the Great Depression, and it is hardly surprising to find them in the photographs that so quickly became an integral part of American culture. The photographs never denied the problems America faced, although like so many other genres of American culture during the period they failed to probe very deeply into their underlying causes and their relationship to other features of American life. If there is a predominant innocence in these photos, however, it is not that of evasion—since few other forms of expressive culture documented the failure of the American economy more graphically or immediately—but the innocence of faith, the belief that Americans had within themselves the qualities and traditions necessary to regenerate themselves and the American dream. Speaking of the photographer Russell Lee, Roy Stryker wrote, "When his photographs would come in, I always felt that Russell was saying, 'Now here is a fellow who is having a hard time but with a little help he's going to be all right.' And that's what gave me courage." Stryker returned to this theme again and again:

> The faces to me were the most significant part of the file. When a man is down and they have taken from him his job and his land and his home— everything he spent his life working for—he's going to have the expression of tragedy permanently on his face. But I have always believed that the American people have the ability to endure. And that is in those faces, too.
>
> Many of these people were sick, hungry, and miserable. The odds were against them. Yet their goodness and strength survived.
>
> You could look at the people and see fear and sadness and desperation. But you saw something else, too. A determination that not even the Depression could kill. The photographers saw it—documented it.[30]

These photos, then, evince Depression culture not only in their images but also in the ideology out of which those images issue. An understanding that these icons reveal not merely the external but also the internal realities, not only appearances but also beliefs, is an important key to comprehending their significance and their meaning. The ubiquitous image of the victim was originally intended to help galvanize public opinion behind the need for governmental help and reform and has served historically to explain the necessity for the massive federal intervention that took place and to justify what happened to the American polity during the thirties. Thus *Midweek Pictorial* utilized Lange's "Migrant Mother" to illustrate its indictment of the inequities inherent in farm tenancy and its demand for change, while the *Buffalo Times* employed an array of Resettlement Administration photos in the before/after format popular throughout the decade to justify federal farm programs (figures 20, 21). The documentary quality of these photos made it difficult to deny the realities of the 1930s, but the photos nevertheless furnished the opportunity of reasserting traditional beliefs. Was "Migrant Mother" a study in despair or in inner strength? Were her face and demeanor symbols of victimization or dignity? It was possible to read into these photographs what one wanted, what one needed, to see in them, and in the 1930s many wanted and needed to see both qualities. It is significant that during these years the image of the victim was never sufficient; it had to be accompanied by the symbols of dignity, inner strength, and ultimate self-reliance. Stryker identified the tension in the images his photographers captured as "dignity versus despair," and commented, "Maybe I'm a fool, but I believe that dignity wins out. When it doesn't then we as a people will become extinct."[31] Characteristically, *Life* magazine had no difficulty in perceiving in Dorothea Lange's photo of a grizzled, impoverished migrant farmer the visage of a traditional American pioneer (figure 22). Though all cultures require icons, they do not require the same ones or use them for the same purposes. That the salient qualities in the icons Depression America used to rationalize massive federal action seem to have been suffering *and* dignity, helplessness *and* self-reliance, tells us much about both the people who created them and the people for whom they were created.

It is particularly important to comprehend the extent to which the ideology represented by these symbols was a shared one. The tendency of recent critics to see Stryker as the author of the worldview that permeated the FSA-OWI file, without adequate reference to the worldviews of his photographers or their subjects, can be misleading.[32] The FSA-OWI file was, after all, reformist and optimistic, embodying a blend of individual and community orientation which was in a long-standing American tradition. Stryker certainly had his priorities, though they were no more totally consistent and successfully implemented than those of his leaders, from Rexford Guy Tugwell to Franklin Delano Roosevelt. There was confusion in Stryker's goals and actions simply because there was confusion and uncertainty in Stryker— the identical body of confusion, hesitation, and ambivalence that ran like a thread through the New Deal from 1933 to 1941. Insofar as Stryker had an ideology, it was not the product of a smoke-filled conference room teeming with politicians and capitalists; it emanated from the same matrix that had long permeated American politics and the American people and was shared by many of Stryker's colleagues and those they photographed: belief in the individual; in voluntary cooperation; in a harmony of interests; in the virtues of the agrarian/small-town way of life; in the future; in the possibilities of

Figure 20: *Midweek Pictorial,* 17 October 1936, from the FSA Scrapbook.

Figure 21: *Buffalo Times,* 14 February 1937, from the FSA Scrapbook.

peaceful, progressive reform; in the superiority and primacy of the American Way. To say that politicians and businessmen often manipulated these beliefs for their own ends is not to prove that they invented them or controlled them. That the FSA-OWI photographs revealed these beliefs is hardly remarkable; so did most of the other major cultural expressions of the period—movies, radio, paintings, magazines, newspapers, music. What needs to be remarked upon is the extent to which the most widely known photographs—as well as many of the creations of the other most popular iconographic form of the period, the movie—went beyond comfortable consensus to show crisis and breakdown. What is equally important is the extent to which the photographers were able to rise beyond a simplistic rendering of their ideological concerns to create a record of those aspects of American life and culture that were generally ignored or downgraded by most cultural and artistic agencies.

Many years ago Robert Louis Stevenson described how he and his schoolmates would place a bulls-eye lantern under their coats, its presence unknown to all but one another, and walk along the links at night, ''a mere pillar of darkness'' to ordinary eyes, but each exulting in the knowledge that he had a hidden lantern shining at his belt. Stevenson used these recollec-

Figure 22: *Life,* 21 June 1937, from the FSA Scrapbook.

DUST BOWL FARMER IS NEW PIONEER

tions as a paradigm for the human condition, commenting that a good part of reality "runs underground. The observer (poor soul with his documents!) is all abroad. For to look at the man is but to court deception. . . . To one who has not the secret of the lanterns, the scene upon the links is meaningless. And hence the haunting and truly spectral unreality of realistic books." [33]

In the same sense, one might speak of "the haunting and truly spectral unreality" of many ostensibly realistic photographs. Indeed, Rexford Guy Tugwell seems to have had something like this on his mind when early in the history of the photography project he advised Stryker, "Roy, a man may have holes in his shoes, and you may see the holes when you take the picture. But maybe your sense of the human being will teach you there's a lot more to that man than the holes in his shoes, and you ought to try and get that idea across." [34] Tugwell's conception was only imperfectly realized. The difficulties were formidable: the photographers' limited vision, the subjects' ability to mask what they felt and thought, the force of ideologies, the intrusion of perceived political necessities. Arthur Rothstein, the first photographer hired by Stryker, observed, "It was our job to document the problems of the Depression so that we could justify the New Deal legislation that was designed to alleviate them." [35] Stryker's instructions to his photographers often bore this out. In January 1936, as Dorothea Lange was preparing for her first major trip for the Resettlement Administration, Stryker wrote her:

> Would you, in the next few days, take for us some good slum pictures in the San Francisco area. (Of course, no California city has slums, but I'll bet you can find them.) We need to vary the diet in some of our exhibits here by showing some western poverty instead of all south and east. . . . When you get to Los Angeles, I think it might be worthwhile to see if you can pick up some good slum pictures there also. Do not forget that we need some of the rural slum type of thing, as well as the urban. [36]

Even in the midst of this ideological and political urge to document suffering, Stryker showed that his mind never strayed too far from the practical. "As you are driving along through the agricultural areas," Stryker wrote Lange in the same letter, "would you take a few shots of various types of farm activities such as your picture showing the lettuce workers. I think Dr. Tugwell would be very appreciative of photographs of this sort to be used as illustrative material for some things which the Department of Agriculture is working on." [37] He could also issue orders to downplay adversity, as he did in his often-quoted letter to Jack Delano in the fall of 1940:

Please watch for autumn pictures, as calls are beginning to come for them and we are short. These should be rather the symbol of Autumn . . . cornfields, pumpkins. . . . Emphasize the idea of abundance—the "horn of plenty"—and pour maple syrup over it—you know, mix well with white clouds and put on a sky-blue platter. I know your damned photographer's soul writhes, but to hell with it. Do you think I give a damn about a photographer's soul with Hitler at our doorstep? You are nothing but camera fodder to me.[38]

In the winter of 1942 Stryker asked Russell Lee and Arthur Rothstein to provide "pictures of men, women and children who appear as if they really believed in the U.S. Get people with a little spirit. Too many in our file now paint the U.S. as an old person's home and that just about everyone is too old to work and too malnourished to care much what happens." Though he quickly added, "(Don't misunderstand the above. FSA is still interested in the lower-income groups and we want to continue to photograph this group.)"[39]

That there is more continuity in these photographs than such gyrating mandates suggest, that Stryker's photographers did not veer wildly from recording victims to recording self-sufficient patriots, was the result both of the photographers' talent and integrity and Stryker's hunger for documentary detail, which provided the underpinning for the entire project and supplied a wealth of information about American culture and belief. He instructed his photographers to record the scenes of everyday life: "How do people spend their evenings," he would ask; "show this at varied income levels." He requested pictures of home life, of leisure pursuits, of people going to church, of group activities, of the woman's world, of backyards and porches, of baseball diamonds, of the way people dressed and decorated their walls, of the differences in their behavior on and off the job. He was proud of the fact that his photographers caught people in everyday situations. He boasted of the fact that "in our entire collection we have only one picture of Franklin Roosevelt, the most newsworthy man of the era. . . . You'll find no record of big people or big events in the collection. There are pictures that say Depression, but there are no pictures of sit-down strikes, no apple salesmen on street corners, not a single shot of Wall Street, and absolutely no celebrities."[40]

This final boast—"absolutely no celebrities"—highlights one of the truths of the FSA-OWI photographs: they paid more attention to regional and folk than to popular and mass culture. While these documents attest to America's complex ethnic, regional, and cultural heterogeneity, they are less successful in depicting the growing uniformity and standardization imposed by the forces of modernization. There are, to be sure, important indications of the intrusion of a national culture onto the local scene: John Vachon's photograph of a long line of cars and parking meters in Omaha, Nebraska, might have been taken in scores of American cities which could have easily supplied not only the cars and meters but also the background replete with a Woolworth's, a chain drug store, and a movie theater (figure 23). Arthur Rothstein's portrait of a young black girl in Gee's Bend, Alabama, peering from a cabin window next to which hangs a newspaper advertisement for Shredded Wheat and another featuring a white woman holding a platter of food above the caption, "Your Baker Offers You a Tempting Variety!" (figure 24), testifies poignantly to the fate of local culture in general and local cuisines in particular.

Nevertheless, one has to supplement these photographs with other sources to grasp fully the truth that by the 1930s all types of Americans from all areas of the country could view identical movies, listen to identical recordings in their homes or on jukeboxes, follow the same soap operas, laugh at the same comedians, be exposed to the same commercial messages, learn from the same news commentators, simultaneously attend the same presidential fireside chats, and listen as a nation to graphic on-the-spot accounts of Babe Ruth hitting his home runs or Joe Louis defending his heavyweight championship. Warren Susman has observed that while the photograph, the radio, and the moving picture were not new to the 1930s, "the sophisticated uses to which they were put created a special community of all Americans (possibly an international community) unthinkable previously. The shift to a culture of sight and sound was of profound importance; it increased our self-awareness as a culture; it helped create a unity of response and action not previously possible; it made us more susceptible than ever to those who would mold culture and thought."[41] Photography was not merely a mechanism for depicting these changes, it was simultaneously their product and their agent, their creation and their creator.

At the end of his life Stryker insisted that his goal had been to "record on film as much of America as we could in terms of people and the land. We photographed destitute migrants and average American townspeople, sharecroppers and prosperous farmers, eroded land and fertile land, human misery and human elation." It was precisely for this documentation of the varied and unspectacular aspects of America that Stryker came more and more to value his collection. *"We introduced America to Americans,"* he asserted. Doubtless this was claiming too much, though it is true that by providing a ready source of photographs for newspapers, government agencies, and national magazines, Stryker's photographic file did constitute one of the many vehicles in the thirties and forties that provided Americans with the opportunity to share experiences, images, and culture. Stryker was more

Figure 23: Cars and parking meters, Omaha, Nebraska, November 1938. John Vachon.

Figure 24: Artelia Bendolph, Gee's Bend, Alabama, 1937. Arthur Rothstein.

accurate when he wrote in 1973, "We provided some of the important material out of which histories of the period are being written."[42] And, it should be added, will continue to be written, for one of the enduring contributions of the photographers of the FSA and OWI is to help to introduce the America of their generation to Americans of ours. They have provided us with an unusually rich historical resource, which is flawed, certainly, as all such bodies of materials are, but which affords us an unusual opportunity to explore many of the past's hidden dimensions if only we have the wisdom to use their legacy with insight and sensitivity.

14

The Folklore of Industrial Society: Popular Culture and Its Audiences

In a sense this essay contains its own introduction. When I was invited to deliver the Merle Curti Lectures at the University of Wisconsin, I decided immediately that the first of the three-lecture series "Patterns of American Culture during the Great Depression," would have to explain *why* popular culture, which I focused on, was an appropriate and effective mechanism for comprehending Depression America in the first place. At the outset of the essay I explain in some detail why I felt it necessary to begin my Curti Lectures with an elaborate rationale. Of course I had—and have—no illusions that a single lecture, or even the entire three lectures, would convince those deeply skeptical of the worth of Popular Culture as historical evidence of what its audiences were thinking and feeling. Certainly I was directing my remarks to those already favorably disposed to using such materials and to those who were agnostic on the issue, but in retrospect I'm equally certain that I was also speaking to myself.

Ultimately, perhaps, everything we write is for ourselves, but the degree to which this is true varies according to the circumstances. Of all the essays in this volume, *this* is the one most definitely aimed at its own author. *I* was the most obvious audience for this piece. This is not to say that I didn't hope or want to convince others, only that before I could do that I had to convince myself that I could make an intellectual case for what I believed was true from my own experiences, observations, and values. I received a reassuringly positive response from my Wisconsin audience when I delivered the lecture on April 2, 1991, and from my colleagues at the Center for Advanced Study in the Behavioral Sciences, where I tried out a very early version in December of 1990. I should add that I found in Wisconsin, as I have in Berkeley, that, while not a few students have already learned to close their minds to the possibility that popular culture has any scholarly value, there is a large reservoir of student interest in, and even hunger for, learning how the materials of Popular Culture might be used in the reconstruction of the past. These various supportive reactions from colleagues and students alike encouraged me to expand the lecture into this essay which is the most recently published piece in this collection and appeared, in slightly different form, along with the commentaries of three scholars, in *The American Historical Review*, 97 (December 1992).

> *My consumers, are they not my producers?*
>
> James Joyce[1]

In his novel *Invisible Man,* Ralph Ellison's protagonist muses about the nature of history:

> All things, it is said, are duly recorded—all things of importance, that is. But not quite, for actually it is only the known, the seen, the heard and only those events that the recorder regards as important that are put down. . . . What did they ever think of us transitory ones? . . . birds of passage who were too obscure for learned classification, too silent for the most sensitive recorders of sound; of natures too ambiguous for the most ambiguous words, and too distant from the centers of historical decision to sign or even to applaud the signers of historical documents? We who write no novels, histories or other books. What about us . . ."[2]

This remains one of the nagging questions for many of us who write history today. What *does* the historian do about what Ellison called "the void of faceless faces, of soundless voices, lying outside history"?[3] There are many approaches to this problem. In *Black Culture and Black Consciousness,* I attempted to use Folk Culture—songs, tales, proverbs, jokes—to re-create the voices and consciousness of the slaves and freedmen who left few if any written sources behind them.[4] I found surprisingly little need for elaborate rationales or heavy theoretical underpinnings. There was an encouraging—and perhaps all too easy—acceptance of the proposition that by examining folklore one could recover the voices of the historically inarticulate. Underlying this acceptance was the widespread agreement that there was a valid correspondence between the creators and the receptors of folklore; since folklore came out of the community, scholars could use it to recover the common voice.

In recent years I've been trying to project this approach into the area of Popular Culture. More specifically, I have been attempting to recover the lost voices of large numbers of Americans during the Great Depression by a detailed examination of the mainstream Popular Culture they were exposed to in the books, magazines, and newspapers they read, the radio programs they listened to, and the movies they watched. I have learned unmistakably, in papers I've given and published, that this time around there will be no easy acceptance; that Popular Culture is seen as the antithesis of Folk Culture: not as emanating from within the community but created—often quite artificially by people with pecuniary or ideological motives—*for* the community or rather for the masses who no longer had an organic community capable of producing culture. Popular Culture, the critics argue—if it has to be invoked at all—should be used primarily to represent the consciousness of its producers not its consumers. I have discovered, for example, that my endeavor to find in the absurdist humor of Groucho, Chico, and Harpo Marx indications of the popular mood of the Great Depression, is precisely the kind of Marxism that distresses many of my colleagues the most. "We went to their movies," a senior historian informed me after one of my lectures, "to be entertained, not to ponder important problems; we went to laugh."

The real question for historians, of course, is less the intentions of the audience than why they laughed at what they did. This is precisely the issue my friend and colleague Gerda Lerner was attempting to get at when, following a paper I delivered on film and politics, she asked how I handled the relationship between the producers of the culture and their audiences. It's an important question to which I gave a flip response: I handled that relationship, I informed her and the audience, just as brilliantly as historians have handled the relationships between the Puritan divine Cotton Mather and his parishioners, between the editor Horace Greeley and his readers, between the politician Franklin Roosevelt and his constituents. In other words, I didn't really handle it at all. Historians, in fact, deal relatively poorly with this question at all levels, and I suppose I was resentful of the fact that it only seemed to be those of us who dealt with Popular Culture who were being importuned to answer it. Nevertheless, resentment and rhetoric are not going to make the question go away. Whether it's fair or not, we are being asked to justify the use of Popular Culture as a historical source; to explain why these materials reflect anything more than what those who produced them were thinking. To put the best possible face on it, I decided that if scholarly attitudes toward Popular Culture made it necessary for historians who used it to grapple with questions other historians were allowed to ignore or soft-peddle with impunity, so be it; it might even prove to be an advantage. Hence the genesis of this article.

We are, of course, not just dealing with an academic question. Scholars may well have their own internal disciplinary reasons for eschewing Popular Culture, but in addition to the academic cubicles they inhabit, scholars are members of a society in which Popular Culture is—and has been for some time—distrusted and denigrated regularly. To the Left, Popular Culture looked like the attempt of the ruling classes to exert hegemony over the masses; to the Right, Popular Culture existed as confirmation of the fear that if the masses and those who cynically catered to their low tastes were given free rein the entire society would be awash in a flood of cultural trivia.

These interpretations were by no means mutually exclusive. An entire range of intellectuals combined the notion that Popular Culture was unvarying trash with the idea that its purpose was hegemonic. Radio, Max Horkheimer and Theodor Adorno asserted in the 1940s, "turns all participants into listeners and authoritatively subjects them to broadcast programs which are all exactly the same," resulting in "the stunting of the mass-media consumer's powers of imagination and spontaneity. The might of industrial society is lodged in men's minds." Similarly, they argued, "The sound film leaves no room for imagination or reflection on the part of the audiences. . . . they react automatically" and "fall helpless victims to what is offered them."[5] A decade later the sociologist Bernard Rosenberg, in a *single* page of his introduction to the collection, *Mass Culture: The Popular Arts in America,* used the words "cretinize," "brutalize," "totalitarianism," "garbage," "ghastliness," "cultural pap and gruel," "illusion," "sub-art," and "pseudo-knowledge" to characterize the subject of the volume and concluded that "the electronic wonderworld and the rulers thereof . . . manage to debar the mass man they have created from any really satisfying experience."[6] The art critic Harold Rosenberg felt so strongly about the debilitating effects of Mass Culture that in 1958 he begged his peers to "quarantine kitsch," to deny it "an intellectual dimension" by refusing to study it. "Every discovery of 'significance' in Li'l Abner or Mickey Spillane," he charged, "helps to destroy the distinction between kitsch and art. . . . If only Popular Culture were left to the populace!"[7] And in our own day Allan Bloom has made a small fortune by disseminating the same views to a receptive public. Rock music, Bloom warned his extensive readership, was "junk food for the soul," a "gutter phenomenon" that transforms the lives of its young listeners "into a nonstop, commercially prepackaged masturbational fantasy," and permanently removes them from the realm of True Culture: "As long as they have the Walkman on, they cannot hear what the great tradition has to say. And after its prolonged use, when they take it off, they find they are deaf."[8]

Indeed, even the practitioners of Popular Culture—who are of course also part of the larger society—have added to this thrust. Thus Groucho Marx was amused at the professors who professed to see significance in the routines he did with his brothers, when in fact they were just improvising without any grand purpose, just trying to make people laugh.[9] The director Frank Capra attributed the success of his first Academy Award–winning film, *It Happened One Night* (1934), to the fact that it was "unfettered with any ideas, any big moral precepts or anything else. Just sheer entertainment, fun.''[10] More recently, the film executive Brandon Tartikoff, when he was head of television programming at NBC, expressed disbelief at academics seriously studying what he himself spent his life doing: ''When I hear about college professors writing books about people who do prime-time shows,'' he told a reporter, ''my natural cynicism says there's got to be courses for all these athletes to make them academically eligible to play football.''[11]

Thus we have found it difficult to study Popular Culture seriously not primarily because of the constraints of our respective disciplines—which are indeed far more open to the uses of Popular Culture than we have allowed ourselves to believe—but because of the inhibitions inculcated in us by the society we inhabit. From an early age we've been taught that whatever else this stuff is, it isn't art and it isn't serious and it doesn't lend itself to critical analysis.

The point of my title and my argument is not that Popular Culture is folklore and that the term ''folklore'' should be defined in such a way as to incorporate it. My intent is not to change definitions, except to the extent that I would like to see us get away from rigid adjectival labels as much as possible and recognize that while culture may not be seamless it is connected; it doesn't exist—at least not outside the academic world—in neatly separate boxes waiting for the scholar's labels. Rather, my intention is to explore the degree to which Popular Culture functions in ways similar to Folk Culture and indeed acts as a form of folklore for people living in urban industrial societies, and can thus be used to reconstruct people's attitudes, values, and reactions.[12]

To accomplish this it is important to regard culture in context. In a modern industrial urban society, people are no more likely to be the exclusive architects of their own expressive cultures than of their own houses or furniture or clothing. Modernity dealt a blow to artisanship in culture as well as in material commodities. But to say this is not to say that as a result people have been rendered passive, hopeless consumers. What people *can* do and *do* do is to refashion the objects created for them to fit their own values, needs, and expectations. We all know from personal experience and observation that people leave their own imprint upon the homes and apartments others build for them and upon the mass-produced furniture, clothing, and accessories they purchase and use. We have to begin to comprehend the extent to which this interactive process also exists between people and the mass-produced expressive culture their society puts at their disposal. Scholars who disregard this process end up with a culture they can neither understand themselves nor interpret for others.

We also must employ the term ''Popular Culture'' in a more consistent and less arbitrary way. What we call Popular Culture has been used most frequently as an aesthetic category—to signify the mudsill of culture, the lowest of the low—and in this sense it has been a very misleading term which, as I've argued elsewhere, has made it virtually impossible to perceive that Shakespearean drama or opera were Popular Culture in the 19th-century United States.[13] My own approach is simple and instrumental: Popular Culture is culture that is *popular;* culture that is widely accessible and widely accessed; widely disseminated, and widely viewed or heard or read. A broad spectrum of Depression film, radio, comics, fiction, and art fits this description and it is this material I am studying to understand American attitudes and culture during the Great Depression. Most of this expressive culture was also what we call Mass Culture since it was disseminated throughout the nation by such centralized mechanisms as national magazines, syndicated newspaper features, Hollywood studios, network radio, Tin Pan Alley, and commercial publishing houses. It is important to remember that all Mass Culture was by no means popular. Many mass-produced books went unread, many films unseen, many radio programs unheard by substantial numbers of people. This distinction is crucial: everything mass-produced for the American people was not popular even if a substantial percentage of what was popular by the 1930s was mass-produced. The significance of this is clear: choices were being made; in every popular genre audiences distinguished between what they found significant and appealing and functional and what they did not. Only the aesthetic hubris of critics and scholars has allowed the automatic equation of Mass Culture with Popular Culture as if everything mass-produced was popular, as if the unwashed masses were incapable of distinguishing and choosing when in fact it was the critics and scholars who were often incapable of making distinctions, of comprehending that the culture they were examining or critiquing was not all one vast sea of formulaic pablum with no substantive or stylistic distinctions.[14]

It is important also to rethink a series of attitudes and images that prevent or at least hamper the serious study of Popular Culture. Let me briefly discuss five of these.

1. The image of the Purely Passive Mass Audience ready to absorb, consciously and unconsciously, whatever ideological message those controlling the Mass Culture industry want to feed them. This image embodies two ideal constructs: the helpless, unknowing, unreflective, all-absorbing consumers of culture on the one hand and the powerful, prescient producers of culture, on the other, who know how to construct cultural products of such "irreducible givenness"[15] that they are impervious to reinterpretation or alteration by the audience. Not until we divest ourselves of these ideal types— just as surely as we have largely disposed of such ideals as the pure hero,

pure villain, pure victim—will we be capable of beginning to use Popular Culture effectively as a tool for comprehending the past.

2. The notion that of all the forms of culture only Popular Culture is so thoroughly formulaic that to know any part of a popular genre is to know all of it. Shortly after I returned from a summer of studying the scripts of radio programs from the 1930s, I was complaining to one of my colleagues about the unwieldiness of the sources I was confronted with, explaining that a single show like *Amos 'n' Andy* had several thousand scripts for the Depression decade alone. My colleague's response: "Oh, but I shouldn't have thought you would need to read more than about eight of them." The difficulty with this statement methodologically, of course, is that even if it were correct you would need to read large numbers of these scripts before you knew you only needed to read eight of them. But the real difficulty is that, although it is an unverified assumption, it is accepted by large numbers of intellectuals and academics. Popular Culture, of course, has no monopoly on the formulaic. The reason we remember Schubert and Beethoven and Dvořák string quartets is not because they are examples of a genre without formulas, but because of what these composers accomplished within those formulas. We have to allow the same possibilities for Popular Culture. If we remember such 1930s writers as Dashiell Hammett, Raymond Chandler, and John Steinbeck; such 1930s directors as Frank Capra, Ernst Lubitsch, John Ford, and Leo McCarey; such 1930s films as *Public Enemy, It Happened One Night, Night at the Opera, The Wizard of Oz,* and *Gone with the Wind,* it is not only because critics and scholars have kept them alive or resurrected them, but often because they were elevated to prominence by audiences of the 1930s who were perfectly capable of distinguishing them from the hundreds of other expressions in their respective genres. Audiences of the Great Depression were able to differentiate and choose among the myriad products of Popular Culture they were confronted with. It is precisely the choices they made that gives us insight into their attitudes and feelings. Having said this, it must be added that even the most solidly formulaic elements of Popular Culture have their satisfactions for the audience and their value for scholars. The obvious analogy here is with the world of games which, as Huizinga observed, gives pleasure by creating a place where the rules still work and where one can count on a certain order.[16] Formulaic culture affords many of the same rewards. But not all is certainty; within the formulas there is room for variation and surprise. The ending may be guaranteed, but the route to it can take twists and turns that not only add the spice of surprise and variation but also have things to teach audiences about the world the genre is supposedly lifting them out of.

3. The notion that Popular Culture was and is invariably "escapist," which depends in turn on the notion that art is an entity apart from the "real" world. In fact, of course, artistic expression is neither detached from the world around it nor just a "reflection" of that world. Rather, it is an inseparable part of the larger world, one of the fundamental forms of communication and expression people engage in and depend upon. Those who attended films and plays, tuned in radio programs, read novels and magazines, attended sporting events, and frequented musical performances of all kinds were not "escaping" from the "real" world; they were partaking of some of its essential features. But even insofar as elements of escape—by which I suppose is meant relief from the pressing matters of everyday life— were involved, we tend to ask the wrong questions. The potential for "escape" is inherent in all forms of expressive culture; thus the fact that it may be a feature of Popular Culture tells us very little. What is essential, as Robert Escarpit has argued, is to "know from what and towards what we are escaping." [17] Even in their escape people can be quite realistic in understanding what it is they need to do to maintain themselves; what kinds of fictions, myths, fantasies they require not primarily to escape reality but to face it day after day after day. Indeed, to "escape" a reality one cannot change is one way of altering that reality, or at least its effects. The question about the Popular Culture of the Great Depression, then, is not merely whether it allowed people to escape from the grim realities of the 1930s, since most forms of expressive culture in the thirties did that, but also whether and in what ways it allowed them to cope with the effects of those realities.

4. The notion that because Popular Culture may not generally be on the cutting edge of knowledge or style it is therefore not truly an art form. Those who understand Folk Culture don't make the mistake of assuming that "artists" are invariably those who break new ground. This is a modern fallacy contradicted by the centuries of folk artists who saw their function as embodying the beliefs and meanings of their cultures in language that could be understood by their fellows. "There is," Raymond Williams has asserted, "great danger in the assumption that art serves only on the frontiers of knowledge." Art can just as legitimately stand near the center of common experience giving its audiences a sense of recognition and community. [18]

5. Finally, in this list of attitudes, let me return to the question of aesthetics. When confronting Popular Culture scholars have been virtually mesmerized by aesthetic matters. Historians, for example, who rarely, if ever, have much if anything to say about the aesthetics of political speeches, religious sermons, reformist pamphlets, legislative committee reports, judicial decisions, even novels and poems which they have tended to mine for content rather than structure and style, seem incapable of treating the materials

of Popular Culture substantively and functionally, as they treat most other materials, rather than aesthetically. This inability to transcend the putative aesthetic poverty of Popular Culture, or kitsch, as intellectuals like to call it, has made it exceedingly difficult for historians to take Popular Culture seriously enough to comprehend the dynamic relationships that exist between the audience and the expressive culture they interact with. Aesthetic worth and substantive complexity are not inexorable partners. The aesthetic quality of an artifact does not necessarily determine its level of complexity or the amount of analysis essential to comprehend its meaning. One does not have to believe that aesthetically Superman rivals Hamlet or that Grant Wood compares to Michelangelo to maintain that Superman and Wood potentially have much to tell us about the Great Depression, that they therefore merit the closest examination, and that they won't necessarily be simple to fathom.

Once we get beyond some of these attitudinal and definitional obstacles, we can begin to perceive the extent to which what we call Popular Culture can and does function in many of the same ways and serves many of the same purposes as what we call Folk Culture. I have been surprised by the degree of antipathy with which folklorists from the turn of the century until at least midcentury tended to treat Popular Culture. If Black children admitted they had learned a rabbit tale from a published Joel Chandler Harris story rather than orally from a member of the community, if blues singers cited a phonograph record as the source for their blues, if a country musician sang a song she first heard on a radio show, it caused great consternation, engendered severe doubts about whether the material collected was really folklore, even if it looked and acted like folklore, and generated still more dire predictions about the imminent demise of the folk and their lore. In my work on Black folk thought I attempted to demonstrate that the effect of commercial blues recordings on folk blues was not at all what some folklorists feared. Undoubtedly, there was a disruptive effect on many local styles and traditions. Nevertheless, what primarily took place was not a total erosion of regional styles in favor of some standard commercial product but a blending process. Through recordings, local traditions could become quickly known to Blacks in every section of the country; the developments in the new urban centers could be spread throughout the South even while the traditional culture could be perpetuated and strengthened among the recent urban migrants. Blacks living far apart could now share not only styles but experiences, attitudes, folk wisdom, expressions. In this sense phonograph records could be seen as bearers and preservers rather than primarily destroyers of folk traditions. And at no point were the folk reduced to the role of mere ciphers; they continued to have a crucial influence. Zora Neale Hurston observed that when the jukebox made its way into the remote work

camps of rural Florida in the 1930s, regional songs began to give way to
the recorded blues but with an interesting twist: "the original words and
music [of the recorded songs] are changed to satisfy the taste of the community's own singers." [19]

Nor was this fascinating blend limited to Black music. At his death in
1936, Dr. Humphrey Bate, one of the most popular country musicians on
the *Grand Ole Opry,* a radio program which began in Nashville in the late
1920s and became a national institution by the Depression years, left a list
of his repertory of 125 songs. Of the 103 that could be traced, 34 were
traditional fiddle tunes, 8 were other traditional tunes, 5 were hornpipes, 2
were marches, 13 were vaudeville and minstrel songs, 20 were popular songs
from the late nineteenth century, 12 were popular songs from the 1920s, and
3 were ragtime tunes. This repertory indicates the dangers of categorizing
Bate too easily. By virtue of appearing on an extremely popular radio program he could certainly be labeled a "popular" rather than a "folk" performer, yet more than half of his material consisted of traditional songs
performed in a traditional style. The very eclecticism of Bate's repertory, in
fact, places him in the tradition of folk performers who were always willing
to utilize appropriate material wherever they found it. Folklorists might have
been purists, the folk rarely were. George Hay, the director of the Opry,
understood this when he observed, "The line of demarcation between the
old popular tunes and folk tunes is indeed slight." [20]

The fragile line between the worlds of Folk and Popular Culture is documented by those in the radio audience who seem to have regarded the radio
as a welcome part of their community. "If I am tired of the voices around
me," a listener testified, "I turn on the radio. There I hear a new voice
. . . it is as if a friend had entered the room." [21] "I feel your music and
songs are what pulled me through this winter," A Chicago listener wrote
station WLS in June 1935. "Half the time we were blue and broke. One
year during the depression and no work. Kept from going on relief but lost
everything we possessed doing so. So thanks for the songs, for they make
life seem more like living." [22] "The radio," one researcher noted,

> is spoken to, cajoled, scolded with apparently little self-consciousness. It
> has become so much a part of the household that using it as another per-
> son—in fact, speaking of it as "company" and as "someone in the house"—
> is neither strange nor unexpected. [23]

These feelings of community were often reciprocated at the other end of the
airwaves. "When I sing for you on the air," the popular country singer
Bradley Kincaid wrote in one of his mail-order songbooks, "I always visualize you, a family group, sitting around the radio, listening and commenting on my program. If I did not feel your presence, though you be a thou-

sand miles away, the radio would be cold and unresponsive to me, and I in turn would sound the same way to you.'' [24]

Testimony like this makes it clear that we need to break through the rigid compartmentalization that automatically and rigorously separates Popular Culture from the oral tradition—which has played a crucial role in the generation and transmission of Folk Culture—when in fact the two intermeshed regularly. ''My husband likes the same things I do,'' one listener testified:

> And if he misses one [radio serial] I tell him what happened—or he'll ask me what happened, or what did Walter Winchell say on Sunday—and I'll tell him. Or what happened to so and so. And then he'll say, ''Oh, for god's sake, we have to wait till next Monday to find out!'' He keeps up with them just the same as I do. . . . We love to talk about the stories and he likes the same ones I do, so it's nice. [25]

Speaking about the popular radio mystery show *Ellery Queen,* Anna B., a twelve-year-old from a lower-middle-class family living on the Lower West Side of New York, observed:

> I listen to it and then I tell the story to the kids around where we live. Some of them don't have radios and some of them have to go to bed early so we all get around and I tell them the story of what happened just like on the radio and then they have to guess who the murderer is. Then I tell them. I tell them the story about some of the other programs too, but mostly Ellery Queen. [26]

Popular Culture could become part not only of folk discourse but of folk performance. In the early 1930s a college sophomore recalled that after she had seen *The Sheik* when she was twelve or thirteen,

> my friend and I enacted the especially romantic scenes out under her mother's rugs, which made excellent tents even though they were hung over the line for cleaning purposes. She was Rudolph and I the beautiful captive, and we followed as well as we could remember the actions of the actors. [27]

Jean S., a nine-year-old middle-class girl living with her mother and sixteen-year-old brother on New York's Upper West Side, described in 1940 how she and her playmates modeled their games on radio programs:

> I started listening to the Lone Ranger when I was four. My brother started me. . . .
>   Then we'd play Lone Ranger in the park. My brother was always the Lone Ranger. I used to play with them. . . . I was the Indian girl or else I married Tonto the Indian. There were two other girls who played with us

too but they were older. I was the youngest and I had to look out for myself. My brother would climb trees and swing on the branches, and shoot Injuns and we'd pull on ropes to make the branches bend. . . .

We stopped playing the Lone Ranger together when my brother was 12. He did not want to play it any more so I played it with girls after that.[28]

Here we have a portrayal of interaction, with members of the audience often imposing themselves upon the expressive culture they're exposed to, restructuring it, changing details—such as giving Tonto women friends and even a wife—molding it to their own needs, and understanding it in terms of their own life experiences. "Yes, I like a happy ending," a twelve-year-old boy told an interviewer, "but once in a while I'd like to see the criminal get away. I have never really seen happy endings in real life."[29]

Roland Barthes has argued that "Mass Culture" has to be distinguished "like fire from water, from the culture of the masses."[30] The testimony quoted above, however, demonstrates how narrow the line between the two can be, and often is. Before we attempt to separate and compartmentalize "Mass Culture" and the "culture of the masses," we need a much clearer and more precise understanding of the interconnections between the two.

This understanding will come not only through examining texts, but also through a clearer perception of audience behavior. Indeed, the audience remains the missing link, the forgotten element, in cultural history. The creation, the creator, and the context are often accounted for; the constituency remains shadowy and neglected. The notion of a profoundly close relationship between the audience and the meaning of a text is hardly new. "Both read the Bible day & night," William Blake observed more than 170 years ago, "But thou read'st black where I read white."[31] Until recently, however, scholars have been strangely diffident about carrying this insight into their studies of culture. Here again Popular Culture resembles Folk Culture. "The history of folklore scholarship," Alan Dundes has written, in terms that could just as easily be addressed to Popular Culture, "is by and large a series of attempts to dehumanize folklore. . . . Considering 'folklore' without reference to 'folk' is commonplace in folkloristics."[32] Just as Dundes has referred to "the folkless study of folklore," we might speak of the "depopulated study of Popular Culture." But the people have not merely been removed from Popular Culture, they have been reduced to uncritical, acquiescent ciphers.

We need more empirical research like that done by Herbert Gans in the Italian working-class homes of Boston's West End in the 1950s. Although the television was on constantly, actual viewing was highly selective and was structured to filter out themes inimical to the life of the peer group and to accept those characters and situations which confirmed the group's values. "West Enders do not enjoy watching satire," Gans comments, "but they do enjoy creating their own in response to what they see." They made fun of the exaggerated claims of commercials, the promises of politicians, the depictions of middle-class people as moral or businessmen as more interested in the community than in profits. They rejected TV detectives who failed to show sympathy to working-class people, and family shows that failed to mirror their own values. "We heckle TV just like we used to heckle the freaks at the circus when we were kids," one of Gans's respondents commented.[33] Janice Radway in her pioneering study of the readers of romance novels, goes even further in exploring how women select novels from among the large number available "by learning to decode the iconography of romantic cover art and the jargon of back-cover blurbs," by insisting upon certain patterns of plot, coherence, and style, by choosing authors who had pleased them in the past, and by consulting each other and forming networks of readers.[34]

I have found much the same patterns of audience selectivity in my own research on the Great Depression. People did not passively accept whatever Popular Culture was thrown their way; they pre-selected the culture they exposed themselves to by learning to decipher reviews and coming attractions, by understanding the propensities of authors, actors, and directors whose work they had been exposed to in the past, and by consulting members of their communities. New York City children queried in 1934, for example, revealed that in choosing radio programs the advice of other children—the peer group whose tastes they trusted most—was by far the most significant influence. Random dialing, advertisements, and parental advice lagged far behind in importance.[35] Even in those cases where listeners had limited or no choice, such as the radio commercials that accompanied the programs they listened to, passive acceptance was not inevitable, as the following three examples illustrate:

> When the advertising comes, sometimes I turn it off. . . . it depends. If it's a short talk I'll leave it running; I might as well. I just don't listen until it's over. But if he keeps talking and talking . . . then I just turn it off.

> I can't remember any of the commercials. . . . because I don't approve of the advertising at all; I hate it. I don't mind it so much when it's really short, but I always turn to another station the moment it comes on, except when it's news. The advertising makes me so darned mad. They talk to you as if you were a child of six.

Chipso, Ivory, Duz and all the others are just too ridiculous for words. They all come on, one after the other, in the morning. They all claim exactly the same things, and yet they do it as if you were too stupid to remember that five minutes ago someone else was claiming the same thing for another product. . . . That's what makes me so mad about it. All they ought to do is to give a straight-forward account of the product, because everyone knows anyway that they are all the same. I often wonder whether they're trying to kid me, or whether they're trying to kid themselves.[36]

Recent literary theory sees neither the reader nor the text as necessarily controlling but rather places emphasis upon the *interaction* between the two.[37] It is precisely in this realm that we have to understand the process of Popular Culture: not as the imposition of texts upon passive people who constitute a kind of tabula rasa, but as a process of interaction between complex texts which harbor more than monolithic meanings and audiences who embody more than monolithic assemblies of compliant people but who are in fact complex amalgams of cultures, tastes, and ideologies. Audiences come to Popular Culture with a past, with ideas, with values, with expectations, with a sense of how things are and should be. One does not have to subscribe to Roland Barthes's dictum that "the text has no memory" to agree with his conclusion that a text is frequently "an old tune to which new words are given," since the creator of a text "can only force himself fragmentarily into a life which is not his."[38] Thus the control any creator has over the manner in which her or his creation is received is always incomplete, always fragmentary. A mechanical one-to-one correlation between the creator's intentions (assuming these were clear to begin with), the shape and meaning of the creation, and the manner in which it is understood by its audience does violence to all three elements in this cultural process: the producer, the thing produced, and the audience for whom it is produced. We seem to have less difficulty understanding this complexity when we enter the realm of what we call High Culture. Many of us have finally come to understand that not only is there no single meaning to Beethoven's late quartets or Shakespeare's tragedies or Hemingway's novels but that there is not even a single *rendition* or reading that is necessarily authentic. Thus both the performer and the audience have a role to play in determining the meaning and nature of the production and become collaborators with the creator. But we balk somehow at transferring this understanding to the realms of Popular Culture. Yet, until we do this we are doomed to misunderstanding the relationship between Popular Culture and its public.

To give a very simple illustration of the ways in which people viewed Popular Culture through the filters of their lives, listeners to *Road of Life,* which began in 1937 and was the Depression's first medical Soap Opera, spoke of the central character, Dr. Jim Brent, in terms which related directly to their own situations. Thus a mother who felt she was sacrificing for an unappreciative family said the show was about "a doctor, his life and how he always tries to do the right thing. Sometimes he gets left out in the cold too." A woman over forty with memories of a sad childhood called Brent "a wonderful man, taking such good care of a poor little orphan boy. He is doing God's work." A sick listener declared, "I like to hear how he cures sick people. It makes me wonder whether he could cure me too."[39]

Soap Operas were one of the Depression's most ubiquitous and popular genres precisely because they were part of what the writer Paddy Chayefsky called "the marvelous world of the ordinary." People could relate to daytime serials in terms of their own existence; could see themselves in them. The actor George C. Scott observed that the radio Soap Operas were the only form of broadcasting that incorporated a "sense of growth and continuity. . . . soap-opera characters grow: They marry, have children, mature, even die."[40] One Depression listener made a similar point by calling Soaps "more real" than such other popular genres as film: "The things that happen in the movies seldom happen to people that I know. I like to listen about plain, everyday people."[41] "I like *Myrt and Marge*," a Manhattan youngster testified in 1934, "because it consists of real life happenings, and they are very exciting to hear."[42] Thus listeners were probably not surprised when the announcer declared at the beginning of each episode of the daytime serial *Rosemary:* "This is *your* story—this is *you*."[43]

The functional similarities between Soaps and genres of folklore are striking. Soaps rarely offered any permanent resolutions; they had neither beginnings nor endings. This of course was one of the characteristics that made Soaps life-like. It was also what made them kin to such folklore cycles as Brer Rabbit stories which also mimicked life itself by having no closure. In any specific tale Rabbit might win a victory over stronger animals but the folk cycle underlined the truth that in life rabbits don't triumph over wolves permanently by beginning the next story in the cycle with Rabbit once again in the weaker position. Thus for the slaves telling and hearing these stories regularly, the message of the entire cycle diverged from the message of the individual tale—and both messages had important lessons to teach. So too the Soaps reminded their listeners incessantly that while people can and do win victories over adversity, adversity is an inherent part of life over which no one wins ultimate triumph. Soaps also bore a striking resemblance to the African-American folk Blues. Both genres often piled crisis upon crisis upon crisis to the point of unreality, but the crises—infidelity, jealousy, failed ambition, sickness, economic distress, betrayal, loneliness—were common enough, and in Soaps as in Blues people learned to handle their frustrations, adversities, and misadventures and cope with life. Like the Blues, Soaps fostered a sense of community, a sense of sharing troubles and solutions. "If you listen to these programs and something turns up in your own life, you would know what to do about it," one listener asserted. "You learn about life from the radio stories," a twelve-year-old New York girl affirmed. "The stories are like life . . . and so you learn how it is when you are grown up." Another listener observed of Soaps, as she well might have said of the Blues: "I learned that if anything is the matter, do not dwell on it or you go crazy." Two other listeners commented more specifically:

> I think Papa David [of *Life Can be Beautiful*] helped me to be more cheerful when Fred, my husband, comes home. I feel tired and instead of being grumpy, I keep on the cheerful side. *The Goldbergs* are another story like that. Mr. Goldberg comes home scolding and he never meant it. I sort of understand Fred better because of it. When he starts to shout, I call him Mr. Goldberg. He comes back and calls me Molly. Husbands do not really understand what a wife goes through. These stories have helped me to understand that husbands are like that. If women are tender, they are better off. I often feel that if my sister had had more tenderness she would not be divorced today. I saw a lot of good in that man.

> I like Helen Trent. She is a women over 35. You never hear of her dyeing her hair! She uses charm and manners to entice men and she does. If she can do it, why can't I? I am fighting old age, and having a terrible time. Sometimes I am tempted to go out and fix my hair. These stories give me courage and help me realize I have to accept it.[44]

This identification between the audiences and the Soap Operas was not fortuitous. Rudolph Arnheim, who studied forty-three daytime serials in the spring of 1941, concluded:

> The producers of radio serials take no chances in trying to meet the taste of their customers. Letters in which the listeners express approbation or protest are carefully studied. Telephone surveys determine the approximate size of the audience of each serial. On the basis of such data, and with a good deal of flair for what suits the purpose, the plots, the characters, the settings of the serials are made to order. That is why a content analysis of the serials can be expected to yield not only something about the programs, but also something about the listeners. These stories are likely to offer a picture of the world such as a particular social group would wish it to be.[45]

Although the evidence certainly points to the validity of Arnheim's conclusion, life was and is not always this cut and dried for Popular Culture audiences. They are not invariably handed meaning on a silver platter. "Writing," Laurence Sterne observed in his novel *Tristram Shandy,* ". . .

is but a different name for conversation." The truest respect an author can pay to the reader's understanding, Sterne insisted, "is to . . . leave him something to imagine, in his turn, . . . For my own part, I am eternally paying him compliments of this kind, and do all that lies in my power to keep his imagination as busy as my own."[46] Sterne was far from unusual in this respect. Whether it is the creator's intention or not, it seems inevitable that the audience's imagination will be kept busy by any work of expressive art simply because so many expressive works are by their very nature incomplete—filled with interstices that need connecting, ambiguities that need resolution, imprecisions that need clarity, complexities that need simplifying. The audience's role in Popular Culture, as it is in Folk Culture, then, is not the passive reception of a given text but rather a question of translation; fitting the text into a meaningful context.[47] Many of those who listened to Orson Welles's radio dramatization of H. G. Wells's *War of the Worlds* on Halloween night, 1938, panicked because they thought the show was an authentic news account of an ongoing invasion. But even in their terror, a substantial number seem to have been able to make the material their own to the extent that they could rule out the things that were not credible to them as these four examples show:

> I never believed it was anyone from Mars. I thought it was some kind of a new airship and a new method of attack. I kept translating the unbelievable parts into something I could believe.

> I knew it was some Germans trying to gas all of us. When the announcer kept calling them people from Mars I just thought he was ignorant and didn't know yet that Hitler had sent them all.

> I felt it might be the Japanese—they are so crafty.

> I worry terribly about the future of the Jews. Nothing else bothers me so much. I thought this might be another attempt to harm them.[48]

But the audience's role extends beyond the act of translation and entails the filling in of gaps or vacancies in the text. "What is missing," Wolfgang Iser has argued, ". . . this is what stimulates the reader into filling the blanks with projections. He is drawn into the events and made to supply what is meant from what is not said."[49] Certainly, this is a central aspect of folklore. Alan Dundes relates the following joke he collected from a black Alabaman in 1964:

> Governor Wallace of Alabama died and went to heaven. After entering the pearly gates, he walked up to the door of a splendid mansion and knocked. A voice inside exclaimed, "Who dat?" Wallace shook his head sadly and said, "Never mind, I'll go the other way."

Dundes's interpretation of this African-American joke centers on the wishful thinking underlying Wallace's death and the sense of justice involved in banning from God's Mansion and consigning to Hell the very man who stood in the doorway of the University of Alabama as a symbol of his opposition to admitting Black students. But this by no means encompasses the entire meaning of the joke which Dundes argues functions for Whites as well as blacks. Some whites interpreted the stereotyped dialect, "Who dat?" as meaning God or Saint Peter was black; others assumed it was a doorman or menial servant. Some Whites understood the joke to mean that Heaven was now integrated; others assumed that Heaven had been completely "taken over" by Blacks. "None of this is articulated in the joke proper," Dundes concludes, "but it is part of the joke as semiotic text." [50]

In this manner folklore encourages listeners to become not merely participants but even creators of meaning where the message is not explicit; to project themselves into the text in order to invest the empty spaces with meaning. Precisely the same process occurs in Popular Culture. Let me suggest a number of examples and begin with one of the Depression decade's most popular forms of expression: photography.

Dorothea Lange's portrait of Florence Thompson, which she called "Migrant Mother" (see figure 6 in essay 13), accomplished precisely what Lange wanted it to when she took it on a March afternoon in 1936: it became an icon of the victimization of millions of Americans during the Great Depression, an argument in favor of substantial federal intervention, and a justification for the transformation of American politics during the 1930s. But Lange's portrait continues to survive and continues to fascinate us because it, like most of the memorable photographs of the decade, is not quite so resolutely one-dimensional. It was possible to see qualities besides that of the victim in photos like this. Roy Stryker, who directed the photographic section for which Lange worked, saw what we can still see: an overriding tension in Lange's portrait; a tension which Stryker, alluding to the work of his photographers in general, referred to as "dignity versus despair." [51] Was "Migrant Mother" a portrait of desperation or fortitude, victimization or resiliency, or was its popularity based upon its astute amalgam of these polarities?

The same conundrums are raised by another popular photograph of the period, Gordon Parks's portrait of Ella Watson, a charwoman who cleaned federal government offices in Washington, D.C. (figure 1). In his autobiography, Parks, the first Black photographer employed by the photographic section, called this photograph "unsubtle" and explained, "I overdid it and posed her, Grant Wood style, before the American flag, a broom in one hand, a mop in the other, staring straight into the camera." Parks remembered that when Roy Stryker saw the photograph "he just smiled and shook

Figure 1: Ella Watson in a government office, Washington, D.C., 1942. Gordon Parks.

Figure 2: Ella Watson with three grandchildren and adopted daughter, 1942. Gordon Parks.

his head'' and urged Parks to capture more of Watson's humanity by following her into her home, her church, her neighborhood. Parks heeded this
advice and was proud of the later pictures he took of Watson (see figure 2
for an example). ''That was my first lesson in how to approach a subject,
that you didn't have to go in with all horns blasting away.''[52] But though
Parks may have achieved greater subtlety in his later pictures of Watson, he
reached far more people with his original photograph which remains to this
day one of his best-known and most popular works. The reason, I think, is
that there is greater nuance in this portrait than either Parks or Stryker initially understood. Parks captured the same dualities Lange had: the victim
and the survivor, vulnerability and strength, exploitation and transcendence.
And he captured these dualities in a format that allowed viewers to enter the
process of investing the image with meaning. The fact that Parks's later
photographs of Watson were less polemical should not blind us to the possibility that they may have also been less open to interpretation. The popularity of Parks's portrait (and indeed of Grant Wood's famous painting
American Gothic, after which it was loosely modeled) may well be linked
not only to aesthetic virtues but also to the scope audiences were given to
project their own world view into the process of unravelling its meaning.[53]

    This discussion makes it clear that even in such relatively finite works
of expression as photographs there is a great deal of room for audiences to
insert themselves. This was even truer of other modes of expressive art,
such as feature films. Two films from different ends of the Depression era
provide instructive examples. *Ann Vickers* (1933) traces the rise of a young
social worker from the beginning of her career in an urban settlement house
during World War One to her great success as the author of a best-selling
exposé of women's penal institutions and as the director of an industrial
home for women where she carries out influential prison reforms. Throughout it all she manifests great pride in being a woman, from going to jail for
suffrage reform activities to her struggle for the safety and dignity of the
women prisoners in her charge. She has an abortion rather than marry a man
who lacks respect for her. Speaking of her unborn ''daughter,'' she declares:
''I've found a new modern virtue to name my daughter: Pride. The pride of
life, the pride of love, the pride of work, the pride of being a woman. These
will be her virtues. Pride Vickers!''[54] She refuses to engage in the pursuit
of a socially prominent man who is interested in her, telling one of her
friends who urges her to be more aggressive: ''I know! If I want a man I
must lure, flatter, be ecstatically impressed by all he says and does. Be
coyly aloof, wistful, be fluttered by his handclasp, arousing him to a conviction that I'm a swooning mystery which he must understand or die. No!
I'll be hanged if I will.'' This film biography of a strong, interesting, intelligent woman ends on a very different note. Her career as a prison admin-

istrator is shattered because of her affair with a married judge who is indicted for accepting bribes. Reunited with her lover, after he has served three years in prison, she declares that now they are *both* out of prison. To his protest, "But you were never in," she replies, "Oh yes I was. You're the man who brought me out of the prison of ambition, the prison of desire for praise and success for myself. We're both out, darling." This dramatic and totally unexpected renunciation of her former life is symbolized by a portrait of family bliss: the two lovers and their young son joyfully embracing as the film fades out.

Sullivan's Travels (1942) ends with a similarly abrupt transition. John L. Sullivan, a Hollywood director famous for such comedic films as *Hey, Hey in the Hayloft,* and *Ants in Your Pants of 1939,* is motivated by the Depression to change moods and make the contemporary drama *Oh Brother Where Art Thou?*. "I want this picture to be a commentary on modern conditions, stark realism, the problems that confront the average man. . . . I want to hold a mirror up to life. I want this to be a . . . true canvas of the suffering of humanity." To obtain material for his epic he disguises himself and becomes another one of the hungry unemployed on the city streets. The bulk of the film concerns Sullivan's attempts to escape his affluent life and experience privation. Through his eyes we see the misery of Depression America depicted with the documentary force characteristic of FSA photographs. In reality Sullivan is never able to become much more than a voyeur until a series of mishaps puts him on a chain gang. Now he personally experiences deprivation and degradation of the worst sort, which is relieved only when he and his fellow prisoners are taken to a black rural church to see a Walt Disney cartoon and they respond with healing, cathartic laughter which so impresses Sullivan that after he escapes from his predicament and is on a plane returning him to the security of Hollywood, he announces to his producers that he is abandoning his project to make a film reflecting the misery of the Great Depression. "I want to make a comedy. . . . There's a lot to be said for making people laugh. Did you know that's all some people have? It isn't much but it's better than nothing in this cockeyed caravan." The film closes with the sights and sounds of the poor, the sick, and the suffering laughing.

The ostensible message of *Sullivan's Travels* may have been an elaborate apologia—a self-interested defense built upon the claim that all Hollywood need do to justify itself was to entertain people; to make them laugh. What is arresting, however, is that the film itself did much more than that: it helped to inform its audiences about the nature and extent of suffering in the United States. *No* final ending, no ultimate apologia could automatically erase the images of misery, despair, and hopelessness the film made available to the audience. Whatever final rationale was on the producers' minds, these images, once released, became the property of the viewers who could do with them what they willed, make of them what their lives and experiences prepared them to make of them. Precisely the same is true of *Ann Vickers*. Its final formulaic ending, no matter how securely it may have fit in with traditional conceptions of woman's fundamental place in society, could not in one fell swoop wipe out everything that preceded it concerning Vickers's strength, talent, independence, competence, the important contributions she made, and the fact that her gender was hardly incidental to all of this but was in fact the basis for much of it. Indeed, this was precisely the judgment of *Time* magazine's reviewer who wrote of Vickers's sudden confession that she had been trapped in the prison of ambition: "Tying the story up with this platitude does not seriously weaken what has preceded it—an intelligent study, over-solemn but affecting, of a mature woman at work and in love." [55]

There is no cultural product—no book or symphony or film or play or painting—so overwhelming, so complete that it binds the audience to a single interpretation, a single angle of vision, a single meaning. *Sullivan's Travels* as an artifact might have been the work of writer-director Preston Sturges, but *Sullivan's Travels* as an affective vehicle, as a mode of meaningful discourse, was a collaborative work depending on the audiences' experiences, needs, and expectations. In this sense Sturges was the singer and his audiences the folk that helped to mold the song and make it their own.

Both *Ann Vickers* and *Sullivan's Travels* are examples of what Umberto Eco has called an "open text" which mandates the cooperation of the audience by compelling it to make a series of interpretive choices that invest the text with meaning and significance. While such choices are obviously not infinite, they are, as Eco puts it, "more than one," and they transform the reader or viewer into "an active principal of interpretation," who becomes "a part of the picture of the generative process of the text." [56] Thus audiences listening to or watching or reading such genres of Popular Culture as the films just discussed were not simply recipients but *participants* engaged in a complex dialogue. They were privy to the *entire* film and not simply at the mercy of formulaic endings which were often in stark contrast to what had preceded them.

It is a mistake, then, to divide the world up too easily into reality and representations of reality. The latter—the representations—when they become embodied in theater, tales, radio, movies, become forms of reality themselves. I don't mean by this that audiences necessarily *confuse* them with reality. Indeed, I think the opposite is more often true. [57] Rather, the entire setting constitutes an important form of reality in which many essential things are realized: lessons are learned, values enunciated and repeated, modes of behavior scrutinized, social institutions and their effects explored, fantasies indulged. We forget far too easily that, as Barbara Herrnstein Smith has put it, "language *is* action, both speaking it and also listening to it." Using, or even simply hearing, other people's words is not invariably a passive act. There are times when what Smith calls "fictive discourse" is the only type of discourse available to people.[58] Throughout history slaves or peasants or workers turned to their lore—their proverbs, tales, songs, religious practices, jokes—to say things they could not say under the normal rules of discourse. Thus Brer Rabbit and Brer Wolf, Moses and Pharaoh could express verities their slave creators and audiences would have had difficulty getting past external and internal censors.[59] There is every reason to believe that people in urban industrial societies use their Popular Culture in precisely the same ways. In this sense, a film, a daytime Soap Opera, a comic strip are all forms of reality, all a structural part of life.

Finally, we have yet to explore sufficiently the ways in which the technologies of the mass media were able to foster and not just weaken or destroy a sense of community. To reiterate a point I made earlier, it is not sufficient merely to focus on the substance of the Popular Culture; we need to understand *how* audiences confronted it. We forget too easily that going to a movie or listening to the radio are in and of themselves *events* and that we may have as much to learn from the process, the ritual, surrounding the expressive culture as from the content of the culture itself. I have argued elsewhere that content is not the sum of the folk process; it is merely an ingredient of it. The antiphonal—call and response—manner of singing, for example, speaks volumes about the state of black community during and after slavery. Similarly, the ways in which tales and jokes were recited makes it clear that African-American culture did not divide easily into creator and audience; the Black folk process was not an individual process but a group process.[60] Similarly, contemporary fan behavior at baseball or football games makes it clear that these are not docile recipients but knowledgeable *participants* who give their advice and opinions and judgments freely and frequently. The *process,* then, can be as enlightening as the substance once we learn to pay more attention to what people do when they watch movies or listen to radio programs and phonograph records.

Radio, for example, was by no means antithetical to a sense of folk or community. We have already seen this by examining the interaction of audiences with daytime serials. The ways in which Father Coughlin, Huey Long, and Franklin Roosevelt used radio to build communities of followers during the Great Depression make the process clearer still. Long, calling himself "Kingfish" after a character in the immensely popular radio show *Amos 'n' Andy,* speaking a vernacular common to many of his listeners, quoting freely from the Bible and from the body of Folk and Popular Culture, would begin his broadcasts by asking his listeners to become participants and reach out to their specific networks of friends and acquaintances:

> I want everybody to get on the radio tonight and listen to me. . . . This here's gonna be the best program on the air tonight. Now you get on the phone right now and ring up your neighbors. Tell 'em Huey P. Long, United States Senator from Louisiana, is got something to tell them. I'm gonna cover everything you ever heard of—and lots of things you ain't never heard of. Get ready to listen to me.[61]

FDR, who was capable of pausing in the midst of a Fireside Chat on the problems of relief, ask for a glass of water, sip it audibly, and remark: "My friends, it's very hot here in Washington," [62] was able to convert his periodic radio reports to the American people into such comfortably familiar events that millions of his listeners wrote him and his wife in terms more often reserved for immediate members of their communities. "Your speech tonight made me very happy," one of his correspondents confided. "You know somehow you seem very close to me like a very old friend." [63] When in the midst of another Fireside Chat, Roosevelt invited his audience to "tell me your troubles," Ira Smith, White House Chief of Mails, testified that large numbers of them "believed implicitly that he was speaking to them personally and immediately wrote him a letter. It was months before we managed to swim out of *that* flood of mail." Hundreds of thousands of letters arrived beginning:

> Dear Mr. President, I am worried about how we are going to . . .
>
> Dear Mr. Roosevelt, The children have no shoes to wear to school . . .
>
> Dear Frank, I've been driving a hack for ten years but now . . .

"They came in so fast," Smith commented, "we couldn't count them, but within a week I had some 450,000 letters stacked all over the office." [64]

Very much related to the sense of community which both charismatic politicians and successful genres like Soaps seem to have evoked, was the fact that people did not necessarily experience the radio in isolation. They often listened in the company of friends or relatives and, as we've already seen, shared the programs they listened to with others. "We live on a ranch in the most remote part of Ontario, Canada," Hugh and Ann MacNabb wrote the Nashville-based magazine *Rural Radio* in 1938. "Radios are not too plentiful here. [We] have seen as many as twenty or thirty [people] gathered in our home on Saturday night to enjoy the Saturday Night Barn Dance." Leone Neises wrote the same magazine in 1936: "I live way up here in the 'sticks' in northwestern North Dakota. Saturday night is the affair of affairs up here. Those who have no radio congregate at the homes of those who have and what an enjoyable evening!''[65] During these same years, Black farmers and workers in and around the town of Stamps, Arkansas, gathered in the general store run by Maya Angelou's grandmother on the nights Joe Louis fought and punctuated the radio announcer's descriptions of the fight with comments and laughter. When an opponent sought refuge from Louis's onslaught by forcing himself into a clinch, someone called out: ''That white man don't mind hugging that niggah now, I betcha.'' When Louis was in trouble, Angelou remembered, ''We didn't breathe. We didn't hope. We waited.'' When Louis was victorious, there were celebrations that lasted more than an hour: ''People drank Coca-Cola like ambrosia, and ate candy bars like Christmas. Some of the men went behind the Store and poured white lightning in their soft-drink bottles, and a few of the bigger boys followed them.'' Those who lived far away stayed overnight with friends rather than risk the ire of Whites who had listened to the fight in *their* communities.[66] Rural living was not a prerequisite for sharing the radio. Azriel Eisenberg found that among the sixth-grade pupils he studied in New York City in 1934, 81 percent of the girls and 72 percent of the boys listened to the radio in the company of their friends or family at least some of the time while 47 percent of the girls and 37 percent of the boys *always* listened with others.[67] Ernest Dichter's study of reactions to radio commercials substantiated the social nature of radio listening:

> The commercial is often the signal for the listener to use this minute for something more important. Even if one family member would want to listen to the commercial, he would have to overcome the social opprobrium attached to such an attitude. He would have to defend his interest in the commercial against the annoying and ridiculing remarks of his family guests.[68]

Similarly, Hadley Cantril and his associates, who studied the listeners who panicked during Welles's Invasion from Mars broadcast in 1938, found that the situation in which people listened helped to determine their reactions. What Cantril called ''the corroboratory effect of other people's behavior: the contagion of other people's fear,'' was crucial. ''I don't think we would have gotten so excited if those couples hadn't come rushin' in the way they did,'' one of Cantril's respondents testified. ''We are both very calm people, especially my husband, and if we had tuned in by ourselves I am sure we would have checked up on the program. . . .''[69]

Radio, of course, was especially susceptible to this pattern since it was the only medium of Popular Culture in the 1930s capable of addressing millions of Americans simultaneously—creating, as Cantril observed, ''the largest grouping of people ever known.''[70] Nevertheless, radio was not unique.

Other forms of Popular Culture—films, plays, sermons, speeches, vaudeville acts, musical performances—were also frequently experienced in social settings where the "contagion" of other people's reactions—their laughter, rumblings, anger, movements, shouts, ecstasies—was a factor as well. Indeed, Janice Radway has shown that even the solitary act of reading could become a social event when the women she studied met regularly to discuss the romance novels they were reading.[71] The point is that before, during, and after the Great Depression people enjoyed Popular Culture not as atomized beings vulnerable to an overpowering external force but as part of social groups in which they experienced the performance or with which they shared it after the fact. In the early 1930s a college sophomore recalled that when he was seven or eight he and his friends would crowd the movie theaters on Saturday mornings to watch the latest episode of an action serial: "All the children of the district used to attend. . . . During the showing of the picture itself we used to be worked up to a terrific high state of emotion, yelling at the hero when danger was near, hissing at the villain, and heaving sighs of relief when the danger was past."[72]

Hollywood regularly made use of audience reaction to give their films a last fine-tuning. "You don't know what you've got until the very last minute," Frank Capra told an interviewer. "Until you've spent all the money and put the picture together, you don't really know what you've got and you worry. . . . you don't know what you've got until you play it before an audience. You really do not know. There's no way of knowing."[73] Capra's own *Lost Horizon* (1937) illustrates his point. Capra previewed the film—which at two million dollars was by far the most expensive movie he or Columbia Pictures had yet made—in Santa Barbara where, following ten minutes of silence, the audience "began to titter, where no titters were intended. The titters swelled into laughs, where no laughs were intended." After several days of anxiety, Capra decided to simply cut the first two reels from the film and held a second preview in San Pedro. "There was not one laugh or titter in the wrong place," Capra reported. "The audience was spellbound." Only then did Columbia release *Lost Horizon* which became one of the most profitable and acclaimed films of the year. For Capra the lesson was evident:

> A motion picture is aimed at communicating with hundreds, or, hopefully, thousands of viewers at each showing; . . . That is why big-time film critics are wrong in insisting they view a film alone in private projection rooms . . . [because they claim] they can be more intelligent, more subjective, in their critical reviews if they are not influenced by the crowd reactions of the great unwashed. But crowd reactions are precisely what the film was made for in the first place, and no proper judgment of a

motion picture can be made without the vital "third dimension" of a large audience being present."[74]

Capra continued to consult the audience throughout his career. When he couldn't decide on an ending for *Meet John Doe* (1941), the final film in his great Depression trilogy, he circulated preview copies with different endings. "In Washington we had one ending, in New York one ending, in San Francisco another ending—trying to see if the audience would tell us which they preferred. None of those three was satisfactory, either to the audience or to me." According to Capra, the ending he finally used was suggested by a fan in a letter signed "John Doe."[75]

Thomas Schatz's careful study of four movie studios makes it clear that Capra was not unique. When preview audiences laughed in surprise at the appearance of the comedic actress Zazu Pitts in the dramatic role of the protagonist's mother in *All Quiet on the Western Front* (1930), Universal Pictures returned the film to production and replaced Pitts with another actress. Audience reaction to the previews of *Frankenstein* (1931) convinced the same studio to delete the deaths of Dr. Frankenstein and his monster and end the film on a more ambiguous note. The responses of preview audiences convinced Darryl Zanuck of Warner Brothers to create a more powerful conclusion for the classic early Depression exposé *I Am a Fugitive from a Chain Gang* (1932). The influential MGM production head Irving Thalberg was so certain of the importance of showing the first cut of a film to preview audiences and of taking their responses seriously that he declared: "I would rather take the picture out [for previews] two thousand feet over length and cut it down afterwards." "They didn't figure when a picture was complete that it was finished," the director Clarence Brown commented. "That was the first cut—the first draft." Thalberg's insistence on audience input before the final cut was released for general viewing led to the Hollywood saying that at MGM movies weren't made, they were remade. Film previews, an MGM story editor observed, were "the equivalent of Broadway's 'taking a show to New Haven.' "[76] Both techniques, of course, were predicated on the existence of the audience as an interactive, independent social entity.

In confronting Popular Culture, audiences did not necessarily encounter a coherent whole but a series of possibilities with which they could interact. The Marx Brothers gave their audiences not truths but situations in which they could *perceive* truths about their society and their lives. Audiences retained the possibility of choice. People could see in Lange's portrait of Florence Thompson the most obvious and compelling truth concerning victimization in the Great Depression or they could also react to the less clearly stated and perhaps more complex truths concerning reactions to victimization. Both possibilities—and doubtless many others—were inherent in the cultural object waiting for viewers to bring them out. This is precisely why creators like Capra and Thalberg understood the necessity of focusing not merely on the cultural artifact they had helped to produce but also on the responses it initiated, the experiences it generated in its audiences. Scholars would do well to learn the same lesson.

The question posed by James Joyce in the epigraph to this essay has remained my point of reference: the boundaries between cultural production and cultural consumption, or, to use terms I find more meaningful, cultural creation and cultural reception. Students and critics of Popular Culture have made the mistake of drawing the lines between Popular Culture and its audiences too rigidly and exclusively and consequently of cutting themselves off from the dynamic cultural relationships that allow us to use Popular Culture to help re-create the attitudes and values of those no longer able to speak to us directly. If the playwright Tom Stoppard went too far in having the Player in *Rosencrantz and Guildenstern Are Dead* declare: "Audiences know what to expect, and that is all that they are prepared to believe in," [77] the statement remains useful in reminding us that audiences *do* have expectations and while they may be willing to transcend them, those expectations constitute boundaries which the creators, producers, and performers of culture cannot afford to ignore completely. The good news, the folklorist Bruce Jackson has announced, is that "all our stories are coauthored."

> No story exists out there by itself. The story takes life from two of us: the teller and the listener, writer and reader, actor and watcher, each a necessary participant in the creation of the space in which the utterance takes life, in which all our utterances take life. [78]

If we interpret Jackson's phrase "two of us" not literally but as symbolic of the dialectic between Popular Culture and its audiences, then Jackson's news is good indeed for those of us seeking additional approaches to a better understanding of people in history.

But the news is not particularly good for those seeking simplicity. Adding the serious study of Popular Culture to the analysis of the past also adds to the complexity of the picture we have to decipher. This is true because Popular Culture seldom comes to us as a unitary voice. We can say of the Popular Culture of Depression America what the anthropologist Edmund Leach has said of the mythology of the Kachin peoples of Northeast Burma: "there can be no possibility of eliminating the contradictions and inconsistencies. They are fundamental." Myth and ritual, Leach continues, constitute "a language of argument, not a chorus of harmony." [79] A language of argument, not a chorus of harmony, is precisely what we face when confronting the Popular Culture of the Great Depression which did not represent one point of view or one segment of the population but had built into it a series of often divergent points of view and competing voices. Disparateness, then, is not aberrant but is in fact Popular Culture's natural state. Those who have seen in Popular Culture an overriding instrument of hegemony have misunderstood its nature. Popular Culture does not present us with a single face or an orderly ideology. Certainly it is true that even in as heterogeneous a society as the United States, there can be deeply internalized points of view and these will inevitably be reflected in the Popular Culture, but there will be myriad fundamental disagreements and contradictions as well, as we've seen in the brief discussion of the photographs and films of the 1930s.

In my study of Black Folk Culture I found that there was no single overarching thematic matrix. Black folk in and out of slavery used different parts of their expressive culture for different purposes. If in matters of style and expression there was a recognizable African-American culture, this was not necessarily the case in matters of content which could vary widely depending on the genre, the situation, and the specific folk involved. If this was true for the Folk Culture of African-American slaves and freedmen, it is still truer for the Popular Culture of a much more diverse mass industrial society. But heterogeneity and variety do not necessarily connote chaos and loss of meaning. One has to look not for an unvarying central message but for *patterns* of meaning and consciousness across the genres and among different segments of the population. This is crucial but it does not negate the fact that whatever patterns we find will have to live alongside the inconsistencies, tensions, and cacophony of voices which help, far more than any putative unanimity and harmony, to reveal the cultural complexity of Depression America. Indeed, it is the very asymmetry and diversity in Popular Culture that should convince us it can be used as an indispensable guide to the thought and attitudes of an asymmetrical and diverse people.

Notes

Chapter 1

1. Quoted in Stephen Lukes, *Marxism and Morality* (Oxford, 1985), 146.
2. Henry James *The American Scene* (1907; rpt. edn., New York, 1946), 182.
3. Marc Bloch, *The Historian's Craft* (New York, 1962), 43.
4. John Higham, "The Cult of the 'American Consensus': Homogenizing Our History," *Commentary* (February 1959):93–100; "Beyond Consensus: The Historian as Moral Critic," *AHR,* 67 (April 1962):609–25.
5. John Higham, "Beyond Pluralism: The Historian as American Prophet," unpublished paper delivered to the Organization of American Historians, April 1983.
6. Lawrence W. Levine, *Defender of the Faith: William Jennings Bryan, The Last Decade, 1915–1925* (New York, 1965); *Black Culture and Black Consciousness: Afro-American Folk Thought from Slavery to Freedom* (New York, 1977).
7. C. Vann Woodward, "A Short History of American History," *New York Times Book Review,* August 8, 1982.
8. Eric Hobsbawm and Terrence Ranger, eds., *The Invention of Tradition* (Cambridge, 1983), 1–14.
9. Carl Bridenbaugh, "The Great Mutation," *AHR,* 68 (January 1963):322–23.
10. Gertrude Himmelfarb, *The New History and the Old* (Cambridge, 1987), 17–18, 25–26, 56.
11. Hamerow's charge is in Theodore S. Hamerow, *Reflections on History and Historians* (Madison, Wis., 1987), 169. Bennett was quoted in the San Francisco *Chronicle,* February 5, 1988.
12. Allan Bloom, *The Closing of the American Mind* (New York, 1987); Lawrence W. Levine. *Highbrow/Lowbrow: The Emergence of Cultural Hierarchy in America* (Cambridge, 1988).
13. *New York Times,* editorials, July 8, 1921, February 6, 1923, January 28, 1928. See also editorials in the issues of April 26, 1920 and January 30, 1922.
14. Nick Herbert, *Quantum Reality: Beyond the New Physics* (Garden City, N.Y., 1985), xi–xii, 246, and *passim.*
15. Quoted in Heinz R. Pagels, *The Cosmic Code: Quantum Physics as the Language of Nature* (New York, 1983), 113.
16. *New York Times,* January 28, 1928.
17. Lawrence W. Levine, *Black Culture and Black Consciousness;* Mark Slo-

bin, *Tenement Songs: The Popular Music of the Jewish Immigrants* (Urbana, Ill., 1982).

Chapter 2

1. Lawrence W. Levine, *Defender of the Faith: William Jennings Bryan, The Last Decade, 1915–1925* (New York, 1965).
2. Carl Bridenbaugh, "The Great Mutation," *American Historical Review,* LXVIII (January 1963), 322–23.
3. Edward Hallett Carr, *What Is History?* (New York, 1962), p. 54.
4. Ernest Nagel, "Relativism and Some Problems of Working Historians," in Sidney Hook, ed., *Philosophy and History* (New York, 1963), pp. 81–82.
5. John Higham, "Beyond Consensus: The Historian as Moral Critic," *American Historical Review,* LXVII (April 1962), 620.
6. Richard Hofstadter, *The American Political Tradition* (New York, 1948), chap. VIII, "William Jennings Bryan: The Democrat as Revivalist."
7. John William Ward, *Andrew Jackson: Symbol for an Age* (New York, 1955); "The Meaning of Lindbergh's Flight," *American Quarterly,* X (Spring 1958), 3–16.
8. Richard Hofstadter, *The Age of Reform* (New York, 1955).
9. John Henrik Clarke, ed., *William Styron's Nat Turner: Ten Black Writers Respond* (Boston, 1968), pp. 29, 32, 36, 43, 50.
10. Roger D. Abrahams, *Deep Down in the Jungle . . . . : Negro Narrative Folklore from the Streets of Philadelphia* (Hatboro, Pa., 1964); Charles Keil, *Urban Blues* (Chicago, 1966); Elliot Liebow, *Tally's Corner: A Study of Negro Streetcorner Men* (Boston, 1967).

Chapter 3

1. Miles Mark Fisher, *Negro Slave Songs in the United States* (New York, 1963, orig. pub. 1953), 14, 39, 132, and *passim.*
2. The contours of this debate are judiciously outlined in D. K. Wilgus, *Anglo-American Folksong Scholarship Since 1898* (New Brunswick, 1959), App. One, "The Negro-White Spirituals."
3. Lucy McKim, "Songs of the Port Royal Contrabands," *Dwight's Journal of Music,* XXII (November 8, 1862), 255.
4. W. F. Allen, "The Negro Dialect," *The Nation,* I (December 14, 1865), 744–745.
5. See, for instance, Henry Edward Krehbiel, *Afro-American Folksongs* (New York, 1963, orig. pub. 1914); James Wesley Work, *Folk Song of the American Negro* (Nashville, 1915); James Weldon Johnson, *The Book of American Negro Spirituals* (New York, 1925), and *The Second Book of Negro Spirituals* (New York, 1926); Lydia Parrish, *Slave Songs of the Georgia Sea Islands* (Hatboro, Penna., 1965, orig. pub. 1942); LeRoi Jones, *Blues People* (New York, 1963).
6. Newman I. White, *American Negro Folk-Songs* (Hatboro, Penna., 1965, orig. pub. 1928); Guy B. Johnson, *Folk Culture on St. Helena Island, South Carolina* (Chapel Hill, 1930); George Pullen Jackson, *White and Negro Spirituals* (New York, 1943).
7. White, *American Negro Folk-Songs,* 11–13.
8. Professor John William Ward gives an excellent example of this process in

his discussion of the different meanings which the newspapers of the United States, France, and India attributed to Charles Lindbergh's flight across the Atlantic in 1927. See "Lindbergh, Dos Passos, and History," in Ward, *Red, White, and Blue* (New York, 1969), 55.

9. George Pullen Jackson, "The Genesis of the Negro Spiritual," *The American Mercury,* XXVI (June 1932), 248.

10. Richard Alan Waterman, "African Influence on the Music of the Americas," in Sol Tax (ed.), *Acculturation in the Americas: Proceedings and Selected Papers of the XXIXth International Congress of Americanists* (Chicago, 1952), 207–218; Wilgus, *Anglo-American Folksong Scholarship Since 1898,* 363–364; Melville J. Herskovits, "Patterns of Negro Music" (pamphlet, no publisher, no date); Gilbert Chase, *America's Music* (New York, 1966), chap. 12; Alan P. Merriam, "African Music," in William R. Bascom and Melville J. Herskovits (eds.), *Continuity and Change in African Cultures* (Chicago, 1959), 76–80.

11. White, *American Negro Folk-Songs,* 29, 55.

12. Jackson, *White and Negro Spirituals,* 266–267.

13. James Miller McKim, "Negro Songs," *Dwight's Journal of Music,* XXI (August 9, 1862), 149.

14. Thomas Wentworth Higginson, *Army Life in a Black Regiment* (Beacon Press edition, Boston, 1962, orig. pub. 1869), 218–219.

15. Henry Russell, *Cheer! Boys, Cheer!,* 84–85, quoted in Chase, *America's Music,* 235–236.

16. Jeanette Robinson Murphy, "The Survival of African Music in America," *Popular Science Monthly,* 55 (1899), 660–672, reprinted in Bruce Jackson (ed.), *The Negro and His Folklore in Nineteenth-Century Periodicals* (Austin, 1967), 328.

17. Natalie Curtis Burlin, "Negro Music at Birth," *Musical Quarterly,* V (January 1919), 88. For Mrs. Burlin's excellent reproductions of Negro folk songs and spirituals, see her *Negro Folk-Songs* (New York, 1918–1919), Vols. I–IV.

18. Clifton Joseph Furness, "Communal Music Among Arabians and Negroes," *Musical Quarterly,* XVI (January 1930), 49–51.

19. Elizabeth Kilham, "Sketches in Color: IV," *Putnam's Monthly,* XV (March 1870), 304–311, reprinted in Jackson, *The Negro and His Folklore in Nineteenth-Century Periodicals,* 127–128.

20. Bruno Nettl, *Folk and Traditional Music of the Western Continents* (Englewood Cliffs, 1965), 4–5; Chase, *America's Music,* 241–243.

21. J. K., Jr., "Who Are Our National Poets?," *Knickerbocker Magazine,* 26 (October 1845), 336, quoted in Dena J. Epstein, "Slave Music in the United States Before 1860: A Survey of Sources (Part I)," *Music Library Association Notes,* XX (Spring 1963), 208.

22. Elizabeth Kilham, "Sketches in Color: IV," *Putnam's Monthly,* XV (March 1870), 304–311, reprinted in Jackson, *The Negro and His Folklore in Nineteenth-Century Periodicals,* 129.

23. White, *American Negro Folk-Songs,* 57.

24. Alan P. Merriam, "Music and the Dance," in Robert Lystad (ed.), *The African World: A Survey of Social Research* (New York, 1965), 452–468; William Bascom, "Folklore and Literature," in *ibid.,* 469–488; R. S. Rattray, *Ashanti* (Oxford, 1923), chap. XV; Melville Herskovits, "Freudian Mechanisms in Primitive Negro Psychology," in E. E. Evans-Pritchard *et al.* (eds.), *Essays Presented to C. G. Seligman* (London, 1934), 75–84; Alan P. Merriam, "African Music," in Bascom and Herskovits, *Continuity and Change in African Cultures,* 49–86.

25. William Francis Allen, Charles Pickard Ware, and Lucy McKim Garrison, compilers, *Slave Songs of the United States* (New York, 1867, Oak Publications ed., 1965), 164–165.

26. *Ibid.*, 43.

27. Harriet Jacobs, *Incidents in the Life of a Slave Girl* (Boston, 1861), 109.

28. Lines like these could be quoted endlessly. For the specific ones cited, see the songs in the following collections: Higginson, *Army Life in a Black Regiment*, 206, 216–217; Allen *et al.*, *Slave Songs of the United States*, 33–34, 44, 106–108, 131, 160–161; Thomas P. Fenner, compiler, *Religious Folk Songs of the Negro as Sung on the Plantations* (Hampton, Virginia, 1909, orig. pub. 1874), 10–11, 48; J. B. T. Marsh, *The Story of the Jubilee Singers; With Their Songs* (Boston, 1880), 136, 167, 178.

29. McKim, "Negro Songs," 148; H. G. Spaulding, "Under the Palmetto," *Continental Monthly*, IV (1863), 188–203, reprinted in Jackson, *The Negro and His Folklore in Nineteenth-Century Periodicals*, 72; Allen, "The Negro Dialect," 744–745; Higginson, *Army Life in a Black Regiment*, 220–221.

30. *Journal of Nicholas Cresswell, 1774–1777* (New York, 1934), 17–19, quoted in Epstein, *Music Library Association Notes*, XX (Spring 1963), 201.

31. Jacobs, *Incidents in the Life of a Slave Girl*, 180.

32. *Life and Times of Frederick Douglass* (rev. ed., 1892, Collier Books Edition, 1962), 146–147.

33. John Lambert, *Travels Through Canada and the United States of North America in the Years, 1806–1807 and 1808* (London, 1814), II, 253–254, quoted in Dena J. Epstein, "Slave Music in the United States Before 1860: A Survey of Sources (Part 2)," *Music Library Association Notes*, XX (Summer 1963), 377.

34. Frances Anne Kemble, *Journal of a Residence on a Georgian Plantation in 1838–1839* (New York, 1863), 128.

35. For versions of these songs, see Dorothy Scarborough, *On the Trail of Negro Folk-Songs* (Cambridge, 1925), 194, 201–203, 223–225, and Thomas W. Talley, *Negro Folk Rhymes* (New York, 1922), 25–26. Talley claims that the majority of the songs in his large and valuable collection "were sung by Negro fathers and mothers in the dark days of American slavery to their children who listened with eyes as large as saucers and drank them down with mouths wide open," but offers no clue as to why he feels that songs collected for the most part in the twentieth century were slave songs.

36. Constance Rourke, *The Roots of American Culture and Other Essays* (New York, 1942), 262–274. Newman White, on the contrary, has argued that although the earliest minstrel songs were Negro derived, they soon went their own way and that less than ten percent of them were genuinely Negro. Nevertheless, these white songs "got back to the plantation, largely spurious as they were and were undoubtedly among those which the plantation-owners encouraged the Negroes to sing. They persist to-day in isolated stanzas and lines, among the songs handed down by plantation Negroes . . ." White, *American Negro Folk-Songs*, 7–10 and Appendix IV. There are probably valid elements in both theses. A similarly complex relationship between genuine Negro folk creations and their more commercialized partly white influenced imitations was to take place in the blues of the twentieth century.

37. McKim, "Songs of the Port Royal Contrabands," 255.

38. Mircea Eliade, *The Sacred and the Profane* (New York, 1961), chaps. 2, 4, and *passim*. For the similarity of Eliade's concept to the world view of West

Africa, see W. E. Abraham, *The Mind of Africa* (London, 1962), chap. 2, and R. S. Rattray, *Religion and Art in Ashanti* (Oxford, 1927).

39. Paul Radin, "Status, Phantasy, and the Christian Dogma," in Social Science Institute, Fisk University, *God Struck Me Dead: Religious Conversion Experiences and Autobiographies of Negro Ex-Slaves* (Nashville, 1945, unpublished typescript).

40. Stanley Elkins, *Slavery* (Chicago, 1959), 136.

41. Allen *et al.*, *Slave Songs of the United States*, 33–34, 105; William E. Barton, *Old Plantation Hymns: A Collection of Hitherto Unpublished Melodies of the Slave and the Freedmen* (Boston, 1899), 30.

42. Allen *et al.*, *Slave Songs of the United States*, 47.

43. Barton, *Old Plantation Hymns*, 19.

44. Marsh, *The Story of the Jubilee Singers*, 132.

45. Fenner, *Religious Folk Songs of the Negro*, 162; E. A. McIlhenny, *Befo' De War Spirituals: Words and Melodies* (Boston, 1933), 39.

46. Barton, *Old Plantation Hymns*, 15; Howard W. Odum and Guy B. Johnson, *The Negro and His Songs* (Hatboro, Penn., 1964, orig. pub. 1925), 33–34; for a vivid description of the "shout" see *The Nation*, May 30, 1867, 432–433; see also Parrish, *Slave Songs of the Georgia Sea Islands*, chap. III.

47. For examples of songs of this nature, see Fenner, *Religious Folk Songs of the Negro*, 8, 63–65; Marsh, *The Story of the Jubilee Singers*, 240–241; Higginson, *Army Life in a Black Regiment*, 205; Allen *et al.*, *Slave Songs of the United States*, 91, 100; Burlin, *Negro Folk-Songs*, I, 37–42.

48. Allen *et al.*, *Slave Songs of the United States*, 32–33.

49. *Ibid.*, 30–31; Burlin, *Negro Folk-Songs*, II, 8–9; Fenner, *Religious Folk Songs of the Negro*, 12.

50. Allen *et al.*, *Slave Songs of the United States*, 128–129; Fenner, *Religious Folk Songs of the Negro*, 127; Barton, *Old Plantation Hymns*, 26.

51. Allen *et al.*, *Slave Songs of the United States*, 70, 102–103, 147; Barton, *Old Plantation Hymns*, 9, 17–18, 24; Marsh, *The Story of the Jubilee Singers*, 133, 167; Odum and Johnson, *The Negro and His Songs*, 35.

52. Allen *et al.*, *Slave Songs of the United States*, 102–103.

53. Mary Allen Grissom, compiler, *The Negro Sings a New Heaven* (Chapel Hill, 1930), 73.

54. Marsh, *The Story of the Jubilee Singers*, 179, 186; Allen *et al.*, *Slave Songs of the United States*, 40–41, 44, 146; Barton, *Old Plantation Hymns*, 30.

55. McIlhenny, *Befo' De War Spirituals*, 31.

56. *Gumbo Ya-Ya: A Collection of Louisiana Folk Tales*, compiled by Lyle Saxon, Edward Dreyer, and Robert Tallant from materials gathered by workers of the WPA, Louisiana Writers' Project (Boston, 1945), 242.

57. For examples, see Allen *et al.*, *Slave Songs of the United States*, 40–41, 82, 97, 106–108; Marsh, *The Story of the Jubilee Singers*, 168, 203; Burlin, *Negro Folk-Songs*, II, 8–9; Howard Thurman, *Deep River* (New York, 1945), 19–21.

58. Thurman, *Deep River*, 16–17.

59. Higginson, *Army Life in a Black Regiment*, 202–205. Many of those northerners who came to the South to "uplift" the freedmen were deeply disturbed at the Old Testament emphasis of their religion. H. G. Spaulding complained that the ex-slaves needed to be introduced to "the light and warmth of the Gospel," and reported that a Union army officer told him: "Those people had enough of the Old

Testament thrown at their heads under slavery. Now give them the glorious utterances and practical teachings of the Great Master." Spaulding, "Under the Palmetto," reprinted in Jackson, *The Negro and His Folklore in Nineteenth-Century Periodicals,* 66.

60. Allen *et al., Slave Songs of the United States,* 148; Fenner, *Religious Folk Songs of the Negro,* 21; Marsh, *The Story of the Jubilee Singers,* 134–135; McIlhenny, *Befo' De War Spirituals,* 248–249.

61. *Life and Times of Frederick Douglass,* 159–160; Marsh, *The Story of the Jubilee Singers,* 188.

62. Higginson, *Army Life in a Black Regiment,* 217.

63. Parrish, *Slave Songs of the Georgia Sea Islands,* 247.

64. "Actually, not one spiritual in its primary form reflected interest in anything other than a full life here and now." Fisher, *Negro Slave Songs in the United States,* 137.

65. Barton, *Old Plantation Hymns,* 25; Allen *et al., Slave Songs of the United States,* 94; McKim, "Negro Songs," 149.

66. Higginson, *Army Life in a Black Regiment,* 201–202, 211–212.

67. Robert Redfield, *The Primitive World and Its Transformations* (Ithaca, 1953), 51–53.

68. Elkins, *Slavery,* chap. III.

69. *Ibid.,* chap. II; Frank Tannenbaum, *Slave and Citizen* (New York, 1946).

70. E. J. Hobsbawm, *Primitive Rebels* (New York, 1959), chap. I.

71. C. M. Bowra, *Primitive Song* (London, 1962), 285–286.

Chapter 4

1. Octave Thanet, "Folk-Lore in Arkansas," *Journal of American Folklore* [cited hereafter as *JAF*], 5 (April–June 1892), 122.

2. The following African tale type and motif indices were used in this comparison: Erastus Ojo Arewa, "A Classification of the Folktales of the Northern East African Cattle Area by Types" (unpublished Ph.D. dissertation, University of California, Berkeley, 1966); Winifred Lambrecht, "A Tale Type Index for Central Africa" (unpublished Ph.D. dissertation, University of California, Berkeley, 1967); Kenneth Wendell Clarke, "Motif-Index of the Folk-Tales of Culture-Area V West Africa" (unpublished Ph.D. dissertation, Indiana University, 1958).

3. R. S. Rattray, *Akan-Ashanti Folk Tales* (Oxford, 1930), pp. x–xii.

4. Janheinz Jahn, *Muntu: An Outline of the New African Culture* (New York, 1961), p. 221.

5. Rattray, *Akan-Ashanti Folk Tales,* p. xiii; Melville J. and Frances S. Herskovits, *Suriname Folk-Lore* (New York, 1936), p. 138; *Standard Dictionary of Folklore, Mythology and Legend* (New York, 1949–1950), I, 52–53.

6. Other primary animal trickster figures in Africa whose geographical distribution is less clear-cut include Antelope, Squirrel, Wren, Weasel, and Jackal. Ruth Finnegan, *Oral Literature in Africa* (Oxford, 1970), pp. 344–354; Richard A. Waterman and William R. Bascom, "African and New World Negro Folklore," *Standard Dictionary of Folklore, Mythology and Legend,* I, 18–24; A. B. Ellis, "Evolution in Folklore: Some West African Prototypes of the 'Uncle Remus' Stories," *Popular Science Monthly,* 48 (Nov. 1895), 93–104. For a refutation of the once widely held thesis that the slaves' rabbit trickster was borrowed from the North

American Indians, see Alan Dundes, "African Tales Among the North American Indians," *Southern Folklore Quarterly,* 29 (Sept. 1965), 207–219.

7. Melville J. and Frances S. Herskovits, *Dahomean Narrative* (Evanston, 1958), pp. 99–101.

8. Constance Rourke, *American Humor* (New York, 1931), chaps. 1–2; Jesse Bier, *The Rise and Fall of American Humor* (New York, 1968), chaps. 1–2; Richard M. Dorson, *American Folklore* (Chicago, 1959), chap. 2; James T. Pearce, "Folk-Tales of the Southern Poor-White, 1820–1860," *JAF,* 63 (Oct.–Dec. 1950), 398–412.

9. Dorson, *American Folklore,* p. 185. In fact, as this essay demonstrates, Anansi stories were present in the nineteenth-century United States in small numbers. Not until the twentieth-century influx of West Indians into the United States are Anansi tales found with any regularity, as the manuscripts of the Federal Writers' Project, New York File, Archive of Folk Song (Library of Congress), indicate. Even then, of course, the spider remains a minor figure in United States black folklore.

10. For an indication of the distribution of Anansi stories in South America, see Terrence Leslie Hansen, *The Types of the Folktale in Cuba, Puerto Rico, the Dominican Republic, and Spanish South America* (Berkeley, 1957).

11. The tar-baby story appears in virtually every collection of black tales in this period. For examples, see Thaddeus Norris, "Negro Superstitions," *Lippincott's Magazine,* 6 (July 1870), 94–95; William Owens, "Folk-Lore of the Southern Negroes," *ibid.,* 20 (Dec. 1877), 750–751; Charles C. Jones, *Negro Myths from the Georgia Coast* (Boston, 1888), pp. 7–11; Louis Pendleton, "Notes on Negro Folk-Lore and Witchcraft in the South," *JAF,* 3 (July–Sept. 1890), 201; *Southern Workman,* 23 (Aug. 1894), 149–150; A. M. H. Christensen, *Afro-American Folk Lore* (New York, 1969; orig. pub. 1892), pp. 62–72.

12. Elsie Clews Parsons, *Folk-Lore of the Sea Islands, South Carolina* (Memoirs of the American Folklore Society, XVI, 1923), p. 78.

13. Jones, *Negro Myths,* p. 35.

14. *Southern Workman,* 22 (June 1898), 125.

15. Jones, *Negro Myths,* pp. 97–99.

16. Federal Writers' Project, Mississippi File, Archive of Folksong (Library of Congress).

17. Emma M. Backus, "Folk-Tales from Georgia," *JAF,* 13 (Jan.–March 1900), 22–24.

18. For examples of the many versions of this tale, see Christensen, *Afro-American Folk Lore,* pp. 73–80; Guy B. Johnson, *Folk Culture on St. Helena Island, South Carolina* (Chapel Hill, N.C., 1930), pp. 138–140; Jones, *Negro Myths,* pp. 53–57; A. M. Bacon and Elsie Clews Parsons, "Folk-Lore from Elizabeth City County, Virginia," *JAF,* 35 (July–Sept. 1922), 253–256.

19. See, for instance, Joel Chandler Harris, *Uncle Remus: His Songs and His Sayings* (New York, 1880), pp. 80–86; Elsie Clews Parsons, "Tales from Guilford County, North Carolina," *JAF,* 30 (April–June 1917), 192–193; Richard Smith, "Richard's Tales," *Publications of the Texas Folk-Lore Society,* 25 (1953), 220–224.

20. Jones, *Negro Myths,* pp. 102–105; Parsons, *Folk-Lore of the Sea Islands,* p. 39.

21. *Southern Workman,* 25 (Sept. 1896), 185–186; (Oct. 1896), 205.

22. Bacon and Parsons, "Folk-Lore from Elizabeth City County, Virginia," 277–278.

23. Jones, *Negro Myths,* pp. 49–53.

24. Christensen, *Afro-American Folk Lore,* pp. 73–80.

25. *Ibid.,* pp. 104–107; Parsons, *Folk-Lore of the Sea Islands,* pp. 30–31.

26. Backus, "Folk-Tales from Georgia," p. 25.

27. For examples, see Anne Virginia Culbertson, *At the Big House* (Indianapolis, 1904); Emma M. Backus, "Animal Tales from North Carolina," *JAF,* 11 (Oct.–Dec. 1898), 288–289; Bacon and Parsons, "Folk-Lore from Elizabeth City County, Virginia," 266; Joel Chandler Harris, *Seven Tales of Uncle Remus* (Atlanta, 1948), tale 7.

28. *Southern Workman,* 27 (April 1898), 76.

29. For various versions of this widely popular tale, see Owens, "Folk-Lore of the Southern Negroes," p. 753; Jones, *Negro Myths,* pp. 27–31; *Southern Workman,* 23 (Aug. 1894), 149–150; Mrs. William Preston Johnston, "Two Negro Tales," *JAF,* 9 (July–Sept. 1896), 194–196; Bacon and Parsons, "Folk-Lore from Elizabeth City County, Virginia," pp. 265–266; Parsons, *Folk-Lore of the Sea Islands,* pp. 53–55.

30. Christensen, *Afro-American Folk Lore,* pp. 36–41; Jones, *Negro Myths,* pp. 99–102; Parsons, *Folk-Lore of the Sea Islands,* pp. 14–19.

31. *Nights with Uncle Remus* (Boston, 1883), p. 330; *Uncle Remus: His Songs and His Sayings,* p. xiv.

32. Christensen, *Afro-American Folk Lore,* pp. ix–xiv.

33. Thanet, "Folk-Lore in Arkansas," p. 122.

34. See, for instance, John Stafford, "Patterns of Meaning in Nights with Uncle Remus," *American Literature,* 18 (May 1946), 89–108; Louise Dauner, "Myth and Humor in the Uncle Remus Fables," *ibid.,* 20 (May 1948), 129–143; Bernard Wolfe, "Uncle Remus and the Malevolent Rabbit," *Commentary* (July 1949), 31–41; Marshall Fishwick, "Uncle Remus vs. John Henry: Folk Tension," *Western Folklore,* 20 (April 1961), 77–85.

35. Christensen, *Afro-American Folk Lore,* pp. 1–5.

36. J. Mason Brewer, *Dog Ghosts and Other Texas Negro Folk Tales* (Austin, 1958), p. 50.

37. See Lawrence W. Levine, "Slave Songs and Slave Consciousness," in Tamara Hareven, ed., *Anonymous Americans* (Englewood Cliffs, N.J., 1971), pp. 99–130.

38. Various versions of this ubiquitous tale can be found in Owens, "Folk-Lore of the Southern Negroes," p. 751; Christensen, *Afro-American Folk Lore,* p. 79; Sadie E. Stewart, "Seven Folk-Tales from the Sea Islands, S. C.," *JAF,* 32 (July–Sept. 1919), 394; Jones, *Negro Myths,* pp. 5–6; B. A. Botkin, ed., *Lay My Burden Down* (Chicago, 1945), p. 23; Backus, "Animal Tales from North Carolina," pp. 284–285; Parsons, *Folk-Lore of the Sea Islands,* p. 79.

39. Jones, *Negro Myths,* p. 105.

40. Christensen, *Afro-American Folk Lore,* pp. 101–103.

41. Parsons, *Folk-Lore of the Sea Islands,* p. 44.

42. Jones, *Negro Myths,* pp. 11–14.

43. Parsons, *Folk-Lore of the Sea Islands,* pp. 66–67.

44. Johnston, "Two Negro Tales," pp. 196–198.

45. Christensen, *Afro-American Folk Lore,* pp. 54–57; Zora Neale Hurston, *Mules and Men* (Philadelphia, 1935), pp. 141–142.

46. *Southern Workman,* 25 (April 1896), 82; Bacon and Parsons, "Folk-Lore

from Elizabeth City County, Virginia," pp. 252–253, 277; Jones, *Negro Myths*, pp. 73–81; Harris, *Nights with Uncle Remus*, pp. 314–319.

47. Emma M. Backus, "Tales of the Rabbit from Georgia Negroes," *JAF*, 12 (April–June 1899), 111–112.

48. Christensen, *Afro-American Folk Lore*, pp. 26–35.

49. Elsie Clews Parsons, "Folk-Tales Collected at Miami, Florida," *JAF*, 30 (April–June 1917), 226.

50. Backus, "Animal Tales from North Carolina," pp. 288–289.

51. Jones, *Negro Myths*, pp. 91–93.

52. *Southern Workman*, 26 (1897), 58.

53. Wolfe, "Uncle Remus and the Malevolent Rabbit," p. 36.

54. Jones, *Negro Myths*, pp. 128–129.

55. Botkin, *Lay My Burden Down*, p. 91.

56. Emma M. Backus and Ethel Hatton Leitner, "Negro Tales from Georgia," *JAF*, 25 (April–June 1912), 127–128; Owens, "Folk-Lore of the Southern Negroes," 752; Bacon and Parsons, "Folk-Lore from Elizabeth City County, Virginia," pp. 262–264; Christensen, *Afro-American Folk Lore*, pp. 19–22, 62–72; Backus, "Folk-Tales from Georgia," pp. 24–25; *Southern Workman*, 28 (March 1899), 113.

57. Dauner, "Myth and Humor in the Uncle Remus Fables," p. 135.

Chapter 5

1. Ulrich B. Phillips, the influential early twentieth-century historian of slavery, quoted with approval the antebellum planters' saying that "a negro was what a white man made him." Phillips, *American Negro Slavery* (1918; reprint ed., Baton Rouge: Louisiana State Univ. Press, 1966), p. 291. Four decades later, the historian Stanley Elkins elaborated upon Phillips's judgment to show how slavery had "infantalized" its victims so that not only was the culture they had brought with them destroyed, but even their aspirations were reduced to fantasies of "catfish and watermelons." Elkins, *Slavery* (Chicago: Univ. of Chicago Press, 1959), p. 136 and passim.

2. Robert E. Park, "The Conflict and Fusion of Cultures with Special Reference to the Negro," *Journal of Negro History* 4 (1919):116–18.

3. Frederick W. Root, "Folk-Music," *International Folk-Lore Congress of the World's Columbian Exposition, Chicago, 1893* 1:424–25; Ambrose E. Gonzales, *The Black Border; Gullah Stories of the Carolina Coast* (Columbia, S.C., 1922), p. 10; John Bennett, "Gullah: A Negro Patois," *South Atlantic Quarterly* 7 (1908):336, 338. The folklorist Louise Pound exemplified the belief that cultural diffusion was a one-way street by arguing that the spiritual, "Weeping Mary," could not have originated among the slaves since her grandmother had learned the song from a white woman who heard it at a white Methodist camp meeting in Hamilton, New York, in the late 1820's. If whites knew the song, Pound was convinced, it must have been they who originated and disseminated it. Louise Pound, "The Ancestry of a 'Negro Spiritual,' " *Modern Language Notes* 33 (1918):442–44.

4. Again, Robert Park stated the position succinctly: "The Negro when he landed in the United States, left behind him almost everything but his dark complexion and his tropical temperament." Robert Park, *Journal of Negro History* 4 (1919):116–18. Like Park, most white scholars in the late nineteenth and early twen-

tieth century were driven to deny Africa any vestige of cultural influence. They were willing to credit Africa only with genetic influences, especially in the areas of movement and rhythm. This compulsive myopia, which obviously is revealing of white American cultural needs and predispositions, is worthy of a study of its own.

5. Peter H. Wood, *Black Majority: Negroes in Colonial South Carolina* (New York: Norton, 1974), pp. 55–62; 119–24. See also Charles Winston Joyner, "Slave Folklife on the Waccamaw Neck: Antebellum Black Culture in the South Carolina Low Country" (Ph.D. diss., University of Pennsylvania, 1977). Labor requirements in South Carolina and other parts of the South allowed the continuation of African cooperative work practices even within the highly individualistic task system. "It is customary *(and never objected to)*" the planter James Sparkman noted, "for the more active and industrious hands to assist those who are slower and more tardy in finishing their daily tasks." Joyner, "Slave Folklife on the Waccamaw Neck," pp. 44–45.

6. C. C. Jones, *The Religious Instruction of the Negroes in the United States* (1842; reprint ed., New York: Arno, 1969), pp. 127–28.

7. Quoted in Dena J. Epstein, *Sinful Tunes and Spirituals: Black Folk Music to the Civil War* (Urbana: Univ. of Illinois Press 1977), pp. 193–94.

8. For a discussion of slave dance, see Lawrence W. Levine, *Black Culture and Black Consciousness: Afro-American Folk Thought from Slavery to Freedom* (New York: Oxford, 1977), pp. 16–18; 38; Marshall Stearns and Jean Stearns, *Jazz Dance: The Story of American Vernacular Dance (New York: Shirmer Books, 1968),* chaps. 2–4; Lynne Fauley Emery, *Black Dance in the United States from 1619 to 1970* (Palo Alto: Arno 1972), chaps. 1–5; Benjamin Henry Boneval Latrobe, *Impressions Respecting New Orleans: Diary & Sketches, 1818–1820* (New York, 1951), pp. 49–51; Henry William Ravenel, "Recollections of Southern Plantation Life," *Yale Review* 25 (1936):768–69.

9. David Macrae, *The Americans at Home* (1870; reprint ed., New York, 1952), p. 318.

10. See Henry Lee Swint, *The Northern Teacher in the South, 1862–1870* (Nashville: Octagon, 1941), and Levine, *Black Culture and Black Consciousness,* chap. 3.

11. J. C. Carothers, "Culture, Psychiatry, and the Written Word," *Psychiatry* (1959):307–20.

12. Mircea Eliade, *The Sacred and the Profane* (New York, 1961). For the importance of the sacred world in Africa, see W. E. Abraham, *The Mind of Africa* (London, 1962), chap. 2; R. S. Rattray, *Religion and Art in Ashanti* (Oxford, 1927); and John S. Mbiti, *African Religions and Philosophies* (Garden City, N.Y.: Doubleday, 1969), chap. 3.

13. Levine, *Black Culture and Black Consciousness,* chaps chap. 1; Albert J. Raboteau, *Slave Religion* (New York; Oxford Univ. Press, 1978); Eugene D. Genovese, *Roll, Jordan, Roll* (New York: Random House, 1974), book 2.

14. Levine, *Black Culture and Black Consciousness,* chaps. 1–2; Theodore Van Dam, "The Influence of the West African Song of Derision in the New World," *African Music* 1 (1954):53–56; William D. Piersen, "Puttin' Down Ole Massa: African Satire in the New World," in *African Folklore in the New World;* Daniel J. Crowley, ed. (Austin: Univ. of Texas Press, 1977), pp. 20–34; Alan Dundes, "African and Afro-American Tales," in ibid., pp. 35–53; William D. Piersen, "An African Background for American Negro Folktales?" *Journal of American Folklore* 84 (1971):204–14.

15. Levine, *Black Culture and Black Consciousness* (New York: Oxford Univ. Press, 1978), chaps. 1–2.

16. Robert Redfield, *The Primitive World and Its Transformations* (Ithaca: Cornell Univ. Press, 1953), pp. 51–53.

17. VèVè Clark, public lecture, Berkeley, Calif., Fall 1973.

18. Richard Alan Waterman, "African Influence on the Music of the Americas," in *Acculturation in the Americas,* Sol Tax, ed. (Chicago: Univ. of Chicago Press, 1952), pp. 207–18; Alan P. Merriam, "African Music," in *Continuity and Change in African Cultures,* William R. Bascom and Melville J. Herskovits, eds. (Chicago, Univ. of Chicago Press 1959), pp. 49–86; Alan P. Merriam, "Music and the Dance," in *The African World,* Robert Lystad, ed. (New York; 1965), pp. 452–68; Levine, *Black Culture and Black Consciousness,* chap. 1; Keith Thomas, *Religion and the Decline of Magic* (New York; Scribner, 1971); John F. Szwed and Roger D. Abrahams, "After the Myth: Studying Afro-American Cultural Patterns in the Plantation Literature," in *African Folklore in the New World,* Crowley, ed., pp. 65–86.

Chapter 6

1. Ralph Ellison, *Shadow and Act* (New York: Random House, 1964), p. 115.

2. Stanley Elkins, *Slavery* (Chicago: University of Chicago Press, 1959), chap. 3.

3. See, for example, Eugene D. Genovese, "The Legacy of Slavery and the Roots of Black Nationalism," *Studies on the Left* 6 (November–December 1966):3–26. Ironically, Genovese has been one of the most perceptive and effective critics of the Elkins thesis for the period of slavery. See his article "Rebelliousness and Docility in the Negro Slave: A Critique of the Elkins Thesis," *Civil War History* 13 (December 1967):293–314, in which he criticizes "Elkins' inability to see the slaves as active forces capable of tempering the authority of the master."

4. Nathan Glazer and Daniel Moynihan, *Beyond the Melting Pot* (Cambridge, Mass.: M.I.T. Press, 1963), p. 53.

5. [Daniel Moynihan], *The Negro Family: The Case for National Action* (Washington, D.C.: Office of Policy Planning and Research, Department of Labor, March 1965), p. 30. Italics added.

6. Thomas F. Pettigrew, *A Profile of the Negro American* (Princeton, N.J.: D. Van Nostrand, 1964), p. 25.

7. E. Franklin Frazier, *The Negro in the United States,* revised ed. (New York: Macmillan, 1957), pp. 680–81.

8. August Meier, *Negro Thought in America, 1880–1915* (Ann Arbor: University of Michigan Press, 1963), chap. 14.

9. See the foreword and "The New Negro," in Alain Locke, *The New Negro* (New York: Albert & Charles Boni, 1925), pp. xv, xvii, 5, 6, 8.

10. August Meier and Elliott Rudwick, "The Boycott Movement Against Jim Crow Streetcars in the South, 1900–1906," *Journal of American History* 55 (March 1969):756–75; "Negro Boycotts of Jim Crow Streetcars in Tennessee," *American Quarterly* 21 (Winter 1969): 755–63; and "Negro Boycotts of Jim Crow Schools in the North, 1897–1925," *Integrated Education* 5 (August–September 1967):1–12.

11. William Muraskin, "Black Masons: The Role of Fraternal Orders in the Creation of a Middle-Class Black Community" (Ph.D. diss., University of California, Berkeley, 1970), p. 186.

12. W. E. B. Du Bois, *The Souls of Black Folk* (1903; reprint ed., New York: Fawcett, 1961).

13. Paul Laurence Dunbar, *The Complete Poems of Paul Laurence Dunbar* (New York: Dodd, Mead, 1922), p. 71.

14. Ellison, *Shadow and Act*, p. xxi.

15. The results of these tests and interviews are conveniently summarized in Pettigrew, *A Profile of the Negro American*, pp. 50–51.

16. Kenneth M. Stampp, *The Peculiar Institution* (New York: Alfred A. Knopf, 1955), chaps. 3, 8.

17. There have been a number of recent studies which have focused upon the central elements of black culture. Among the most notable are Charles Keil, *Urban Blues* (Chicago: University of Chicago Press, 1966); LeRoi Jones, *Blues People* (New York: William Morrow, 1963); Roger D. Abrahams, *Positively Black* (Englewood Cliffs, N.J.: Prentice-Hall, 1970); and Bruce A. Rosenberg, *The Art of the American Folk Preacher* (New York: Oxford University Press, 1970).

18. Paul Oliver, *Conversation with the Blues* (New York: Horizon Press, 1965), pp. 29–30, 121–23.

19. Bruno Nettl, *Folk and Traditional Music of the Western Continents* (Englewood Cliffs, N.J.: Prentice-Hall, 1965), pp. 4–5.

20. Howard W. Odum and Guy B. Johnson, *The Negro and His Songs* (1925; reprint ed., Hatboro, Pa.: Folklore Associates, 1964), pp. 2–3.

21. Oliver, *Conversation with the Blues*, pp. 34–35.

22. John A. Lomax, "Self-Pity in Negro Folk-Songs," *Nation* 105 (9 August 1917):141–45.

23. Howard W. Odum and Guy B. Johnson, *Negro Workaday Songs* (Chapel Hill: University of North Carolina Press, 1926), pp. 120–21.

24. Newman I. White, *American Negro Folk Songs* (1928; reprint ed., Hatboro Pa.: Folklore Associates, 1965), pp. 30, 258, 286, 382, 384, 377, 27.

25. Harold Courlander, *Negro Folk Music, U.S.A.* (New York: Columbia University Press, 1963), p. 145. For similar arguments, see James Weldon Johnson's preface to *The Second Book of Negro Spirituals* (New York: Viking Press, 1926) and Jones, *Blues People*, p. 28. Jones goes even further and argues: "Even the purely instrumental music of the American Negro contains constant reference to vocal music. Blues-playing is the closest imitation of the human voice of any music I've heard; the vocal effects that jazz musicians have delighted in from Bunk Johnson to Ornette Coleman are evidence of this."

26. Oliver, *Conversation with the Blues*, pp. 24, 33–34.

27. Lawrence W. Levine, "Slave Songs and Slave Consciousness," in Tamara Hareven, ed., *Anonymous Americans* (Englewood Cliffs, N.J.: Prentice-Hall, 1971).

28. Howard W. Odum, "Religious Folk-Songs of the Southern Negroes," *American Journal of Religious Psychology and Education* 3 (July 1909):269. Odum and Johnson, *The Negro and His Songs*, pp. xvii, 9.

29. Guy B. Johnson, "Double Meaning in the Popular Negro Blues," *Journal of Abnormal Psychology* 22 (April–June 1927):12–20.

30. Odum and Johnson, *The Negro and His Songs*, pp. 41, 42, 124, 131, 120, 116. For many similar songs, see chaps. 2–4.

31. For many examples of "John Henry" songs, see Guy B. Johnson, *John Henry: Tracking Down a Negro Legend* (Chapel Hill: University of North Carolina Press, 1929).

32. Lomax, *Nation* 105 (9 August 1917):144.

33. Odum and Johnson, *Negro Workaday Songs*, pp. 121–22.

34. Ibid., pp. 112, 115.

35. Dorothy Scarborough, *On the Trail of Negro Folk-Songs* (1925; reprint ed., Hatboro, Pa.: Folklore Associates, 1963), p. 99. White, *American Negro Folk Songs.*, p. 161.

36. Odum and Johnson, *Negro Workaday Songs*, pp. 115–16.

37. Odum and Johnson, *The Negro and His Songs*, p. 253.

38. Ibid., pp. 171, 257. Odum and Johnson, *Negro Workaday Songs*, pp. 76, 128. White, *American Negro Folk Songs*, pp. 255, 258. Scarborough, *On the Trail of Negro Folk-Songs*, p. 190.

39. White, *American Negro Folk Songs*, pp. 255, 302. Scarborough, *On the Trail of Negro Folk-Songs*, p. 235. Odum and Johnson, *The Negro and His Songs*, p. 163.

40. Odum and Johnson, *The Negro and His Songs*, p. 255.

41. For example, see Odum and Johnson, *Negro Workaday Songs*, chap. 4; and Paul Oliver, *Blues Fell This Morning* (New York: Horizon Press, 1960).

42. White, *American Negro Folk Songs*, p. 355.

43. Ibid., p. 316.

44. Odum and Johnson, *The Negro and His Songs*, p. 193.

45. White, *American Negro Folk Songs*, p. 326.

46. Odum and Johnson, *Negro Workaday Songs*, p. 146.

47. Odum and Johnson, *The Negro and His Songs*, p. 162. Odum and Johnson, *Negro Workaday Songs*, p. 40.

48. Odum and Johnson, *The Negro and His Songs*, pp. 171, 176. Odum and Johnson, *Negro Workaday Songs*, pp. 46, 112–13.

49. White, *American Negro Folk Songs*, p. 259.

50. Lomax, *Nation* 105 (9 August 1917):144.

Chapter 8

1. Mark Twain, *The Adventures of Huckleberry Finn* (New York, 1884), 190.

2. Laurence Hutton, *Curiosities of the American Stage* (New York, 1891), 157, 181–86; Stanley Wells, ed., *Nineteenth-Century Shakespeare Burlesques*, 5 (London, 1978):xi–xii; Charles Mathews, *Trip to America* (Baltimore, 1824), 9, 25; Charles Haywood, "Negro Minstrelsy and Shakespearean Burlesque," in Bruce Jackson, ed., *Folklore and Society: Essays in Honor of Benj. A. Botkin* (Norwood, Pa., 1976), 88; and Ray B. Browne, "Shakespeare in America: Vaudeville and Negro Minstrelsy," *American Quarterly*, 12 (1960):381–82. For examples of parodies of *Hamlet*, see *An Old Play in a New Garb: Hamlet, Prince of Denmark*, in Wells, *Nineteenth-Century Shakespeare Burlesques;* and *Hamlet the Dainty*, in Gary D. Engle, ed., *This Grotesque Essence: Plays from the Minstrel Stage* (Baton Rouge, 1978). For the popularity of parodies of *Hamlet* in the United States, see Ralph Leslie Rusk, *The Literature of the Middle Western Frontier*, 2 vols. (New York, 1925), 2:4n; Louis Marder, *His Exits and His Entrances: The Story of Shakespeare's Reputation* (Philadelphia, 1963), 295–96, 316–17; and Esther Cloudman Dunn, *Shakespeare in America* (New York, 1939), 108–12, 215–16.

3. For examples, see Wells, *Nineteenth-Century Shakespeare Burlesques;* and Engle, *This Grotesque Essence*. For a contemporary view of nineteenth-century parodies, see Hutton, *Curiosities of the American Stage*, 145–204. Also see Marder, *His Exits and His Entrances*, 316–17; Alice I. Perry Wood, *The Stage History of*

Shakespeare's King Richard the Third (New York, 1909), 158; Browne, "Shakespeare in America," 380, 385–90; David Grimsted, *Melodrama Unveiled: American Theater and Culture, 1800–1850* (Chicago, 1968), 240; and Constance Rourke, *Troupers of the Gold Coast* (New York, 1928), 221.

4. Haywood, "Negro Minstrelsy and Shakespearean Burlesque," 80, 86–87; and Browne, "Shakespeare in America," 376–79.

5. John Quincy Adams, who was born in 1767, wrote of Shakespeare, "at ten years of age I was as familiarly acquainted with his lovers and his clowns, as with Robinson Crusoe, the Pilgrim's Progress, and the Bible. In later years I have left Robinson and the Pilgrim to the perusal of the children; but have continued to read the Bible and Shakespeare." Adams to James H. Hackett, printed in Hackett, *Notes and Comments upon Certain Plays and Actors of Shakespeare, with Criticisms and Correspondence* (New York, 1864), 229. See Alfred Van Rensselaer Westfall, *American Shakespearean Criticism, 1607–1865* (New York, 1939), 45–46, 50–55; Wood, *The Stage History of Shakespeare's* King Richard the Third, 134–35; Charles H. Shattuck, *Shakespeare on the American Stage: From the Hallams to Edwin Booth* (Washington, 1976), 3, 15–16; and Hugh Rankin, *The Theater in Colonial America* (Chapel Hill, 1960), 191–92.

6. Arthur Hobson Quinn, *A History of the American Drama* (New York, 1943), 162; Dunn, *Shakespeare in America*, 133, 171–72; and Carl Bode, *The Anatomy of American Popular Culture, 1840–1861* (Berkeley and Los Angeles, 1960), 16–17. For the reception of Shakespeare in specific Eastern and Southern cities, the following are useful: T. Allston Brown, *A History of the New York Stage from the First Performance in 1732 to 1901*, 3 vols. (New York, 1903); James H. Dorman, Jr., *Theater in the Ante-Bellum South, 1815–1861* (Chapel Hill, 1967); W. Stanley Hoole, *The Ante-Bellum Charleston Theatre* (Tuscaloosa, Ala., 1946); Reese Davis James, *Cradle of Culture, 1800–1810: The Philadelphia Stage* (Philadelphia, 1957); Martin Staples Shockley, *The Richmond Stage, 1784–1812* (Charlottesville, Va., 1977); Eola Willis, *The Charleston Stage in the XVIII Century* (Columbia, S.C., 1924); and Joseph Patrick Roppolo, "Hamlet in New Orleans," *Tulane Studies in English*, 6 (1956):71–86. For tables showing the popularity of plays in the first half of the nineteenth century, see Grimsted, *Melodrama Unveiled*, apps. 1–2.

7. Towle, *American Society*, 2 (London, 1870):22. The migration of English stars to America is demonstrated throughout Shattuck's *Shakespeare on the American Stage*.

8. Bernard, *Retrospections of America, 1797–1811* (New York, 1887), 263; and Tocqueville, *Democracy in America*, pt. 2 (Vintage edn., New York, 1961), 58.

9. Knortz, *Shakespeare in Amerika: Eine Literarhistorische Studie* (Berlin, 1882), 47.

10. James G. McManaway, "Shakespeare in the United States," *Publications of the Modern Language Association of American*, 79 (1964):514; and Bernard DeVoto, *Mark Twain's America* (Boston, 1932), 142–43.

11. Rusk, *The Literature of the Middle Western Frontier*, 1:398–400, 411–14; William Bryan Gates, "Performances of Shakespeare in Ante-Bellum Mississippi," *Journal of Mississippi History*, 5 (1943):28–37; Ashley Thorndike, "Shakespeare in America," in L. Abercrombie *et al.*, eds., *Aspects of Shakespeare* (Oxford, 1933), 116–17; Westfall, *American Shakespearean Criticism*, 59; William G. B. Carson, *The Theatre on the Frontier: The Early Years of the St. Louis Stage* (1932; reprint edn., New York, 1965); West T. Hill, Jr., *The Theatre in Early Kentucky, 1790–*

1820 (Lexington, Ky., 1971); Sol Smith, *Theatrical Management in the West and South for Thirty Years* (New York, 1868); and Noah Ludlow, *Dramatic Life as I Found It* (St. Louis, 1880).

12. Rourke, *Troupers of the Gold Coast* 33, 44, 101–2; George R. MacMinn, *The Theater of the Golden Era in California* (Caldwell, Idaho, 1941), 23–24, 84, 87–88; and Margaret G. Watson, *Silver Theatre: Amusements of the Mining Frontier in Early Nevada, 1850–1864* (Glendale, Calif., 1964), 73.

13. Leman, *Memories of an Old Actor* (San Francisco, 1886), 212–13, 260–62, 276–77; Ludlow, *Dramatic Life as I Found It*, 89–90, 113, 116, 242–43, 256, 258, 303; and Smith, *Theatrical Management in the West and South for Thirty Years*, 90–91.

14. Place, as quoted in Dorman, *Theater in the Ante-Bellum South*, 257n; Cooper, *Notions of the Americans*, 2 (London, 1828):100, 113. For the theater in Iowa, see Joseph S. Schick, *The Early Theater in Eastern Iowa: Cultural Beginnings and the Rise of the Theater in Davenport and Eastern Iowa, 1836–1863* (Chicago, 1939). Schick's appendixes contain a list of all plays performed in either English or German in Iowa during these years.

15. Playbill, American Theatre, Philadelphia, May 13, 1839, Folger Shakespeare Library, Washington [hereafter, FSL]. For the prevalence of this format in the eighteenth century, see Rankin, *The Theater in Colonial America*, 150, 193–94; Kenneth Silverman, *A Cultural History of the American Revolution* (New York, 1976), 62; and Garff B. Wilson, *Three Hundred Years of American Drama and Theatre* (Englewood Cliffs, N.J., 1973), 19–27.

16. Playbills, St. Charles Theatre, New Orleans, November 30, 1846, Alexandria, Virginia, July 12, 1799, and Arch Street Theatre, Philadelphia, March 2, 1857, FSL.

17. Playbills, American Theatre, Philadelphia, August 30, 31, September 1, 11, 1838, June 24, 1839, FSL.

18. Davenport, as quoted in Lloyd Morris, *Curtain Time: The Story of the American Theater* (New York, 1953), 205.

19. Playbills, Walnut Street Theater, Philadelphia, November 30, 1821, Military Hall, Newark, N.J., August 15, 1852, Montgomery Theatre, Montgomery, Alabama, March 21, 1835, and American Theatre, Philadelphia, June 25, 1839, December 14, 1837, FSL; and MacMinn, *The Theatre of the Golden Era in California*, 90. Nevertheless, it was not uncommon for *Catharine and Petruchio,* an abridged version of *The Taming of the Shrew,* to serve as an afterpiece; see playbills, American Theatre, New Orleans, April 20, 1827, American Theatre, Philadelphia, September 26, 1838, and St. Charles Theatre, New Orleans, March 25, 1864, FSL. *Catharine and Petruchio* also served as an afterpiece when plays other than Shakespeare's were presented; see playbills, American Theatre, New Orleans, April 20, 1827, and American Theatre, Philadelphia, September 26, December 8, 1838, FSL.

20. John S. Kendall, *The Golden Age of the New Orleans Theater* (Baton Rouge, 1952), 210.

21. Hudson, *Lectures on Shakespeare,* 1 (New York, 1848):1–41.

22. Smith, *The Sentinel and Other Plays,* ed. Ralph H. Ware and H. W. Schoenberger (Bloomington, Ind., n.d.), 101–14.

23. Power, *Impressions of America,* 2 vols. (London, 1836), 2:189–92. Shakespeare's contemporary is quoted in Alfred Harbage, *Shakespeare's Audience* (New York, 1941), 84–85. For an excellent discussion of theater audiences in the first half of the nineteenth century, see Grimsted's indispensible *Melodrama Unveiled,*

chap. 3. For a comparison with audiences in eighteenth-century England, see James T. Lynch, *Box, Pit, and Gallery: Stage and Society in Johnson's London* (New York, 1971). Claudia Johnson deals with a neglected part of the American audience in "That Guilty Third Tier: Prostitution in Nineteenth-Century Theaters," *American Quarterly,* 27 (1975):575–84.

24. Alan S. Downer, ed., *The Autobiography of Joseph Jefferson* (Cambridge, Mass., 1964), 286; Whitman, "The Old Bowery," in Justin Kaplan, ed., *Walt Whitman: Poetry and Prose* (New York, 1982), 1189–90; and Irving, *Letters of Jonathan Oldstyle,* ed. Bruce I. Granger and Martha Hartzog (Boston, 1977), 12–25.

25. Trollope, *Domestic Manners of the Americans,* 2 vols. (London, 1832), 1:179–84, and 2:87–88, 194–95.

26. Power, *Impressions of America,* 2:171–74. Also see *ibid,* 1:62–66, 87–89, 123–26, 210–11.

27. Irving, *Letters of Jonathan Oldstyle,* 14; the Virginia and New York editors are quoted in Grimsted, *Melodrama Unveiled,* 63–64; and the French reporter's account is reprinted in Barnard Hewitt, *Theatre U.S.A., 1665 to 1957* (New York, 1959), 164–66.

28. Smith, *Theatrical Management,* 137–38; and Rourke, *Troupers of the Gold Coast,* 149–50, 209–10.

29. Sacramento *Union,* as quoted in MacMinn, *The Theatre of the Golden Era in California,* 90–91.

30. Playbill, Walnut Street Theatre, Philadelphia, November 30, 1821, FSL.

31. As quoted in Nancy Webb and Jean Francis Webb, *Will Shakespeare and His America* (New York, 1964), 84.

32. San Francisco *Chronicle,* January 1854, as quoted in MacMinn, *The Theater of the Golden Era in California,* 100.

33. New York *Mirror,* December 29, 1832, reprinted in Hewitt, *Theatre U.S.A.,* 122.

34. Grimsted, *Melodrama Unveiled,* 60; and *Harper's New Monthly Magazine,* December 1863, p. 133.

35. Marder, *His Exits and His Entrances,* 317–18.

36. Nachman, "Break a Leg, Willy," San Francisco *Chronicle,* November 30, 1982; and Papp, as quoted in Gerald M. Berkowitz, *New Broadways: Theatre Across America, 1950–1980* (Totowa, N.J., 1982), 37.

37. Young, *The Community Theatre and How It Works* (New York, 1957), 126; and George McManus, *Bringing Up Father,* ed. Herb Galewitz (New York, 1973), 37.

38. Plunkitt, *Plunkitt of Tammany Hall: A Series of Very Plain Talks on Very Practical Politics,* recorded by William L. Riordon (1905; reprint edn., New York, 1963), 52, 71.

39. Richardson, *The Long Day: The Story of a New York Working Girl* (1905), reprinted in its entirety in William L. O'Neill, ed., *Women at Work* (Chicago, 1972), 300, chap. 6.

40. Playbills, American Theatre, San Francisco, May 29, 1855, Varieties Theatre, New Orleans, December 30, 1869, California Theatre, San Francisco, April 4, 1873, Mechanics Hall, Salem, Mass., February 12, 1868, San Jose Opera House, August 22, 1870, Roberts Opera House, Hartford, Conn., November 1869, Academy of Music, Providence, R.I., November 24, 1869, Leland Opera House, Albany, N.Y., September 27, 1880, April 15, 1882, Opera House, Albany, N.Y., January

21, 22, 1874, Piper's Opera House, Virginia City, Nevada, July 29, 1878, Walnut Street Theatre, Philadelphia, November 5, 1875, Duquesne Theatre, Pittsburgh, December 23, 24, 25, 1890, Murray Hill Theatre, New York, May 4, 1903, Garden Theatre, New York City, December 24, 1900, Forty-fourth Street Theatre, New York City, February 22, 1915, Schubert Memorial Theatre, St. Louis, November 9, 1914, Olympic Theatre, St. Louis, January 6, 1902, May 6, 1907, and National Theatre, Washington, D.C., October 2, 1939, FSL.

41. Dorman, *Theatre in the Ante-Bellum South,* 256–59. Esther Dunn studied the "indifferent and vulgar stuff" accompanying Shakespeare in the theater and concluded that, "if the public could stand for this sort of entertainment, night in and night out, they could not have derived the fullest pleasure from the Shakespearean portion of the programme"; *Shakespeare in America,* 133–35, 142–45, 175. In 1926 Poet Laureate Robert Bridges spoke for many on both sides of the Atlantic when he attributed the "bad jokes and obscenities," "the mere foolish verbal trifling," and such sensationalism in Shakespeare's plays as the murder of Macduff's child or the blinding of Gloucester to Shakespeare's need to make concessions "to the most vulgar stratum of his audience, . . . those wretched beings who can never be forgiven their share in preventing the greatest poet and dramatist of the world from being the best artist"; Bridges, *The Influence of the Audience* (New York, 1926), 3, 23.

42. Hudson, *Lectures on Shakespeare,* 1:54; and Kenneth S. Lynn, *William Dean Howells: An American Life* (New York 1971), 67–68.

43. Whitman, *Specimen Days,* in Kaplan, *Whitman: Poetry and Prose,* 702–03; Mark Twain, *Is Shakespeare Dead?* (New York, 1909), 4–7; William S. McFeely, *Grant: A Biography* (New York, 1982), 29; Robert N. Reeves, "Abraham Lincoln's Knowledge of Shakespeare," *Overland Monthly,* 43 (1904):333–42; Westfall, *American Shakespearean Criticism,* 227–29; and Henry W. Simon, *The Reading of Shakespeare in American Schools and Colleges: An Historical Survey* (New York, 1932).

44. Ludlow, *Dramatic Life as I Found It,* 234, 690–91, 694–95; Richard Moody, *America Takes the Stage: Romanticism in American Drama and Theatre, 1750–1900* (Bloomington, Ind., 1955), 195–96; and Whitman, "The Old Bowery," in Kaplan, *Whitman: Poetry and Prose,* 1187–88.

45. Alger, *Life of Edwin Forrest: The American Tragedian,* 2 (Philadelphia, 1877; reprint edn., New York, 1972):786.

46. For Whitman's musings about the effects of Shakespeare's "aristocratic perfume," see his "A Thought on Shakespeare" and "A Backward Glance o'er Travel'd Roads," in Kaplan, *Whitman: Poetry and Prose,* 1150–52, 663–64. Eighteenth-century depictions of Shakespeare as a moral playwright are described in Bernard, *Retrospections of America,* 270–71; Westfall, *American Shakespearean Criticism,* 30–31; and Shattuck, *Shakespeare on the American Stage,* 16. And see Jefferson, as quoted in Lawrence A. Cremin, *American Education: The Colonial Experience, 1607–1783* (New York, 1970), 438; Lincoln, as quoted in Alan Bloom, *Shakespeare's Politics* (New York, 1964), 5; and Adams, "The Character of Desdemona," *American Monthly Magazine,* 1 (1836):209–17, reprinted in Hackett, *Notes and Comments,* 234–49, and "Misconceptions of Shakespeare upon the Stage," reprinted in Hackett, *Notes and Comments,* 217–28.

47. Hudson, *Lectures on Shakespeare,* 1:79; and playbill, Varieties Theatre, New Orleans, January 3, 4, 1870, FSL. Also see Ruth Miller Elson, *Guardians of*

Notes for pages 159–63

Tradition: American Schoolbooks of the Nineteenth Century (Lincoln, Neb., 1964), 242, 283; and Simon, *The Reading of Shakespeare in American Schools and Colleges,* 19, 26, 44.

48. Downer, *The Autobiography of Joseph Jefferson,* 166–67; and Hudson, *Lectures on Shakespeare,* 1:69.

49. For the New York reaction to Sophocles, see Doris M. Alexander, "Oedipus in Victorian New York," *American Quarterly,* 12 (1960):417–21.

50. Grimsted, *Melodrama Unveiled,* chap. 6; George C. Branam, *Eighteenth-Century Adaptations of Shakespearean Tragedy* (Berkeley and Los Angeles, 1956), chap. 1; and Rankin, *The Theater in Colonial America,* 83–84, 191–92.

51. In 1909 Alice Wood reported that Cibber's version of *Richard III* "is still holding the stage and is still preferred by a large part of the community," and thus "the struggle for the 'Richard the Third' of Shakespeare is still 'on' "; *The Stage History of Shakespeare's* King Richard the Third, 133, 165. As late as 1930, Arthur Colby Sprague attended a performance of *Richard III* in Boston and was treated to "the Cibber text, practically in its entirety" although Cibber's name was nowhere mentioned; Sprague, *Shakespearian Players and Performances* (1953; reprint edn., New York, 1969), 151, 212 n.3.

52. Cibber, *The Tragical History of King Richard III,* in Christopher Spencer, ed., *Five Restoration Adaptations of Shakespeare* (Urbana, Ill., 1965), 275–344. For an excellent discussion of Cibber's adaptation, see Wood, *The Stage History of Shakespeare's* King Richard the Third, chaps. 4, 6; also see Frederick W. Kilbourne, *Alterations and Adaptations of Shakespeare* (Boston, 1906), 107–12.

53. Hackett, *Notes and Comments,* 227n. For John Quincy Adams's critique of Tate, see *ibid.,* 226–28.

54. As quoted in Grimsted, *Melodrama Unveiled,* 119–20.

55. Tate, *The History of King Lear,* in Spencer, *Five Restoration Adaptations of Shakespeare,* 201–74. Also see Kilbourne, *Alterations and Adaptations of Shakespeare,* 157–72.

56. For a first-hand account of the changes the theater underwent, see Otis Skinner, *Footlights and Spotlights: Recollections of My Life on the Stage* (Indianapolis, 1924), esp. chap. 23.

57. Joshua A. Fishman, *Language Loyalty in the United States* (1966; reprint edn., New York, 1978), 59.

58. For Denney's phrase, see his essay, "The Discovery of Popular Culture," in Robert E. Spiller and Eric Larrabee, eds., *American Perspectives: The National Self-Image in the Twentieth Century* (Cambridge, Mass., 1961), 164–65. The relationships between recitation of the King James Bible and performances of Shakespeare and between the transformation of nineteenth-century religious style and the transformation of Shakespeare need further thought and research.

59. Higham, "The Reorientation of American Culture in the 1890's," in John Weiss, ed., *The Origins of Modern Consciousness* (Detroit, 1965), 25–48.

60. The questioner was the young actor Otis Skinner; see his autobiography, *Footlights and Spotlights,* 93. As he was preparing for his first portrayal of Shylock in 1893—the year of Booth's death—Skinner discovered the extent of Booth's influence: "I found myself reading speeches with the Booth cadence, using the Booth gestures, attitudes and facial expressions, in short, giving a rank imitation. The ghost of the dead actor rose between me and the part." *Ibid.,* 213. For other evidence of Booth's influence, see Hutton, *Curiosities of the American Stage,* 293–94; Henry Austin Clapp, *Reminiscences of a Dramatic Critic* (1902; reprint edn., Freeport,

N.Y., 1972), chap. 15; and Charles H. Shattuck, *The Hamlet of Edwin Booth* (Urbana, Ill., 1969).

61. Hackett, "After the Play," *New Republic*, March 24, 1920, p. 122.

62. For the suitability of Shakespeare to modern media, see Roger Manvell, *Shakespeare and the Film* (New York, 1971), 9–10; Jan Kott, *Shakespeare, Our Contemporary*, trans. Boleslaw Taborski (Garden City, N.Y., 1964), 231–35; and John Wain, *The Living World of Shakespeare* (London, 1978), 2–7.

63 Goffman, *Encounters: Two Studies in the Sociology of Interaction* (Indianapolis, 1961); Whitman, "Miserable State of the Stage," *Brooklyn Eagle*, February 8, 1847, reprinted in Montrose J. Moses and John Mason Brown, eds., *American Theatre as Seen by Its Critics* (New York, 1934), 70–72; and Power, *Impressions of America*, 1:141.

64. Curtis, "Editor's Easy Chair," *Harper's New Monthly Magazine*, December 1863, pp. 131–33. For the contrast between the two actors portraying Hamlet, see Hutton, *Curiosities of the American Stage*, 281.

65. Payne, as quoted in Grimsted, *Melodrama Unveiled*, 56–57.

66. Somer, *Personal Space: The Behavioral Basis of Design* (Englewood Cliffs, N.J., 1969), chap. 2; Bledstein, *The Culture of Professionalism: The Middle Class and the Development of Higher Education in America* (New York, 1976), 58–64, 80; and Taylor, "Public Space, Public Opinion, and the Origins of Mass Culture," paper presented to a joint meeting of the American Council of Learned Societies and the Hungarian Academy of Sciences, held in Budapest, August 1982.

67. Irving, *Letters of Jonathan Oldstyle*, 12.

68. Francis Courtney Wemyss, *Twenty-Six Years of the Life of an Actor and Manager* (New York, 1847), 97–99, 113–15; and Shattuck, *Shakespeare on the American Stage*, 2–43.

69. Power, *Impressions of America*, 1:351–55.

70. My account of the Astor Place Riot is based on Richard Moody, *The Astor Place Riot* (Bloomington, Ind., 1958), 12, 172; William Toynbee, ed., *The Diaries of William Charles Macready*, 2 (London, 1912), 404–29; and Peter G. Buckley, "The Astor Place Riot and Jenny Lind," paper presented at the Ninety-sixth Annual Meeting of the American Historical Association, held in Los Angeles, December 28–30, 1981, and " 'A Privileged Place': New York Theatre Riots, 1817–1849," paper presented at the annual meeting of the Organization of American Historians, held in St. Louis, April 8–11, 1982. I am extremely grateful to Buckley for sharing with me not only his unpublished papers but also a chapter from his draft dissertation. Moody sets the number of dead at thirty-one—twenty-two during the riot itself and nine more as a result of wounds received during the riot; in his more recent research Buckley has only been able to account for a total of twenty-two dead—eighteen during the riot and four more as a result of wounds received.

71. New York *Tribune*, May 12, 1849; New York *Herald*, May 12, 1849; *Home Journal*, May 12, 1849, as quoted in Montrose J. Moses, *The Fabulous Forrest: The Record of an American Actor* (Boston, 1929), 262; and Philadelphia *Public Ledger*, May 16, 1849.

72. Arnold, *Culture and Anarchy* (New York, 1875), 44, 47; and James, as quoted in Moses, *The Fabulous Forrest*, 246.

73. Brooks, *America's Coming-of-Age* (New York, 1915), 6–7. Brooks popularized rather than coined the terms. According to the *Supplement* to the *Oxford English Dictionary*, "highbrow" was first used in the 1880s to describe intellectual or aesthetic superiority, while "lowbrow" came to mean someone or something

neither "highly intellectual" nor "aesthetically refined" shortly after 1900. The term "middlebrow" seems to have come into use in the 1920s.

74. Whitman, *Democratic Vistas,* in Kaplan, *Whitman: Poetry and Prose,* 950–51, 961–62. For an excellent discussion of Whitman and culture after the Civil War, see Alan Trachtenberg, *The Incorporation of America: Culture and Society in the Gilded Age* (New York, 1982), 158–60.

75. Veblen, *The Theory of the Leisure Class* (1899; Penguin edn., New York, 1979), 45, 397–98.

76. My sense of late nineteenth-century American culture was enhanced by the following: Trachtenberg, *The Incorporation of America;* Lewis A. Erenberg, *Steppin' Out: New York Nightlife and the Transformation of American Culture, 1890–1930* (Westport, Conn., 1981); Daniel Walker Howe, "American Victorianism as a Culture," *American Quarterly,* 27 (1975):507–32; John F. Kasson, *Amusing the Million: Coney Island at the Turn of the Century* (New York, 1978); John G. Sproat, *"The Best Men": Liberal Reformers in the Gilded Age* (New York, 1968); Arthur M. Schlesinger, *Learning How to Behave: A Historical Study of American Etiquette Books* (New York, 1946); John Tomisch, *A Genteel Endeavor: American Culture and Politics in the Gilded Age* (Stanford, 1971); T. J. Jackson Lears, *No Place of Grace: Antimodernism and the Transformation of American Culture, 1880–1920* (New York, 1981); Stow Persons, *The Decline of American Gentility* (New York, 1973); Robert R. Roberts, "Gilt, Gingerbread, and Realism: The Public and Its Taste," in H. Wayne Morgan, ed., *The Gilded Age: A Reappraisal* (Syracuse, N.Y., 1963), 169–95; Robert Wiebe, *The Search for Order* (New York, 1967); and George Frederickson, *The Inner Civil War: Northern Intellectuals and the Crisis of the Union* (New York, 1965).

77. See Albert F. McLean, Jr., *American Vaudeville as Ritual* (Lexington, Ky., 1965), 16–17; Foster Rhea Dulles, *A History of Recreation: America Learns to Play* (New York, 1965), 219; Russel Nye, *The Unembarrassed Muse: The Popular Arts in America* (New York, 1970), 170; and Wilson, *Three Hundred Years of American Drama and Theatre,* 301.

78. Sennett, *The Fall of Public Man* (New York, 1978), esp. 261. For the argument that by the 1880s Americans became preoccupied with the private rather than the public taste, also see Russell Lynes, *The Tastemakers: The Shaping of American Popular Taste* (1955; reprint edn., New York, 1980), 117.

79. Towle, *American Society,* 4. For a discussion of opera as popular music in nineteenth-century America, see Charles Hamm, *Yesterdays: Popular Song in America* (New York, 1983), chap. 4.

80. This account of chromolithography is based upon Peter C. Marzio, *The Democratic Art: Pictures for a Nineteenth-Century America* (Boston, 1979). For the Columbian Exposition of 1893, see Reid Badger, *The Great American Fair: The World's Columbian Exposition and American Culture* (Chicago, 1979); David F. Burg, *Chicago's White City of 1893* (Lexington, Ky., 1976); and John C. Cawelti, "America on Display: The World's Fairs of 1876, 1893, 1933," in Frederick Cople Jaher, ed., *The Age of Industrialism in America* (New York, 1968), 317–63.

Chapter 9

1. Lawrence W. Levine, *Highbrow/Lowbrow: The Emergence of Cultural Hierarchy in America* (Cambridge, Mass., 1988), 224–225.

2. Richard Sennett, *The Fall of Public Man* (New York, 1978), 230, 261.

3. Sydney Smith, "Review of Adam Seybert, Statistical Annals of the United States of America," *Edinburgh Review* 33 (1820):79–80.

4. Henry James, *Hawthorne* (1879; New York, 1967), 34–35; Marc Pachter, "American Cosmopolitanism, 1870–1910," in *Impressions of a Gilded Age: The American Fin de Siècle,* eds. Marc Chenetier and Rob Kroes (Amsterdam, 1983), 29.

5. "Criticism in America," *The Outlook* 48 (1893):990.

6. Matthew Arnold, *Culture and Anarchy* (New York, 1875), 44–47.

7. Van Wyck Brooks, *America's Coming-of-Age* (New York, 1915), 6–7.

8. Charles E. Ives, *Memos,* ed. John Kirkpatrick (New York, 1972), 52, 71, 131–32.

9. Joseph A. Mussulman, *Music in the Cultured Generation: A Social History of Music in America* (Evanston, Ill., 1985), 109.

10. Ives, *Memos,* 88–89.

11. Antonín Dvořák, "Real Value of Negro Melodies," *New York Herald,* 21 May 1893.

12. Mussulman, *Music in the Cultured Generation,* 115.

13. John Philip Sousa, *Marching Along: Recollections of Men, Women and Music* (Boston, 1928), 341.

14. "Our Window," *Putnam's Magazine* 10 (1857):133.

15. Thomas Wentworth Higginson, "A Plea for Culture," *Atlantic Monthly* 19 (1867):33.

16. Mussulman, *Music in the Cultured Generation,* 106.

17. Sidney Lanier, "The Proper Basis of English Culture," *Atlantic Monthly* 82 (1898):165–74.

18. Henry Adams, *The Education of Henry Adams,* (1918; New York, 1931), 237.

19. Levine, *Highbrow/Lowbrow,* 221–23.

20. "Jass and Jassism," *New Orleans Times-Picayune,* 20 June 1918.

21. Macdonald Smith Moore, *Yankee Blues: Musical Culture and American Identity* (Bloomington, 1985), 75.

22. "Rector Calls Jazz National Anthem," *New York Times,* 30 January 1922.

23. "A Subject of Serious Study," *New York Times,* 8 October 1924.

24. "His Opinion Will Not Be Accepted," *New York Times,* 13 November 1924.

25. Robert Haven Schauffler, "Jazz May Be Lowbrow, But—," *Collier's* 72 (1928):10.

26. "Where Is Jazz Leading America?: Part II of a Symposium," *The Etude* 42 (1924):595.

27. Don Knowlton, "The Anatomy of Jazz," *Harper's* 152 (1924):578; *The Etude* 42 (1924):593.

28. Moore, *Yankee Blues,* 106.

29. *Ibid.,* 108.

30. Maude Cuney-Hare, *Negro Musicians and Their Music* (Washington, D.C., 1936), 156.

31. Dave Peyton, "The Musical Bunch," *Chicago Defender,* 28 January 1928.

32. Lucien H. White, *New York Age,* 23 April, 7 May, 23 July 1921, 8 July 1922; Richard Aldrich, "Drawing a Line for Jazz," *New York Times,* 10 December 1922, sec. VIII.

33. "Where Is Jazz Leading America?: Opinions of Famous Men and Women in and out of Music," *The Etude* 42 (1924):518.

34. Moore, *Yankee Blues*, 90.

35. "Where Is Jazz Leading America?," 595.

36. Henry O. Osgood, *So This Is Jazz!* (Boston, 1926), 247.

37. "Buying American in Music," *Literary Digest* 118 (1934):24.

38. Gilbert Seldes, *The Seven Lively Arts* (New York, 1924), 83–84, 95–97.

39. Lawrence W. Levine, *Black Culture and Black Consciousness: Afro-American Folk Thought from Slavery to Freedom* (New York, 1977), 294.

40. *Ibid.*, 294–95.

41. *Ibid.*, 295.

42. Benjamin Brawley, *The Negro Genius* (New York, 1937), 10.

43. Alain Locke, *The Negro and His Music* (Washington, D.C., 1936), 88.

44. Ira Gitler, *Swing to Bop: An Oral History of the Transition in Jazz in the 1940s* (New York, 1985), 303, 311.

45. Sidney Bechet, *Treat It Gentle* (New York, 1960), 102.

46. William R. Dixon, "The Music in Harlem," in *Harlem: A Community in Transition,* ed. John Henrik Clarke (New York, 1964), 70; emphasis in original.

47. Erik Wiedemann, *Jazz i Danmark—ityverne, trediverne og fyrrerne* [Jazz in Denmark—Past, Present, and Future] (Copenhagen, 1985), 395.

48. Dizzy Gillespie with Al Fraser, *To Be, or Not . . . to Bop: Memoirs* (New York, 1979), 424n.

49. Josef Skvorecky, "Jamming the Jazz Section," *New York Review of Books* 30 June 1988:40–42.

50. Phillipe Adler, "La Saga du Jazz," *L'Express* 17 May 1976:52–56.

51. George Harmon Knoles, *The Jazz Age Revisited: British Criticism of American Civilization During the 1920s* (New York, 1968), 120.

52. Georges Duhamel, *America the Menace: Scenes from the Life of the Future* (London, 1931), 121–22.

53. S. Frederick Starr, *Red and Hot: The Fate of Jazz in the Soviet Union, 1917–1980* (New York, 1983), 12.

54. Ernst Krenek, *Music Here and Now,* trans. Barthold Fles (New York, 1939), 260.

55. Hughes Panassié, *Hot Jazz: The Guide to Swing Music,* trans. Lyle and Eleanor Dowling (New York, 1936), 2; emphasis in original.

56. Edmund Wilson, *The American Earthquake: A Documentary of the Twenties and Thirties* (Garden City, 1958), 114.

57. Osgood, *So This Is Jazz!,* 249–50; *New York Times,* 11 August 1924.

58. Stanley Dance, *The World of Earl Hines* (New York, 1977), 74.

59. Cuney-Hare, *Negro Musicians and Their Music,* 148.

60. Francis Newton [Eric Hobsbawm], *The Jazz Scene* (Harmondsworth, Eng., 1961), 41.

61. Margaret Just Butcher, *The Negro in American Culture* (New York, 1966), 95.

62. "He Has No Scorn for Jazz?," *New York Times,* 28 January 1925.

63. U.S. State Department, *Semi-Annual Reports* (Washington, D.C., 1956), 5–6.

64. "United States Has Secret Sonic Weapon—Jazz," *New York Times,* 6 November 1955.

65. Margo Jefferson, "Jazz Is Back," *Newsweek* 82 (1973):52.

66. Jacques Barzun, *Music in American Life* (Garden City, N.Y., 1956), 85–86.

67. Virgil Thomson, *A Virgil Thomson Reader* (Boston, 1981), 498–500.

68. Constant Lambert, *Music Ho!: A Study of Music in Decline* (London, 1934), 206.

69. "Jazz Goes to College," *Time* 97 (1971):67.

70. Ross Russell, *Bird Lives!: The High Life and Hard Times of Charlie (Yardbird) Parker* (New York, 1973), 293.

71. Gillespie, *To Be, or Not. . .* , 142.

72. *Ibid.*, 492–93.

73. Scott E. Brown, *James P. Johnson: A Case of Mistaken Identity* (Metuchen, N.J., 1986), 86–87.

74. Dance, *The World of Earl Hines,* 14.

75. Gene Lees, "Jazz: Pop or Classical," *High Fidelity* 27 (1977):22.

76. Ian Carr, *Miles Davis: A Biography* (New York, 1982), 115.

77. Bernard Holland, "By Head or by Heart?: A Musician's Dilemma," *New York Times,* 30 May 1987.

78. Benny Goodman, "I Lead a Double Life," *House and Garden,* April 1951, p. 181.

79. Milton "Mezz" Mezzrow and Bernard Wolfe, *Really the Blues* (New York, 1946), 124–25; emphasis in original.

80. Carr, *Miles Davis,* 77.

81. A. B. Spellman, *Four Lives in the Bebop Business* (New York, 1966), 34.

82. Edward Kennedy Ellington, *Music Is My Mistress* (Garden City, 1973), 192–93.

Chapter 10

1. See, for example, Henry Nash Smith, *Virgin Land* (Cambridge, 1950); R. W. B. Lewis, *The American Adam* (Chicago, 1955); John William Ward, *Andrew Jackson—Symbol for an Age* (New York, 1955); Marvin Meyers, *The Jacksonian Persuasion* (Stanford, 1957); Richard Hofstadter, *The Age of Reform* (New York, 1955).

2. Leon Festinger, Henry W. Riecken, Stanley Schachter, *When Prophecy Fails* (New York, 1964).

3. Stanley Coben, "A Study in Nativism: The American Red Scare of 1919–1920," *Political Science Quarterly* LXXIX (March 1964), pp. 52–75.

4. Milton M. Gordon, *Assimilation in American Life* (New York, 1964), chap. 4. See also chapters 5–6 for incisive discussions of the melting pot and cultural pluralism.

5. Lawrence W. Levine, *Defender of the Faith: William Jennings Bryan, The Last Decade, 1915–1925* (New York, 1965), chaps. 5–9.

6. Joseph Gusfield's important analyses of the prohibition movement can be found in his study, *Symbolic Crusade: Status Politics and the American Temperance Movement* (Urbana, 1963) and his article, "Prohibition: The Impact of Political Utopianism," in *Change and Continuity in Twentieth-Century America: The 1920's,* edited by John Braeman *et al.* (Columbus, Ohio, 1968).

7. John William Ward, *Red, White, and Blue: Men, Books, and Ideas in American Culture* (New York, 1969), chap. 3.

8. Here and in much of what follows on the movies of the twenties, my inter-

pretations have been heavily influenced by Arthur Knight, *The Liveliest Art* (New York, 1959); David Robinson, *Hollywood in the Twenties* (New York, 1968); Lewis Jacobs, *The Rise of the American Film* (New York, 1939, 1968); Gilbert Seldes, *The Seven Lively Arts* (New York, 1924, 1957).

9. My analysis of the comic strips of the twenties follows the interpretations of Stephen Becker, *Comic Art in America* (New York, 1959); Coulton Waugh, *The Comics* (New York, 1947); Pierre Couperie, Maurice C. Horn, *et al.*, *A History of the Comic Strip*, translated from the French by Eileen B. Hennessy (New York, 1968).

Chapter 12

1. Louise Tanner, *All the Things We Were* (Garden City, N.Y.: Doubleday, 1968), p. 266.

2. During the 1980 campaign, Reagan spoke about the affinities between the New Deal and fascism, and asserted that key members of Roosevelt's Brains Trust admired the fascist system. See Robert Dallek, *Ronald Reagan: The Politics of Symbolism* (Cambridge, Mass.: Harvard University Press, 1984), p. 58.

3. "Thomas Predicts Dictatorship Here," *The New York Times,* February 7, 1933; E. Francis Brown, "The American Road to Fascism," *Current History,* July 1933, pp. 392–398; Harold Loeb and Selden Rodman, "American Fascism in Embryo," *The New Republic,* December 27, 1933, pp. 185–87; "Roosevelt—Dictator?" *The Catholic World,* April, 1934, pp. 1–8; Roger Shaw, "Fascism and the New Deal," *The North American Review* 238:6 (December 1934), pp. 559–564; George E. Sokolsky, "America Drifts Toward Fascism," *The American Mercury* 32:127 (July 1934), pp. 257–264; "The Great Fascist Plot," *The New Republic,* December 5, 1934, pp. 87–89; V. F. Calverton, "Is America Ripe for Fascism?," *Current History* 38 (September 1933), pp. 701–704; J. B. Matthews and R. E. Shallcross, "Must America Go Fascist?" *Harpers Magazine,* June 1934, pp. 1–15; Hugh Stevenson Tigner, "Will America Go Fascist?" *The Christian Century,* May 2, 1934, pp. 592–594; "Need the New Deal Be Fascist?" *The Nation,* January 9, 1935, p. 33.

4. Raymond Gram Swing, *Forerunners of American Fascism* (New York: Julian Messner, 1935), pp. 19, 28–29.

5. Sinclair Lewis, *It Can't Happen Here* (1935; reprint ed., New York: Dell Publishing Co., 1961), pp. 86, 97.

6. John O'Connor and Lorraine Brown, eds., *Free, Adult, Uncensored: The Living History of the Federal Theatre Project* (Washington, D.C.: New Republic Books, 1978), pp. 58–67.

7. Lawrence Dennis, *The Coming American Fascism* (New York: Harper & Brothers, 1936), chaps. 1–10, 14, 16–17, 23.

8. Except where otherwise noted, all quotations from films come directly from my viewing of the film.

9. Press Release for *Washington Merry-Go-Round,* in Division of Motion Pictures, Broadcasting, and Recorded Sound, Library of Congress. Cited hereafter as Division of Motion Pictures, LC.

10. Advertisement in *New York Daily News,* March 31, 1933.

11. *Literary Digest,* April 22, 1933; *The New Republic,* April 19, 1933; *The Nation,* April 26, 1933; *The New York Times,* April 1, 1933; *The Chicago Tribune,*

April 7, 1933; *The San Francisco Chronicle,* April 1, 1933; *The Commonweal,* May 5, 1933; *The Hollywood Reporter,* March 2, 1933.

12. *The New Republic,* April 19, 1933.

13. *Inaugural Addresses of the Presidents of the United States* (Washington, D.C.: Government Printing Office, 1974), pp. 235–239.

14. Quoted in Arthur M. Schlesinger, Jr., *The Coming of the New Deal* (Boston: Houghton Mifflin, 1959), pp. 1–2.

15. See the March 5, 1933, editions of *The New York Times, The New York Herald Tribune, The Washington Post, The Washington Evening Star, The Chicago Tribune,* and *The Los Angeles Times.*

16. *Barron's,* February 13, 1933. Smith and Landon are quoted in Schlesinger, *The Coming of the New Deal,* p. 3.

17. *Fortune,* July 1934, p. 45 *et passim.*

18. *Time,* December 3, 17, 1934; Press Book for *The President Vanishes,* in Division of Motion Pictures, LC.

19. *The New Republic,* December 26, 1934; *The New York Daily News,* December 8, 1934.

20. Dialogue Cutting Continuity for *The Man Who Dared,* in Division of Motion Pictures, LC.

21. *The Washington Post,* October 22, 1939; Press Release for *Washington Merry-Go-Round,* in Division of Motion Pictures, LC.

22. Dialogue Cutting Continuity for *Gabriel Over the White House,* in Division of Motion Pictures, LC.

23. Press Book for *This Day and Age,* in Division of Motion Pictures, LC.

24. Press Book for *Song of the Eagle,* in Division of Motion Pictures, LC.

25. For more on this theme, see Lawrence W. Levine, "American Culture and the Great Depression," *Yale Review* 74:2 (Winter 1985), pp. 196–223.

26. For an excellent discussion of this strain of thought in the 1930s, see Michael C. Steiner, "Regionalism in the Great Depression," *Geographical Review* 73:4 (October 1983), pp. 430–46.

27. For evidence of Capra's popularity in the 1930s, see the polls in *Increasing Profits with Continuous Audience Research* (Princeton, N.J.: Audience Research Institute, 1941), pp. 42–43. Robert Sklar has made the point that among the decade's filmmakers only Capra and Walt Disney shared the acclaim of all three of the significant audiences for movies: the ticket-buying public, the critics, and their Hollywood colleagues. While no other director won the Academy Award for Best Director more than once in the 1930s, Capra won it three times. Sklar, *Movie-Made America* (New York: Random House, 1975), pp. 197–198.

28. Patrick Gerster, "The Ideological Project of 'Mr. Deeds Goes to Town,' " *Film Criticism,* Winter 1981, pp. 35–48.

29. Leonard Quart, "Frank Capra and the Popular Front," *Cinéaste,* Summer 1977, p. 6.

30. Frank Capra, *The Name Above the Title: An Autobiography* (New York: Macmillan, 1971), p. 186; James Childs, "Capra Today: An Interview," *Film Comment,* November–December 1972, p. 23.

31. For more on the importance of the spoken word in Hollywood films, see Charles Affron, *Cinema and Sentiment* (Chicago: University of Chicago Press, 1982), chap. 5.

32. Capra made these remarks in a conversation with Richard Glatzer held in August and December 1973. See Richard Glatzer and John Raeburn, eds., *Frank*

Capra: The Man and His Films (Ann Arbor: University of Michigan Press, 1975), p. 34.

33. *The San Francisco Chronicle,* October 29, 1939.

34. Stephen Handzo, "A Decade of Good Deeds and Wonderful Lives UNDER CAPRACORN," *Film Comment,* November–December 1972, p. 10.

35. Dialogue Cutting Continuity for *Thanks a Million,* in Division of Motion Pictures, LC.

36. Dialogue Cutting Continuity for *Stand Up and Cheer,* in Division of Motion Pictures, LC.

37. John Clellon Holmes, "A Decade of Coming Attractions," in Arthur F. McClure, ed., *The Movies: An American Idiom* (Rutherford, N.J.: Fairleigh Dickinson University Press, 1971), pp. 114–116.

Chapter 13

1. William James, *Selected Papers on Philosophy* (New York: E. P. Dutton, 1917), 1–2.

2. Ralph Ellison, *Shadow and Act* (New York: Random House, 1964), 303–17.

3. The newspaper and magazine clippings collected by the FSA and OWI indicate how immediate and persistent the impact of Lange's photo was. See the Written Records of the Farm Security Administration, Historical Section—Office of War Information, Overseas Picture Division, Washington Section Collection, in the Prints and Photographs Division, Library of Congress.

4. Lange left no record of the order in which she took her photos of the Thompsons. I have followed the interpretation of James C. Curtis, who has tried to establish the sequence of the shots from internal evidence ("Dorothea Lange, Migrant Mother, and the Culture of the Great Depression," *Winterthur Portfolio* 21 [Spring 1986]:1–20).

5. William Stott, *Documentary Expression and Thirties America* (New York: Oxford University Press, 1973), 58–59.

6. Maurice Berger, *FSA: The Illiterate Eye: Photographs from the Farm Security Administration.* Berger curated and wrote an essay for an exhibition held 26 November 1985–10 January 1986 at Hunter College Art Gallery, New York City.

7. Arthur Schlesinger, Jr., *The Crisis of the Old Order, 1919–1933* (Boston: Houghton Mifflin, 1957), 231, 241–42; Stott, *Documentary Expression and Thirties America,* 67–73; and Robert S. McElvaine, *The Great Depression: America, 1929–1941* (New York: Times Books, 1984), chap. 4.

8. Irving Bernstein, *A Caring Society: The New Deal, the Worker, and the Great Depression* (Boston: Houghton Mifflin, 1985), 17–18.

9. Lawrence W. Levine, "American Culture and the Great Depression," *Yale Review* 74 (Winter 1985):201.

10. Ibid.

11. James Agee and Walker Evans, *Let Us Now Praise Famous Men* (Boston: Houghton Mifflin, 1941); and Stott, *Documentary Expression and Thirties America,* 286–87.

12. Interestingly, the photographer of the Burroughs family, Walker Evans, has been criticized for the opposite tendency as well: for posing his subjects and rearranging the belongings in their homes "to show the order and beauty that he believed lay beneath the surface of their poverty. . . . Evans sought to ennoble the share-

croppers." See James C. Curtis and Sheila Grannen, "Let Us Now Appraise Famous Photographs: Walker Evans and Documentary Photography," *Winterthur Portfolio* 15, no. 1 (Spring 1980):1–23. In his 1942 review of *Let Us Now Praise Famous Men* Lionel Trilling faulted James Agee for refusing to "see these people as anything but good" (Trilling, "Greatness with One Fault in It," *Kenyon Review* 4 [Winter 1942]:102).

13. Bruno Bettelheim, "Individual and Mass Behavior in Extreme Situations," *Journal of Abnormal Psychology* 38, no. 4 (October 1943):417–52; and Stanley Elkins, *Slavery: A Problem in American Institutional and Intellectual Life* (Chicago: University of Chicago Press, 1959), chap. 3.

14. Halla Beloff, *Camera Culture* (Oxford and New York: B. Blackwell, 1985), 18.

15. Alan Sekula, *Photography Against the Grain: Essays and Photo Works, 1973–1983* (Halifax: Press of the Nova Scotia College of Art and Design, 1984), 7.

16. Roy E. Stryker and Nancy Wood, *In This Proud Land: America 1935–1943 as Seen in the FSA Photographs* (Greenwich, Conn.: New York Graphic Society, 1973), 8.

17. Dorothea Lange, "The Assignment I'll Never Forget: Migrant Mother," *Popular Photography* 46, no. 2 (February 1960):42–43, 126.

18. "Report and Notes on Experiences in Collecting Yugoslav Folk Material, December 13, 1938," Sylvia Diner folder, in Works Progress Administration, Federal Writers' Project Life Histories, Library of Congress.

19. Stott, *Documentary Expression and Thirties America,* 92. Throughout his study, and especially in part 2, Stott describes this documentary urge with great intelligence and insight.

20. Bernstein, *A Caring Society,* 257.

21. Bill Ganzel, *Dust Bowl Descent* (Lincoln: University of Nebraska Press, 1984), 124–25.

22. This summary of the culture of the twenties and thirties is derived from my articles "Progress and Nostalgia: The Self Image of the 1920s," in *The American Novel and the 1920s,* ed. Malcolm Bradbury (London: Edward Arnold, 1971); "American Culture and the Great Depression," *Yale Review* 74 (Winter 1985):196–223; "Hollywood's Washington: Film Images of National Politics in the Great Depression," *Prospects* 10 (1986):169–95.

23. Bernstein, *A Caring Society,* chap. 4; William E. Leuchtenburg, *Franklin D. Roosevelt and the New Deal, 1932–1940* (New York: Harper and Row, 1963), 243–45.

24. Ganzel, *Dust Bowl Descent,* 122–23; Samuel A. Stouffer et al., *The American Soldier: Combat and Its Aftermath,* Studies in Social Psychology in World War II, vol. 2 (Princeton: Princeton University Press, 1949), 598.

25. Stryker and Wood, *In This Proud Land,* 7.

26. Caroline Bird, *The Invisible Scar* (New York: D. McKay, 1966), 22–23.

27. Warren I. Susman, "History and Film: Artifact and Experience," *Film & History* 15 (May 1985):30.

28. John Steinbeck, *The Grapes of Wrath* (New York: Viking Press, 1939; reprint, Bantam, 1946), 378; Margaret Mitchell, *Gone with the Wind* (New York: Macmillan, 1936; Pocket Books, 1968), 862.

29. This theme is further explored in my article "American Culture and the Great Depression."

30. Stryker and Wood, *In This Proud Land,* 14, 17.

31. Ibid.

32. See, for example, John Tagg, "The Currency of the Photograph," in *Thinking Photography,* ed. Victor Burgin (London: Macmillan, 1982), 126, 128. For a more interesting and subtle argument along these lines, see Sally Stein, "Marion Post Wolcott: Thoughts on Some Lesser Known FSA Photographs," in *Marion Post Wolcott: FSA Photographs* (Carmel, Cal.: Friends of Photography, 1983), 3–10.

33. Robert Louis Stevenson, *Across the Plains* (London: C. Scribner's Sons, 1892), 206–28.

34. Stryker and Wood, *In This Proud Land,* 11.

35. Arthur Rothstein, *Documentary Photography* (Boston: Focal Press, 1986), 36.

36. F. Jack Hurley, *Portrait of a Decade: Roy Stryker and the Development of Documentary Photography in the Thirties* (Baton Rouge: Louisiana State University Press, 1972), 70.

37. Ibid.

38. Stryker and Wood, *In This Proud Land,* 16.

39. Stryker to Lee and Rothstein, 19 February 1942, reprinted in ibid., 188.

40. Stryker and Wood, *In This Proud Land,* 8, 14, 15, 187, 188; Rothstein, *Documentary Photography,* appendix A, 163–68.

41. Warren I. Susman, *Culture as History: The Transformation of American Society in the Twentieth Century* (New York: Pantheon Books, 1984), 160.

42. Stryker and Wood, *In This Proud Land,* 8, 9, 14.

Chapter 14

1. Quoted in Marshall McLuhan, *From Cliché to Archetype* (New York: Viking, 1970), 28.

2. Ralph Ellison, *Invisible Man* (New York, Random House, Modern Library ed., 1952), 332.

3. Ibid., 331.

4. Lawrence W. Levine, *Black Culture and Black Consciousness: Afro-American Folk Thought from Slavery to Freedom* (New York: Oxford University Press, 1977).

5. Max Horkheimer and Theodor W. Adorno, *Dialectic of Enlightenment,* translated by John Cumming (1944; reprint ed., New York: Continuum, 1987), 122, 126, 133–134.

6. Bernard Rosenberg, "Mass Culture in America," in Bernard Rosenberg and David Manning White, eds., *Mass Culture: The Popular Arts in America* (New York: Free Press, 1957), 9.

7. Harold Rosenberg, "Pop Culture and Kitsch Criticism," *Dissent* 5 (Winter 1958), 15–16.

8. Allan Bloom, *The Closing of the American Mind* (New York: Simon and Schuster, 1987), 68–81 and passim. That this rather extreme traducer of Popular Culture, in his very act of traducing, ended up writing the second best-selling hardcover nonfiction book of 1987 and became for a time an icon in the popular press with the concomitant photo-journalism spreads replete with such lifestyle minutiae as his apartment furnishings and his compact disc collection, is one of the paradoxes that make studying culture so fascinating. See, for example, James Atlas, "Chicago's Grumpy Guru: Best-Selling Professor Allan Bloom and the Chicago Intellectuals," *New York Times Magazine,* Jan. 2, 1988.

9. The source for this is my memory of remarks Marx made in his later years to a reporter. I have not been able to find the exact quote.

10. See Capra's interview with Richard Schickel in Schickel, *The Men Who Made the Movies* (New York: Atheneum, 1975), 73.

11. "Yesterday's Boob Tube Is Today's High Art," *New York Times*, Oct. 7, 1990.

12. These comparisons were not totally unknown during the Great Depression itself. In a study published in 1941, two psychiatrists concluded: "Comic books can probably be best understood if they are looked upon as an expression of the folklore of this age. They may be compared with the mythology, fairy tales and puppet shows, for example, of past ages." See Lauretta Bender, M.D. and Reginald S. Lourie, M.D., "The Effect of Comic Books on the Ideology of Children," *The American Journal of Orthopsychiatry* XI (1941):540–550.

13. See Lawrence W. Levine, *Highbrow/Lowbrow: The Emergence of Cultural Hierarchy in America* (Cambridge: Harvard University Press, 1988), chaps. 1, 2.

14. After receiving a number of passionate letters protesting derogatory remarks he had written about detective stories, Edmund Wilson undertook a new review of the genre. He concluded that there were no substantial distinctions within it and advised his correspondents to stop importuning him to read novels and stories which were "wasteful of time and degrading to the intellect." "With so many fine books to be read, so much to be studied and known, there is no need to bore ourselves with this rubbish." Wilson, "Who Cares Who Killed Roger Ackroyd?," in Rosenberg and White, eds., *Mass Culture*, 149–153.

15. The term is Janice Radway's. See her superb discussion of how the adoption of such assumptions has caused critics to be "hermetically sealed off from the very people they aim to understand." Janice Radway, *Reading the Romance: Women, Patriarchy, and Popular Literature* (Chapel Hill: University of North Carolina Press, 1984), Introduction.

16. J. Huizinga, *Homo Ludens: A Study of the Play-Element in Culture* (Boston: Beacon Press, 1955), 10.

17. Robert Escarpit, *The Sociology of Literature*, translated by Ernest Pick (London: Frank Cass, 1971), 91.

18. Raymond Williams, *The Long Revolution* (New York: Columbia University Press, 1961), 30.

19. Levine, *Black Culture and Black Consciousness*, 217–239.

20. Charles Wolfe, *The Grand Ole Opry: The Early Years, 1925–35* (London: Old Time Music, 1975), 17.

21. Ernest Dichter, "On the Psychology of Radio Commercials," in Paul F. Lazarsfeld and Frank N. Stanton, eds., *Radio Research, 1941* (New York: Duell, Sloan & Pearce, 1941), 471.

22. Reprinted in Charles Wolfe, "The Triumph of the Hills: Country Radio, 1920–50," in Paul Kingsbury and Alan Axelrod, eds., *Country: The Music and the Musicians* (New York: The Country Music Foundation and Abbeville Press, 1988), 63.

23. Ruth Palter, "Radio's Attraction for Housewives," *Hollywood Quarterly* III (Spring 1948), 251, 254.

24. Quoted in Wolfe, "The Triumph of the Hills: Country Radio, 1920–50," in Kingsbury and Axelrod, eds., *Country*, 87.

25. Palter, "Radio's Attraction for Housewives," *Hollywood Quarterly* III (Spring 1948), 251, 254.

26. Herta Herzog, *Survey of Research on Children's Radio Listening* (New York: Columbia University, Office of Radio Research, 1941), 77.

27. Interview in Herbert Blumer, *Movies and Conduct* (New York: Macmillan, 1933), 16.

28. Herzog, *Children's Radio Listening*, 74–75.

29. Katherine M. Wolfe and Marjorie Fiske, "The Children Talk About Comics," *Communication Research, 1948–1949*, Paul F. Lazarsfeld and Frank N. Stanton, eds. (New York: Harper & Brothers, 1949), 15.

30. Roland Barthes, *The Pleasure of the Text*, translated by Richard Miller (New York: Hill and Wang, 1975), 38.

31. William Blake, "The Everlasting Gospel" (*c.* 1818), in *William Blake: Selected Poetry*, W. H. Stevenson, ed. (London: Penguin Books, 1988), 275.

32. Alan Dundes, "Projection in Folklore: A Plea for Psychoanalytic Semiotics," in Dundes, *Interpreting Folklore* (Bloomington: Indiana University Press, 1980), 34–35.

33. Herbert Gans, *The Urban Villagers* (Glencoe, Ill.: Free Press, 1962), chap. 9.

34. Radway, *Reading the Romance*, 46 and passim.

35. Azriel L. Eisenberg, *Children and Radio Programs: A Study of More Than Three Thousand Children in the New York Metropolitan Area* (New York: Columbia University Press, 1936), 51–52.

36. Ernest Dichter, "On the Psychology of Radio Commercials" in Lazarsfeld and Stanton, *Radio Research, 1941*, 478, 473, 474.

37. See for example Wolfgang Iser: "The literary text activates our own faculties, enabling us to recreate the world it presents. The product of this creative activity is what we might call the virtual dimension of the text, which endows it with its reality. This virtual dimension is not the text itself nor is it the imagination of the reader: it is the coming together of the text and imagination." "The Reading Process: A Phenomenological Approach," in Ralph Cohen, ed., *New Directions in Literary History* (Baltimore: Johns Hopkins University Press, 1974), 130.

38. Roland Champagne, *Literary History in the Wake of Roland Barthes: Re-Defining the Myths of Reading* (Birmingham, Ala.: Summa Publications, 1984), 58–60.

39. Herta Herzog, "On Borrowed Experience: An Analysis of Listening to Daytime Sketches," *Studies in Philosophy and Social Science* IX (February 1941), 67–68.

40. Jeff Greenfield, "Passion Once Removed," *Wilson Quarterly* II (Summer 1978). Chayevsky is quoted on p. 95; Scott on p. 93.

41. Herzog, "On Borrowed Experience," *Studies in Philosophy and Social Science*, IX (February 1941), 85.

42. Eisenberg, *Children and Radio Programs*, 91.

43. Madeleine Edmonson and David Rounds, *From Mary Noble to Mary Hartman: The Complete Soap Opera Book* (New York: Stein and Day, 1976), 17–19.

44. Herta Herzog, "What Do We Really Know About Daytime Serial Listeners?," in Paul F. Lazarsfeld and Frank N. Stanton, eds., *Radio Research, 1942–43* (New York: Duell, Sloan and Pearce, 1944), 25, 27–28, 31; Herzog, *Children's Radio Listening*, 80–81.

45. Interestingly, his own conclusion that these shows were what their audiences wanted made Arnheim uneasy and he held out a standard for Popular Culture that one assumes he would not have advocated for High Culture. After protesting

against "presenting the world as one huge, catastrophic mess," he insisted that "There is no point in describing the problems and tragedies of life unless such a description is based on a belief in its positive values. Discord and conflict must be evaluated against the background of man doing his job constructively, peacefully, and cheerfully." In a footnote to this remark, he continued: "Why not apply some lightheartedness? View with detached, smiling wisdom these problems now overburdened with pathetic seriousness? Why the masochistic insistence on the moaning of despair, the Wagnerian vibrations of the pipe organ which so aptly create the hot, stuffy atmosphere of sterile emotion?" Rudolf Arnheim, "The World of the Daytime Serial," in Lazarsfeld and Stanton, eds., *Radio Research, 1942–43*, 34–35, 82–83.

46. Laurence Sterne, *The Life and Opinions of Tristram Shandy* (1759–67; Penguin Books edition, London, 1967), 127.

47. "The text, in other words, supplies me with words, ideas, images, sounds, rhythms, but I make the poem's meaning by a process of translation. That is what reading is, in fact: translation." Robert Crosman, "Do Readers Make Meaning?," in Susan R. Suleiman and Inge Crosman, eds., *The Reader in the Text: Essays on Audience and Interpretation* (Princeton: Princeton University Press, 1980), 152.

48. Hadley Cantril, *The Invasion from Mars: A Study in the Psychology of Panic* (1940; Harper Torchbook ed., New York: Harper & Row, 1966), 100, 116, 160–161.

49. "Communication in literature, then, is a process set in motion and regulated, not by a given code, but by a mutually restrictive and magnifying interaction between the explicit and the implicit, between revelation and concealment. What is concealed spurs the reader into action, but this action is also controlled by what is revealed; the explicit in its turn is transformed when the implicit has been brought to light. Whenever the reader bridges the gaps, communication begins. The gaps function as a kind of pivot on which the whole text-reader relationship revolves." Wolfgang Iser, "Interaction Between Text and Reader," in Suleiman and Crosman, eds., *The Reader in the Text*, 110–11.

50. During World War II a version of this joke featured Hitler attempting to enter Heaven only to be confronted by a voice with a Yiddish accent. Dundes, "Projection in Folklore," in Dundes, *Interpreting Folklore*, 59–60.

51. Roy E. Stryker and Nancy Wood, *In This Proud Land: America 1935– 1943 as Seen in the FSA Photographs* (Greenwich, Conn.: New York Graphic Society, 1973), 14, 17.

52. Gordon Parks, *A Choice of Weapons* (1966; reprint ed., St. Paul: Minnesota Historical Society Press, 1986), 231; interview with Gordon Parks by Richard Doud, 28 April 1964, Archives of American Art, Smithsonian Institution, quoted in Carl Fleischhauer and Beverly W. Brannan, eds., *Documenting America, 1935–1943* (Berkeley: University of California Press, 1988), 228.

53. For a more extended discussion of some of these questions, see Lawrence W. Levine, "The Historian and the Icon: Photography and the History of the American People in the 1930s and 1940s," in Fleischhauer and Brannan, eds., *Documenting America*, 15–42.

54. This quote and my later quotes from *Ann Vickers* and *Sullivan's Travels* come directly from my viewing of the films.

55. *Time,* Oct. 9, 1933.

56. Umberto Eco, *The Role of the Reader: Explorations in the Semiotics of Texts* (Bloomington: University of Indiana Press, 1979), 4, 9–10, 22–23.

57. Barbara Herrnstein Smith has put this well: "As we view the canvas, the

myriad spots of paint assume the guise of natural objects in the visual world, but we are nevertheless always half-conscious of them as spots of paint. As we watch the play, the stage recedes and the personal identities of the actors yield to those of the fictions whom they portray, but when, at the final curtain, we clap our hands, it is not Hamlet whom we are applauding, but the performers and the playwright himself. The illusions of art are never *de*lusions. The artwork interests, impresses, and moves us both as the thing represented and as the *representing* itself: as the actions and passions of Prince Hamlet and as the achievement of William Shakespeare, as the speech of men—and as the poet's fiction." Smith, *On the Margins of Discourse: The Relation of Literature to Language* (Chicago: University of Chicago Press, 1978), 39–40. See also Roland Barthes, *Writing Degree Zero & Elements of Semiology* translated by Annette Lavers and Colin Smith (London: Jonathan Cape, 1967), 29–34, in which Barthes observes of the novel: "Its task is to put the mask in place and at the same time to point it out." "The whole of Literature," he adds, "can declare *Larvatus prodeo*. As I walk forward, I point out my mask."

58. "Fictive discourse allows us to speak the unspeakable—but only if we agree not to *say* it. . . . Produced in the theaters of language or displayed in its galleries, fictive discourse is not subject to the economics of the linguistic marketplace. Thus, the poet can use language and his audience can respond to it without the constraints that would otherwise shape and confine the behavior of each of them. Though this may appear to be a tendentious way of describing 'poetic license,' its implications are considerably more far-reaching than what the cliché suggests. For the licensing that I am speaking of here extends to the audience as well as to the poet, and it involves not merely formal or even thematic features of the utterance, but quite fundamental aspects of the linguistic transaction itself." Smith, *On the Margins of Discourse*, 105, 110–111.

59. For copious examples, see Levine, *Black Culture and Black Consciousness.*

60. Ibid.

61. Ernest G. Bormann, "This Is Huey P. Long Talking," *Journal of Broadcasting* II (Spring 1958), 111–122.

62. Erik Barnouw, *The Golden Web: A History of Broadcasting in the United States, Volume II—1933 to 1953* (New York: Oxford University Press, 1968), 7–9.

63. Leila A. Sussmann, *Dear FDR: A Study of Political Letter-Writing* (Totowa, N.J.: Bedminster Press, 1963). 114.

64. Ira R. T. Smith with Joe Alex Morris, *"Dear Mr. President . . ."*: *The Story of Fifty Years in the White House Mail Room* (New York: Julian Messner, 1949), 156, 213–214.

65. Reprinted in Wolfe, "The Triumph of the Hills: Country Radio, 1920–50," in Kingsbury and Axelrod, eds., *Country,* 63.

66. Maya Angelou, *I Know Why the Caged Bird Sings* (New York: Bantam Books, 1971), 111–115.

67. A study conducted in 1934 among secondary school students in Oakland, California, found similar patterns of listening behavior. Eisenberg, *Children and Radio Programs,* 29–30, 162–163.

68. Ernest Dichter, "On the Psychology of Radio Commercials," in Lazarsfeld and Stanton, *Radio Research, 1941,* 477.

69. Cantril, *The Invasion from Mars,* 139–149.

70. Ibid., xii.

71. Radway, *Reading the Romance.*

72. Blumer, *Movies and Conduct,* 120.

73. American Film Institute, "Frank Capra: 'One Man—One Film,'" in Richard Glatzer and John Raeburn, eds., *Frank Capra: The Man and His Films* (Ann Arbor: University of Michigan Press, 1975), 22–23.

74. Frank Capra, *The Name Above the Title: An Autobiography* (New York: Macmillan, 1971), chap. 10.

75. Capra discusses his difficulties with *John Doe* in his interview with Richard Schickel in Schickel, *The Men Who Made the Movies*, 78, and in his autobiography, *The Name Above the Title*, chap. 16.

76. Thomas Schatz, *The Genius of the System: Hollywood Filmmaking in the Studio Era* (New York: Pantheon, 1988), 37, 85, 94–95, 116–119, 147; Neil Gabler, *An Empire of Their Own: How the Jews Invented Hollywood* (New York: Crown, 1988), 224.

77. Tom Stoppard, *Rosencrantz and Guildenstern Are Dead* (New York: Grove Press, 1967), 84.

78. Bruce Jackson, "The Perfect Informant," *Journal of American Folklore* 103 (Oct.–Dec. 1990), 416.

79. Edmund Leach, "Myth as a Justification for Faction and Social Change," in Robert A. Georges, ed., *Studies on Mythology* (Homewood, Ill.: Dorsey Press, 1968), 186, 198.

Index